SCHOOLING
FOR SUCCESS

COLUMBIA UNIVERSITY SEMINAR SERIES

The University Seminars at Columbia University welcomes this study, *Schooling for Success* edited by Laura Randall and Joan B. Anderson, to the Columbia University Seminars Series. The study has benefited from Seminar discussions and reflects the advantages of scholarly exchange provided by the Seminar Movement.

Aaron W. Warner
Director, University Seminars
Columbia University

SCHOOLING
FOR SUCCESS

Preventing Repetition and Dropout in Latin American Primary Schools

LAURA RANDALL
JOAN B. ANDERSON
Editors

Routledge
Taylor & Francis Group

LONDON AND NEW YORK

First published 1999 by M.E. Sharpe

Published 2015 by Routledge
2 Park Square, Milton Park, Abingdon, Oxon OX14 4RN
711 Third Avenue, New York, NY 10017, USA

Routledge is an imprint of the Taylor & Francis Group, an informa business

Library of Congress Cataloging-in-Publication Data

Schooling for success : preventing repetition and dropout in Latin American primary
schools / [edited by] Laura Randall and Joan B. Anderson.
p. cm. — (Columbia University seminar series)
Papers in this book were presented at a conference sponsored by the University Seminars,
the Brazil Seminar, the Latin American Seminar and the Institute of Latin American and
Iberian Studies of Columbia University.
Includes bibliographical references and index.
ISBN 0-7656-0238-5 (hc. : alk. paper); ISBN 0-7656-0239-3 (pbk. : alk. paper)
1. Elementary school dropouts—Latin America—Prevention—Congresses.
2. Grade repetition—Latin America—Prevention—Congresses.
3. Education, Elementary—Social aspects—Latin America—Congresses.
4. Schools—Decentralization—Latin America—Congresses.
5. Education, Elementary—Latin America—Curricula—Congresses. 6. Teaching—
Latin America—Congresses. 7. Education and state—Latin America—congresses.
I. Randall, Laura. II. Anderson, Joan B. III. Series.
LC45.8.L29S36   1999
372.12′913′098—dc21   98–46625
CIP

ISBN 13: 9780765602398 (pbk)
ISBN 13: 9780765602381 (hbk)

Contents

List of Tables and Graphs

Tables

Graphs

Acknowledgments

We wish to thank the Spencer Foundation, the Ahlers Center for International Business of the University of San Diego, the Brazilian Ministry of Education and Sport, the Mexican Cultural Institute, the Research Foundation of the City University of New York, and the University Seminars of Columbia University for their timely and generous support of our project and of the conference at which the initial version of the papers in this book were presented. The conference was sponsored by the University Seminars, the Brazil Seminar, the Latin American Seminar, and the Institute of Latin American and Iberian Studies of Columbia University. The kind, effective, and continuing support of Dr. Aaron W. Warner, director of the University Seminars of Columbia, is greatly appreciated.

Part I

Introduction and Overview

Joan B. Anderson and Laura Randall

Introduction: Education and Development

This book addresses the issues of educational quality, grade repetition, and early school dropout in primary school in Latin America. The importance of primary school education is universal: primary school education is a fundamental ingredient for creating economic development and growth. In the United States, it has been more important than increased capital in accounting for worker productivity and U.S. economic growth (Denison 1974, 1985). In developing countries, social returns to education are at least as high as any reasonable measure of the opportunity cost of capital and are greater for primary education than for secondary and higher education (Tilak 1989). The social returns to primary education in Latin America are more than 17 percent, according to a 1990s estimate for fourteen Latin American countries (Wolff, Schiefelbein, and Valenzuela 1994). In Brazil, a literate man earns about 50 percent more than an illiterate one; a man with elementary school education earns about 130 percent more; and a man with at least a secondary school education earns almost 550 percent more (Thomas and Strauss 1997).

Designing and implementing programs to ensure the completion of a quality primary education may be the single most important measure that can be taken to achieve continuing economic development, global competitiveness, and well-being. It is a major contributor to the level of productivity. Latin America's integration into the global economy has increased the need for an educated labor force to be globally competitive.

Education plays an important role in maintaining or transforming political and social structure. It is a significant determinant of the distribution of income and wealth. In Latin America, the structure of education has maintained "social, political and economic domination of subordinate groups" (Akkari and Pérez 1998, p. 3) Inequities are derived from unequal access to quality education, inequalities in school readiness, in attendance, in educational environment, and in learning outcomes (Fields 1997a and b; dos Reis and de Barros 1991).

Increasing the access to education of the poorest in society is essential to improve income distribution for present and future generations. Educating women is an important part of breaking the cycle of poverty. The level of maternal education affects a child's access to information, literacy, and health services. High family income increases the ability of the family's children to be well nourished and stay in school, increasing their chances of earning higher wages and educating their children (Kassouf and Senauer 1966).

The most effective education is concentrated among the wealthy and upper-middle classes who attend private schools (World Bank 1998). The children of the poor attend public schools that have been underfunded, are overcrowded, often lack basic supplies and materials (including such essentials as paper and pencils), and are staffed by poorly paid teachers, many of whom do not have sufficient training. A UNESCO study shows that most public school students fail to meet national curricula objectives as a result of the poor quality of inputs (REPLAD 1994). Very poor children are those least likely to be enrolled in school, although the expense of their enrollment could be covered by an expenditure of much less than 1 percent of gross domestic product (Van der Gaag and Winkler 1996). Thus, restructuring public education to provide a quality education to even the poorest children is one of the best hopes for raising productivity, decreasing inequality of wages and increasing incomes and, subsequently, the size of the market for goods and services (Lam and Levisen 1992; Lau et al. 1993).

By 1996, most Latin American countries had expanded average net enrollment for the region to 88 percent. Given the relatively high initial access to primary school education, emphasis is shifting to the quality of education, its impact on what students learn, and the education system's ability to retain them in school. High primary school dropout rates perpetuate a low-productivity workforce and the consequent economic inequality. The high rate of grade repetition, 40 percent in the first grade and an overall average of 29 percent for primary education in Latin America (1990 data) cost an estimated extra $2.5 billion per year to educate the approximately 20 million repeaters (Schiefelbein and Wolff 1992).

This book, *Schooling for Success* examines the factors leading to the educational panorama described above. It starts with a general section of five essays that discuss broad issues, followed by sections that examine key issues in Argentina, Brazil, Chile, and Mexico. The chapters in each of these sections, while adapted for the specific issues of a particular country, are written with a common outline in mind in order to provide the reader with cross-country comparisons. They are: an overview of the educational system, prevention of repetition and dropout, centralization/decentralization of school systems, curricula and materials for teaching and learning, and teacher training and careers.

The general section of the book begins with an essay by Donna Barnes about the influence of educational style on student achievement, distinguishing between "transmission" and "transaction" models. The transmission method includes the teacher as authority, a "one size fits all" approach to teaching, based on lecturing, with competition as the motivating strategy to induce children to learn. In contrast, the transaction model has a more democratic classroom management style in which the teaching of subjects is placed in contexts from daily life. Grouping is heterogeneous, and teaching methods are adapted to the needs of individual children. Emphasis is based on cooperative learning by students. Barnes indicates that schools can retain students by moving to a transaction model of teaching.

Ruth Sautu indicates that poor, rural children are least likely to succeed in school; however, school quality may compensate for the negative effect of poverty. Sautu argues that when children's school failure is explained almost exclusively by family and neighborhood characteristics, social responsibility is implicitly transferred from the school context and society to the individuals. She asserts that disruptive behavior is often confused with poor academic achievement, resulting in grade repetition and eventual dropout. Intervention should therefore be based on psychological, cultural, and behavioral aspects of schooling, and should include the active participation of parents, teachers, and students.

Marcela Latorre and John Swope indicate that use of a transaction model of education in schools for poor children is an important part of Fe y Alegría schools, which operate in several Latin American countries. These schools are run by Jesuits, using non-religious personnel. They incorporate participation of the local community, the aid of private groups, and agreements with governments. Fe y Alegría's policies include improvement in health and nutrition, remedial programs, community participation, flexible or multiple promotion programs, economic incentive programs, preschool education, and secondary technical education that includes paid jobs. Fe y Alegría schools do not always have better "on time" promotion rates than public schools in their nations, but in almost all nations they do have noticeably lower drop out rates.

The role of the state in education is that of implementing institutional mechanisms. Lúcia Avelar argues that in countries with diverse regions one must speak of various roles of the state in a complex structure of regional diversities and differing power structures. Smaller regions and those on the periphery have a low Human Development Index and high grade repetition and school dropout rates. Avelar traces the "collapse of public basic education" to the sharp decline in teacher pay, following the debt crisis up to the present, which caused many qualified teachers to leave the field and others to work at more than one job. She recommends that teachers' salaries and promotion rules be made equal to those of other professionals, and administration of education be reorganized.

The failure of national governments to raise education of the poorest to desired levels has elicited an international response. Regina Cortina indicates that the World Bank and the Inter-American Development Bank have made loans for primary education. The World Bank stresses greater involvement of parents and the community, decentralization, and privatization, although in the absence of adequate public funding, privatization will not help poor children. The World Bank and UNICEF are funding new teaching materials. UNESCO favors cultural pluralism, educational opportunities for women and girls, and partnerships for education reform. It emphasizes secondary and vocational education. The large fund available from international organizations makes their work especially visible.

Overviews of the Educational Systems of Argentina, Brazil, Chile, and Mexico

Argentina, Brazil, Chile, and Mexico have common educational patterns but different national policies. In the first grade in 1989, the share of primary school age children in school in Argentina reached 99 percent, in Brazil 91 percent, in Chile 94 percent, and in Mexico 90 percent. Once in school, however, for Latin America as a whole, 35 percent repeated the first grade in 1997, but varied from a low of 10 percent in Chile to 31 percent in Argentina, 33 percent in Mexico and to a high of 53 percent in Brazil (Wolff, Schiefelbein, and Valenzuela 1994).

Educational policy in Argentina stresses decentralization; in Brazil, ensuring that every child attends primary school and obtains textbooks; in Chile, increasing hours of schooling per year and special measures to help the poorest schools; and in Mexico, decentralization, increasing the amount of required schooling and providing new, free textbooks. All four nations have recently begun to emphasize preschool education and reorganization of schools into cycles of several years, often with a recommendation for automatic promotion until the end of the cycle (see Table 1.1).

In Argentina, Sautu and Babini indicate that the Federal Education Act of 1993 reformed basic education to include preschool education, comprising kindergarten for children between three and five years old. Attendance of five-year-old children is compulsory with nine years of compulsory basic general education. This is followed by two tracks, one offering vocational education and another preparing students for university study. Nine and one-quarter percent of education costs are wasted because of grade repetition, varying from a low of 3.1 percent in Buenos Aires to a high of 33.5 percent of educational cost in Santiago del Estero. The accumulated actual costs of overaged pupils is estimated at $650 million.

Brazil's educational system is undergoing major changes and initiating new programs described by Minister of Education and Sports Paulo Renato Souza. Brazilian education has two levels, basic and superior. The basic level is divided into fundamental and middle school. The first lasts eight years and is compulsory. Fundamental education assumes special characteristics in the first four grades in order to be more adequate for the special needs of the age group of the respective students. Grade repetition and the resulting age/grade distortions have resulted in 5.3 million students in the 15 to 19 year old bracket still in primary school. Half of the children, ages 7 to 14, who are not in school are in the Northeast—Brazil's poorest region.

Chile's educational system is described by Ernesto Schiefelbein and Paulina Schiefelbein. It is divided into preschool education, basic education (eight grades), middle school education (four grades), with humanistic scientific and technical-professional tracks, and higher education. Primary and secondary

Table 1.1

Structure of Educational Systems of Argentina, Brazil, Chile, and Mexico

Ages	Argentina	Brazil	Chile	Mexico
3	PS			
4	PS	PS	PS	PS
5	PS	PS	PS	PS
6	P1	PS	P1	P
7	P1	P	P1	P
8	P1	P	P1	P
9	P2	P	P1	P
10	P2	P	P2	P
11	P2	P	P2	P
12	P3	P	P2	S
13	P3	P	P2	S
14	P3	P	S	S
15	S	S	S	S
16	S	S	S	S
17	S	S	S	S
18		S		

Source: McMeekin 1998.
Notes: PS=Pre-Primary; P=Primary; P1=Primary First Cycle; P2=Primary Second Cycle; S=Secondary.
Argentina: Primary (grades 1–9); General Basic Education. Secondary (grades 10–12) Polimodal Education.
Brazil: Primary: Fundamental Education. Secondary: Intermediate Education.
Chile: Primary; General Basic Education (grades 1–8).

schools have been transferred to municipalities, and are divided into free municipal, private subsidized, private tuition paid schools, and corporations, which are public institutions administered by private nonprofit organizations. In the 1960s, educators in Chile recognized student failure as a problem that was at least in part the responsibility of the school and one that was not always solved by grade repetition so they switched to an "automatic promotion" policy. The first grade repetition rate fell from 40 percent in the 1960s to around 10 percent in the 1980s, where it has remained for the past decade.

Teresa Bracho describes the restructuring of the Mexican educational system, which is now governed under the General Education Law of 1993, which indicates that basic education covers ten years of schooling: one year of preschool, and three years of secondary school. Primary and Secondary school are compulsory, while preschool may last more than one year. Educational responsibilities were transferred to the states, but many aspects of educational finance and administration continue to be centralized. The share of federal government expenditure on basic education has been expanded to almost 50 percent. Early results indicate success, with the national primary school repetition rate falling from 18 percent in 1990–91 to 10 percent in 1996–97.

Programs for Improving Quality and Lowering Repetition and Dropout Rates

The next section of the book analyzes the scope of repetition and dropout and presents programs to prevent them and to increase achievement. Ruben Klein indicates that dropout rates were overestimated. Corrections indicate that dropout rates have decreased over time, and that dropout rates were only 1 percent in the first grade in Brazil. Some 88 percent of a school cohort finished the fourth grade, taking an average of 6.5 years to do so. Repetition occurs most often at the beginning of a school cycle. According to Klein, automatic promotion within a school cycle of several grades postpones repetition to the last grade in the cycle, but does not eliminate repetition.

In Argentina, María Celia Agudo de Córsico points out that grade repetition is closely correlated with low socioeconomic levels. She indicates that a social educational plan to improve schools in lower-class environments has reached more than 3 million children. New schools were built and old ones repaired, books and didactic materials were distributed. Special projects include in-service training for teachers. At the same time current economic policies have caused high unemployment and an increase in the poverty rate. Córsico postulates that the consequent negative impact on school children will be greater than the positive effect of these programs.

Ivany Rodrigues Pino and Mariane Campelo Koslinski describe new government programs to lower Brazil's high grade repetition and dropout rates. Brazil has organized basic education into school cycles in which promotion is continuous within the cycle. Summer school and "accelerated learning" programs with smaller class size, more hours in school, new materials and teacher training have been established for students who are having difficulties and/or are over age in their grade level. An "Every Child in School" program is designed to assure access to school and to prevent early dropout. In São Paulo, the Family Educational Supplement program pays poor families (with income under seven-tenths of minimum wage) one minimum wage if all the family's children ages 7 to 14 are attending school.

Cecilia Cardemil O. points out that in Chile from 1990 to 1997, policy decisions were oriented to improve the quality of education, offering more opportunities to the neediest children, and encouraging community participation and investment in education. Chile increased teachers' salaries, provided help to schools to design and carry out their own educational projects, and directed special programs to schools in poor communities, which led to improvement in students' achievement, except in cases in which school principals acted as bureaucrats, rather than as educational leaders.

Sylvia Schmelkes notes that Mexico reformed the structure of basic education in 1992 with a "back to basics" approach. Starting in 1993–94, teachers were asked to give children two years to learn to read and write, and principals were asked to let the first grade teacher teach the same children in the second grade. This led to a reduction of repetition rates for the first grade, and second grade repetition rates did not rise in the following year. In 1996, the Mexican government created 300 teacher centers for in-service training, and, in 1997, it reformed initial training in normal schools. Mexico also established the Children in Solidarity Program to help children in the poorest parts of the nation in 1990, but neither this nor a World Bank loan to aid education in the four poorest states led to a significant improvement of education.

Decentralization of Educational Systems

The need to adapt program design to local needs, the desire to reduce the central government's size and, in some cases, the central government's financial support of education have contributed to decentralization of education. Ana María Brigido indicates that although the Argentine constitution grants provinces the autonomy to manage primary education, many provinces lack the resources to do so, forcing the national government to provide subsidies and create schools. Participation of the "educational community" in school boards is limited in practice by a lack of persons trained to participate and by the absence of a tradition of such participation. The 1978 decentralization has had a negative impact on Argentine educational quality, equity, and effectiveness. It is too soon to evaluate the effect of the 1993 Federal Education Act.

Maria Ligia de Oliveira Barbosa places the decentralization of education in Brazil in the context of the battle for redemocratization of the nation. Emphasis was placed on election of principals and on participation of school councils in decision making, but until the administration of President Fernando Henrique Cardoso (1995–) there was no clear central government policy favoring decentralization. The state of Minas Gerais provides an example of decentralization. It attempted to place students in the schools closest to their homes; create school councils consisting of parents, students, and school employees, which were especially important in small communities; and developed new auditing systems. School funds were increasingly spent on purchases of teaching materials rather than on support of needy students. Nonetheless, testing indicates that the index of student achievement has increased.

According to Jaime Vargas S., the reduction of the state in Chile began in 1974. The educational reforms of 1981 transferred primary and secondary schools to municipalities and resources to municipal and private subsidized schools, based on a per-student attendance subsidy, popularly called a "voucher system." Municipalities did, however, have to follow pedagogic norms and obey general labor laws in their dealings with teachers. The curriculum was to be modified to meet local needs. As a result of the new "voucher" subsidy, students transferred massively from municipal to private subsidized schools.

Alec Gershberg indicates that in Mexico, the federal government historically provided 80 percent and the states 20 percent of funds for basic education, this proportion varying among states. State education systems were independent of the federal system. In addition, between 1978 and 1992, the national Secretariat of Education was decentralized. The 1992 educational reform transferred civil service and management systems to the states, while much of education finance and administration remained centralized. State officials emphasized preschool education, and also arranged for young women, some without teacher training, to work in understaffed schools in their local communities.

School centralization/decentralization issues may not be the key to understanding student achievement. Local control may either increase parent participation and responsiveness to local needs or lead the way to inadequate management, highly responsive to political rather than educational requirements. The content and style of teaching and the ability to attract and keep excellent teachers may be more important in explaining student achievement than the level of government that controls the educational system.

Curriculum and Textbook Development

Development of curriculum and the materials that implement it are crucial for a successful education program. A World Bank study shows that excellent curriculum with clear teacher guides can partially substitute for teacher training. Edith Litwin indicates that in Argentina common basic contents were issued for initial and basic education for the entire nation. They define fields of study, and provide teaching and learning strategies. New subjects such as civics and technology were introduced into the curriculum, although few teachers are able to teach technology. To remedy this situation, educational personnel must complete several courses, chosen at the educator's discretion. Textbooks are provided primarily by two private publishers with little competition. The introduction of computers is limited and inefficient; school libraries are just beginning to be introduced. There is a clear need for teachers to have greater influence in curricular reform, which should be adapted to local needs.

Ana Lúcia Amaral indicates that in Brazil, curriculum varies among the regions, reflecting their differing levels of human development. In the 1960s in Brazil, mass education led to a dilution of the curriculum; materials adequate for lower-class students were not available; rates of failure in school skyrocketed. In the 1970s, educational theory focused on social and political themes. In 1996, new guidelines for education required study both of traditional subjects and of democratic multi-cultural values. A new organization of schooling facilitated continuous evaluation of students and increased required annual school time from 180 to 200 hours.

In Chile, Francisco Álvarez indicates that teaching materials are being revised to stress language and mathematics, and how to learn and to cooperate with others. Computers, which enabled schools in rural areas to use the Internet to obtain greater knowledge of the world, have been introduced. Another innovation is the use of games simulating daily life. The games require cooperative behavior and use of skills learned in school to solve practical problems. In addition, teacher learning guides that encourage students to investigate their daily life and their families as part of school work have been developed.

Margarita Gómez Palacio states that Mexico desires to prevent failure, rather than remedy it by stressing the teaching of reading and writing. A national program to strengthen reading and writing incorporates teacher training, especially continuing education for current teachers, newly designed curriculum materials, and evaluation of the program's impact on student achievement. Teaching is to be organized into two-year cycles, implying automatic promotion from the first to the second grade. New textbooks were produced, along with plans to improve school libraries and initiate mass programs to promote adult literacy.

The Teaching Profession: Training and Salaries

In Latin American nations, teaching conditions in public schools are often governed by a teaching statute, defining a "teaching career," which sets minimum qualifications for teachers and establishes pay scales and promotion ladders. These conditions, as well as the way teachers are trained, determine teaching conditions and practice. The disastrous decline in teachers' wages throughout Latin America both in real terms and in relation to wages in other occupations has made it harder to attract qualified highly educated people to teach in primary school.

Emilio Tenti Fanfani writes that Argentina has more than 700 diverse teacher training institutions that depend on provincial educational administrations. However, one-fifth of teachers have not received formal teacher training. In addition, the training teachers receive is obsolete; teachers are not prepared for teaching new subjects or for using a transaction model of teaching. Limited job tenure among primary school teachers, lack of control over decisions about classroom behavior, acquisition of irrelevant credentials for promotion combined with deteriorating salaries that vary widely among provinces have demoralized teachers. In 1997, Argentina increased the requirements for teacher training. Unions, however, may impede school improvement by emphasizing spending on salaries rather than on school supplies. Moreover, the best teachers are in schools accessible to middle- and upper-class families; poor teachers are in schools for low-income children, which contributes to these children's low achievement and perpetuates a cycle of poverty.

María Umbelina Caiafa Salgado analyzes the 1990s reformulation of teachers' salaries and work conditions in Brazil. Teacher training is shifting from high school to higher-level educational institutions. By the year 2006, higher-level or in-service training will be required. Teachers in the 1990s had diverse levels of training, but approximately 20 percent had only completed basic education. An important innovation is the use of satellite television, with the aid of written materials, to train teachers. Teachers' salaries and careers are determined by the public or private school system that employs them. Increased incentives are now given to job performance compared to the acquisition of academic degrees. Low teachers' salaries result in the attraction of women rather than men to the teaching profession, which creates problems among teachers who work at more than one job and also have domestic responsibilities, leading to "burnout." Nonetheless, teaching is attractive to those from humble origins for whom it represents upward social mobility. Teachers' social status remains low, and there are conflicts between teachers and educational specialists.

Gabriel Castillo Inzulza focuses on in-service teacher training in Chile. He identifies the transaction model of education as a successful way of increasing student achievement. "Anticipation schools," designed to contribute to the formation of a new society, involve significant learning by all students. Teachers, principals and supervisors committed to "anticipation learning" were given new study guides and trained to use them. The guides are modified, based on their use in the classroom. They are likely to be useful to schools in many other nations, including those with a somewhat different history.

Regina Cortina describes the training and employment of teachers in Mexico. Diminished government spending on education reduced teachers' real salaries by more than 50 percent from 1981 to 1995, which allowed the government to avoid firing teachers, prevented highly qualified people from entering the teaching profession, and forced teachers to seek additional jobs. Teachers are mainly women, and lack an advanced degree, having been trained in five-year normal (secondary) schools. When schools expanded rapidly, untrained teachers were hired. They then needed in-service training. Normal advancement requires teachers to move into government or teachers' union administration. This was modified in 1992 legislation, which increased compensation for classroom teaching. Teacher training is now the responsibility of the states, and union power in determining promotion has been reduced.

Teachers are central to implementing educational reform. For this reform to be effective, high-quality personnel must be attracted to and retained in primary schools. The complementary step needed is improved career and especially salary opportunities for teachers. Improved working conditions for teachers are a necessary ingredient for improved educational quality.

In summary, increasing the quality of education, especially for the poor, is essential for economic development in Latin America. The rich and upper middle class send their children to private schools, while public schools serve most of the population. Improving public schools can help increase economic equality, increase the efficiency and productivity of the labor force and provide an educated populace for democratic participation. Latin America leads all developing nations in the proportion of repeaters in primary school. To correct this Argentina, Brazil, Chile, and Mexico are addressing issues of educational structure, curriculum, methods of preventing repetition and dropout and teacher training.

References

Akkari, Abdeljalil, and Soledad Pérez. 1998. "Educational Research in Latin America: Review and Perspectives." *Education Policy Analysis Archives* 6, no. 7, March 30.

Denison, Edward. 1974. *Accounting for United States Economic Growth, 1929–1969.* Washington, DC: Brookings Institution.

———. 1985. *Trends in American Economic Growth, 1929-1982.* Washington, DC: Brookings Institution.

dos Reis, José Guilherme Almeida, and Ricardo Paes de Barros. 1991. "Wage Inequaltiy and the Distribution of Education: A Study of the Evolution of Regional Differences in Inequality in Metropolitan Brazil." *Journal of Development Economics* 36: 117–143.

Fields, Gary. 1997a. "Accounting for Income Inequality and Its Change." Unpublished, July.

———. 1997b. "A Note on Inequality Decompositions." Personal communication.

Kassouf, Ana L., and Benjamin Senauer. 1996. "Direct and Indirect Effects of Parental Education on Malnutrition Among Children in Brazil: A Full Income Approach." *Economic Development and Cultural Change* 44: 817–838.

Lam, David, and Deborah Levison. 1992. "Declining Inequality in Schooling in Brazil and Its Effects on Inequality in Earnings." *Journal of Development Economics* 37: 199–225.

Lau, Lawrence J., Dean T. Jamison, Shu-Cheng Liu, and Steven Rivkin. 1993. "Education and Economic Growth. Some Cross-Sectional Evidence from Brazil." *Journal of Development Economics* 41: 45–70.

McMeekin, R.W. 1998. *Education Statistics in Latin America and the Caribbean.* Washington, DC.: Inter American Development Bank, Sustainable Development Department Education Unit Technical Study, January.

REPLAD. 1994. *Medición de la calidad de la educación básica,* Vol. I, Chile: UNESCO, Oficina Regional de Educación para América Latina y El Caribe.

Schiefelbein, Ernesto and Laurence Wolff, 1992. "Repetition and Inadequate Achievement in Latin America's Primary Schools: A Review of Magnitude, Causes, Relationships, and Strategies. A Brief LATHR No. 31. Technical Department, Latin America and the Caribbean, The World Bank.

Thomas, Duncan, and John Strauss. 1997. "Health and Wages: Evidence on Men and Women in Urban Brazil." *Journal of Econometrics* 77: 159–185.

Thomas, Duncan, John Strauss, and Maria-Helena Henriques. 1990. "How Does Mother's Education Affect Child Height?" *The Journal of Human Resources* 26: 183–211.

Tilak, Jhandvala B.G. 1989. "Education and Its Relation to Economic Growth, Poverty and Income Distribution," *World Bank Discussion Papers* 46. Washington, DC: World Bank.

Van der Gaag, Jacques, and Donald Winkler. 1996. *Children of the Poor in Latin America and the Caribbean.* Washington, DC: World Bank, LASHC Paper Series, No. 1, July.

Wolff, Laurence, Ernesto Schiefelbein, and Jorge Valenzuela. 1994. *Improving the Quality of Primary Education in Latin America and the Caribbean Toward the Twenty First Century.* Washington, DC: World Bank Discussion Paper 257.

World Bank, Human Development Network, Latin America and the Caribbean. 1998. *Education and Technology at the Crossroads: A Discussion Paper.* April.

2

DONNA BARNES

Causes of Dropping Out from the Perspective of Education Theory

Why Do Students Drop Out of School?

The reasons that students choose to drop out of school are varied and complex and can be categorized as "in-school reasons" and "out of school reasons." Out of school reasons are influenced by political, economic, and family issues as well as involvement in drugs, alcohol, gangs, and/or criminal activity. This chapter addresses only those issues that pertain to the school environment. However, it is important to acknowledge that all of these issues affect each other and are inextricably bound together in a complete context that affects each individual student who makes the decision to either continue his/her formal schooling or to drop out of school.

History of Failure

One of the major reasons that students drop out of school is that they "fail to learn," as reflected by poor grades, low test scores, and teacher assessment. When students do "poorly," they are frequently retained or flunked, and required to repeat a grade level in the hope that they will do better by being in the same environment for a longer period of time. It does not matter why they did not do well; the fact is that they have not acquired the information and should, therefore, spend more time at acquiring the necessary information so that their chance of success in later school years is enhanced.

The educational practice of grade repetition—which is sometimes called retention—is practiced in many countries. Whether or not a student is retained is the single best predictor of the students's eventually dropping out of school or staying in school. Forty percent of those students who are retained subsequently drop out of school, compared to a 10 percent dropout rate for those who are not retained (Alexander, Entwisle, and Dauber 1994). Therefore, it is important to look at the issues surrounding grade repetition as a fundamental cause of dropping out of school.

The incidence or frequency with which children are held back in or "flunk" a grade in school can be dependent on the set of beliefs incorporated into each educational system that creates policy with regard to the practice. As we try to assess the frequency of grade repetition, which correlates with student dropout in various countries, an attempt should be made to try to understand and document the philosophy of education or set of beliefs about education and learning that directs and informs policymakers and hence practitioners.

Clearly, there are many different ways of looking at the goals of education and purposes of schooling, and many different beliefs about how those goals and purposes are best accomplished. However, it is useful to present two basic models of learning that can be compared and contrasted and that have implications for the practice of grade repetition. How do we learn language and develop literacy? Is learning oral language the same as or different from learning written language (reading and writing)? Is learning written language a more difficult process than learning oral language? The ways in which these questions might be answered are varied and reflect either a transmission model of education or a transaction model.

This chapter summarizes theories about school failure and why children drop out, contrasting methods of teaching. At one extreme are "transmission" methods, in which knowledge is transmitted from the teacher to the student, and at the other, "transaction" methods. The difference is sometimes summarized as that between teaching facts and teaching "how to learn," on the part of students, parents, teachers, and administrators. Most school systems include methods based on each of these theories. The theories are presented as opposite ends of a spectrum to help evaluate the educational systems and practices in the nations studied.

Brief Descriptions of the Transmission and Transaction Models of Education

The contrasting characteristics of the transmission and transaction models of education are shown in Table 2.1.

The Transmission Model

The transmission model of education assumes that education is about acquiring information from a knowledgeable source. Information is imparted to the learner, who acquires the information through memorization or study. Knowledge is transmitted from one to another: there is a giver (teacher) and a receiver (student). Evaluation of knowledge acquisition can be done with testing because learning is defined as acquiring information. In this model there is the belief that learning happens sequentially and that information can be organized in a specific scope and sequence from easier to more difficult concepts. Knowledge is most

Table 2.1

A Comparison of Transmission and Transaction Models of Education

Transmission Model	Transaction Model
Teacher is the authority.	Classroom management is democratically based.
Classroom management style is authoritarian, with the use of punishments and rewards.	Teacher uses multiple strategies including demonstrating, inviting, discussing, challenging, creating real-life problem situations, and experimentation in order to engage learners.
Errors are considered undesirable and are often punished.	
There are homogeneous grouping patterns.	There are heterogeneous grouping patterns.
All children are taught the same thing at the same time using the same materials in a specific scope and sequence.	Instruction is based on the assumption that all learners learn and develop differently.
Teaching techniques include a large amount of lecturing, direct teaching, paper and pencil activities, and copying information from a blackboard.	Teaching techniques use many hands-on and varied materials.
Learning is characterized as the mastery of isolated skills in specific subject areas.	
Competition is used as a motivation strategy for learning.	Emphasis is placed on collaborative and cooperative learning.
Controlled vocabulary materials are used which are "graded."	
Assessment is usually limited to tests.	Assessment is seen as diagnosis and is done frequently. Decisions about placement or advancement are not based on the outcome of only one measure

easily learned when it is broken down into easier parts and acquired in a step-by-step fashion. Scope and sequence indicators are often framed in terms of grade levels. For example, all first graders will be able to read at a pre-primer reading level at the end of first grade. If these standards are not met, then the solution is that the student should be kept in the same grade in order to have the time to learn the material. Connie Weaver, one of the foremost literacy educators in America today, clearly summarizes the transmission model of education when she says this model

> . . . leads to curricula that require them [learners] to practice skills, memorize facts, and accumulate information, typically in isolation from the uses to which the skills and information might be put. Students do worksheets and workbooks on reading and writing skills, but spend little time reading or writing for enjoyment or other real-world purposes. Errors are to be avoided and are therefore penalized to discourage the formation of inappropriate habits. Learning is expected to be uniform; that is students are treated and tested as if they are all expected to learn the same things at the same time. Therefore, many students will necessarily "fail," though in varying degrees. (Weaver, 1988, p. 87)

A common outcome of a transmission model of education is high rates of repetition because students fail to learn at the same pace and may not benefit from the strategies of teaching most often associated with this philosophical stance toward what constitutes learning.

The Transaction Model

The transaction model of education assumes that learners construct their own knowledge by actively making sense out of what seems to be a mass of information relating new information to prior knowledge, and that they learn about the parts of language by grappling with the whole. It asserts that (1) learning written language is quite similar to learning oral language; consequently, the conditions in which we learn oral language ought to be replicated for learning written language; (2) learning is messy, not easily sequenced or quantified; and (3) meaning is created as a transaction between the learner and the information and social context.

Teachers who believe in a transaction model of learning "try to create rich environmental contexts and situations from which students can learn. Such teachers understand that taking risks, developing and refining hypotheses (often unconscious ones), and making errors are all necessary aspects of growth. . . . They know that mastery of processes like speaking a language, reading, writing, spelling . . . takes years, and will never reach perfection. The learning (or acquisition) of such processes is expected to be individual and idiosyncratic" (Weaver, 1988, p. 87). Reading and writing are taught within a real-world context. Writing is taught as a tool of expression for writing letters, stories, and so forth, rather than merely doing workbook exercises. Basic to this perspective is that the learner constructs his or her own knowledge based on background knowledge and experience.

Failure in Schools

Those educators who subscribe primarily to a transmission model of learning are likely to insist that students acquire certain knowledge before they may be passed to the next grade. This perspective is a partial explanation of why the grade repetition rates are so high in Latin and South American countries. Since this is so, it becomes imperative that we understand why children are not learning and thus being held back in the grades.

Failure in schools is seen in two forms: grade repetition and dropping out. However, planners, policymakers, and government officials rarely gauge the failure of schools as measured by their students' failure to learn. "It is common to assign the cause of failure to the students themselves. This is a mistake. The students' failure to learn is often a failure of the school, and to attribute failure to the students themselves is to blame the victim, and to lose sight of the purpose of schools. The failure of children to learn what is expected of them is a failure of the school to teach effectively" (McGinn et al. 1992).

Why Don't Students Learn?

Student Factors

Some children simply do not go to school or they have very high absence rates. If they are not present they miss the opportunity to learn. Reasons for not attending school include the direct and opportunity costs compared to the benefits of attending school as well as the quality of the school experience. Families consider the direct costs of school books and materials, uniforms, and the time needed and difficulty of getting to school. They estimate the income that students could earn if they were not in school. In rural areas, there may not be jobs available that provide higher pay for more highly educated workers. An implicit cost of educating girls is that when they are in school they cannot take care of their younger siblings, and, in some cases, it is believed that when girls have more education, they become less marriageable.

Schools do not meet the needs of the students if the curriculum is irrelevant, if the students do not have positive relationships with the counselors and teachers at school, if they are harassed at school and consequently do not want to attend. In these cases, too often, those who do attend school are not successful academically, which results in poor grades, discouragement, grade repetition, and, finally, giving up.

Teacher Factors

In Latin America, teachers are generally underpaid and undervalued. They are undereducated in some of the fields that they teach, in pedagogy, and in how to meet the needs of diverse learners. Consequently, they often use the one-size-fits-all model (transmission model) of education. In most cases they are not required to participate in, nor do they benefit from, in-service or ongoing education. There is high absenteeism among teachers. Many do not believe that children can really learn in school (McGinn et al. 1992). Teachers' low expectations of their students results in low achievement of their students. McGinn et al. (1992) found that rural teachers in Honduras had higher expectations for children who came from literate families, who lived in larger and better constructed houses, who were clean, well-dressed, and wore shoes. This is a huge area of concern given what we know about the impact of teachers' expectations and the issues of poverty in Latin American countries.

We know from research that supplies affect learning; greater learning occurs when teachers have chalk and writing paper. In many schools, especially those in poor districts, there is a lack of basic supplies ranging from pencils, pens, markers, paper, construction paper scissors and glue, to the more basic school materials such as books, libraries, math materials, and others. There is a lack of equipment including Xerox machines, typewriters, overhead projectors, and computers.

Other environmental constraints that affect student learning include: (1) time in school: there is wide variation across schools and students in the amount of time provided for learning, including the length of the school day and school year (McGinn et al. 1992), as well as how the time is spent. (2) Students' learning is handicapped when there are very large classes and when the next grade is not available (Schiefelbein 1991).

Regardless of the reasons why students fail to learn, a common response to the situation is to have the student repeat the grade so that they may acquire the information necessary to achieve ultimate success. How has the research literature contributed to our knowledge of the effects of this practice?

Grade Repetition or "Flunking" of Students and Its Effects

Years of research in this area of inquiry indicate almost uniformly that the choice to retain a student in the same grade for an extra year is not a helpful long-term strategy to encourage children to learn more or stay in school. In most Latin American countries, students take examinations in order to enter the next grade. It is not uncommon for children to have been retained three times before they are in sixth grade. In the United States, policies with regard to "social promotion" (being sent to the next grade regardless of academic achievement) vary according to locations, however, there is a current move to "return" to a non-promotion policy whereby students are not passed if they fail to acquire the necessary information of any specific grade level. Educators with this view argue that by not passing students on, the students learn more and high standards are maintained.

The research shows that high standards prevail and we push our students out of schools, which indicated by higher dropout rates. If a student drops out of school, then he or she has absolutely no chance of increased learning within a school environment. We must ask ourselves, is it more important to have high standards and lose students, or to try to teach our students as we find them and as they are able? How can we find the balance between maintaining high academic standards and meeting the needs of our students in ways that do not drive them away? This issue is particularly complicated because the public, families, teachers, school and government personnel all have their views about the efficacy of this practice, whether it is research based or not. Research, however, favors not repeating years in primary school. For example, Holmes and Matthews (1984) reviewed data from forty-four studies on grade-level retention effects on elementary and junior high students in the areas of academic achievement and personal adjustment. Their conclusion was that the outcomes for promoted pupils were more positive than for retained students. Also, contrary to expectations, the negative effects of retention were greater on achievement measures than on measures of self-concept, attitude toward school and personal adjustment.

Holmes updated this original review (Shepard and Smith 1989) adding nineteen newer studies to the original forty-four. He described fifty-four negative effects for students who were retained and nine positive effects. The negative effects of grade repetition in primary school on student ability to learn and on achievement, as well as the high cost of repeating school years, have led to an increased search for ways to enhance learning, and to avoid repetition and dropout.

Programs and Practices That Can Reduce Grade Repetition and Dropout

U.S. initiatives similar to those in Latin America indicate the importance of preschool education programs such as Head Start, and of programs to prevent repetition and dropout. A brief summary is presented for comparison to Latin American programs.

Head Start is a U.S. federally funded comprehensive program designed to meet the emotional, social, health, nutritional, and psychological needs of low-income families, specifically serving children ages three to five. It offers preschool education. It provides health care, which includes medical and dental care, nutrition counseling for parents, a free lunch program for children, and access to mental and health professionals. It involves parents in program planning, in volunteering at the school, and in learning about child development and educational activities that can be carried out at home through staff visits and workshops. Parents also are encouraged to enroll in adult education classes. Head Start also assists families in assessing their needs and helps families to avail themselves of community resources.

The results of participation in Head Start for students include: higher academic scores for three or four years; fewer grade retentions and special class placements; more high school graduates (67 percent who attended preschool graduated as compared to 47 percent who did not attend preschool); better behavior in the classroom and greater interest and curiosity than their counterparts (Schweinhart and Weikart 1980). At age nineteen, the students who had attended preschool had higher levels of employment, higher earnings, received less public assistance, and had fewer arrests and fewer pregnancies (Weikart et al. 1984).

Programs to Prevent Repetition and Dropout

Shirley Wells has done extensive work on student dropouts and potential dropouts, identification systems, and evaluation of programs of dropout prevention. In her book, *At-Risk Youth: Identification, Programs, and Recommendations* (Wells 1990), she includes over 100 pages of descriptions of programs for "at-risk" children. The successful programs have characteristics that coincide with the transaction school model. In addition to those mentioned in Table 2.1, they include systematic attendance and defined discipline procedures; peer tutoring; mentor programs; interpersonal and life skills; work/study programs; staff development to better teach all at-risk children, including cultural sensitivity; role models in the classroom (teachers, counselors, business and community leaders) who are from the same population group as the students; student access to schools of their choice; student assistance programs to address substance abuse, teen pregnancy and young parenthood, suicide prevention, and other mental and physical health issues; health centers; quality after-school care and/or extended day programs; partnerships with businesses and with the community, including business incentives to student employees to stay in school and community-based youth activities and community service.

Conclusion: What Can We Do To Prevent School Failure?

The continuing debate about the best way of making elementary school education more attractive and successful while increasing student achievement has led to the redesign of educational systems, administration, teaching methods, and curriculum. The transaction and transmission models described provide a means of organizing knowledge of educational practices and facilitate the comparison of Latin America to educational systems throughout the world.

The measures urged to increase achievement and prevent repetition correspond to a move toward the transaction model of education. They consist of the following:

1. Make school more interesting and relevant.
2. Help students to improve their health by providing them with free meals

or snacks. This increases students' attendance at school. In addition it is difficult for a child to learn if he or she is hungry.
3. Provide free textbooks and uniforms. This decreases the economic costs of attending school, consequently increasing students' attendance.
4. School performance is enhanced by the provision of preschool, which should be offered when possible beginning with three-year-old children and involving the community in their education.
5. Pay teachers more: their effectiveness is increased by doing so, for then they do not need to work at additional teaching or other jobs.
6. Offer and require more education for teachers, including in-service education.
7. Tie primary school systems to universities and teacher training schools.
8. Develop materials to facilitate individualized learning and train teachers to use them.
9. Maintain high expectations for students, offering them an academically challenging curriculum.

References

Alexander, Karl L., Doris R. Entwisle, and Susan L. Dauber, 1994. *On the Success of Failure: A Reassessment of the Effects of Retention in the Primary Grades.* Cambridge: Press Syndicate of the University of Cambridge.

Holmes, C. Thomas and Kenneth M. Matthews, 1984. "The Effects of Non-Promotion on Elementary and Junior Hich School Pupils: A Meta-Analysis," *Review of Educational Research*, Vol. 54 No. 2, pp. 225–236, summer.

McGinn, Noel F., María del Carmen Soto, Sagrario Lopez, Armando Loera, Tom Cassidy, Ernesto Schiefelbein, and Fernando Reimers, 1992. *Attending School and Learning or Repeating and Leaving: A Study About the Determinants of Grade Repetition and Dropout in Primary School in Honduras.* Cambridge, MA: Harvard University.

———. 1991. *Efficiency and Quality of Latin American Education.* Santiago, Chile: OREALC-UNESCO.

Schweinhart, Lawrence J. and David Weikart, 1980. *Young Children Grow Up: The Effects of the Perry Preschool Program on Youths Through Age 15.* Ypsilanti, MI: High/Scope Press.

Shepard, Lorrie, and Mary L. Smith. 1989. *Flunking Grades: Research and Policies on Retention.* London: Falmer Press.

Weaver, Constance. 1988. *Reading Process and Practice: From Socio-Psycholinguistics to Whole Language.* Portsmouth, NH: Heinemann.

Weikart, David P., John R. Berrueta-Clement, Lawrence J. Schweinhart, Steven Barnett, and Ann S. Epstein, 1984. *Changed Lives: The Effects of Perry Preschool Program on Youths through Age 19.* Ypsilanti, MI: High/Scope Press.

Wells, Shirley E. 1990. *At-Risk Youth: Identification, Programs, and Recommendations.* Englewood, NJ: Teacher Ideas Press.

3

Ruth Sautu

Poverty, Psychology, and Dropouts

The quantitative expansion of schooling in Latin America and the Caribbean after World War II has been the result, first, of the growth in number and location of new schools in rural and marginal areas, and second, of the material improvement of housing and sanitation in addition to a growing consciousness on the part of families of the value of education (CEPAL 1992, 43). Nevertheless, regional and intra-country disparities in school performance remain. Differences in the rates of repetition and dropout show that the quantitative expansion of elementary school attendance has been reached at the expense of quality. Deficient teachers training and low pay, obsolete curricula and formalistic pedagogic practices may account for low learning achievement, especially in rural areas and among children from poor households (CEPAL 1992, 44–46). The persistence of grade repetition and low average scores in language and mathematics achievement tests have stirred up the debate on the role of schools and on the need to improve their quality.[1]

This chapter discusses the role of schools among children who have failed achievement tests or have been involved in events of so-called disruptive behavior, and whose parents are unable to cope with their education either because they themselves are uneducated, they have low expectations about their children's future, or they are deprived of economic means to meet their family's basic needs. In contrast to previous studies, this study focuses on interactions between teachers, students, and the family as crucial to improving educational achievement.

One recent research report issued by the Economic Commission for Latin America and the Caribbean (ECLAC) states that in the 1990s the percentage of children from low-income households who are delayed in their studies is between ten and forty times higher than that of children from non-poor homes (CEPAL 1993a, 45–48). In addition to low income, the report indicates that the level of schooling of the household members who are fifteen years of age and over, the marital status of the family, and the number of people in the household per room are all explanatory factors of children's school performance, measured for children seven to fourteen years old by their regular grade attainment or their delayed attendance or dropping out of school, and for young people fifteen to twenty-four years old by their enrollment in any educational institution.

A second ECLAC report (CEPAL 1993b, 87–98) analyzes the influence of family organization on children's school performance when the household per capita income and the average years of schooling of family members are held constant, combining the two variables into twelve strata. Three indicators of family organization are: female or male head of household, extended or nuclear families, and legal marriage or marital union. School performance is measured by the average years of schooling of two subpopulations: children ten to fourteen years old and young dependent people fifteen to twenty-four years old living in the household.

In all strata, children from homes of unmarried couples have a lower school performance than children from homes of married couples; the majority of free marital unions is concentrated in the lower strata, and their effect on children's schooling is negative. The effect of female head of household is less clear. In some countries they concentrate in the lower strata and affect children's schooling negatively. Extended family households are overrepresented in the middle strata of several of the countries under study, and their influence on children's schooling is positive, even in those families with a low average of members' years of schooling. Finally, none of the independent variables has a higher effect on children education than low income and rural place of residence.

An earlier study in Brazil (Psacharopoulos and Arriagada 1989, 702–703) incorporates region and urban/rural place of residence as independent variables. The other independent variables are: the availability of piped water and toilets in the household, family income, the presence of other school-age children, parental education and occupation, and gender and working status of the children themselves. Their conclusion is that in comparing the rural Brazilian North and Northeast to the urban Southeast, regional disparities in school participation and literacy can be immense. When regional differences are controlled, the existence of piped water supply increases the probability of children's attending school and completing their education, while children's labor status increases their chances of dropping out of school.

Neither the ECLAC (CEPAL) studies nor Psacharopoulos and Arriagada incorporates the quality of education in their explanatory schemes, although the differences by place of residence (rural/urban) and by region implicitly suggest the existence of a great diversity in the supply of education, which has been proved significant by other sources.

Opinions with regard to the influence of home and family, on the one hand, and the quality of school on the other, disagree on the importance attributed to each. One way in which Latin America differs from developed areas is that there is no systematic research on the contribution of school and family to the educational achievement of children. The existing partial research is not conclusive. Some studies find that family resources have a stronger explanatory power than school characteristics (Simmons and Alexander 1978).[2] On the other hand, a comparison of the results of achievement tests applied in schools of twenty-nine developed and developing countries conclude that the lower the per capita income of a country, the weaker the influence of pupils' social status on achievement; and that the effect of school and teacher quality is comparatively greater. For example, the proportion of the explained achievement variance due to schools and teachers is well over 50 percent in Argentina, Brazil, Peru, Mexico, and Chile, while in the United States it is 36 percent, in Sweden 27 percent and in England 26 percent (Heyneman and Loxley 1983). Bustillo (1993, 192) studies the case of Brazil and concludes that children from lower-income homes benefit proportionally more from improvements in the quality of teaching than children from higher-income homes.

School quality may compensate for the negative effect of poverty. In a study of the educational performance of the poor in rural Northeast Brazil, Harbison and Hanushek (1992, 196–198) state that "providing quality basic facilities and adequate writing materials and textbooks improves student performance" and although measuring teachers quality is difficult, "the results suggest that the difference between an average teacher and one of the best can be sufficient to move a student more than 30 percentile ranks in the achievement distribution in just a two year period."

Along the same line of thought, a World Bank discussion document on improving the quality of primary education in Latin America and the Caribbean proposes three investment measures that maximize learning and school retention in relation to cost: First, implement specific policies for poor children; second, induce a change in the behavior of teachers in the classroom (new teaching techniques and systems of promotion); and third, expand the supply, in both quantity and quality, of textbooks and didactic materials (Wolff, Schiefelbein, and Valenzuela 1994, IX).

School Practices, Disciplinary Codes, and Children's Performance

Awareness of the school's compensatory role among children who live in poverty and policy efforts to improve school quality have basically rested upon increasing investment in infrastructure, didactic materials, and the provision of meals at school. Little attention has been paid to psychosocial and cultural school environments associated with repetition and low learning achievement among children from poor family backgrounds. The studies quoted above assigned a larger explanatory power to household variables and school structural characteristics than to interaction among teachers and pupils and their families. The latter is the focus of our discussion.

Drawing on education experts' experiences and research evidence from Latin America, the United States, and Great Britain, we shall begin by discussing teaching and organizational practices and, subsequently, disciplinary codes, all of which affect children's behavior and learning achievement.

School is a microcosm that shapes knowledge and life chances, including children's own self-expectations, once the influence of family background and community context have been considered. To many poor children, school constitutes a unique source of formal experiences and training for the performance of adult economic and social roles; the most important of these is gainful employment.

Meaningful long-term knowledge, like any social experience, is sorted out and stored by the individual self, processed, and mobilized during further social interaction (Turner 1988, 43–46). Thus, learning is an accumulative situational process that involves selves and their emotions. While malnutrition and certain drugs influence attention, and anxiety is detrimental to learning, there also exist situational training techniques that improve perception, encoding and storing of information and its further processing and mobilization (Abadzi 1990, 12–13).

Like other meaningful life experiences, school trains children in selective perception, recognition, categorization, problem solving, reasoning and decision making; these processes also include training in abstract inferential reasoning. Children and teachers bring to the classroom their own experiences, developing an interaction "taken as shared meanings. Teaching and learning are a constructive building process of meaning-making that results in reflective abstractions, producing symbols within a medium. These symbols then become part of the individual's repertoire of assimilatory schemes, which in turn are used when perceiving and further conceiving" (Fosnot 1996, 27). This cognitive constructivist perspective focuses attention on "the students' active construction of their way of knowing as they strive to be effective by restoring coherence to the worlds of their personal experience" (Cobb 1996, 34). In schools located in poor neighborhoods, indigenous communities, or rural areas, there may exist a difference between what teachers intend to teach and their students' meaningful interpretations when their life experiences are significantly different from those of the teachers. Social class, ethnicity, and neighborhood are a central component of children's affiliation and experiences either through their own families or peer significant groups.

A study based on student records for Dallas, Texas, in 1986 indicates that African-American and Mexican-American children from low income households fall behind their peers in basic skills (language and mathematics), habits (measured by unexcused absenteeism), and teachers' evaluation of both their work habits and their style and demeanor, which refers to students' disruptiveness and appearance (also a teacher's judgment). As long as these children advance in grade attendance, differences in achievement compared to their peers increase (Farkas 1996, 74–75; 137–144).

In grading children's achievement and assessing their behavior at school, teachers reproduce society's standards through their expectations about cognitive achievement and compliance with behavioral norms. Societal association between performance and social class, gender, ethnicity, or national origin often replaces actual direct experience in judging students. "Teachers may give lower grades to students who challenge discipline standards, who question commonly held viewpoints, who appear to be uninterested or uninvolved in activities the teacher organizes, who through frequent absence seem to indicate a lack of commitment to school" (Leiter and Brown 1985, 167).

Social class, ethnicity, national origin, and gender are dealt with as sociocultural categories frequently associated with low learning achievement and in many cases with so-called disruptive behavior. When children's school failure is explained almost exclusively by family and neighborhood characteristics, social responsibility is implicitly transferred from the school context and society to individuals. This may be an expression of the prejudice and discrimination deeply rooted in Latin American tradition.

One case in point are children from indigenous communities. In bilingual or multilingual countries many children are schooled in a language different from their mother language. Spanish, for example, is alien to many young children of Central America and the Andean countries. The fact that their abstract language representation has a different content and meaning prevents them from being fully integrated into the official language system of thought. Several proposals focus education in the native mother language and on teaching Spanish as a second language. These programs are a reaction against teaching all children exclusively in Spanish (Hernández 1995, 535). Pedagogic practices like behavior codes and symbolic rituals—for example, teaching about national heroes—are relative and part of a hegemonic society and culture (Bracho 1995, 279). These facts set up standards of achievement and proper behavior that are difficult to reach for those children labeled as "marginal." Psycho-social withdrawal or challenging behavior may be responses of self-defense in a school context that is not perceived as a field of belongingness and identification.

What is school doing to make children of different social, ethnic, or national affiliations become part of the education community? The Inter-American Dialogue has sponsored an education development project for the secondary and university levels that pursue social equity and economic competitiveness in Latin America (Puryear and Brunner 1995). The idea of promoting a quantitative expansion of education has been replaced by the realization that the quality of schooling has to be improved for those children who deserve special program commitments. This volume includes several of these experiences and their evaluation. They accept that schools are partly responsible for the low level of children's learning achievement.

"Escuela Nueva" in Colombia and the "Fe y Alegría" network of non-elitist Catholic schools in several Latin American countries represent new participatory experiences in which teachers and administrators receive special instructional materials as well as training in new pedagogic standards and in promoting children's self-esteem and creativity (Psacharopoulos, Rojas, and Vélez 1993; Wolff, Schiefelbein, and Valenzuela 1994, 94–95).

The inclusion of psychosocial, cultural, and behavioral aspects of schooling are crucial to understanding children's school performance. The fact that most research in Latin America is quantitatively oriented and includes structural explanatory variables that are correlated with quality of schooling, makes it difficult to discover the role played by those variables at an aggregate level. For Brazil, Gomes-Neto and Hanushek (1994, 136) recognize that "the dearth of information about the entire process of promotion, repetition, and dropping-out behavior implies that informed decision making is extremely difficult."

This entire process at a micro level requires us to study teachers' and pupils' interactions with regards to learning and behavior codes, how they categorize events, what associations among categories they stress, and what their subjective meaning is.

Those pupils labeled as troublesome require headmasters and teachers who establish the difference between a minority with special psychological and pedagogic needs, and the troublemakers. Most of them are children who are experiencing emotional difficulties or who are not oriented to achievement, with consequent adverse effects on attendance, learning, and expected school behavior. Blyth and Milner (1996, 12–13) explained the increase in the rate of exclusion in Great Britain in terms of the unwillingness of headmasters and teachers to cope with troublesome pupils, particularly due to pressures on the school to improve their assignment of resources and productivity in terms of school average scores in the achievement tests.

The same type of pressure is exerted on the majority of Latin American schools. Outside a targeted school program, this emphasis on quality and achievement to face the challenges of a globalized society may lead to discrimination and exclusion. The needs and demands of children in poverty, migrant or rural residents, and non-hegemonic ethnic or national groups have to be articulated with standards of higher achievement.

Low performance at school, measured by evaluation tests, is one cause of repetition that when it is chronic eventually leads to early dropout. The labeling of behavior as disruptive also leads to exclusion from schools or transfers to schools for problematic children. In both cases, dropping out is a probable outcome.

The confusion between grading achievement and assessing proper behavior at school is so frequent that most of the literature on school performance and proposals of change is basically pedagogic. Projects of change based on participatory and conscientization ideas, like community or popular schools, or those designed for indigenous children, very rarely emphasize dealing with disruptive behavior as an issue directly relevant to learning achievement.

It seems likely that behind low achievement test scores in language and mathematics is the application of behavior codes designed for an ideal of children, a design which is alien to children from poor households. Participation in school tasks cannot be dissociated from learning opportunities. Psychosocial self-withdrawal, apathy, and absenteeism may be responses to an environment that children feel as threatening, while teachers interpret these symptoms as troublemaking or disruptive behavior. Psychological counseling programs are expected to treat children in extreme need of help due to emotional stress generated in their daily lives. Generally, it is assumed that their daily lives take place exclusively at home and in the community, thus relieving school contexts from responsibility in fueling children's stress.[3]

Public policies, practices, conventions, and rituals shape school cultures which for many groups may be felt as oppressive and discriminatory. The burden of adaptation is placed on pupils (Watkinson 1997, 8). Some authors, like Paulo Freire, have blamed the education system as a source of violence against children. Discipline and control may take diverse forms, from corporal punishment to injurious or humiliating treatment. Records in the performance notebook that eventually lead to temporal suspension from school or the compulsory participation in psychological counseling services are different ways to deal with problematic children. In general it is assumed that these problems originate outside the school context.

In a study conducted in Australia, Slee (1995, 167) concludes that "policy has predominantly been framed within a control paradigm which limits the potential for addressing the culture, curriculum, organization and pedagogy of schooling which contribute to indiscipline. Education authorities' concern tends to revolve around questions of after-the-fact responses to disruption and is beholden to political dynamics of competing professional cultures within the education organization and to electoral politics which shape governments and, in turn, bureaucratic agendas." Teacher's trade union pressures should be added to this analysis.

Disruptive behavior takes different forms of expression that may be traced to different psychosocial origins. Troublemaking, apathy, absenteeism, and self-withdrawal may be associated with the lack of adequate material resources and deficient teachers' training to interpret and deal with this type of behavior. Bullying is the most frequent form of violence at school. It reflects conflicts and tensions that have their origin in family rearing practices and are favored in certain school contexts.

> The degree to which a school's students will manifest bully/victim problems is not only dependent on the amount of aggression-generating factors in the area, which includes family and neighborhood, it is also largely contingent on the strength of the countervailing forces. The attitudes, routines, and behaviors of the school personnel, particularly those of the teachers, are decisive factors in preventing and controlling bullying activities, as well as in redirecting such behaviors into more socially acceptable channels. . . . [T]he reactions of students who do not participate in bullying can have a major influence on both the short-term and long-term outcome of the situation. (Olweus 1996, 46–48)

Research on the incidence of disruptive behavior at school shows that certain categories of pupils are more vulnerable to a range of disciplinary sanctions including exclusion. In England, Blyth and Milner (1996, 74) question why African-Caribbean boys are more vulnerable to exclusion than girls or boys from other ethnic groups, including whites. They conclude that beyond ethnicity it seems that "there may be more gender effects operating rather than racial ones: that senior teachers (who are mostly male) may find particular difficulties in tolerating masculine assertiveness on the part of older male pupils—in terms of this being a challenge to themselves or to their more junior female colleagues. It is also tentatively suggested that white male teachers may find the masculine assertiveness of black pupils to female teachers more difficult to tolerate than that of white pupils."

A study of violence at primary schools in a very poor neighborhood of Buenos Aires arrives at similar conclusions. Boys nine to ten years of age are more likely to be sent to a psychological counseling service on the basis of their disruptive behavior (Sautu et al. 1997). The specific situations in which they are involved may be troublemaking, truancy, or more serious violent behavioral expressions. Younger children or girls are more likely to be sent to that counseling service on the exclusive basis of their learning difficulties. Only in some cases are children's disruptive behaviors explained by their family's violent experiences. Among children from non-violent homes, behavior problems may be due to their individual temperament or, most probably, to their social experiences related to peer and school interactions. The school climate, for example, may be one that transmits and reinforces power-assertive aggressive model of behavior that affects some children more than others. The research design based on the content analysis of clinical records could not capture either features of the school climate that may foster aggressive behavior or the inability of teachers and headmasters to inhibit this type of behavior.

Conclusion

In this article I have emphasized the role of psychosocial and cultural factors in the explanation of school performance of children from poor families and neighborhoods. My contention has been that achievement of learning abilities and school behavior standards are developed both at home and at school. Reading practices and dispositions are crucial links between family, social class, and ethnicity on the one hand, and school models and practices on the other. The specificity and complexity of these interactions call for a profound investigation of each case before designing interaction programs to alleviate school failure and dropouts in Latin America. General policies may settle the parameters for intervention, but each solution has to be specific for each district and school. Programs should include the actual active participation of family, teachers, and pupils and should be able to create a trustful atmosphere based on the individuals' capacity to find solutions on common-sense grounds, and on the recognition of mutual rights to participate in school decisions.

Notes

1. In 1989, 29 percent of all elementary school children repeated a grade; in the first grade this percentage was 42 percent of enrolled children. The rates of grade repetition and graduation were negatively correlated for eighteen Latin American countries.

2. Heyneman (1980) critizes the conclusions of Simmons and Alexander (1978) on the basis of the evidence not considered by the authors. His own review of the literature concludes that "it is simply not true that the determinants of school achievement are basically the same in both developing and developed countries."

3. It would be misleading to confound poverty, ethnicity, or national origin with school disruption and failure. We cannot ignore children from middle-class or wealthy households. The crucial difference is that school behavior and performance problems among more affluent children find private solutions and therefore are not part of the official statistics.

References

Abadzi, H. 1990. *Cognitive Psychology in the Seminar Room.* Washington, DC: Economic Development Institute of the World Bank, Seminar Paper no. 41.

Blyth, E., and J. Milner. 1996. "Black Boys Excluded from School: Race or Masculinity Issues?" In *Exclusion from School. Inter-Professional Issues for Policy and Practic,* ed. E. Blyth and J. Milner. London: Routledge.

Bracho, T. 1995. "Pobreza educativa." In *Educación y pobreza,* ed. E. Pieck Gochicoa and E. Aguado López. Zinacantepec, Mexico: UNICEF and El Colegio Mexiquense.

Bustillo, I. 1993. "Latin America and the Caribbean" in King, E.M. and M.A. Hill, ed. *Women's Education in Developing Countries: Barriers, Benefits and Policies.* World Bank.

CEPAL. 1992. *Educación y conocimiento: Eje de la transformación productiva con equidad.* Santiago de Chile: U.N. CEPAL.

———. 1993a. *Panorama social de América Latina.* Santiago de Chile: U.N. CEPAL.

———. 1993b. *Cambios en el perfil de las familias. La experiencia regional.* Santiago de Chile: U.N. CEPAL.

Cobb, P. 1996. "Here Is the Mind? A Coordination of Sociocultural and Cognitive Constructivism Perspectives." In *Constructivism, Theory, Perspectives, and Practice,* ed. C. Towney Fosnot. New York: Teachers' College Press.

Farkas, G. 1996. *Human Capital or Cultural Capital. Ethnicity and Poverty Groups in an Urban School District.* New York: Aldine de Gruyter.

Fosnot, C. Twoney. 1996. "Constructivism: A Psychological Theory of Learning." In *Constructivism, Thory, Perspectives, and Practice,* ed. C. Twoney Fosnot.

Gomes-Neto, J. B. and E. A. Hanushek. 1994. "Causes and Consequences of Grade Repetition: Evidence from Brazil." *Economic Development and Cultural Change,* 43:1, 117–148.

Harbison R.W., and E.A. Hanushek. 1992. *Educational Performance of the Poor.* New York: Oxford University Press.

Hernández, J. 1995. "Una approximacion a la educacion indigena como objeto de estudio," in E. Pleck Godicoa and E. Aguado Lopez (eds.), *Educacion y Pobreza.* Zinacantepic, Mexico: UNICEF and El Colegio de Mexico.

Heyneman, S.P. 1980. "Differences Between Developed and Developing Countries: Comment on Simmons and Alexander's Determinants of School Achievement," *Economic Development and Cultural Change* 28, 2: 403–406.

Heyneman, S.P., and W. Loxley, 1983. "The Effect of Primary School Quality on Academic Achievement Across Twenty-nine High and Low Income Countries." *The American Journal of Sociology* 88: 1162–1194.

Leiter, J., and J.S. Brown. 1985. "Determinants of Elementary School Grading." *Sociology of Education* 58: 166–180.

Olweus, D. 1996. *Bullying at School.* Oxford: Blackwell.

Psacharopoulos, G., and A.M. Arriagada. 1989. "The Determinants of Early Age Human Capital Formation: Evidence from Brazil." *Economic Development and Cultural Change* 37, 4: 683–708.

Psacharopoulos, G., C. Rojas, and E. Vélez. 1993. "Achievement Evaluation of Colombia's Escuela Nueva." *Comparative Education Review* 37: 263–277.

Puryear, J.M., and J.J. Brunner. 1995. *Educación, equidad y competitividad económica en las Américas: Un proyecto de diálogo interamericano.* Volume 2, Case studies. Washington DC: Organization of American States.

Sautu, R., S. Slapak, M.M. Di Virgilio, A.M. Luzzi, and R. Martínez Mendoza. 1997. "Pobreza, violencia y fracaso escolar: el papel de la familia y la escuela." *Anuario.* Buenos Aires: School of Psychology, University of Buenos Aires.

Simmons, J., and E.L. Alexander. 1978. "The Determinants of School Achievement in Developing Countries. A Review of the Research." *Economic Development and Cultural Change* 26, 2: 341–357.

Slee, R. 1995. *Changing Theories and Practices of Discipline.* London: The Falmer Press.

Turner, Jonathan H. 1988. *A Theory of Social Interaction.* Stanford: Stanford University Press.

Watkinson, A.M. 1997. "Administrative Complicity and Systemic Violence in Education." In *Systemic Violence in Education: Promise Broken*, J. Ross Epp and A.M. Watkinson eds. Albany: State University of New York Press.

Wolff, L., E. Schiefelbein, and J. Valenzuela. 1994. *Mejoramiento de la calidad de la educación primaria en América Latina y el Caribe. Hacia el Siglo XXI.* Washington DC: The World Bank.

4

Marcela Latorre and John Swope, S.J.

Fe y Alegría: An Alternative Proposal for Primary Education in Latin America

This chapter presents some results of the study "Evaluation of the Internal Efficiency of the Primary Schools of Fe y Alegría (FYA)," carried out by the Centro de Investigación y Desarrollo de la Educación (CIDE) of Chile. It evaluates the schools in the public system with the FYA primary schools with respect to levels of promotion, repetition, and dropout rates, and is based on Codina (1994), Fe y Alegría (1992), Reimers (1992), Schiefelbein (1997), and Swope and Latorre (1998). Attention will be focused on the strategies for retention of students in the school system that Fe y Alegría has been developing since its foundation in 1955.

The Fe y Alegría Movement

Fe y Alegría, FYA, is a non-governmental organization that originated in Venezuela in 1955, the product of a private initiative to increase the educational coverage of the least advantaged groups in society. With the participation of the local community, the aid of private groups, and on the basis of agreements with the respective governments, FYA has been able to grow rapidly and with greater force after 1972, transforming itself into a viable educational alternative for the children in underprivileged sectors.

FYA defines itself as an "integrated popular education movement" that includes formal and informal education, but focuses on primary school in suburban or rural areas. It is an institution of the Catholic Church, backed by the Jesuits, even though it is made up almost exclusively by non-religious personnel. The countries in which FYA operates make up the International Federation of FYA. Its primary education system operates autonomously as a private non-profit institution, within the framework of the respective agreements with the Ministry of Education of each country.

Today, this organization functions in twelve Latin American nations, meeting the educational needs of more than 500,000 students and more than 17,000 teachers and collaborators.

In Latin America, 50 percent of FYA students are matriculated in primary formal education, 30 percent in secondary education, and 14 percent in preschool teaching establishments. The largest coverage of FYA can be observed in Bolivia, where 3 percent of all school age children attend the organization's schools. In Venezuela, 1 percent attend.

In each one of the countries where FYA operates, the cost of the teachers' wages is covered by the Ministry of Education. The local communities partici-pate in the construction of buildings and infrastructure. The National Office of FYA in each country oversees the quality of education given and offers training to its teachers and center directors, administers, the educational centers, and coordinates the activities in such a way that it becomes a development strategy for the local area (Reimers 1992).

The Educational Project of FYA

For FYA, education is a fundamental right of all people. Its principal strategy that cements its programs is oriented toward transferring education and other benefits to those sectors of the population who have been denied the right to a quality education. It is a response to marginal social conditions of broad sectors of the population in the Latin American and Caribbean region.

FYA uses a variety of educational approaches. The initial reading of the social situation of Venezuela in the second half of the 1950s led to the formation of the first educational centers. Soon after, educational centers that included community and social service programs were formed and integrated into the functioning of FYA (FYA prefers to call its schools "educational centers"). FYA showed and continues to show a considerable flexibility in its search for efficient and cost-effective solutions to the multiple problems faced by children and adults from its target population.

The accelerated growth observed between 1972 and 1996 resulted from:

1. *The necessity of responding to social demand for education:* This consti-tuted a source of popular mobilizations in marginal urban sectors. The com-munity was becoming a protagonist, giving land for construction of the educational centers, as well as participating in their construction.
2. *The inability of the state to increase educational coverage:* This factor was crucial in establishing a relationship between FYA and the governments of the respective nations. FYA decided to operate within the public system. The agreements made between FYA and the governments of the respective nations allow FYA to enjoy a relatively high level of autonomy, which has permitted the introduction of school innovations. In exchange for this auton-omy, FYA promises to cover the costs of infrastructure, equipment, and the implementation of innovative educational programs. The fiscal saving con-tributed by FYA has been calculated for the first time in this study.

    Annual unit investment: FYA produces public savings. The comparison of the annual unit investment of FYA to that of public education is of considerable interest. Each of the respective systems of Guatemala and Paraguay generate additional resources. In Guatemala, FYA adds up to US$76 to the state subsidy of US$95 per student. The general unit investment of FYA was US$171, which was higher by US$41 per student than the total unit investment in the public sector. In Paraguay, FYA added an investment of US$49 to the government subsidy of US$119. The general unit investment in FYA reached US$168, which was US$114 per student higher than the total unit investment in the public sector.

This provides a model of private management of public education that makes concerted efforts with the aim of increasing total unit investment beyond the level of public spending. In Guatemala, the total spending per student in FYA schools is US$171, and in public schools it was US$136. In Paraguay, total investment per student reached US$168, and in public schools it was US$133.

FYA provided an important saving of public sector resources. Formal primary school education in public schools cost the government US$136 per student in Guatemala, and US$133 in Paraguay. And the public cost of formal education in FYA schools is, in these countries, US$95 and US$119, respectively. This results in savings. In 1995, FYA-Guatemala reduced public spending on education by US$41 per student, and in Paraguay by $US14 per student. Multiplying these savings by the number of students, we can better appreciate the size of FYA's economic contribution. In 1995, total government saving in primary school education, brought by FYA-Guatemala, was approximately US$350,222, while in Paraguay this saving reached US$89,502.

The projected savings that will be generated by FYA in each nation during 1995–2004, anticipating an annual rate of inflation of 10 percent, will reach US$4,983,806 for the government of Guatemala and US$1,504,681 for that of Paraguay.

3. *The changes in the focus of the Catholic Church:* With the thrust of the Second Vatican Council beginning in 1965, the Latin American Episcopal Conference (CELAM) proceeded to invite both the secular religious as well as religious congregations to reorient their mission toward the poor masses in the Latin American and Caribbean region. FYA provided a context in which these groups dedicated to the poorest would later work.

FYA constitutes an interesting case of concerted public and private action, as well as of mobilization of a range of diverse resources. This approach was confirmed explicitly in the 1990 "Education for All" conference in Jomtien. In alliance with the state, with the support of the local community and through the combination of resources donated at the local and international levels, FYA has been converted into an interesting model of an educational system privately managed and financed on a shared basis. The institutional characteristics of FYA's primary education are:

Strategic Alliances: concerted aid from the private sector, the national and local government, and international granting agencies;

Participation of the local community, becoming protagonists in educational processes;

Diversified and relevant education, which relates education to the satisfaction of basic learning needs and the improvement of the quality of life of the beneficiaries;

Selection of directors of schools and of educational programs, as well as the selection of teachers (whenever possible) and the organization of training programs for teachers and directors;

Public credibility through true leadership and good management of public and private resources;

Spirit of innovation, which has been the source of the development of alternative educational models and of micro-innovations;

Value added of FYA: a sense of mission, strong institutional identity, and the option of offering quality education to the poorest sectors; and

Policy of optimization of resources: in all the nations covered by FYA and where the state subsidizes teachers' salaries, the large number of students per class does not lead to greater direct subsidies. The number of students per class could be lowered without affecting government subsidies. However, FYA tries to maintain a high number of students per class as a response to the low proportion of the age cohorts receiving education in the various nations.

Data on Fe y Alegría

An overview of the FYA's levels of coverage shows that the total number of primary school educational centers varies considerably among the countries evaluated (see Table 4.1). Only eight FYA centers were closed between 1990 and 1995.

This accomplishment is even more meaningful given that the state resources obtained by FYA cover only the salaries of the teachers and some administrators, and that, therefore, its survival depends on financial and administrative management of FYA in each country.

FYA's Strategies for the Retaining Primary School Students

The Ministries of Education of the entire region have developed a great many strategies to reduce rates of grade repetition and school dropout during the first years of schooling of children coming from the most unprotected sectors of society. FYA's strategies to retain students include six types of programs aimed at confronting school failure:

Preventive programs destined to improve and change the health and nutrition status of poor children can be efficient although expensive, given the large number of students in poverty.

Table 4.1

Characteristics of Fe y Alegría Schools

Country	Number of educational centers in 1995	Number of educational centers closed since the beginning of FYA	Number of matriculated students in 1995	Survival Index — Educational centers closed in relation to the number of centers functioning in 1995
Bolivia	115	5	78, 576	.95
Colombia	54	1	35, 321	.98
Ecuador	48	2	14, 827	.95
Guatemala	33	0	8, 542	1.00
Peru	41	0	29, 225	1.00
Nicaragua	11	0	6, 143	1.00
Venezuela	169	0	NA	1.00
Paraguay	43	0	47, 438	1.00
Totals	514	8	220, 241	.98

Remedial programs for children with learning problems are effective in reducing school dropout rates, especially when the school calendar and daily hours are adapted to the needs of the students and their community.

Flexible or multiple promotion programs are especially effective. At the same time, multiple promotion programs offer students more opportunities to be promoted to the next grade.

Economic incentive programs attempt to influence the parents' decision to withdraw their older children from school in order to make them take care of their younger siblings or to directly enter the labor force in order to supplement family income. Preschool programs not only offer an initial advantage in basic learning abilities, but also could reduce the dropout of girls, since preschool education programs provide a supervised activity for all children between three and six years of age, thus reducing the demand for older girls as a domestic alternative for the care of younger siblings. Sixty-five percent of FYA schools have preschool programs.

Active community participation in the institutional process, especially during preschool, not only can stimulate the intellectual development of the child, but also can generate positive relationships among the teachers, families, and students that result in a better educational outcome.

Secondary education technical education programs—"education with work"—offer parents with primary school age children a concrete example of children of slightly older school ages receiving education and, at the same time, developing income-generating work. The Colegio Marista in

Table 4.2

Average Number of Years of Service of Teachers in FYA Educational Centers

Country	Total cases	5 or less	6–10	11–20	21 or more
Peru	28	18.5	66.7	14.8	—
Bolivia	90	44.6	41.3	12.0	2.2
Venezuela	64	20.0	52.3	24.6	3.0
Nicaragua	10	60.0	40.0	—	—
Ecuador	28	34.6	52.1	11.5	3.8
Guatemala	14	46.2	15.4	38.5	—
Colombia	31	17.2	34.5	37.9	10.3
El Salvador	4	50.0	25.0	25.0	—
Paraguay	24	91.3	8.7	—	—

Cochabamba, Bolivia, offers preschool, primary, and lower secondary technical education (seventh to ninth grades) in the same school. In the lower secondary technical program, the students produce furniture in the carpentry workshop for the school itself, as well as for a number of clients in the city of Cochabamba. This small business finances the cost of supplies for the workshops, as well as a small stipend for the student-workers. According to interviews with groups of parents in each level of the school, this acts as a strong stimulus to keep their children in school.

A necessary condition for the successful implementation of any strategy for retaining students is the stability of the teaching team. As indicated in Table 4.2, for all the countries except Nicaragua, at least 50 percent of the teachers had five or more years of service.

In the cases of Guatemala and Paraguay, a significant percentage of the FYA directors considered that the years of service in their respective schools was rather brief, 46 percent in the case of Guatemala and 37 percent in that of Paraguay. In the remaining countries, between 75 percent and 90 percent considered that the average number of years of service of their teachers was "reasonable." Within this institutional context of the relative stability of the teaching team, FYA developed seven types of student retention strategies, including preventive and compensatory educational programs, multiple promotion policies, economic incentives, integration of the community, preschool programs, and secondary education programs. The theme of the community and its integration into educational processes is the axis of FYA's action in all of the countries. It is the take-off point for and the nucleus of action. We can also indicate that the educational model implemented by FYA gives great importance to preschool attendance, which is indispensable for the development of abilities and basic skills that facilitate learning processes and scholastic success.

Preventive Strategies

These strategies are a fundamental aspect of the plan for retaining students in certain nations. We include here preventive programs to take care of students' health and nutrition, which are present in more than 50 percent of FYA schools. Only 20 percent of student dropouts in these nations were attributed to health (59 of 285 dropouts). This could be precisely because the preventive programs are in place.

Together with preventive strategies, FYA implements remedial strategies, and compensatory strategies to retain students in schools and improve the possibilities of their timely progress.

Remedial Strategies

Remedial strategies consist of programs whose aim is to confront the complex problems related to school failure, as well as to aid students with learning problems. The most specialized remedial strategy is the professional service of a psychologist. However, the special services for those students with deficits in learning are not quickly arranged for extremely poor urban neighborhoods and even less for rural areas, places where FYA centers usually are located.

Thus, a large share of FYA remedial strategies are carried out in large part by non-professional teams, with programs that usually are not highly specialized. The most frequent strategies are programs to stimulate parents' awareness, encouraging them to participate actively in their children's education (especially those with learning difficulties). Specialized therapeutic interventions by a psychologist with groups or individual students are less frequent.

Multiple or Flexible Promotion Policies

Teachers in general are unhappy with rigid promotion policies, and believe that flexible promotion policies would aid in reduction of repetition and dropout, in part because students' maturity levels could change during the school vacation after they had failed and been assigned to repeat a grade. The flexible promotion policies are structured to provide more opportunities to students for progressing from one grade to another, thus avoiding school failure. An additional measure that aids in reducing repetition is adjusting the school year to permit students to work during the harvest periods without slowing their educational progress.

An example of flexible promotion is that of FYA schools in Guatemala. Students from preschool education through the sixth grade of basic education can advance to the next grade by (1) normal promotion: at the end of the school year and based on grade averages; (2) delayed promotion: at the end of a remedial period after which special promotion tests are administered; and (3) final promotion: students from the third to the sixth grades have the opportunity to take an exam for promotion when they return to school the following year.

In some FYA educational centers, teachers give a test to preschool, first and second grade students who failed the previous year. This test is not approved by the Ministry of Education. The educational centers in which the final promotion test is applied report that 50 percent of those repeaters from the first and second grade pass the exam at the beginning of the new school year. The teachers believe that the students who fail during the normal and postponed promotion processes but are approved in the final promotion phase often exhibit a greater emotional and physical maturity when they return to school the following year.

Strategies of Economic Incentive Programs

Economic incentive programs provide direct or indirect economic incentives for parents to maintain their children in school. Sending minors into the labor force during the normal primary school year is a family strategy, based on the analysis of "immediate economic benefit versus long-term personal cost" frequently utilized by families in extreme poverty. In this case, the immediate benefit goes to the family and the cost is paid later by the child who leaves school.

In various countries FYA provides indirect economic incentives including: (1) school food programs, especially free lunches, which are a powerful incentive for families in extreme poverty to maintain their children in schools; (2) payment of direct school costs, such as transportation, school uniforms and school suppl- ies; and (3) free textbooks.

Strategies of Community Integration

An active commitment of the community to the school is central to FYA's student retention strategy. At the same time, the pursuit of the active engagement of the community overtakes these more restricted educational objectives, trans- forming itself into a local development strategy in which the educational center includes political-territorial, productive, cultural, and educational projects. The active participation of the family in a child's education is only one of the charac- teristics of a larger strategy for the community. The creation of an educational center has various steps, even though they vary from country to county. These generally are:

1. Representatives of the community invite FYA to establish a school in the area. FYA tends to be introduced in highly marginal urban areas in which there is no school, exclusively by invitation by a group from the local community.
2. FYA strives to initiate classes immediately, with whatever resources that are at hand.
3. Contact is made with community organizations in order to construct a broad alliance to aid the school.

4. Community groups and parents participate in the construction of the school, which significantly reduces the cost of labor. The community often has to finance to finish carpentry, windows, and electrical installation of the school building.
5. The parents' center begins operation immediately and tends to collaborate closely with the director.
6. FYA is aware of the challenges faced by the family and seeks to involve it actively in the school.

This focus on centers that provide multiple educational and social services tends to create a vast range of learning situations for children and various community groups. The preschool programs increase the level of educability, and programs of "education combined with work" connected with technical education in secondary school provide parents with another powerful incentive, although indirect, for keeping their children in school.

Programs for Technical Education in Secondary School: "Education with Work"

Education with work in the high school technical education programs and programs for apprentices, which provide education with work and/or education with income on the same premises as the school itself, offer parents an example of the benefits of postponing early dropout from the school system. Given the problems of coverage of primary education, and the devastating economic effects of dropout and repetition, no type of secondary education has been a priority of FYA. However, in some countries a significant number of programs exist, some of which combine education with work. Some programs even include education work and income: "businesses with a base in the school" have appeared, offering products for the local market and providing an attractive image to parents who are tempted to withdraw their children from school. In other cases, these "businesses with a base in the school" have been converted into a source of income for the worker-students, bringing, in this way, a powerful economic incentive without blocking their capacity of benefiting from education. This kind of educational activity has considerable impact on a school community fighting to reduce school dropouts.

Conclusions

Of the programs and factors mentioned above that have an impact on student retention in the FYA primary schools, the most important ones are the following: parent-centered strategies based on an open school environment that promotes effective parent involvement in the learning process and community involvement in the management of the school; and student-centered strategies based on remedial strategies that depend on an intensive conversation among teachers and recognition of a variety of learning styles. Together with these two factors, we should also mention an overall organizational strategy in which the FYA educational offer in each school is comprehensive, including preschool, primary and lower secondary technical education. This organizational strategy operates as a strong stimulus for parents to keep their children in school because it helps them to envision more clearly the return of education, and provides a basis for the economic and social development of extremely poor local communities.

References

Codina, G. 1994. "La experiencia de Fe y Alegría en Bolivia." In *Cooperación internacional y desarrollo de la educación*, pp. 321–346. Santiago: Agencia de Cooperación Internacional de Chile.

Fe y Alegría. 1992. "Ideario Internacional de Fe y Alegría." *Identidad de Fe y Alegría: procesos educativos* 1: 513.

Reimers, F. 1992. "Fe y Alegría: una innovación educativa para proporcionar educación básica con calidad y equidad." *Revista paraguaya de sociología* 85.

Schiefelbein, E. 1997. *School-Related Economic Incentives in Latin America: Reducing Drop-Out and Repetition, and Combating Child Labor.* Inocenti Occasional Papers, Child Right Series, No. 12. Bogotá: UNICEF-TACRO.

Swope, J., and M. Latorre. 1998. "El aporte de Fe y Alegría a la educación primaria en América Latina: un estudio comparativo longitudinal de la educación primaria impartida por Fe y Alegría y las escuelas públicas en nueve países en América Latina." Financed by the Academy of Educational Development.

5

LÚCIA AVELAR

The Role of the State in Education

Introduction

In all the developing nations on the periphery of the capitalist world, and, in general, under political authoritarian regimes, problems of education are well known: basic education of low quality, high rates of repetition and dropout, pauperization of teachers with loss of status as educational professionals, an enormous contingent of teachers without adequate professional preparation, inefficiency in the management of public resources for education, excessive numbers of bureaucrats, absence of evaluation of administrative school units, political interference in educational management, especially in the context of strong local power, inadequate investment in works, and other undertakings to the detriment of professional formation.

The present discussion starts with the fact that educational policy is made by political actors who are profoundly different, representing the differences among towns and regions in the same nation, especially where there exists enormous social and regional inequality and differentiated structures of political power; education thus feels the impact of varied political and administrative mechanisms. During the 1990s, education is considered basic for the recovery of economic growth, re-entry into international competitiveness, and recuperation of citizenship rights that had been lost by large masses of the population. It is this field in which the answers to questions about the role of the state in education are most important. In this chapter we undertake a policy analysis of the role of the state in education, discussing the depth and nature of the socio-educational question, and indicating the recommendations found in national and international debates.

Depth and Nature of the Socio-Educational Question

It is misleading to confuse the state with its government apparatus, the public sector, or the combination of public bureaucracies, which are part of it, but not the whole. The state is also a conjunction of social relations that are established in a given territory, formalized in a legal/constitutional system. In nations with strong social and regional inequalities, that the effectiveness of the law does not always extend itself throughout the territory. Many nations, for example Brazil, Argentina, and Mexico, have many "peripheral" areas in relation to the national center, present weak bureaucracies, particular rules of local power, personalism, and patrimonialism. These "peripheral areas" refer as much to cities in distant regions of the developed nations as to the periphery of large cities, in the area of urban decay, where the state is not capable of implementing the law and enforcing its decisions for the public good.

If we were to draw a picture of the regions according to the greater or lesser effectiveness of state laws, with differentiated degrees of private power, we would imagine a map showing high, medium, and low areas of the Human Development Index, with differences so highly marked that we refer to "three Brazils," the first being the richest region of the nation. The high human development areas have effective laws and bureaucracies. The medium areas have a high grade of territorial penetration and lower presence of state functionaries. The low areas have neither effective bureaucracies, nor state functionaries, nor legality, nor true public action tied to the public interest (O'Donnell 1994). Using the case of Brazil as an example, the figures of current social inequalities present an enormous correspondence with the areas in which differential penetration of the state in the territory is observed.

Center–Periphery Relations and Mechanisms of Political Intermediation

If we take each one of the "three Brazils," would the role of the state be the same in education? If we know that the smaller the locality, the lower the Human Development Index, and that in the poorest subregion, the third Brazil, there are numerous localities with strong local power bases, what should be the action of the state for an efficient action in education? Table 5.1 indicates the Human Development Index and rank of amount of schooling. By way of illustration, the average number of years of schooling for the first Brazil is 4.23, for the second Brazil it is 3.02, and for the third Brazil, it is 2.18 years of study.

Does not the role of the state have to be that of a strong regulator, as a means of correcting large deficiencies and giving priority to areas of exclusions, discrimination, and vulnerability, particularly in poor regions like those of third Brazil? Or, similarly, in these regions, does not the state have to act organically and efficiently, to reach "high" objectives? This posited, we avoid speaking of a role of the state in education, and instead speak of its various roles in a complex structure of diversities, privileges, and differing degrees of citizenship.

Growth in the Periphery of the Capitalist World

In the postwar period in Latin America, state capitalism became the motor of economic development, implementing activities that would preferentially con-

Table 5.1

Classification of Brazilian States According to the Human Development Index

State	Value of HDI	Rank of Schooling
First Brazil		
Rio Grande do Sul	0.871	3
Distrito Federal	0.858	1
São Paulo	0.850	2
Santa Catarina	0.842	5
Rio de Janeiro	0.838	4
Paraná	0.827	6
Mato Grosso do Sul	0.826	7
Espirito Santo	0.816	8
Second Brazil		
Amazonas	0.797	15
Amapá	0.781	10
Minas Gerais	0.779	11
Mato Grosso	0.769	12
Goiás	0.760	9
Roraima	0.749	14
Rondônia	0.715	13
Third Brazil		
Pará	0.688	16
Acre	0.665	20
Sergipe	0.663	19
Bahia	0.609	21
Pernambuco	0.577	17
Rio Grande do Norte	0.574	18
Maranhão	0.512	22
Ceará	0.506	24
Piauí	0.502	23
Alagoas	0.500	26
Paraíba	0.466	25

Source: Relatório Sobre o Desenvolvimento Humano. IPEA/PNUD. 1996.

tribute to the domestic product, controlling investments by defining the firms and productive sectors that would direct the economy. Government policy succeeded well in the field of industrialization for many Latin American countries, but, with the exception of Cuba, it neither consistently redistributed income nor promoted social democracy in the nation.

Authoritarian Regimes and Interest Groups

For development to occur under state capitalism, authoritarian regimes act simultaneously to centralize clientelistic practices, and to centralize and strengthen the capacity of institutional innovation. Using patrimonialist bureaucracies and meritocracies in a peculiar and successful economic model, some policies are created that benefit regional interest groups composed of middle and upper middle class segments who are their political bases. As a result, development modifies class structure, also deepening the distance between classes.

Traditionalism and Modernization: Traditional Political Elites and Their Role

All analyses have indicated the perseverance of traditional elites throughout the processes of modernization, with enormous access of oligarchic groups to the governmental and bureaucratic area of the state. Government political and bureaucratic relations can be obstacles to the implementation of social policies of national interest, given the fragmented attention to the demands made on the political system and the consequent pulverization of resources destined to education (Faria 1997).

Moreover, regions of the second and third Brazil have more conservative municipal political power than do municipalities with better social development (Avelar 1997). What is the consequence for educational policies? Up to what point are the local oligarchic elites the efficient channels of application of public resources in the local area?

Economic Modernization and Political Change

Economic modernization does not necessarily bring political change. In the least developed regions of Latin America, clientelism rather than ideology or interest groups tend to dominate policymaking and practice. The ties between the political center and local politics are the dorsal spine of an undemocratic restrictive system, which characterizes the way the state responds to political demands for education. For example, in Brazil the perpetuation of the power of agrarian elites in the state is guaranteed by the electoral rules of proportional representation, by means of which the least populated states are over-represented, and the most highly developed regions are under-represented. In general, resources for education are distributed through political-oligarchic networks to the areas which control it. Moreover, the educational policies that deal with nationally defined priorities may encounter difficulties of implementation at the municipal level, among other reasons, because implementation is done by state-level administrators who are functionaries of the advisory government bodies and the state technicians. Further, client-oriented decision making, especially in rural areas, has not adapted to the demands of varied interest groups expressed through non-governmental organizations, although political parties have incorporated these demands in order to attract urban voters (Keck 1991; Sandoval 1994; Przeworski 1985).

The Political Use of Bureaucracies

State bureaucracies are used as sources of special benefits to redistribute government resources to benefit organizations or politicians loyal to the president.

Payment of the foreign debt reduced government financial resources and increased clientelism, contributing to the pauperization of teachers and the collapse of primary education. The smallest towns tended to suffer greatly during the economic crisis and became more dependent on the federal network.

Consequence: Collapse of Teaching and Pauperization of Teachers

One of the most delicate social consequences of the collapse of public basic education was the pauperization of teachers. This occurred in the epoch in which policy discourses emphasized the importance of education for national and international competitiveness in industry and, also, for improving impoverished workers' salaries. The real process of educational policy was different: teachers in public schools at the basic school level were paid less as time went on, especially following the Latin American debt crisis beginning in the early 1980s and continuing into the 1990s. A large share of them, the most qualified, left in search of other jobs and income, while others worked not only in public but also in private teaching jobs. Others, still, looked for commercial jobs in their own schools to make up for their increasing loss of income. For example, average annual salaries of Rio de Janeiro teachers of the first and second segments of the first grade indicate that from 1979 to 1996, the salary of an experienced teacher with higher education was, in 1994, barely 15.07 percent of that which had obtained in 1979 (Paiva et al. 1997). For the entire category, there was a loss of one-third of the earnings; the professors of first grade lost more than two-thirds, which shows, among other things, their smaller capacity for mobilization to defend their status and self-esteem (see Table 5.2). The same rapid decline in salaries occurred in Argentina, Mexico (see chapters 24 and 27), and other Latin American countries. The "pauperization of teachers" demonstrates a situation of profound consequence in the daily life of schools, and is reflected in repetition and dropout.

In Brazil recent reforms by the Ministry of Education aimed at addressing the inequalities in the distribution of educational resources have created a national, value added tax–financed fund to supplement state and municipal resources used, in part, to improve teachers' salaries.[1] The distribution of the resources would be made in proportion to students' annual enrollment, based on the number of students in the prior year's census.

One of the most polemic points is related to the training of teachers without full credentials, which would absorb 60 percent of the resources destined to the payment of salaries, thus resulting in teachers' pay continuing at low levels.

Disparities in teachers' salaries, school supplies, and school attendance are all closely related to the distribution of income. In Brazil, 80 percent of adolescents from families with income above two minimum wages go to school while barely 40 percent of those from poor families are able to stay in school (PNUD/IPEA 1996).

Table 5.2

Average Annual Salaries (in 1996 reais)

	IPC-RJ*			ICVT-DIEESE**	
Year	Lowest salary	Highest salary	Year	Lowest salary	Highest salary
1979	637.18	1,818.64	1979	1,169.00	3,332.96
1980	806.64	1,657.65	1980	1,485.75	3,053.37
1981	640.82	1,314.36	1981	1,208.37	2,478.45
1982	572.17	1,173.55	1982	1,103.93	2,264.22
1983	499.77	2,005.62	1983	941.47	3,774.45
1984	532.28	1,760.84	1984	1,039.05	3,423.98
1985	489.47	1,572.07	1985	957.52	3,073.99
1986	561.36	1,730.02	1986	1,022.32	3,157.85
1987	455.69	1,453.00	1987	740.24	2,360.92
1988	395.02	1,310.00	1988	699.65	2,320.24
1989	385.25	1,277.28	1989	534.27	1,771.37
1990	512.98	1,406.63	1990	644.48	1,767.20
1991	429.08	958.47	1991	503.86	1,125.52
1992	327.66	709.11	1992	390.21	844.32
1993	281.44	545.24	1993	342.52	663.66
1994	239.67	442.79	1994	283.60	524.10
1995	316.93	472.66	1995	334.69	499.73
1996	385.81	537.95	1996	384.56	536.21

Source: Vanilda Paiva, Célia Junqueira, Leonardo Muls. *Prioridade ao ensino básico e pauperização docente.*
*Consumer price index, calculated by the Fundaçáo Gétulio Vargas of Rio de Janeiro.
**Cost of living index calculated by the Departmento Intersindical e Estadistica e Estudus Sócioeconomicus which is an entity of the government of the State of Sâo Paulo.

The regional disparities bear directly on the rates of repetition and on the pauperization of teachers. In 1990, the national rate of grade repetition was 46 percent; in the "third Brazil" (the Northwest and Northeast), it was 60 percent; in the Southeast, 23 percent, the South, 30 percent; the Center, 44 percent; and the Center West, 44 percent. Considering the distinct socioeconomic levels, these rates were 23 percent for the highest level of income, 48 percent for the middle level, and 63 percent for the lowest level.

This Brazilian example illustrates the distributional problem of educational policies and its social consequences, which are a major challenge to the state. Can the state change the picture to create perspectives of effective changes of its role, becoming truly redistributive? The discussion, then, is centered on which mechanisms should govern the distribution of resources, diminishing the possible amount of policy negotiation.

It is important to compare Brazil to other nations analyzed in this volume. In Mexico the situation is similar to that of Brazil. Mexico is a federal state with strong provincial power; it was centralized during the nineteenth century, strengthened by the postrevolutionary regimes to obtain national unity, and today has changes in the mechanisms for collecting and distributing taxes among the federal government, states, and municipalities. The transparency of fiscal collections has been an important theme of debate, as well as the division of the proceeds. There were serious problems that directly affected social policies owing to the practices of political intermediation of a clientelistic or semiclientelistic nature; the people lacked autonomy to organize their interests (Vega 1995; Fox 1995).

In Chile, the major challenges of fiscal federalism seem to have been overcome. The central government establishes general rules for a minimum curriculum, and for the tasks of administrative and technical supervision. The financing of school units obeys market principles, subsidized per student, in a way to promote competition between schools to attract and retain the students. Implanted before the other countries, it is considered one of the success cases in overcoming the observed challenges.

Argentina, with the political instability it has undergone in recent decades, has alternated between democratic and dictatorial regimes, with shifting amount of central and local power. In the 1990s, the picture is that of profound regional inequalities. Educational decentralization that is now taking place is, therefore, part of a long history related to the institutional and fiscal shaping of Argentine federalism. Here the provincial jurisdictions are those that receive the financing, with a traditional mechanism of laying out money according to vacancies, which by all indications is resulting in a greater dispersion of funds than is true for Chile.

The rules of electoral representation in Brazil are the true institutional source of corruption and of clientelism, the ways par excellence by which the politicians, allied to the political center, obtain government funds for the execution of their political plans at the local level. This situation is made worse because highly competent people often refuse to work in the government. Some suggest that transformation of the state can be achieved by decentralization, a process that will incorporate increased access to information made possible by increased access to the Internet, which is a feature of current educational policy in some Latin American nations.

Another challenging question is how to resolve the balance between public and private responsibility for financing education. It is well known that private primary and high schools are of superior quality, with low rates of repetition and dropout, and better qualified, better paid teachers. The contrast between private and public school teachers' salaries has had slight alterations owing to the diminution of teachers' salaries, and lower sums for stipends for research and postgraduate studies. On the other hand, the private and semiprivate institutions in many Latin American nations claim that they have given greater service to the population with the worst socioeconomic condition (Velloso 1995), for example, in the Fe y Alegría schools. In any case, this is another point of tension in the field of negotiations of the state in education.

Recommendations for State Policies on Education

The quality of state intervention depends on the quality of democracy, and this, in turn, depends on the effectiveness of accountability by which the governments are forced to justify their acts to the population (Przeworski 1995). The question of greater inclusion is how to make the state a real instrument for serving common objectives (Sartori 1991).

The state should coordinate decentralization, so that it does not reinforce inequalities; it should develop shares with the various institutions of civil society, calling on them to carry out their social functions; decentralize without corporatization for greater participation of special interests and solidarity groups, conditions essential for the promotion of the collective good of education; adopt modern systems of social protection, with responsible bureaucracies. It is clear that the means of decentralizing education should be distinct and adapted to the needs of the country, considering the regional distribution of income and wealth. Where resources are much greater, the teachers are much better trained and have much better material conditions.

There is no way of postponing the question of salary policy in the educational field. The consequences of extremely low teacher salaries is profound. The salary scales and promotion rules for teachers should be made equal to those of other professionals, such as those of the Judiciary, for example, whose incentives are progressive, including the promise of working in distant locations and, little by little, moving closer to these professionals' place of origin.

Greater sensitivity is needed for the implementation of teachers' training programs, especially for teachers from the lowest socioeconomic segments. In the municipalities of subregions, especially those of strong local power, the government should break with conservative structures, understanding that their elites are not interested in educating the masses. The educational bureaucracies in these municipalities should be transformed in order to serve their respective populations.

Educational policies should center themselves on mechanisms of institutional innovation for a new political pact in the field of education, giving rise to new forms of management that take account of its role in the social area of education, establishing conditions for the implementation of changes whose necessity already is too well known. The role of the state in education is that of active agent in the implementation of institutional mechanisms, intervening effectively in redistribution. It is in this sense that social policy cannot be delayed, with the responsibility of bringing to effective citizenship the thousands of individuals excluded from basic social rights. Finally, the essential role of the state is to prepare the individual for citizenship and for democracy.

Note

1. One reason for the pauperization of primary school teachers in Brazil was that there was an expansion of the unionization of teachers at the middle and high school levels, with effective political organization. This did not happen in the same way for primary

school teachers: the federal expenditures for salaries for primary education fell 39 percent between 1986 and 1989; for higher education, they rose 59 percent. The competition for scarce resources ended up favoring the most organized segments of education.

General References

Arretche, Marta. 1996. "Mitos da descentralização: mais democracia e eficiência nas políticas públicas?" *Revista Brasileira de Ciências Sociais,* número 31 (junho).

Berger, Suzanne. 1981. *Organizing Interests in Western Europe: Pluralism, Corporatism and the Transformation of Politics.* New York: Cambridge University Press.

Carciofi, Ricardo, Centrángolo, and O. Larrañaga. 1996. *Desafíos de la descentralización.* Naciones Unidas.

Cintra, Antônio Octávio. 1972. "A política tradicional brasileira: uma interpretação das relações entre o centro e a periferia." *Cadernos do DCP.*

Gouveia, Gilda. 1994. *Burocracia e elites burocráticas no Brasil.* ace of Pub Paulicéia. São Paulo.

Hagopian, Frances. 1986. "The Politics of Oligarchy." Unpublished Ph.D. dissertation. Massachusets Institute of Technology.

Inter-American Development Bank. 1996. *Opportuniy Foregone—Education in Brazil,* ed. Nancy Birdsall and Richard Sabot. Baltimore: Johns Hopkins University Press.

Klein, Ruben. 1997. "Indicadores educacionais: disparidades regionais e socioeconômicas no Brasil." Mimeograph.

Lamounier, Bolívar." 1992. "O modelo institucional dos anos 30 e a presente crise brasileira." *Estudos Avançados,* 6, no. 14.

Linz, Juán, and Alfred Stepan. 1996. *Problems of Democratic Transition and Consolidation: Southern Europe, South America, and Post-Communist Europe.* Baltimore: Johns Hopkins University Press.

Monlevade, João, and Eduardo Ferreira. 1997. *O FUNDEF e os seus pecados capitais.* Brasília: Idéia Editora.

Pizzorno, Alessandro. 1966. "Introduzione allo studio della partecipazione politica." *Quaderni di Sociologia* 15.

Programa das nações Unidas para o desenvolvimento. Instituto de Pesquisas Elonômicas Aplicadors Ministerio de Planejamento.

Przeworski, Adam. 1989. *Capitalismo e Social Democracia.* Ed. Companhia das Letras. São Paulo.

Przeworski, Adam. 1995. "Reforming the State: Political Accountability and Economic Intervention." Paper presented at conference entitled "Inequality, the Welfare State and Social Values." Spain.

Reis, Fábio Wanderley. 1974. "Solidariedade, interesses e desenvolvimento político." *Cadernos do DCP,* 1.

———. 1984. *Política e racionalidade.* Belo Horizonte: Edição UFMG/PROED/RBEP.

———. 1989. "Cidadania, estado e mercado—democracia social e democracia política no processo de transformação capitalista." In *Para a década de 90: prioridades e perpesctivas de políticas públicas,* ed. Sônia Draibe. Rio de Janeiro: IPEA/IPLAN.

Tenti, Emilio. 1989. "Estado y sociedad—Discutir el estado en la Argentina." *Conces* año 1, número 1 (abril).

Sartori, G. 1991. *International Social Science Journal* vol. 48. August.

United Nations. 1994. *Coping with Crisis: Austerity, Adjustment and Human Resources.* Monograph.

World Bank. 1992. *Governance and Development.* Washington, DC: World Bank.

Works Cited

Avelar, Lúcia. 1996. "Clientelismo de estado e política educacional brasileira." *Revista Educaçã e Sociedade* (Ano XVII—abril). Campinas: Ed. Cedes/Papirus.

Faria, Vilmar. 1997. Conferência sobre Políticas Sociais, feita na Fundaçao Konrad-Adenauer-Stiftüng, setembro. São Paulo.

Keck, Margaret E. 1991, PT: A lógica da difernça: o Partido dos Trabahadores na construção de democracia brasileira São Paulo Editora Atica.

O'Donnell, Guillermo. 1994."On the State, Democratization and Some Conceptual Problems." *World Politics.*

Paiva, Vanilda, Célia Junqueira, and Leonardo Muls. 1997. "Prioridade ao ensino básico e pauperização docente." *Cadernos de Pesquisa da Fundação Carlos Chagas,* número 100 (março). São Paulo.

PNUD/IPEA. 1996. *Relatório sobre o Desenvolvimento Humano no Brasil.*

Sandoval, Salvador. 1994. *Os trabalhadores param.* São Paulo: Atica.

6

Regina Cortina

The Impact of International Organizations on Educational Policy in Latin America

Latin America, compared to Africa and Asia, has made tremendous progress in providing access to elementary education; nevertheless, education in the region is still in great need of improvement. Primary schools have high attrition rates, a high incidence of grade repetition, and are characterized by low achievement standards and poor quality. Success rates in Latin American schooling are much lower than one might expect in view of the priority given to increased access for all. Among policymakers in Latin America and officials within international organizations, there is growing concern about how to improve primary education in the region.

International organizations such as the World Bank and UNICEF are funding an array of projects in a concerted effort to improve Latin American education. Education has become increasingly important to these organizations, which provide aid and assistance from Western countries to less developed countries. During this decade, there has been a shift in the aid agenda toward partnerships with private investors, local government, and citizens' groups with the objective of fighting poverty and improving education and health systems. As a result, international organizations are playing a more prominent role in the direction of education reform in Latin America.

Latin America has the lowest rate of primary school completion in the world, which in part is the result of the high percentage of students who repeat a grade (see Table 6.1). Only three countries in the region—Argentina, Chile, and Uruguay—are providing education beyond elementary school to more than 70 percent of the eligible population (Naciones Unidas, Comisión Económica Latino América Latino y el Caribe, 1996).

The full scope of the problem of repetition and attrition needs to be seen in contrast to the recent success of education in the region. Although countries in Latin America have achieved almost universal access to elementary education,

Table 6.1

Internal Efficiency Percentage of Repeaters at First Level, Selected Countries*

Country	Male/Female	Male	Female
Argentina	5.6	—	–
Belize	10.5	11.8	9.0
Brazil	18.4	—	—
Colombia	9.2	9.6	8.8
Costa Rica	8.7	9.9	7.5
Cuba	2.8	—	
Ecuador	4.5	4.8	4.1
Guyana	4.1	4.7	3.4
Honduras	12.0	—	—
Mexico	7.0	8.1	5.9
Nicaragua	15.0	16.4	13.6
Paraguay	8.1	9.2	6.9
Uruguay	9.9	11.5	8.2

Source: UNESCO, *UNESCO Statistical Yearbook*, 1994.
*Percentage of repeaters: Total number of pupils who are enrolled in the same grade as the previous year, expressed as a percentage of the total enrollment at the first level.

Latin America is wasting precious public resources by expanding the physical plant of schools while not sufficiently investing in improving quality and retention and the training of teachers.

Research and Recommendations for Education in Latin America by International Organizations: The World Bank, UNICEF, and UNESCO

This section focuses on the international aid organizations that are having the greatest impact on education issues in Latin America, not only in the amount of their financial contributions, but the kinds of change they are sponsoring. The World Bank has been shifting its loans away from big infrastructure projects toward the funding of educational programs. As a result, the World Bank has become the largest funder of education worldwide and an important player in educational reform both because of the size of its financial contributions and because its loans carry the Bank's technical assistance criteria in implementing change. The direction for change that the Bank sponsors is part of the international debate on ways to reform education.

In contrast to the World Bank and its setting of policy guidelines and funding parameters is UNESCO, an organization more explicitly devoted to educational concerns. UNESCO promotes public and private investment in education at a time when public investment in education is sharply declining. It disseminates an international dialogue among scholars and government representatives and seeks to reexamine prevailing economic models used to evaluate the benefits of education, calling for rethinking education along sociopolitical and cultural lines.

UNICEF is one of UNESCO's specific funds mandated to promote the well-being of children worldwide. The priority of UNICEF's efforts is "the universal participation of children in quality primary education, with girls as the special target population" (UNICEF 1995).

The World Bank

The reform recommendations that international organizations have made for dealing with repetition and dropout need to be seen against the broader program of the reforms they recommend. Latin America is experimenting with an economic model that emphasizes free trade, privatization, and decentralization. Along with this new strategy in achieving economic growth comes a certain philosophy of educational reform, which includes emphasis on basic education, decentralization, and privatization.

Investing in basic or elementary education rather than secondary or higher education: The recommendation is to focus public funding on basic education and to rely on private and family sponsorship for higher education. Many of the most outspoken writers in the current wave of reform are economists who argue in favor of redirecting funding from higher education to basic education because the rates of return on investment are better for basic education than for higher education. In most countries, public spending on higher education is larger than it is for basic education.

One important aspect of higher education that must be expanded in order to achieve better education in Latin American countries is the training of teachers. As the new generation prepares to participate in an information age and global economy, the training of teachers needs to be improved considerably; however, this will be harder to accomplish with increasingly decentralized educational systems and a decreasing commitment to public investment in higher education. At present, the teaching profession serving poor and marginalized populations in Latin America has a strikingly low academic profile. Reliance on in-service training might be cost-effective in terms of the projects funded by international organizations, but in the long run, an entire overhaul of teacher training institutions is necessary. Moreover, projects supported by international organizations are experimenting with teacher training models that are shorter and specific rather than the multi-year and stratified training systems that exist in the region today. The evidence that emerges points toward the conclusion that well-planned but shorter and more focused training models can produce the same results as long training programs. Without doubt, teacher training is one of the priorities in the agendas of education reform in Latin America.

Decentralization: The World Bank report stresses greater involvement of parents and community, and decentralization is perceived as the solution to most of the current problems in education. The model has been imported from North America, which has long enjoyed a successful and decentralized educational system. Latin America, influenced by European models, has always had centralized and national systems of education; decentralization, therefore, is seen as a cure for bureaucratic and wasteful systems to manage education. However, in the countries of Latin America, where specific cultural and historical conditions have concentrated human capital in national systems, it might be inadvisable to decentralize resources too abruptly when local capacity to manage such rapid change remains severely restricted.

Privatization: Private finance and autonomous institutions are recommended to lower the pressure that education expenditures currently exert on national spending. The contribution of the private sector to public education in Latin America has always been minimal and in some respects the civic traditions of a colonial past are still present today. Considering that Latin American elites have never seriously invested in public education, it is probably short-sighted to think that the privatization of basic or higher education in Latin America will ameliorate the present situation. Public funding is pivotal to maintaining the national university system and other levels of education across the region.

Latin America, Mexico, Brazil, and Argentina are the largest borrowers for education from the World Bank. During the six years between 1992 and 1997, Latin America and the Caribbean received the largest share of World Bank funding devoted to education, 45 percent of which was devoted to basic education (World Bank 1997). For 1999, the World Bank estimates that it will lend $2.3 billion to Latin America and increase the number of projects being funded from twenty-four to twenty-eight, showing a funding increase from $2.08 billion in 1998 (World Bank 1998).

UNICEF

Four current UNICEF strategies to improve primary education include:

1. Increased access to preschooling. In many countries, preschooling is primarily an option for the children of the middle and upper classes. One year of preschool before first grade helps children to become accustomed to the routine of school and reduces learning disparities. But preschool alone is not the solution, since grade repetition can also be a problem at this level. In the case of Brazil, the rapid expansion of preschool education with nonformal programs and untrained teachers explains the high proportion of black and poor students in the North and Northeast still in preschool even though they are seven years old or more. Fúlvia Rosenberg (1997) found that the highest levels of preschool repetition are in the poorest states, with lower performance in education, lower academic profiles among teachers, and a higher percentage of black children, thereby correlating grade repetition with other socioeconomic indicators and reflecting inequalities within the education system.

2. Quality of teaching. A widespread belief among teachers and parents is that repetition is necessary for children. Uninspired teaching styles, lack of pedagogical training, and the need to improve the training of teachers working in the schools are variables that have a direct influence on high repetition rates. An important element of reform is to change the pedagogical practices of teachers through the use of in-service training.

3. Quality of education materials. Both UNICEF and the World Bank are financing projects across the region to increase the quality, availability, and pedagogical content of educational materials in addition to making the production of such materials more cost-effective. The distribution of these materials is focused primarily on the poorest groups in society, since these groups must contribute a greater proportion of their family resources to buy educational materials for their children.

4. Education financing and management. The current literature sees community involvement as an important element to foster school reform. Many recent projects have proven successful in training community members as teachers and in creating community involvement in the schools. Along with community involvement, there is a push to increase the involvement of private-sector and non-governmental organizations in the delivery of educational services.

UNESCO

Overall, decentralization and privatization as strategies of education reform in Latin America have resulted in a reduced responsibility of the public sector to improve the performance and quality of the systems. In a recent publication, UNESCO emphasizes the central role of education for human and social development to create a "learning society founded on the acquisition, renewal and use of knowledge" (Delors 1996, 24). Policy recommendations include cultural pluralism in education around the world, strong encouragement for the provision of educational opportunities for girls and women, and partnerships to foster programs of education reform. Moreover, the report argues in favor of committing one-fourth of all international aid to education.

In contrast to World Bank recommendations, UNESCO emphasizes the importance of secondary and vocational education. Graduating from secondary school is related to the alleviation of poverty and increasing levels of social equality. The UNESCO report insists on looking at secondary education as preparation for work life and a life of learning, and not only as preparation for higher education. It also focuses on achieving basic and universal education and on increasing educational opportunities for girls in those regions of the world with marked differences in access such as Africa and the Middle East.

UNESCO clearly stresses the paradoxes of education reform in the region. While there is an increasing emphasis on universal access and quality basic education, in most countries there has been a clear deterioration in the training and working conditions of teachers. Hiring teachers with increasingly deficient general educational backgrounds and providing them with reduced training clearly contradicts the overall objective of improving the quality of education. A recent report provides a model to transform teacher education programs and an expanded description of programs in Chile, Ecuador, and Colombia, and states: "Self-reflection and horizontal exchange among teachers are increasingly acknowledged today as key components of teacher education and professional development" (UNESCO/UNICEF n.d., p. 5).

Projects Funded: Escuela Nueva

Colombia's creation in the mid-1960s of the Escuela Nueva program which was applied in rural areas is often cited as an example of successful education reform. It includes multi-grade teaching, automatic promotion from first grade, and the expansion of preschool programs, making Colombia one of several countries in the region that has been able to decrease repetition rates in the first grade. The Escuela Nueva is one model program financed by international organizations to exemplify how a cost-effective approach to education, community involvement, multi-grade teaching, and improved pedagogical practices are able to increase the quality of education for the urban and rural poor in Latin America.

The philosophy of education reform behind the Escuela Nueva has been tried in many other Latin American countries with the same type of results. The contribution of the Escuela Nueva program can be summarized as the creation of an active pedagogy for multi-grade schooling with flexible promotion from one grade to the next (Schiefelbein 1991). In many rural areas of the world this model is a cost-effective way to provide basic education. One of the innovations of this program is to transform the traditional system in which teachers are repeaters of facts exercising rigid authority to one where teachers are actively involved with children pursuing the joy of learning. This new role for teachers can only be achieved with well-prepared instructional materials and a classroom with the necessary resources, such as a small library, tables and chairs for group projects, and so forth.

An evaluation in the late 1980s comparing achievement for Spanish and mathematics between traditional schools and the Escuela Nueva showed significant differences in achievement. Among the factors explaining these differences was that teacher training expenditures were at least three times higher in Escuela Nueva than in traditional schools. The study was cautious about the massive implementation of this program, beyond the pilot programs with careful implementation and devoted professionals who can guarantee quality (Psacharopoulos et al. 1993).

Among the lasting contributions of the Escuela Nueva program is the implementation of a rural education system that focuses on schooling as a learning process and moves away from an exclusive concern with outcomes, as is the case of most systems of education across the region. In addition, contrary to the conditions in other countries in Latin America, the Escuela Nueva effort was focused on the rural population and its efforts were directed at increasing the social and economic opportunities of an unprivileged sector of the population, since in Latin America, education is highly subsidized by the state but mostly the wealthy benefit as roughly half of the children that enter school never go beyond fifth grade.

Conclusion

When viewed in terms of repetition and dropout rather than initial access, the grim reality that primary education indicators portray is that compulsory education laws and tuition-free primary schooling are not sufficient to achieve equity and quality. The chief strategy of international organizations has been to fund non-formal community school projects and local partnerships, and this has permitted the people involved to develop some interesting new solutions. For the first time, Latin America is experimenting with models of educational change that are not centrally controlled. We are left, however, with a troubling question: How will the learning that is happening in these disparate projects across the region influence the prospects of a better education for the millions of Latin American children unable to benefit from the newly initiated reforms?

The trends toward decentralization and decreased social spending could severely disrupt the previous two decades of increasing educational opportunities for children in Latin America. As we approach the end of the decade, the continuation of this trend is increasing the risk of marginalization for the poor in these societies. For that reason, international organizations are focusing their educational efforts on providing health and education to the poorest in society.

References

Delors, Jacques. 1996. *Learning: The Treasure Within*. Report to UNESCO of the International Commission on Education for the Twenty-First Century. Paris: UNESCO.

International Labour Organization. 1996. *Impact of Structural Adjustment on the Employment and Training of Teachers*. Geneva: ILO.

Mogallón, Oscar. 1998. "New Knowledge: Studies in Girls' Education." Paper presented at the conference entitled "Educating Girls: A Development Imperative." International Trade Center, Washington, DC, May 6–8.

Naciones Unidas. Comisión Económica para América Latino y el Caribe. 1996. *Rol estratégico de la educación media para el bienestar y la equidad*. LC/G.1919. Santiago de Chile: CEPAL.

Psacharopoulos, George, Carlos Rojas, and Eduardo Vélez. 1993. "Achievement Evaluation of Colombia's *Escuela Nueva*: Is Multigrade the Answer? *Comparative Education Review* 37, no. 3: 263–276.

Rosenberg, Fúlvia. 1997. "Educaçâo, gênero e raça." Paper presented at the XX International Congress of the Latin American Studies Association. Guadalajara, Mexico, April 17–19.

Schiefelbein, Ernesto. 1991. *In Search of the School of the XXIst Century: Is the Colombian Escuela Nueva the Right Pathfinder?* Santiago de Chile: UNESCO/UNICEF.

UNESCO/UNICEF. 1995. *The Learning of Those Who Teach: Towards a New Paradigm of Teacher Education.* UNESCO/UNICEF Project on Innovations in Basic Education. New York: United Nations, Economic and Social Council, United Nations Children's Fund. "UNICEF Strategies in Basic Education," April 7.

Wolff, Laurence, Ernesto Schiefelbein, and Jorge Valenzuela. 1994. *Improving the Quality of Primary Education in Latin America and the Caribbean: Towards the 21st Century.* Washington, DC: World Bank.

World Bank. 1995. *Priorities and Strategies for Education: A World Bank Review.* Washington, DC: World Bank.

———. 1997. *The World Bank and Education.* Washington, DC: World Bank.

———. 1998. *Latin America and the Caribbean.* World Bank Presentation at the United Nations, February 13.

Part II

Basic Education Systems

7

RUTH SAUTU AND ANA MARÍA EICHELBAUM DE BABINI

Argentina: Elementary School Enrollment and Attainment

Argentina has placed great efforts in improving education at the elementary, secondary, and higher levels. Until 1997, seven years of primary school were required. From then on, basic education was extended to ten years, and included one year of pre-primary school education and compulsory basic general education lasting nine years, although some provinces delayed implementation of the ten–year requirement until 1998. The governance and administration of the educational system is concurrently the responsibility of central and local powers. Consequently, although the school year extends for ten months, the length of the school day and number of days of school per year varies among the provinces. Despite the increase in education coverage and a reduction in dropouts and illiteracy in the nation overall, primary school repetition and low learning achievement remain serious problems in several of the poorest provinces and among children from low-income homes (Eichelbaum de Babini 1995, 41–64; 1996, 25–41).

According to the last National Population Census of 1991, the gross elementary school enrollment rate (number of children enrolled in a grade divided by the number of children of the age appropriate for that grade) was 109, a little lower than in the previous census (112 in 1980) probably due to the decrease of over-age students. The net enrollment rate was 95 percent for 1991, higher than that of 1980 (91 percent), which is consistent with most of the educational data showing progress in the last intercensal periods. Unlike education level enrollment rates, age-specific rates are computed on the basis of the number of children in a given age group. Initial enrollment, mostly preschool and a few in first grade, takes place at the age of five; elementary and secondary education, between six and twelve and thirteen and seventeen, respectively; finally, higher education between ages eighteen and twenty-two. Thus enrollment rates computed on the basis of each of these age groups are valid indicators of primary (99 percent), secondary (83 percent), and higher education (63 percent).

At first sight, education for the first level looks like a relatively homogeneous block, which allows only for qualitative differences. However, there are notorious deficits among the less economically and socially developed Northern provinces, especially those in the Northeast (see Table 7.1). The deficits of education are associated with the infant mortality rate, life expectancy at birth, percentage of population living in households with "unsatisfied basic needs," and the adult illiteracy rate. The last two indicators are the most important. Illiteracy is an essential means for measuring adult education. "Unsatisfied basic needs" is an index that includes those households with poor housing and sanitary conditions, low education and unemployment of the household head, and the presence of children ages six to twelve who do not attend school (INDEC 1984).

Most of the educational indicators were computed from census sources. They refer to specific ages or age intervals so as to avoid distortions derived from the demographic structure. The names given to the indicators are clearly specified in each case, since dropouts, repetition, and achievement can be measured differently depending on the goals and the availability of data.

The educational gap refers to children who have not had access to the school system. It will be measured in terms of the population ages ten to fourteen who have never attended school. Those excluded from the system have little or no opportunity of receiving further formal education. Dropping out can be measured in terms of the early dropouts (between ages six and twelve). It is not unusual that part of the group should start school again. Dropouts aged fourteen to nineteen have fewer opportunities for completing their education than early dropouts, especially after fifteen. As regards repetition, we will draw mainly from total figures for primary education in 1994 (Ministerio de Cultura y Educación 1996). We will also take into account school life expectancy. This refers to the total number of years of future schooling for a child at a given age, assuming that his probability of being enrolled in a school is equal to the schooling rate for that age group. This school life expectancy covers not only grade attainment levels but repetitions as well (UNESCO 1995).

Youngsters ages fourteen to nineteen attending primary school are considered low achievers just because of their age, which seriously jeopardizes their future schooling, no matter the results of their school activity or their teachers' evaluations. The size of this group is an indicator of the educational deficit of a social unit, which should be compared to other theoretically more significant indicators such as those of dropouts and the excluded.

Without yet considering other types of information (such as results of achievement tests, which we will see below) an indicator of the good performance of a geographical unit could be the proportion represented by the "norm" that is the expected standard for the group aged twelve which complies (or complied, since at present the Argentine school system is in a process of change) with the expectations of attending or having finished the seventh grade. The closer a province comes to having 100 percent of the children of that age reach or surpass seventh grade, the closer is that province to the expected school "norm." The "norm" was two-thirds or more of the expected value in the Federal

Table 7.1

Argentina, Selected Provinces. Socioeconomic and Education Indicators (circa 1990)

Provinces and Federal District

	Total country	With great deficits					More educationally developed			
		Corrientes	Chaco	Formosa	Misiones	Santiago del Estero	Federal District	Conurbano	Córdoba	Mendoza
Infant mortality rate	23.6	27.7	33.5	32.3	27.0	28.7	14.9	22.4	19.6	22.1
Life expectancy at birth	71.9	70.0	69.0	69.4	69.5	69.8	72.7	72.1	72.8	72.7
Percent of population living in povery	19.9	31.4	39.5	39.1	33.6	38.2	8.1	18.9	15.1	17.6
Adult illiteracy (15+ years old)	4.0	10.3	12.3	9.2	9.1	9.5	0.7	2.5	3.5	5.0
Norm 7th grade at age 12	65.1	41.4	42.2	43.2	42.2	45.4	83.6	70.8	71.1	63.0
School life expectancy	13.0	12.8	11.3	12.6	11.2	11.6	15.4	12.7	13.8	13.0
Percent repetitions 1994	5.6	13.4	10.5	12.1	12.1	15.3	2.2	3.0	4.5	4.7
14- to 19-year-olds attending primary school	5.1	13.0	9.0	10.9	8.8	8.1	1.9	3.8	3.7	4.6
Dropping out: 6 to 12	2.3	3.8	9.5	3.8	5.6	4.7	1.2	1.5	1.5	2.2
Dropping out: 15 to 19	7.0	14.9	18.6	12.5	19.0	17.4	1.4	4.5	5.8	8.0
Education gap	0.6	1.3	3.2	1.2	1.6	1.5	0.2	0.3	0.4	0.6

Sources: INDEC (1994–1995), Ministerio de Cultura y Educación (1996).

District, Greater Buenos Aires (the area surrounding the Federal District), the rest of the province of Buenos Aires, Córdoba, Santa Fe, Santa Cruz, Tierra del Fuego, and La Pampa. The national mean was 65 percent.

A short look at the respective age-specific enrollment rates is revealing. Between ages six and twelve the highest enrollment is at age nine, 98 percent for the whole country. Below and above those ages (six and twelve) enrollment is always lower: 84 percent at age five; and decreasing year by year between ages thirteen and twenty-three (from 89 to 20 percent). The high enrollment in basic education shows little variation among provinces. There is a slightly higher variation in elementary enrollment; somewhat higher between ages thirteen and seventeen, and even higher between ages eighteen and twenty-three.

In spite of its relative homogeneity, elementary enrollment shows a difference between a large portion of the country and a few provinces characterized by educational deficits (see Table 7.1). The enrollment gap, children ages ten to fourteen who never attended school, is a highly marginal category. The country mean was always below 1 percent but it was higher than that figure in the provinces with the greatest educational deficits: Chaco (3.2 percent), Misiones (1.6 percent), Santiago del Estero (1.5 percent), Corrientes (1.3 percent), and Formosa (1.2 percent). For the same age group, the proportion of dropouts was higher than 10 percent in some cases (Chaco, Misiones, and Santiago del Estero).

School life expectancy does not show great variation among provinces. The figures are between eleven and fifteen years of school life, including repetitions; the latter very exceptional figure is for the Federal District.

Differences in education for boys and girls at the primary school level are of little significance (Eichelbaum de Babini 1991, 174–195). Educational inequalities by gender have not been very serious in Argentina, at least in the past few decades. They are limited now to differences in courses taken and areas of specialization, which, in spite of their importance, cannot be compared to disparities in literacy and basic education that have more serious social consequences (Deblé 1980, 91).

Starting with enrollment at age five, it is possible to observe that the differences by gender among provinces are usually not significant (83.7 percent for boys and 84.2 percent for girls for the whole of the country). The net enrollment rates for the elementary school level do not vary significantly by gender either. Generally, they are slightly higher for girls. The small differences among provinces are not consistent. For the whole of the country, 95.7 percent of the boys and 95.6 percent of the girls attend school. At the secondary level, however, there is a distinct and generalized higher female enrollment, which in the census of 1991 amounted to 61.9 percent for females and 56.6 percent for males. There is also higher female enrollment in higher education, especially in the case of non-university higher education.

With regard to school life expectancy (ages five to twenty-three), differences are also of little significance, although it is 13.2 years for females and 12.8 years for males, because it covers secondary and higher education where female enrollment is higher. As to differences by gender in what we have called the "norm," they are a little higher than those mentioned above: 62 percent of males and 68 percent of females of age twelve attend or have completed the seventh grade.

The Socioeconomic Correlates of Education Indicators

Using information for the years around 1990, we see that enrollment between ages five and seventeen has a high to moderately high association with social variables. Using provinces as units of analysis, the correlation coefficient between percent age of the population living in poverty and adult illiteracy rate is .861; and those between the latter and initial elementary and secondary enrollment are respectively $-.831$, $-.852$, and $-.815$. Adult illiteracy correlates with early dropping out of school (.849), while the percentage of population living in poverty constitutes a good predictor of early dropping out (children six to twelve). However, neither life expectancy at birth nor infant mortality is strongly associated wtih early dropping out of school. They do show moderately high correlations with the educational gap, that is, the percentage of children ages ten to fourteen who have never attended school.

Repetition rates are negatively correlated to life expectancy at birth ($-.689$) and positively correlated with the percentage of poor population (.776) and with adult illiteracy (.833). Similarly, the percentage of youngsters ages fourteen to nineteen who are still attending primary schools is associated with both poverty and adult illiteracy (respectively .788 and .793)

The expected "norm" is negatively associated with adult illiteracy ($-.907$), percentage of population living in poverty ($-.866$), infant mortality ($-.634$), and positively associated with life expectancy at birth (.748). At an aggregate level the "norm" is one of the best indicators of the educational performance of a province or social or geographical unit. It also shows the relevance of including age in measures of educational outcomes. High correlations between different socioeconomic indicators and education variables show that education deficits come together with economic deficiencies; poor economic development also implies poor development of the education system. Moreover, the association of adult illiteracy rates with children's enrollment and attainment indicates that education deficits remain over time and affect more than one generation, thus making change a slow process that requires permanent, persistent, and very active public policies.

Differences Among Provinces

Taking into account both cross-sectional data and last decade changes in the educational profile of elementary, secondary, and higher education of the twenty-four Argentine provinces and the Federal District, we have designed five empirical categories of educational development:

1.   Well-developed provinces that have relatively high values in all indicators for each of the three levels of education. The Federal District and the provinces of

Córdoba and Buenos Aires rank at the top of this category. Greater Buenos Aires, which forms part of the homonymous province, Santa Fe, Mendoza, and San Juan with somehow lower values, are also part of this category.

2. Poorly developed provinces that show low or very low values in the indicators analyzed herein (see Table 7.1). Formosa, Misiones, and Santiago del Estero make up this category.

3. Provinces that have relatively well developed higher education because in addition to some provincial or private universities, they have national universities supported by federal funds. In contrast, these provinces have serious deficits in primary and secondary education. Tucumán and especially Corrientes are part of this category. With an intermediate development of higher education and very low values in primary and secondary education, the province of Chaco is also included together with Salta, which has a very low rank in primary school development and an intermediate one in the other levels.

4. La Pampa and the Patagonia provinces of Santa Cruz, Tierra del Fuego, Chubut, and Neuquen. These provinces have achieved reasonably good standards in their primary and secondary schools and an incipient development of higher education.

5. La Rioja and Entre Ríos, with intermediate education development at the three levels; a little behind in this category are the provinces of Catamarca and San Luis. Jujuy and Río Negro are included in this category although their higher education attendance rates are still very low. Misiones, Santiago del Estero, Formosa, Chaco, and Corrientes have the highest deficits because of their very low values in primary school indicators; their primary school net enrollment rates are among the lowest in Argentina: respectively 92 percent, 93 percent, 94 percent, 88 percent, and 94 percent (Eichelbaum de Babini 1994). These five provinces with the highest educational deficits differ in the degree of development of their primary, secondary, or higher education systems. Chaco is an extreme case because of its high rate of exclusion (children six to twelve who have never attended school) and its dropout rate. Corrientes, instead, with a high repetition rate and a high proportion of youngsters over fourteen years of age who are still attending primary schools, is somehow nearer to Formosa, although the later has a higher school life expectancy. Misiones and Santiago del Estero, with low school life expectancies, rank near the province of Chaco.

The Effects of Family Background and Type of School on Children's Grade Repetition and Achievement

Since 1993 seventh graders of public and private schools all over the country have been tested in language, mathematics, and social and natural sciences. The evaluation tests were designed by the Federal Education Authority and applied to samples of schools in each province and the Federal District. In 1996 with a maximum grade of 100 and a passing grade of 40, the national means were 60.6

in language and 58.8 in mathematics (Ministerio de Cultura y Educación 1996, 40–50). The Federal District of Buenos Aires, the province of Mendoza and Greater Buenos Aires occupied the first ranks while provinces in the North were among the last. In this analysis we have selected the already mentioned districts in addition to the provinces of Córdoba, Santiago del Estero y Corrientes. Data for this analysis come from a pupils' self-administered survey that includes individual and family information and their scores in language and mathematics evaluation tests (see Table 7.2). At the state level (provinces and the Federal District), in both tests, children in urban private schools do systematically better than children in urban public or rural schools.[1]

Gender and the family's standard of living also affect children's school performance. Girls' mean scores in both tests are higher than those of boys; and children living in poor housing conditions scored lower than better-off children.[2] As the dispersion of children's scores in each province and type of school is very high (in some cases as high as 50 percent of the mean value), we shall analyze here the proportion of children who failed at the evaluation tests because their scores were lower than 40 (see Table 7.2). At public schools, among pupils who enjoy good standards of living, failures in language tests may be double, sometimes triple, the figures of private schools. Between 20 percent and 60 percent of children in rural schools were not able to pass the tests. In a rich province like Córdoba and a poor one like Santiago del Estero, at least one-fifth of better-off private school boys failed; the proportion in public schools was respectively, 42.5 percent and 31.9 percent.

Failures among children from poor households are even more critical. As very few attend private schools, we have excluded them from Table 7.2. By far, Mendoza shows the highest performance for boys and girls; in Greater Buenos Aires the level of failures is about one-fifth, and in Córdoba, Corrientes, and Santiago del Estero the proportions reach 30 to 40 percent.

The same pattern of failure is observed in mathematics evaluation tests. The number of failures is particularly alarming among boys from public schools of Córdoba, Corrientes, and Santiago del Estero. Public schools do worse than private ones. Failure among poor children is in general higher than among the better off. However, in both tests the education systems of the Federal District, Greater Buenos Aires, and Mendoza seem to work more efficaciously than those of Córdoba, Corrientes, and Santiago del Estero.

The case of Córdoba is surprising because it is a province with a good education system and a high education level of the adult population. In this province, failure in language and mathematics among seventh graders seems to be a problem of the past few years. While the mean scores in language and mathematics in 1993 and 1994 were above the national mean in 1995 and 1996 they ranked below that mean (Ministerio de Cultura y Educación 1995, 27–28; 1996, 49–50).

Low achievement in language and mathematics is negatively associated with age in all provinces and types of schools. Among males and females the average

Table 7.2

Seventh Grade Primary School Pupils: Percentage Who Failed at Evaluation Tests and Percentage Who Repeated at Least Once, by Province of Residence, School Type, and Housing Conditions by Gender

Province and school type	Males						Females					
	Percent failures				% Repetition		Percent failures				% Repetition	
	Language		Mathematics				Language		Mathematics			
	Non-poor	poor	Non-poor	poor	Non-poor	poor	Non-poor	poor	Non-poor	poor	Non-poor	poor
Federal District												
Public	11.9	*	16.6	*	13.5	*	7.3	*	21.3	*	11.1	22.2
Private	13.6	*	3.5	*	2.8	*	4.8	*	2.7	*	0.0	*
Great Buenos Aires												
Public	12.3	26.2	18.1	19.5	14.4	41.0	10.3	17.8	20.0	26.7	11.5	23.9
Private	11.1	*	6.7	*	4.4	*	1.6	*	3.6	*	2.6	*
Córdoba												
Rural	42.1	*	26.3	*	31.6	*	28.6	*	26.1	*	18.2	*
Public	42.5	45.5	28.7	39.6	18.0	29.2	20.2	31.9	25.1	33.3	12.8	28.6
Private	22.9	*	7.9	*	6.5	*	7.8	*	7.2	*	3.0	*
Mendoza												
Rural	30.5	25.0	27.0	10.0	32.8	52.4	20.8	5.9	20.3	15.8	32.2	40.0
Public	12.6	0.0	9.3	19.2	20.0	43.3	7.8	10.5	6.0	20.9	16.4	36.4
Private	0.0	*	0.0	*	16.7	*	0.0	*	0.0	*	7.7	*

Corrientes												
Rural	48.0	30.8	42.2	15.4	50.0	69.2	26.7	50.0	17.4	65.0	43.5	65.0
Public	21.7	35.7	17.1	14.5	34.1	50.0	12.7	30.9	20.4	24.7	28.8	54.7
Private	6.3	*	6.3	*	6.4	*	7.0	*	18.0	*	4.9	*
Santiago del Estero												
Rural	60.9	61.5	65.1	91.7	39.7	53.8	42.6	66.7	55.2	75.0	16.2	33.3
Public	31.9	41.0	34.4	55.3	24.6	60.0	28.0	46.2	36.6	57.0	22.8	50.0
Private	21.6	*	16.2	*	8.3	*	8.2	*	17.1	*	8.2	*

Source: Ministerio de Cultura y Educación. 1996. Unpublished.
*Few cases.

age is higher in rural and public schools than in private ones; this would indicate that low learning achievement might antecede repetition. In addition, remaining longer at school is no guarantee of good achievement. This correspondence is shown on Table 7.2: provinces and schools with high proportions of failures in the evaluation tests also have high repetition rates.

Unlike evaluation tests that were designed by the Federal Education Authority, criteria to promote a pupil from one grade to the next depend exclusively on the district authorities and they are very much influenced by headmasters' and teachers' perceptions and evaluations of learning and behavior performances. Again, private schools have lower rates of repetition than public or rural schools, and girls do better than boys.

Although local and school criteria may affect repetition rates, the high rates observed among poor children may not be due exclusively to differences of criteria. In every district, in public schools, between one-quarter and one-half of pupils in the seventh grade have repeated at least once. In rural schools these rates were even higher.

Conclusions

The conclusions stemming from this overview deal with the meaning and validity of aggregate education indicators and their relevance to policymaking.

In Argentina, the values of age-specific enrollment rates show that, with the exception of early schooling at age five, there do not exist serious deficits in schooling opportunities. Achieving the "norm" is far more problematic; the proportion of children age twelve who are attending or have completed the seventh grade, in less developed provinces, is two-thirds the figure of the educationally most developed ones.

Deficits in schooling are shown with high repetition rates that accompany low learning achievement, as measured by evaluation tests and subsequent overage attendance (children ages fifteen to nineteen). The most deficient provinces are those with dropout rates that double the national average. Learning achievement and grade attainment are indicators of the returns to investment in education; grade repetition, over-age attendance, and eventually dropping out increase costs and reduce the rate of return to education investment. In Argentina as a whole, 9.25 percent of education costs are wasted because repeaters have to remain at school longer than seven years. In the Federal District this percentage is 3.1 percent and in Santiago del Estero 33.5 percent of the local education cost (Ministerio de Cultura y Educación 1996, Table 3). The accumulated actual costs of over-aged pupils (those who have repeated grades) is estimated at $650 million. An improvement in achievement and grade attainment would mean a significant reduction in these costs.

The fact that adult illiteracy is highly associated with children's school outcomes indicates the existence of an intergenerational reproduction of school quality. Those provinces that have comparatively failed more in educating a past generation do worse in educating the present generation than other provinces that have worked more efficaciously in the past and in the present.

Living in a poor household and attending a non-private school in a poor province increases children's chances of failing at learning tests and/or repeating grades. These unequal outcomes in school performance are a challenge to equity because the place of residence and type of school make a crucial difference in the opportunity to receive a good education, thus adding school disadvantages to children's underprivileged family position.

Notes

1. In the sample under study, the proportion of all children in public schools is 72 percent in Santiago del Estero and 79 percent in Greater Buenos Aires. The Federal District is an exception because that proportion is 56 percent. Private schools represent between 3.4 percent in Mendoza and 10 percent to 20 percent in the rest of the provinces. In the Federal District the figure is 44 percent. In Mendoza, Corrientes, and Santiago del Estero the proportion of children who attend rural schools, both public and private, is respectively 19 percent, 11 percent, and 18 percent. Córsico in this volume compares sample to census data on the number of pupils in each province and the Federal District.

2. The only indicator of standard of living is the ratio achieved by dividing the number of members in the household by the number of rooms in the house. This rate of room overcrowding has proved to be a good predictor of family's socioeconomic conditions. The Permanent Households Survey estimates as non-poor a ratio of less than three persons per room and as poor three or more persons per room.

General Bibliography

Argentina. Instituto Nacional de Estadística y Censos (INDEC). 1994–1996. *Censo nacional de población y vivienda de 1991. Series B y C.* Buenos Aires: INDEC.
———. 1994. *Anuario estadístico de la República Argentina 1994.* Buenos Aires: INDEC.
———. 1994–1996. *Anuario estadístico de la República Argentina 1996.* Buenos Aires: INDEC.
———. *Secretaría de programación y evaluación educativa, 1995. Establecimientos Educativos '94.* Buenos Aires.
Deblé, Isabelle. 1980. *La escolaridad de las mujeres.* Paris: UNESCO.
———. 1995. *La medición de la educación de las unidades sociales.* Buenos Aires: Academia Nacional de Educación.
Sautu, R., and A.M. Eichelbaum de Babini. 1996. *Los pobres y la escuela. Trabajos de investigación.* Buenos Aires: La Colmena.

Works Cited

Argentina. Instituto Nacional de Estadística y Censos (INDEC). 1984. *La pobreza en la Argentina.* Buenos Aires: INDEC.

Argentina. Instituto Nacional de Estadística y Censos (INDEC). N.d. *Censo nacional de población y vivienda 1980. Serie D.* 1984. Buenos Aires: INDEC.

Argentina. Ministerio de Cultura y Educación. Secretaría de Programación y Evaluación Educativa. Morduchowicz, A. et al. 1996. *Tres análisis de indicadores de la demanda educativa.* Buenos Aires: Ministerio de Cultura y Educación.

Argentina. Ministerio de Cultura y Educación de la Nación. 1996. *Censo nacional de Docentes y Establecimientos Educativos '94.* Buenos Aires: Ministerio de Cultura y Educación.

Eichelbaum de Babini, 1991. *Sociologia de la educación.* Buenos Aires: El Ateneo.

———. 1994. "La educación argentina en 1990. Las cifras en la comparación internacional." In *La educación en la Argentina. Trabajos actuales de investigación,* ed. R.E. Gibaja and A.M. Eichelbaum de Babini. Buenos Aires: La Colmena.

———. 1996. "La educación en la Argentina en 1970 y 1990." In *Los pobres y la escuela. Trabajos de investigación,* ed. R. Sautu and A.M. Eichelbaum de Babini. Buenos Aires: La Colmena.

UNESCO. 1995. *Informe mundial sobre la educación 1995.* Madrid: Santillana/UNESCO.

Operativo Nacional de Evaluación 1995, Buenos Aires.

———. 1996. Buenos Aires.

8

PAULO RENATO SOUZA

Primary Education in Brazil: Changes and Prospects

The profile of the Brazilian education system has changed sharply in the 1990s. In response to the aspirations of a society not only more demanding but also more aware of the rights of citizenship, all three levels of government—federal, state, and municipal—have given priority to providing more and better public educational services.[1] Among the most positive aspects of the recent development of Brazilian education, the following deserve emphasis: steady declines in illiteracy rates; strong growth in enrollments at all levels; gradual reductions in failure and dropout rates; and systematic improvement in the average rates of schooling of the population in general.

Despite advances already achieved, Brazilian education is still far from satisfactory, particularly in qualitative terms. This means there is still a relative lag between society's growing expectations and the public system's real short-term capacity to satisfy them. However, aside from the demand on public authorities to expand educational supply and improve its quality, Brazil must cope with still other educational challenges now common to all countries, independent of their respective development levels. These are difficulties borne of the process of globalization and the speed of technological innovation.

Within this framework of rapid social and economic transformation, the education policy agenda has incorporated an increasingly varied and complex array of problems for which there are no easy solutions nor ready-made models to be copied. Governments in all countries are coming under growing pressures to reform their education systems and increase public investments in this sector.[2] With this, efforts have been intensified to foster pedagogical and curricular innovations aimed at enhancing school efficiency and preparing students to face a world of fierce competition. There is a consensus today that education does not only define the individual's chances of success, but is a component vital to the destiny of nations.

As Brazil attempts to face up to the challenge of building a school system for the twenty-first century, urgent measures are required to guarantee universal access to basic education, retention of students within the system, and effectiveness in delivering the educational product. With this goal in mind, the government of President Fernando Henrique Cardoso (1995–) chose primary schooling as its number one priority in the education sector, and has adopted a series of policies aimed at attaining new standards of efficiency, equity, and quality. Concrete results have already been forthcoming and are clearly reflected in the major education performance indicators analyzed in this chapter. In the first place, one must stress that despite budget restrictions imposed by the economic adjustment program followed by Brazil since 1994, public sector outlays in education were not reduced. Furthermore, measures have been adopted to ensure effective redistribution of available funding and to guarantee greater efficacy and transparency in the use of resources.[3]

This general, current overview of the Brazilian education system focuses on primary education and is presented from the point of view of someone who bears government responsibilities rather than an independent or academic analysis.[4] It represents the vision of someone deeply involved in and committed to resolving the nation's educational difficulties. However, our involvement in no way hinders us from making a rigorous and unbiased diagnosis of the current condition of our schools, followed by a brief description of the basic education policies and programs put forward by the federal government. Finally, one should stress the fact that the emphatic tone of the position defended in this chapter is due more to our desire to ensure high quality education to all Brazilians than to any misplaced presumption of infallibility in the decisions taken as Brazilian Minister of Education.

Primary education in Brazil in 1995 displayed characteristics common to developing areas that led to the reforms outlined below. These characteristics include students not learning enough. For fourth grade students, the probability of a student giving a correct answer to a question about reading Portuguese was 49.95 percent, and about mathematics was 30.6 percent. One-fifth of these students had reading or mathematics achievement above the level (225) at which three-fourths of eighth grade students reached a similar performance. High student achievement was associated with high education of parents, attendance in private school, and location in a capital city. Students who repeated a grade achieved less than first-time students; girls were better at language, while boys were better at math. The performance of students in Brazil is greatly influenced by social-economic and cultural conditions. Students who identified themselves racially as "white" or "yellow" outperformed those who said they were of "mixed race" or "black." And the better educated the teacher, the better the students' results.

Although 38 percent of students were in elementary schools that had no library, more than 90 percent received textbooks. Most of the physical plant of the schools was in good condition. Some two-thirds of students were in schools that had television, giving them access to Brazil's educational television network, which aids teachers. There is regional variation in primary education. Extensive survey research and public debate contributed to recent policy initiatives for primary education.

In Search of a New Financing Structure

The efforts of public authorities to implement education policies, coupled with the mobilization of Brazilian society, have already begun generating results. Most recent statistics point to significant improvements in basic public education,[5] in terms of both coverage and efficiency. However, in the hope of hastening this process, the government is making every effort to correct certain structural distortions, particularly with respect to financing primary education.

According to the Brazilian Constitution, this level of education is obligatory and must be provided free of charge at public institutions, even for those who did not have access to it at the proper age (seven to fourteen). In the second half of 1996, the National Congress approved a constitutional amendment bill sent to it by the Executive Branch, aimed at clearly defining the division of responsibility for providing educational services among the three levels of government.

The federal government was given responsibility for performing "a redistributive and supplementary function in educational matters, in such a way as to ensure equal educational opportunity and minimum standards of quality, through technical and financial assistance rendered to the states, Federal District and municipalities."[6] To ensure the effectiveness of this redistribution of responsibilities and resources, Constitutional Amendment no. 14 created the Fund for the Maintenance and Development of Primary Education and Teacher Improvement, to be implemented in all Brazilian states as of January 1, 1998. The sole exception is the state of Pará, which decided to get a head start on the rest of the nation and implemented its program early.[7]

The Fund, which is composed of 15 percent of the principal state and municipal revenue sources,[8] redistributes resources proportionately to the number of students enrolled in the respective state and municipal primary education systems. Another important equalizing mechanism that the Fund possesses is the guarantee that a specified minimum value defined by the federal government will be spent per student/year. The poorer states of the Federation that are unable to reach the targeted level will receive the required complementary resources from the federal government. Finally, a third innovative aspect of the Fund is the obligation that 60 percent of its resources be channeled into wage payments for teachers working in the classroom.

With the latter measure, an immediate improvement in teacher wage levels is expected. The Fund's regulations (Law no. 9,424/96) demand that state and municipal education systems adopt career and wage plans based on the new national guidelines to be defined in resolutions issued by the National Education Council. The intention is to raise the quality of the nation's teachers through a three-pronged approach: career, continued training, and adequate wages.

This is the major educational reform now going forward in Brazil. According to estimates issued by the Secretariat of the Federal Treasury, the Fund will channel approximately R$13.5 billion into primary education in 1998. This evidently reflects significant growth in the volume of investments at this level of education, coupled with a more equitable redistribution of available funding. Councils will be created with the participation of the different segments of the education sector at all three levels of government with the task of guaranteeing that these resources be invested correctly.

Aside from the immediate redistributive impact of these resources on teacher wages, particularly in the North and Northeast regions, the Fund is also stimulating a process of shifting control of primary education toward municipalities. Though this is not one of the priority objectives of the reform, it will obviously be beneficial since it will tend to draw local governments and communities into a more active role in ensuring the quality of primary schools, while freeing state authorities to give greater attention to the expansion of secondary school facilities.[9]

Universal Access to Primary Education

In 1996, the national primary school structure consisted of 195,767 schools, 92 percent of which were public schools, with 33.1 million enrollments, 88.8 percent of which were concentrated in public schools. Despite the fact that the vast majority of students attend urban schools (82.6 percent), more than two-thirds of the nation's schools are actually located in rural areas.[10]

Though primary schools have an average of 169.2 students, there are 85,200 schools with less than 30 students, representing 43.6 percent of total primary schools but accounting for only 4.3 percent of enrollments. In contrast to these figures, large-scale schools with more than 250 students account for only 19.4 percent of total institutions but 76.7 percent of primary school enrollments. These schools average 670 students and, as a consequence of the rapid demographic shift from rural to urban areas that has marked Brazil in recent decades, are concentrated in the urban areas.

From 1991 to 1996, the net rate of schooling of the 7- to 14-year-old population, which corresponds to the eight grades of primary education, expanded from 86 percent to about 91 percent. In the same period, the proportion of overall school-age population served increased from 91.6 percent to 96 percent, while the gross rate of schooling (those enrolled in school in proportion to the total population of the age group that should in a given level [or grade] in school) climbed from 106 percent to 116 percent. That it is greater than 100 percent due to over-age children in that grade level, mainly due to repetition. In order to better understand the major problems faced by Brazilian education, the indicators used to measure the breadth of coverage from varied standpoints require conceptual definition.

The net rate of schooling indicates the percentage of children in the 7- to

Table 8.1

Rates of Gross and Net Schooling in the 7- to 14-Year Age Bracket: Brazil and Regions, 1991 and 1996

Region/Year	Population ages 7–14 years	Primary enrollment	Gross %	Primary enrollment ages 7–14 years	Net %
Brazil					
1991	27,611,850	29,203,724	105.8	23,777,428	86.1
1996	28,525,815	33,131,270	116.1	25,909,860	90.8
North					
1991	2,248,157	2,246,339	99.9	1,780,876	79.2
1996	2,417,649	2,820,531	116.7	2,171,209	89.8
Northeast					
1991	9,010,532	8,650,747	96.0	6,528,914	72.5
1996	9,180,333	10,475,469	114.1	7,601,089	82.8
Southeast					
1991	10,737,330	11,965,480	111.4	10,185,214	94.9
1996	11,127,665	12,958,674	116.5	10,558,852	94.9
South					
1991	3,811,860	4,201,369	110.2	3,589,194	94.2
1996	3,899,007	4,475,774	114.8	3,773,730	96.8
Central–West					
1991	1,803,701	2,140,062	118.9	1,693,230	93.9
1996	1,901,161	2,400,822	126.3	1,804,980	94.9

Source: MEC/INEP/SEEC IBGE.
Notes: Population 1991, Demographic Census, IBGE.
Enrollments 1991 and 1996, School Census, MEC/INEP/SEEC.
Population 1996, Estimate, MEC/INEP/SEEC.

14-age bracket enrolled in primary schools in relation to the total population in the same age group. As shown above, this index suggests that Brazil is moving toward universal access to primary education. However, regional differences are still quite accentuated. Despite strong growth of 11 percentage points in the North and Northeast regions in the 1991–96 period, these two regions still have the worst overall schooling rates in the country (Table 8.1).

In turn, the coverage rate indicates the percentage of enrollments in the obligatory school-age bracket of seven to fourteen years, independent of school level. Therefore, this index includes those children who, even though they are seven or older, are still in preschool or the so-called literacy classes still very common in the North and Northeast.[11] To these totals, one must also add enrollments in special education and, to a much lesser extent, students who reach the secondary level at a precocious age, that is, before the age of fifteen.

Finally, the gross rate of schooling shows the ratio between primary school enrollments independent of student ages, and the total number of children in

7- to 14-year age bracket. The fact that this rate reached the significant level of 116 percent indicates that a highly important share of the students enrolled in primary school is marked by age/grade distortions or, in other words, the chronological age of these students has already passed the age that would normally correspond to the grades in which they are enrolled. Evidently, this phenomenon is directly related to high levels of repetition, particularly in early grades. This explains why the number of enrollments at this level is far superior to the numbers in the seven to fourteen year population, despite the fact that a significant share of children in this bracket still remains outside school (Table 8.1).

Consequently, increased demand for primary schooling has been generated more by students repeating the school year than by new enrollments. In the 1994 to 1997 period, enrollments in the first to fourth grades expanded by only 1.9 percent, reflecting a situation of stability since access to primary education is becoming increasingly universalized. This rate of growth in enrollments in the early years of primary education is quite close to the rate of Brazilian demographic expansion. In contrast to this trend in the initial grades, enrollments in the fifth to eighth grades climbed by a full 10 percent in the same period, clear evidence of progressive improvement in system performance.

With this data, it is evident that the overloading of the primary education system is a direct consequence of age/grade distortions. According to the 1996 School Census, more than 63 percent of students enrolled in primary school had already passed the age level corresponding to their respective grades. In the Northeast, the situation is even more dramatic with over 80 percent of the students in this situation (see Table 8.2). This is an indication of the precise dimensions of the inefficiency of Brazilian education: students take an average of 11.2 years to complete the eight grades of primary schooling, reflecting an average per student rate of three repetitions.

Grade repetition causes grave problems for the students themselves—age/grade distortions are a major cause of dropping out of school—and generates significantly higher additional costs for the system as a whole. In 1996, total primary school enrollments were almost 20 percent higher than the total population of 7- to 14-year olds. The excess consists of approximately 5.3 million students in the fifteen to nineteen years of age bracket still in primary school when, in reality, they should be in secondary school or even college.

The principal strategy to be used in turning this situation around is accelerated learning programs, already tried with great success in a number of Brazilian states. The Ministry of Education is now encouraging expansion of these initiatives, financing production of specific pedagogical materials together with teacher training courses.

Aside from the excess enrollments that have already clogged up the early grades of primary education, the Population Count of 1996 carried out by the Brazilian Institute of Geography and Statistics (IBGE) indicates that there are an additional 2.7 million 7- to 14-year old children not enrolled in school at all. This

Table 8.2

Grade/Age Distortion Rates. Primary Education, by Grade: Brazil and Its Regions, 1996

Region	Median	1st grade	2nd grade	3rd grade	4th grade	5th grade	6th grade	7th grade	8th grade
Brazil	47.0	40.0	44.1	46.4	46.6	55.6	53.2	49.2	49.0
North	62.3	54.7	63.1	65.0	64.9	69.1	67.5	60.7	60.8
Northeast	65.7	58.4	66.9	68.0	67.3	72.8	70.2	67.1	67.0
Southeast	34.8	16.7	26.5	32.1	34.4	47.4	46.1	42.9	42.7
South	27.8	12.8	20.0	23.8	26.7	38.2	38.1	34.7	34.8
Central–West	47.1	30.0	40.0	44.9	47.4	60.6	58.9	55.6	55.5

Sources: MEC/INEP/SEEC, IBGE.

figure corresponds to almost 10 percent of the population in this age bracket. The 1996 School Census pointed to a slightly smaller number of children not enrolled in school. This survey is carried out annually at the start of the school year and registers total initial enrollments or, in other words, the number of children enrolled in school at that specific moment in time. In contrast to this, the School Census calculated by IBGE utilizes August 1 as its base date and is carried out on a home-by-home basis. For this reason, the results of the two surveys do not coincide. The fundamental difference is found in the number of first-semester dropouts. Even though this figure has declined in recent years to the point that it is not particularly high in the period between March and July of each year, it is still sufficient to inject a significant difference between the numbers produced by the School Census and those presented by the IBGE.

The importance of this discussion is not found in a quantitative definition of the exact number of children not enrolled in school. Its value is in contrasting the two surveys and analyzing the varied results generated. The population in the obligatory schooling age bracket not enrolled in school varies during the course of the year. The differences are generated by the nature of the problem itself, since the percentage of children in the seven to fourteen year age bracket who never attended school is much lower than the percentage who attended school but later dropped out. From the point of view of regional distribution, approximately half of the children from 7- to 14-years of age still not in school are concentrated in the Northeast region.

To cope with this problem, in October 1997, the Ministry of Education launched a program called "Every Child in School,"[12] with the goal of ensuring a place in school to every child in the compulsory age bracket as a national priority. In pursuing this target, the principal reasons for exclusion were identified and differentiated strategies designed to eliminate their causes. At the same time, measures have been taken to mobilize society and create highly flexible mechanisms of support to state and municipal systems, since they are at the forefront in efforts to provide educational opportunities.

Improvement in Repetition and Dropout Rates

Despite the dramatic nature of the age/grade distortion, positive—albeit moderate—growth is occurring in primary education transition rates.[13] As a matter of fact, in the last decade, repetition and dropout rates have declined, while promotion rates have moved up. In the past decade, aggregate approval rates in primary education have improved, rising from 55 percent in 1984 to 66 percent in 1995, accompanied by a reasonable decline in aggregate rates of failure and dropouts, which closed the same year at 30 percent and 4 percent, respectively (Table 8.3).

Notwithstanding improvement in dropout rates, promotion, and repetition rates in the first grade of primary school are still far from satisfactory: only 55 percent of total students are promoted and 44 percent repeat the year, thus continuing the vicious cycle that will eventually push these students out of the

Table 8.3

Aggregate Promotion and Repetition Rates in Primary Education: Brazil, 1981–1995

Year	Promotion rates (%)	Repetition rates (%)	Dropout rates (%)
1981	58	36	6
1982	56	38	6
1983	55	38	7
1984	55	37	8
1985	58	36	6
1986	56	37	7
1987	58	36	6
1988	57	36	7
1989	59	35	6
1990	60	34	6
1991	62	33	5
1992	62	33	5
1995	66	30	4

Sources: MEC/INEP/SEEC, IBGE.

system. Another primary education bottleneck is found in the fifth grade, marking the transition from the first to the second cycle. In that grade, the promotion rate is 61 percent and the rate of repetition is still a very high 34 percent (Graphs 8.1, 8.2, 8.3).

From the regional point of view, with the exception of the North and Northeast, the regions have managed to achieve gradual increases in promotion rates and declines in repetition and dropout rates, thus pointing to gradual improvement in system efficiency. However, one should underscore the fact that dropout rates have also declined in the North and Northeast regions and are quite close to the national average.

With these developments, the average time students take to complete the primary level has dropped, at the same time that there has been strong growth in expected rates of completion from 55 percent in 1993 to 65 percent in 1995. Other positive aspects that deserve mention are the progressive increases in the average number of school years completed and improvement in the average time during which students remain within the primary education system.

Recent improvement in primary education has had a positive impact on enrollment growth at the secondary level. As a consequence, this level is now going through a process of dizzying expansion. In the period from 1985 to 1996, enrollments at this level of education increased by a full 90.28 percent and this has accelerated in the last five years, reaching more than a 10 percent growth in 1996 alone.

Here, one should emphasize that the Brazilian Constitution affirms that it is

Graph 8.1 **Promotion Rates in Primary Education, By Grade** (%)

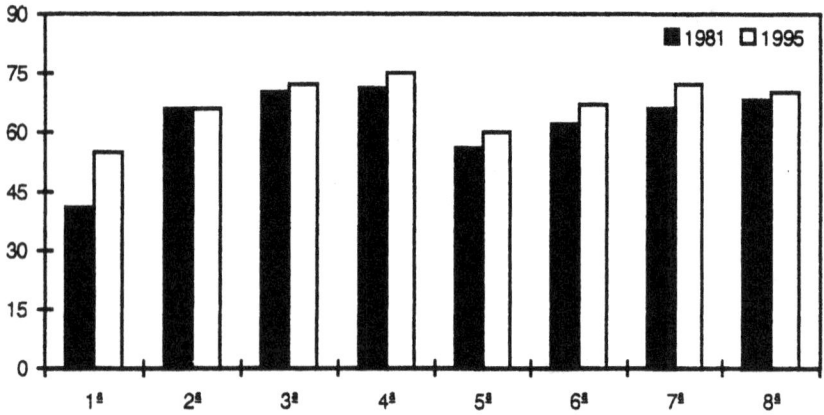

Source: MEC/INEP/SEEC.

Graph 8.2 **Repetition Rates in Primary Education, By Grade** (%)

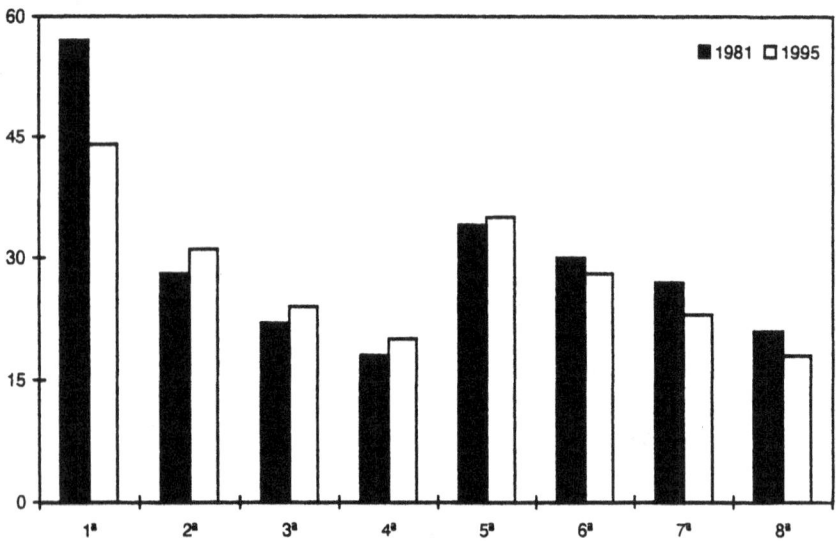

Source: MEC/INEP/SEEC.

Graph 8.3 **Dropout Rates in Primary Education, By Grade** (%)

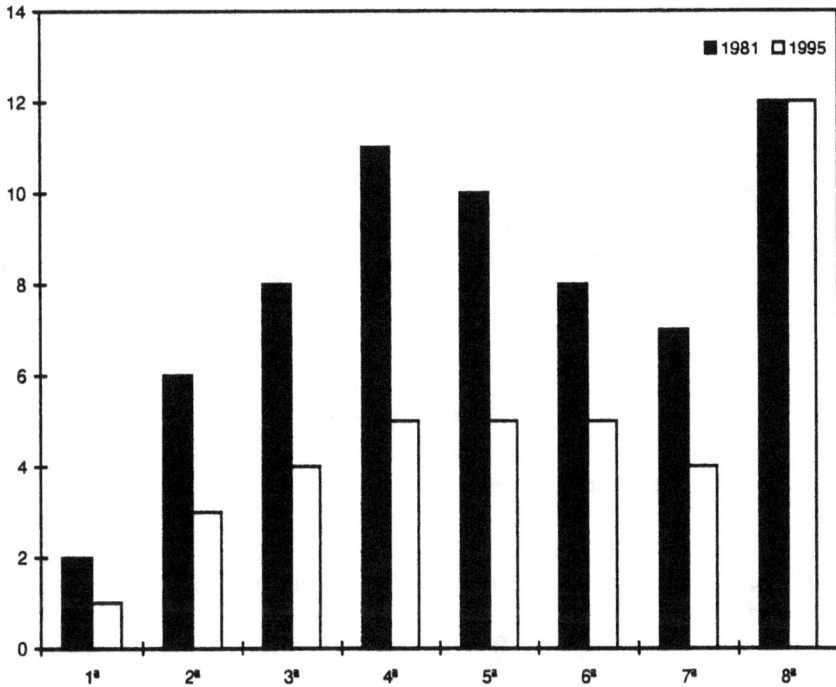

Source: MEC/INEP/SEEC.

the duty of the state to extend the obligatory period of schooling progressively into the years of secondary education. The public sector already provides about 80 percent of enrollments at this level of education, and this has required a tremendous effort to meet rapidly increasing demand. In coming years, the continued expansion of secondary level education is expected to be one of the Brazilian system's primary challenges.

Policies on Basic Education Quality

For the reasons already stated in this analysis, the pursuit of quality in basic education is a national priority. In keeping with the federal system, the federal government, states, and municipalities have the task of fostering educational development in a collaborative framework. As already noted, the federal government has a redistributive and supplementary role, particularly in dealing with primary education. To fulfill this obligation, the Ministry of Education has implemented a series of basic education policies, with the following results:

- expansion and consolidation of the National System of Basic Education Evaluation (SAEB);
- implementation of a system of textbook evaluation, with measures to orient teacher preferences and foster higher quality;[14]
- definition of National Curricular Parameters (PCN) for the first four grades of the primary level and preparation of a similar initiative for the final grades, with the overall aim of fostering curricular renewal in state and municipal systems and innovation in curricular content;[15]
- implementation of the School TV Program through creation of an exclusive education channel and distribution of technological kits capable of receiving such programming to approximately 45,000 public primary schools, making it possible to provide teacher training and improvement courses coupled with new pedagogical instruments to support classroom activities;
- creation of the Accelerated Learning Program and development of specific didactic-pedagogical material for accelerated classes, offering students in situations of age/grade lag an opportunity to make up for lost time;
- implementation of the program "Money at School," designed to distribute financial resources directly to schools in such a way as to enhance their autonomy, foster greater efficiency in the use of these funds, and stimulate the organization and participation of the local community in school management;
- growth in the agility and efficacy of the Northeast Basic Education Project, which channels federal resources and funding provided by World Bank loans into efforts to reduce regional inequalities in the supply and quality of primary education;[16]
- decentralization of the school lunch program and expanded funding for the program;
- launching of the "Every Child in School" program, mobilizing the three levels of government and society in general with the goal of ensuring that every child in the obligatory schooling age bracket of 7 to 14 years will not only have access but will remain in school;
- reorganization and modernization of the system of educational indicators and statistics, providing information to be used in formulating, implementing and evaluating educational policies and monitoring the performance of education systems.

Defining an Education Scenario for the Twenty-first Century

The convergence of the education priorities of the three levels of government coupled with the increasing value attributed to education by Brazilian society in general has created a synergetic environment capable of driving an intense process of reform in the nation's public education system. Today, concern with the question of quality improvement is the major priority of the public policy agenda in the field of education.

To meet the demand defined by the New Law of Guidelines and Bases of National Education (LDB)—Law no. 9,394, dated December 24, 1996—in 1997, the Ministry of Education coordinated elaboration of the new National Education Plan (PNE), projecting a series of goals to be attained over the next ten years. The first stage of this debate was a wide-ranging process of consultation with all segments of the education sector. The National Education Plan had its first public hearing in Congress November 26, 1998. It is expected that the hearing will be concluded in 1999. Moreover, on defining a deadline of one year for formulation of the PNE, the LDB simultaneously instituted the Decade of Education, scheduled for the period from 1998 to 2007.

Brazil is now immersed in a profound process of debate on education policies and reforms that has mobilized not only the different levels of government authority, but also various segments of society, all with the fundamental aim of fostering a quality leap in Brazilian education. The conditions are highly favorable since a broad consensus has already been reached on the strategic importance of education as a fundamental requirement for the full exercise of citizenship and as the underlying capital for the nation's economic and social development.

Notes

1. This demand also extends to the private education sector, as the clientele exerts pressure to obtain educational quality compatible with the value of monthly payments.
2. Taking the three spheres of government as a whole, 1995 public investments in Brazilian education came to 4.6 percent of gross domestic product.
3. Among the measures taken with this in mind, special mention should be made of decentralization of the National School Lunch Program, initiation of funding transfers directly to public schools, and creation of the Fund for the Maintenance and Development of Primary Education and Teacher Improvement, instituted by Constitutional Amendment no. 14, dated September 12, 1996, and regulated by Federal Law no. 9,424, dated December 26, 1996.
4. The author has been Minister of Education and Sports since January 1, 1995.
5. The concept of basic education used in Brazil encompasses three levels of education: preschool, primary, and secondary.
6. Constitutional Amendment no. 14, promulgated on September 12, 1997.
7. Federal Law no. 9,424, dated December 26, 1996, regulated this fund and granted states the right to anticipate implementation provided authorizing legislation was approved at the state level. The northern state of Pará took the initiative and implemented the fund on July 1, 1996. Its work since that time has served as a reference for the other states.
8. These principal resources include the following funds and taxes: State Revenue Sharing Fund (FPE), Municipal Revenue Sharing Fund (FPM), state quota of the Industrialized Products Tax (IPI) and Tax on the Circulation of Merchandise and Services (ICMS), and also include transfers from the federal government to the states, Federal District and municipalities effected in the form of financial compensation for revenue losses consequent upon the removal of taxation from export operations (Complementary Law no. 87, dated December 13, 1996).

9. Exponential growth in demand for secondary education is the principal challenge faced by Brazil in the education field in this decade. Enrollments in this level have expanded by an average of more than 10 percent per year. This growth has been almost totally absorbed by state education networks, which account for 72.5 percent of enrollments.

10. The fact of the matter is that these schools are concentrated in the Northeast region (50 percent) due not only to the social and economic characteristics of that area but also to a lack of planning in the process of physical expansion.

11. The Ministry of Education has encouraged abandonment of this anachronistic pedagogical practice, which results in late entry into regular primary education. The overcrowding of the first grade of primary education and the consequent lack of vacancies is one of the factors that accounts for the continued existence of literacy classes.

12. The conditions required to achieve the goal of the "Every Child in School" program are concentrated in four fundamental principles of current education policy: (1) Constitutional Amendment no. 14/1996, which defines the sharing of education responsibilities among the three levels of government and implements a mechanism designed to redistribute funding in such a way as to prioritize primary education; (2) the new Law of Guidelines and Bases of National Education gives concrete form to this objective by permitting adoption of specific learning acceleration programs for students with grave age/grade lags, while also encouraging other forms of pedagogical innovation; (3) recent advances in the modernization of systems of education statistics and information have made it possible to achieve a better grasp of the reality and nature of the problem; and (4) measures taken to improve the quality of primary education based, among other elements, on the following policies: National System of Basic Education Evaluation (SAEB), National Curricular Parameters, School TV, Textbooks, and Money at School.

13. Transition rates (promotion, repetition, and dropouts) are defined by: (1) the rate of promotion in grade S is the ratio between total students promoted from that grade to S+1 and initial enrollments in grade S; (2) the repetition rate in grade S is the total of students repeating that grade divided by the number of students enrolled in the same grade in the previous year; and (3) the dropout rate in grade S is obtained by dividing the number of dropouts in that grade by total students enrolled in that grade. It is defined by: (i) students promoted in grade S—those who enrolled at the start of the year in the grade (S+1) following that in which they were enrolled in the previous year; (ii) students repeating in grade S—those who enrolled at the start of the year in the same grade S in which they were enrolled in the previous year; and (iii) students who dropped out in grade S—those who were enrolled in this grade in the previous year and did not enroll in any school at the start of the following year. In this article, these rates are calculated in percentage terms and were estimated by researcher Ruben Klein (CNPq/LNCC).

14. The Textbook Program was expanded to encompass all eight grades of the primary level. With this, the number of textbooks distributed each year increased by 83 percent and reached the very significant number of 110 million books in 1996.

15. National Curricular Parameters for the first four grades define the common core of Portuguese language, mathematics, sciences, history, geography, arts, and physical education. However, the important innovation here was inclusion of transverse subjects, such as ethics, sex education, environment, health, economic studies, and cultural plurality. These themes are integrated into the basic subjects and in this way are to permeate course content in general with questions not previously discussed in school.

16. The Brazilian government has already finalized an agreement with the World Bank to finance the second stage of the Northeast project, now called the School Development Fund (FUNDESCOLA). The program will now incorporate the North and Central-West regions of the country. This project will begin in 1999 in the development of

primary education in the three most needy regions of the country. FUNDESCOLA Projects will have a total of $1.3 million for the next six years: FUNDESCOLA I, in the amount of $125 million will be in action for two and a half years, and will cover the North and Central West regions; FUNDESCOLA II, which will also include the Northeastern region, will be in action from 1999 to 2002, and will have a budget of $600 million; FUNDESCOLA III is to benefit all three region's from 2001 to 2003, with an expected budget of $575 million. Continuation to FUNDESCOLA Projects II and III are dependent on the physical and financial development of projects I and II, respectively. It is expected that FUNDESCOLA funds will be maintained in the face of 1998 government budget reductions.

9

ERNESTO SCHIEFELBEIN AND PAULINA SCHIEFELBEIN

Repetition and Quality of Education in Chile

Repetition, failure to learn adequately, and dropout in primary school in Chile take place in the context of a school system that has undergone considerable modification during the last twenty years. The school system is divided into preschool education for students from four to six years old, basic education school (eight years), middle school (four years), university (three to seven years) and postgraduate studies. The first enrollment in primary school takes place at six years of age. Students are not required to complete a given number of years of school; instead, they must attend school until they are fourteen years old, and they most frequently leave to enter the work force at that age. University or technical institutes follow secondary school, and three to five years are required to obtain the equivalent of a B.A. *(licenciado)* degree. Postgraduate studies are available. Approximately 30 percent of secondary students continue their studies, and 2 percent of the *licenciados* (equivalent to college graduates) continue to study for higher academic degrees.

In this chapter, emphasis is placed on repetition and quality of education in primary school. There is automatic promotion from the first to second grade. The school year consists of 180 days of school (ten days have been added since 1995), of five hours, including two rest periods of fifteen minutes daily. It will be extended to almost six hours in the next three years. There are usually two shifts of school. In small schools, there are classes in which students in many different grades are taught in the same classroom. In order to achieve these aims, an estimated 4 percent of GDP is spent on education. For the primary school level, 9 percent of expenditure is private, 32 percent is private subsidized, and 59 percent is municipal, but funded by the central government. Federal spending on education is 15 percent of the federal budget, a number lower than the historically high 17.9 percent in 1972. The reduction is the result of privatization of education, which, however, includes elements of subsidy from the central government. Repetition, however, is the result of educational as well as financial factors.

Chile decreased its index of repetition of the first grade to practically half during the 1970s. It fell from 40 percent in 1964 to 23 percent at the end of the

1970s (Schiefelbein and Grossi 1978) and has been maintained at about 10 percent during the last ten years (Table 9.1).

Although repetition affects students from all socioeconomic groups, the students who are affected are those with an inadequate preparation for learning from an ideal curriculum—occasioned by inadequacies that can be traced to their marginal living conditions—and whose parents have low levels of education. This situation becomes worse among children who live in isolated rural zones, who go to multi-grade classes, or who only speak an indigenous language and are required to educate themselves in Spanish.

In the 1960s, high rates of repetition were detected; this generated a collective effort to increase the quality of education. Teachers, and to a certain extent parents and administrators, changed their attitudes, feeling a greater personal responsibility for students' failure and recognizing that repetition would not always overcome learning problems (Schiefelbein and Davis 1974). In 1967, legislation established "automatic promotion" (for students attending more than 75 percent of class days), accompanied by national measures that tended to improve the quality of education: teacher training, rest periods, distribution of texts, parent participation, timely enrollment below the age of seven years, changes in the curriculum, student scholarships, school food programs, and other stimuli.

The rate of repetition in Chile is considerably less than the average in Latin America and the Caribbean. The Latin American rate reached 35 percent in the first grade in 1997. The decrease of repetition in the region has been slow. In the first grade it fell from 50 percent to 43 percent in the 1980–90 period (UNESCO 1996). At this rate, Latin American nations would have to wait until 2022 to reduce repetition to 10 percent (if present policies remain unchanged). Chile and Uruguay in South America and other countries of the English-speaking Caribbean, which have other educational traditions, have repetition rates of less than 15 percent in the first grade of primary school (UNESCO 1996). The two South American countries reduced repetition (Schiefelbein and Wolff 1995) by combining the stimulus of promotion based on age, or "flexible promotion," accompanied by solid in-service training of teachers and the provision of educational materials (Wolff et al. 1994).

School Pyramid and Repetition

In Chile, a significant number of students in each of the first three grades are of an age that corresponds to students having repeated a grade (Table 9.2). Practically 98 percent of Chilean students enter the school system on time for basic education; 91 percent of each group of the age cohort enters at the age of six years, and the other 7 percent enters at seven years (Table 9.2). If most of the class were of the same age, this would facilitate the traditional work of the teachers, in the sense that it would permit them to work with a homogeneous group of students. For example, a great number of first grade students who are

Table 9.1

Chile: Estimates of the Repetition Rate for First and Second Grades, 1970–1996

Year	New admissions First grade	Enrollment First grade	Repeaters First grade	Promotions Second grade	Enrollment Second grade	Repetition rate for first grade Maximum	Minimum	Promotion rate
1970	276,800	395,400	165,600	229,800	338,300	41.9	41.1	58
1971	270,500	436,100	131,400	304,700	349,500	30.1	29.3	70
1972	271,000	402,400	137,334	265,066	375,800	34.1	33.3	66
1973	269,866	407,200	135,759	271,441	355,900	33.3	32.5	67
1974	267,565	403,324	109,490	293,834	347,717	27.1	26.3	73
1975	265,901	375,391	90,594	284,797	345,995	24.1	23.3	76
1976	264,151	354,745	96,506	258,239	323,971	27.2	26.4	73
1977	262,514	359,020	105,215	253,805	312,473	29.3	28.5	71
1978	256,614	361,829	103,108	258,721	314,626	28.5	27.7	72
1979	255,585	358,693	85,648	273,045	318,011	23.9	23.1	76
1980	254,785	340,433	69,497	270,936	312,509	20.4	19.6	80
1981	253,383	322,880	36,583	286,297	300,535	11.3	10.5	89
1982	252,077	288,660	(1,296)	289,956	295,565	-0.4	-1.2	100
1983	250,342	249,046	(5,721)	254,767	273,902	-2.3	-3.1	102
1984	248,978	243,257	41,664	201,593	241,143	17.1	16.3	83
1985	247,782	289,446	35,509	253,937	237,428	12.3	11.5	88

Year							
1986	247,789	283,298	28,166	255,132	274,981	9.9	9.1	90
1987	249,585	277,751	38,929	238,822	269,153	14.0	13.2	86
1988	251,367	290,296	26,768	263,528	265,981	9.2	8.4	91
1989	254,377	281,145	16,014	265,131	280,968	5.7	4.9	94
1990	258,728	274,742	1,660	273,082	275,837	0.6	-0.2	99
1991	264,886	266,546	(6,412)	272,958	268,102	-2.4	-3.2	102
1992	269,244	262,832	22,641	240,191	263,796	8.6	7.8	91
1993	275,671	298,312	22,594	275,718	257,083	7.6	6.8	92
1994	281,704	304,298	25,178	279,120	284,359	8.3	7.5	92
1995	287,150	312,328	29,652	282,676	298,135	9.5	8.7	91
1996	289,991	319,643			308,492			

Sources: Author's estimates using data from the Depto. de Estadística de MINEDUC and population estimated by CELADE. Period 1995–2005; Año 30, No. 60, 1997.

Notes: The new entrants in the first year of primary school correspond to the annual increase in enrollment of population older than six years of age.

The negative figures correspond to the sudden reduction in enrollment generated by the economic crisis of the 1980s and the return to democracy at the beginning of the 1990s.

Using three-year moving averages allows for more stable estimates, eliminating the effects of annual crises.

Table 9.2

Chile: Student Enrollment by Age and Grade, 1995

Age	Preschool	1	2	3	4	5	6	7	8
0–1	3,119	0	0	0	0	0	0	0	0
2	13,243	0	0	0	0	0	0	0	0
3	31,186	0	0	0	0	0	0	0	0
4	64,480	0	0	0	0	1	0	1	0
5	126,143	468	2	1	2	1	0	0	0
6	150,786	113,368	952	28	2	1	1	0	0
7	4,880	175,402	99,474	825	40	1	1	6	1
8	0	17,734	162,649	84,223	817	43	25	63	0
9	0	3,651	25,672	157,296	69,896	1,028	58	1,369	1
10	0	1,607	6,563	28,785	135,779	77,480	1,316	72,943	15
11	0	431	2,489	8,245	27,153	126,477	77,648	115,540	118
12	0	178	762	3,548	10,486	32,026	117,407	42,616	1,280
13	0	86	403	1,466	5,227	15,279	35,888	15,192	65,610
14	0	46	143	555	1,859	6,205	15,104	3,671	110,470
15	0	19	57	190	549	1,923	5,418	963	40,223
16	0	3	9	40	141	418	1,516	158	11,564
17	0	3	8	19	36	119	314	19	3,347
18	0	0	3	2	7	19	52	20	592
19	0	0	0	1	4	2	22	0	118
20	0	0	2	2	3	10	27	0	50
21	0	0	0	0	0	0	0	0	0
22	0	0	0	0	0	0	0	0	0
23	0	0	0	0	0	0	0	0	0
24	0	0	0	0	0	0	0	0	0
25	0	0	0	0	0	0	0	0	0
26 and older	0	0	0	0	0	0	0	0	0
Total	393,837	312,996	299,188	285,226	252,001	261,032	254,796	252,561	233,389

eight years or older indicates the presence of repeaters, which transforms the class into a heterogeneous group. This variance in the age distribution of each grade has repercussions on teaching practices and on the quality of education, since it makes it difficult to apply the traditional verbal transfer of information, known as the frontal or transmission method of teaching—generally applied in the country—a method efficient for groups of students with homogeneous characteristics.

Underestimation of Repetition During the 1960s

At the end of the 1960s, it was demonstrated for the first time that repetition was underestimated by one-third—by at least 10 percentage points (Schiefelbein and Davis 1974). The official statistics for 1964 indicated 30.4 percent repetition in first grade but the simulation models used to reconstruct the flow of students in the prior eight years showed that repetition in this grade would be at least 40.9 percent. Later it was shown that the difference was generated because the school principals considered those who dropped out temporarily and returned to matriculate the following year in another school in the same grade as "dropouts," and the students who left before the year-end exams also were not included (Schiefelbein and Heikkinen 1991).

Five main causes could lead to an underestimation of repetition: (1) temporary dropout by some students (for illness or to work at harvest time in rural zones), or transfer to others schools who were reported as "dropouts" even when they entered the same grade the next year either in another school, or even in the same school. The major part of these temporary dropouts would repeat the grade, but would not be registered as repeaters; (2) statistical questionnaires filled out badly by teachers—whether for lack of time, or because they completed them from memory (and when in doubt, omitted students), because they did not understand the questionnaires, or because it is not an educational priority; (3) problems with records in badly managed schools made it hard to verify the accuracy of data; (4) the phenomenon of the "re-enrolled," that is to say a child with grades sufficient to pass the class, whose teacher and parents agreed to keep him in the same grade for another year in order to "mature" (these students were not considered repeaters, but "re-enrolled"); and (5) students whose parents presented them as recently arrived, but who in fact had been expelled from another school for repeating more than once or for bad behavior.

Factors Influencing Repetition and Quality

Learning problems make many children repeat. However, the main cause of repetition in Chile (and in Latin America) is low quality of education, especially because of poor (usually obsolete) teaching methods and because of the lack of adequate teaching materials. However, the decrease in repetition does not necessarily imply an improvement in the quality of education, since it could be the result of reducing the standards for promotion, whose limiting case corresponds to automatic promotion (Schiefelbein and Wolff 1993). An increase in learning could result as much in an increase in the requirements for passing as in an increase in promotion rates.

The results of research about the probable causes of repetition suggest problems relative to the:

1. Lack of Preschool Education. Two-thirds of students enter the school system without appropriate preparation. Preschool is only available to one-third of the population between three and five years of age and to one-half of the age six population (Table 9.2), a figure that is considerably lower in the isolated rural and marginal urban areas than urban areas, so that the children most in need of preschool education are least likely to receive it. Children who lack preschool education (Myers 1992) have lower school achievement levels than those who attended preschool, and this increases the level of repetition. Paradoxically, a minority of the children who are taught with flexible methods in preschool have difficulty adjusting to the rigid frontal method that predominates in basic education.

2. "Average student" and variance of ages in each grade. Teachers are used to targeting their message to an "average student" despite the great heterogeneity of ages that is observed in each grade of primary school (Table 9.2). The heterogeneity of the class-group, compounded by the repetition rates, makes it hard for students to learn, given that many remain "below the capacity of the average student" and need some personalized attention to learn. This would require the utilization of teaching materials that are designed for diversity (Avalos 1986). The vicious cycle of inadequate teaching for heterogeneous groups increases repetition and requires personalized attention to break it.

3. Fixed time of year in which school curriculum is offered. Some youths temporarily leave school to work during the harvest and other seasonal jobs and then return to classes, but usually cannot catch up and, therefore withdraw before the school year ends and then re-enter the following school year in the same grade. The same pattern of interrupted study takes place when students repeat the grade, so that they never are able to see the material that is handed out during the harvest or work season, thus generating another vicious cycle of continual repetition (Schiefelbein and Heikkinen 1991).

4. Multi-grade classrooms. Schools in rural zones or in lightly populated areas have few students and few teachers, and some 10 percent of schools have only one teacher who teaches all the students. In schools with less than 100 students it is necessary to work in multi-grade classrooms with twenty to twenty-five students per teacher. Multi-grade classes in Chile usually have low student achievement and high repetition rates. But in developed nations there is no empirical evidence that multi-grade and multi-age classes interfere with children's learning (Veenman 1995), and at times this system benefits social development and emotional attitude (Miller 1990). This would suggest that in Chile, the low achievement and high repetition rates could be due to the lack of individualized teaching to address the students' basic needs. When personalized methods of teaching are applied, with more interactive educational techniques, better results are obtained than with traditional methods (Psacharopolos et al. 1993).

5. *"Incomplete" schools.* Chile has achieved almost universal attendance rates among the school age population. However, in some rural areas there are schools that do not offer complete schooling (they do not wish to have multi-grade classes). When the incomplete primary school is located far from the nearest complete primary or continuation school, or when travel is very expensive, some children repeat the last grade offered in their local school convinced that they will at least learn something. Some teachers work with them on additional assignments on a personalized basis. These students are listed as repeaters in the last grade of school.

6. *Poor quality of teaching.* The teaching methods most frequently observed in Chile do not address the learning problems of students, thus generating excessive repetition. Methods applied give priority to the verbal transfer of information and to the passive memorization by a whole-class group. These methods minimize: (i) use of prior knowledge of students; (ii) time-on-task, since the professor has to maintain order in the classroom (which results in about 30 percent less time spent in actual instruction); (iii) thinking about the meaning of concepts; (iv) applications related to the context in which the students live; (v) stimulation of written communication—in class or as homework for class. As mentioned above, "frontal" education usually is effective in homogeneous groups—where the majority of students coincides with the "imaginary average student"—but it is not effective for heterogeneous groups (a frequent characteristic in classrooms in the poorest districts of the country), where many students are not capable of following the rhythm with which knowledge is "deposited" (Schiefelbein 1994). If teaching is not individualized for these students, the level of reading comprehension falls and the rates of repetition increase, which in turn causes the heterogeneity of ages in the classroom to increase, which increases the problems of applying these methods (Thomas and Shaw 1992; Ezpeleta and Weiss 1994).

7. *Problems of management and finance.* Repetition is linked in Chile to: (i) low teachers' salaries, meaning that few high school graduates want to study teaching and most choose that career when they are not accepted in other careers; (ii) teachers learn to teach in a passive manner; (iii) low quality of texts and study guides (Eyzaguirre and Fontaine 1997); (iv) delay in reassigning teachers when the number of students enrolled in a school changes (from those in which the number of students falls to schools in which enrollment increases and requires more teachers); (v) failure to find teacher replacements in a timely manner in case of sickness or pregnancy; and (vi) lack of incentives for the best teachers. Finally, in rural districts there is absenteeism of teachers and this generates poor learning and repetition.

8. Time available for learning. In Chile the school day in public schools used to last five hours for 170 days per year (Schiefelbein et al. 1997). The 850 hours of class offered by public education are far fewer than the 1,200 hours offered by private schools, which limits the possibility of improving the quality of education and diminishing repetition (Schiefelbein 1995). The time spent on bureaucratic activities needs to be decreased and dedicated to teaching. Since 1997, Chile is extending the school day by one hour, to increase the available time for learning; to implement this strategy additional classrooms have been created and salaries to cover the expanded time have been secured. Still, there are many ongoing problems that range from lack of lunchrooms to lack of suitable activities to keep students busy at school.

9. Bilingualism. In Chile, around 5 percent of students come from indigenous cultures and usually have learning difficulties, since they must be taught in a different language and culture from their own (Tedesco 1990). This problem is manifested in higher repetition levels in the regions in which indigenous population is concentrated (North and Center-South). For example, in Malleco province (where the largest share of indigenous population is found) repetition rates are twice as high as the national average.

10. "Culture of repetition." Many teachers share the view that a given percentage of students should be failed each year and that, as a result, even if they were to increase their learning, a similar percentage would continue to be failed. This probably originated in the initial teacher training, which endorses rigid standards in both teaching methods and in achievement levels. This is based on teacher training schools in France and Germany at the end of the century, which emphasized that professional teachers should only promote students capable of achieving the desired level. This tradition has gradually changed since the adoption of "automatic promotion" rules in Chile, which effectively generated a decrease in repetition rates in the late 1960s.

11. Student characteristics and problems of nutrition. Poor nourishment, lack of assistance from the family, lack of family resources, and the cultural level of parents all influence the students' learning process and impact the repetition rates (Gajardo and de Andraca 1988). Although it is known that the ability to learn is directly related to nutrition and the students' health (Pollit 1990; Lockheed and Verspoor 1991), it is not possible to verify whether programs of supplying food in public schools could be sufficient to improve the quality of learning and diminish eventual repetition (Schiefelbein and Clavel 1983).

12. Too stringent standards for promotion. It could be assumed that repetition is the result of evaluation standards that are too high, imposed by elite schools that wish to maintain their national prestige. However, the students of elite schools for the most part meet their requirements. Even if it is possible to reject the notion that the standards are too high, it should be noted that repeaters in elite schools usually have a higher level of learning than many students who are promoted in the rest of the system.

Consequences of Repetition

1. Heterogeneity of student age and older-than-average students in the class-room. As we have already mentioned, a by-product of repetition is greater heterogeneity in the age of students in the same grade. Both the lower self-esteem of the repeater—who feels himself "inferior" to those who pass the course—and the difficulty of adjusting the "average" which determines the level at which "frontal" classes are conducted in rural areas, negatively affect learning in the classroom, because teachers do not use personalized teaching methods, which would allow them to meet the specific needs of different students.

2. Poor results obtained by students who repeat. Various studies have shown that the achievement scores of repeaters usually are lower than those of their classmates (Schiefelbein and Clavel 1983). In the United States, the reading achievement of children who have repeated is 18 percent lower than that of those who did not repeat (Wolff et al. 1994). Repetition, moreover, reduces the probability of completing the entire primary school cycle, given that from fourteen years of age economic pressures require the least favored students to abandon the school system in order to enter the workforce.

3. Early dropout from school. In Chile, dropout from school begins at fourteen years of age (2 percent) and is accentuated at sixteen (12 percent). Dropouts have usually repeated several grades in primary school, and entrance into the labor market seems more stimulating to them than continuing in school with such poor results. A better quality education that generated higher rates of promotion would probably help students to complete primary education before dropping out, which would substantially increase the total educational yield in the nation.

4. Greater annual cost per student borne by the state. Chile spends $300 million per year in educating repeaters. That a student repeats a grade implies that he occupies that same place twice and, therefore, duplicates the cost of his education. This signifies a greater monetary effort, both on the part of the parents and that of the state. There are 400,000 repeaters in the first eight grades of basic education and 130,000 in the four middle school grades.

5. Social inequality and the quality of education. Although repetition affects students from all socioeconomic groups, its greatest impact is on students from poor families. This is because, principally, the teaching process is especially deficient in schools located in rural and marginal urban areas (Wolff et al. 1994). This situation is negatively influenced if the parents are illiterate or lack formal education and if access to public services is difficult. For this reason, among students coming from families of a low socioeconomic level, those that live in isolated rural areas usually have twice the average probability of repeating. In this subgroup of poverty and isolation, repetition will be even greater among children belonging to indigenous groups who speak a language other than Spanish at home.

Effective Strategies to Decrease Repetition

In order to improve teaching methods it is necessary to change the teaching strategies and self-teaching materials: use "flexible" promotion strategies, introduce bilingual education in the cases where it is necessary, offer early (preschool) education, and increase the time spent learning.

1. Change of teaching strategies. Research suggests that it is possible to improve the quality of learning, by (i) reducing educational processes centered in exposition and repetition of information; (ii) using materials that would stimulate individual, cooperative, and interactive learning; (iii) training teachers in teaching methods for multi-grade classes by means of active learning processes (Purves 1973; Costa 1977; Husen et al. 1978; Jamison et al. 1981; Farrell and Heynemann 1989).

2. Teaching and learning materials. Investment in effective educational materials is one of the best investments in terms of cost-efficiency. The use of self-study guides facilitates the change from the educational process employed by teachers to a personalized and group process (Schiefelbein and Tedesco 1995) and also facilitates the use of students' previous knowledge or the family culture as an active part of the learning process. Providing a minimum of a reading text and a mathematics text (both with a self-study guide format) for each student and other texts in social sciences and natural sciences for the last grades, plus a small "classroom library" of one or two books per student, would cost approximately $5 per student, that is to say around 4 percent of the estimated average cost per student of $118 for 1989 (Wolff et al. 1994).

3. Flexible promotion. Colombia's "Escuela Nueva" is characterized by multi-grade education and promoting of students to the extent that they achieve minimal educational objectives, regardless of when they achieve them, rather than only at the end of the school year, which increases learning and decreases the repetition rate.

4. Bilingual education. Children belonging to ethnic or cultural minority groups usually have learning difficulties because they have to be schooled in the official language of Chile, which is different from their own language and culture (Tedesco 1990). When the native language of the students is used in informal communication—in recreation and also in the classroom—it seriously interferes with the process of educating in Spanish. These cases require a bilingual focus on learning, so that the students can relate new signs with sounds and well-known meanings and then transfer their knowledge to the official language. This should be discussed with (and explained to) Spanish-speaking parents who complain when their children are placed in bilingual classes.

5. Improving the prior preparation of the student. The growing evidence with respect to the importance of developing students from early infancy implies expanding preschool education to improve the yield of basic education and reduce repetition (Grawe 1979; Myers 1992, 1995; Loera 1995).

6. *Time dedicated to learning.* It is necessary to increase the time available to students for learning (Schiefelbein 1995). This could be achieved in two complementary ways: (i) enforcing the current norms on length of the school day and year and curbing teachers' absences; and (ii) modifying teaching strategies in the classroom to improve effective learning. The second alternative would have a high cost, but would favor not only the increase of time employed, but also the improvement of the educational process in the classroom.

7. *Complete multi-grade schools.* As pointed out earlier, there are appropriate methods to generate effective multi-grade learning processes. By means of multi-grade classes it is possible to offer eight years of education in all the primary schools.

References

Avalos, Beatriz. 1986. *"Enseñando a los hijos de los pobres: un estudio etnográfico en América Latina."* Ottawa: IDRC.
Costa, M. 1977. "School Outputs and the Determinants of Scholastic Achievment." Ph.D. dissertation. Stanford University.
Eyzaguirre, Barbara, and Loreto Fontaine, eds. 1997. *El futuro en riesgo: nuestros textos escolares.* Santiago, Chile: Centro de Estudios Públicos.
Ezpeleta, J., and E. Weiss. 1994. "Programa para abatir el regazo educativo. Evaluación cualitativa del impacto. Informe final." Mexico: Instituto Politécnico Nacional; DIE.
Farrell, J.P., and S.P. Heyneman. 1989. "Textbooks in the Developing World: Economic and Educational Choices." Paper presented at the EDI Seminar of the World Bank. Washington, D.C.
Gajardo, M., and A.M. de Andraca. 1988. *Trabajo infantil y escuela. Las zonas rurales.* Santiago, Chile: FLACSO.
Grawe, R. 1979. "Ability in Pre-Schools. Earning and Home Environment." Working paper No. 322. Washington, D.C.: World Bank.
Husen, T., L. Saha, and R. Noonan. 1978. "Teacher Training and Student Achievement in Less Developed Countries." Staff Working Paper No. 310, World Bank.
Jamison, D., B. Searle, S.P. Heynemann, and K. Galda. 1981. "Improving Elementary Mathematics Education in Nicaragua: An Experimental Study of the Impact of Textbooks and Radio on Achievement." Discussion Paper No. 81-5 of the Population and Human Resourses Division, World Bank.
Lockheed, M., and A. Verspoor. 1991. *Improving Primary Education in Developing Countries.* New York: Oxford University Press.
Loera Varela, Armando. 1995. "Los indicadores de la educación básica en México: Bases para conformar un sistema." Mexico, DF: Secretaría de Educación Pública.
Miller, B.A. 1990. "A Review of the Quantitative Research on Multigrade Instruction." *Research in Rural Education* 7, no. 2: 1–8.
Myers, Robert G. 1992. *The Twelve Who Survive.* New York: Routledge.
———. 1995. "La educación preescolar en América Latina. El estado de la práctica." Documentos de PREAL.
Pollit, E. 1990. "Malnutrition and Infection in the Classroom." Paris: UNESCO. Ed. Pollit, Haas, and Levitsky. 1989. "International Conference on Iron Deficiency and Behavioral Development." *The American Journal of Clinical Nutrition* 3.
Psacharopoulos, G., J. Valenzuela and M. Arends. 1993. "Teacher's Salaries in Latin

America: A Comparative Analysis." Working Paper No. 1086, Departamento Técnico de América Latina y el Caribe, World Bank.

Purves, A. 1973. *Literature Education in Ten Countries.* New York: Almqvist and Wiksell.

Schiefelbein, E., 1983. "Variables exógenas que inciden en el rendimiento escolar en 40 y 60 años de la escuela básica y que convendría usar en futuros análisis del PER." Serie de Estudios No. 91. Lo Barnechea, Chile: CPEIP y OEA.

Schiefelbein, Ernesto. 1994. "Estrategias para elevar la calidad de la educación." *Revista Interamericana de Desarrollo Educativo de OEA.* no. 117. Washington, D.C.

———. 1995. "Education Reform in Latin America and the Caribbean." Santiago, Chile: UNESCO-OREALC, Bulletin no. 37.

Schiefelbein, E., and C. Clavel. 1977. "Stability over Time of Educational Input–Output Relationships." Programa ECIEL del PIIE—Depto. de Economía de la Universidad de Chile. Santiago, Chile.

Schiefelbein, E., and R.G. Davis. 1974. *Development of Educational Planning Models and Application in the Chilean School Reform.* New York: Lexington Books.

Schiefelbein, E., and M.C. Grossi. 1978. "Análisis de la matrícula escolar en Chile." Documento de Trabajo 10/78 del CIDE. Santiago, Chile.

Schiefelbein, E., and S. Heikkinen. 1991. "Chile: acceso, permanencia, repetición y eficiencia en la educación básica." Santiago, Chile: OREALC.

Schiefelbein, E., and J.C. Tedesco. 1995. "Una nueva oportunidad. El rol de la educación en el desarrollo de América Latina." Buenos Aires: Editorial Santillana; Aula XXI.

Schiefelbein, E., and L. Wolff. 1993. "Repetición y rendimiento inadecuado en escuelas primarias de América Latina: magnitudes, causas, relaciones y estrategias." Place? UNESCO/OREALC, Bulletin no. 30.

———. 1995. "Repetition and Poor Achievement in Latin America Primary Schools." Place: UNESCO/OREALC, Bulletin no. 24.

Schiefelbein, Paulina, Benno Sander, Leonel Zuñiga, Gefulio Carvalho, Beatrice Edwards, Laurence Wolff, and Michael H. Alleyne. 1997. "Education in the Americas: Quality, Equity and Citizenship." Washington, DC: OAS.

Tedesco, Juan Carlos. 1990. "Intercultural Bilingual Education in Latin America." *Prospects 75.* Paris.

Thomas, C., and C. Shaw. 1992. "Issues in the Development of Multigrade Schools." Technical Paper no. 172. Washington, DC: World Bank.

UNESCO. 1996. "State of Education in Latin America and the Caribbean, 1980–1994." Santiago, Chile: OREALC.

Veenman, Simon. 1995. "Cognitive and Noncognitive Effects of Multigrade and Multi-Age Classes: A Best Evidence Synthesis." *Review of Educational Research* 65, no. 4: 319–321.

Wolff, L., E. Schiefelbein, and J. Valenzuela. 1994. "Improving the Quality of Primary Education in Latin America and the Caribbean." World Bank No. 257S, Washington D.C.

10

TERESA BRACHO

Basic Education in Mexico: An Overview

Introduction

Advances in the Mexican educational system have been important during the last fifty years. Increases in the literacy rates and the average years of school per capita, the expansion of all levels of education, and the increase in the quantity of people involved in offering educational services have been accompanied by changes associated with other social processes such as increasing urbanization, changes in the composition of employment, and a slowing in the rate of population growth, among others. However, even today the constitutional edict of basic education for all has not been achieved, and the conditions of the supply of relevant and high quality education, and the improvement of opportunities for access to post-basic education are disputed. Thus, although it is certain that educational efforts are important, they have not, however, been sufficient to achieve the objectives hoped for from the national educational system.

It must be remembered that in Mexico, as in other countries in the region, education was not a priority in the government's agenda during the last decade: the economy suffered a severe crisis and faced heavy payments to service the foreign debt. Educational indicators, including those related to public expenditure, show this toward the end of the 1980s and the beginning of the 1990s. From then on, Mexico has not only tried to give priority to education in public discourse, but also has witnessed some advances in educational indices.

The present chapter describes the national education system and the distribution of schooling in the Mexican population, focusing the analysis on the recent evolution of basic education and of its principal indices of efficiency. The period covered is 1990–95 when, based on evidence from the census, it was evident that the system was excluding important contingents of young children. It was evident that the decreases in public spending on education were affecting human development for the future, and, with it, the viability of national development.

Two factors are important to note before introducing the national educational system. The first is the volume of potential demand for education in Mexico. According to the most recent estimates available, by 1997 the population reached approximately 95 million people of when slightly more than 56 percent were twenty-four years old or younger. That is, despite the tendencies toward stabilization in population growth, the large numbers of people that could place demands on the educational system are important. On the other hand, conditions of backwardness, poverty, and marginality, together with the territorial dispersion of the poorest populations, are phenomena to keep in mind in analyzing shortcomings in the educational system. According to the most recent available information, the 1996–97 school year included about 27.5 million people in different education levels, systems, and modalities.[1]

The second factor is the new structure of the national educational system. Until 1992, the control, administration, and regulation were the responsibility of the federal government. From May of that year, educational administration and labor relations with approximately 700,000 teachers were decentralized. With the new administration, different systems of information and calculation were introduced that at times could make it difficult to analyze the recent evolution of the educational system.

The modification of the Mexican Political Constitution in 1992, and the promulgation of the General Law of Education in 1993, extended basic education to ten years, including preschool and secondary education, both of which are now required. For many decades, the required primary school cycle in Mexico covered six school years, beginning at six years of age. Education that precedes it is preschool, with a variable duration of one to three years. This cycle is not required, although it has had a very recent and important expansion in public school supply.

The "secondary" school cycle refers to what before was called the first cycle of middle level school. It includes three school years after primary school. It continues to be administratively and operationally independent of primary school, even though it is now formally part of required basic education.

Post-basic education includes the higher middle school levels and higher (post–middle school) general and technical education. It has much greater institutional, administrative, and funding diversity than basic education does.

The Results of the 1990 Census

Despite about fifteen years in which the educational system prided itself on covering 100 percent of educational demand, despite advances in systems of adult literacy education and similar achievements, the results of the 1990 population census cast doubt on many of the assertions about the achievements of the educational system. Census results indicated that though the average years of schooling had increased, there were important shortfalls in basic education. We summarize some of these results below.[2]

Table 10.1 summarizes the principal educational indices for the adult population between twenty and sixty-five years of age. The proportion of adults who never went to school are important for the nation as a whole. The regional distribution fluctuates between 6 percent of adults without education in the national capital, to one-third in the South; and, when one looks at the youngest part of the adult population (between twenty and thirty-four years of age), the figures fall to 3 percent in the capital and one-fifth among the youth in the south of the country. At the other extreme for the population that has some post-basic education, only in the Federal District has almost half of its adult population gone beyond basic education (42.5 percent). The North has proportions around 30 percent. The South has very low shares (12.8 percent), together with the Center-Periphery (17.1 percent).

Distribution by size of locality shows that post-basic education is concentrated in the largest cities, although for mid-sized cities conditions are better in the North than the rest of the nation. There is a strong concentration of population with post-basic education in the largest cities of the South.

The age distribution shows that for almost all states, the proportion of youth with secondary education is over one-fifth of the population, much below that of the capital, where more than half the youths have post-basic education.

The average schooling of adults in the nation is six and a half years. Only the Federal District has an average educational level equivalent to secondary school (nine years). In the northern states, average schooling surpassed seven years, with a slightly higher average in the Northwest. In the Center and Center-West, schooling was higher than the basic six years; in the Center-Periphery and the Southeast there was a little more than five years of education on average; the states in the South had barely more than an average of four years of primary school. Schooling of the youngest group of adults (between twenty and thirty-four years) in comparison with the entire adult population showed higher averages: the national average is 7.9 school years, reflecting the recent expansion of the educational system and the improvements in the general rates of school participation.

While young people in the capital have achieved an average of ten years of education, those of the South do not even achieve the average of elementary school education. The Southeast shows an important increase in this indicator when compared to the national average. For their part, the distance increased between states in the Center-Periphery in relation to the other regions of the southern zone.

The rural population has an average of 3.5 years of schooling; that is, it does not reach the level of "functional literacy" established as four years by UNESCO decades ago, and there are entities that do not achieve even an average of three years of average schooling.[3] Only two entities in the North Pacific exceed five years. The average schooling of the indigenous population is even lower than the average for the rural population in general. By regions, the highest average is registered in the North Pacific (3.8 years), followed by the Southeast (3.5), the West Center (3.4), the North (3.3), the Center (3), the Center-Periphery (2.6), and finally the South (2.4).

Table 10.1

Educational Levels and Average Years of School (adults, ages 20–65 years)

Region	Adults Total (1,000s)	No schooling (%)			With post-basic education (%)			Average years of school				
		Total	Rural	Youth	Total	Rural	Youth	Total	Indige-nous	Rural	Urban	Youth
Pacific Northwest	1,798.8	8.9	15.3	4.2	29.5	10.2	39.7	7.5	3.8	5.0	8.3	8.9
North	4,681.8	8.7	16.4	4.3	28.2	5.7	38.0	7.4	3.3	4.4	8.3	8.8
Federal District	4,325.8	5.8	14.3	2.5	42.5	24.1	51.9	9.1	6.0	6.9	9.1	10.2
West	4,719.4	12.4	20.1	5.8	23.2	6.6	32.5	6.6	3.0	4.1	8.1	8.0
Center	5,851.1	12.0	27.6	6.0	24.9	6.9	32.6	6.9	3.4	4.0	7.9	8.2
Center, perifery	9,917.8	21.8	32.1	11.8	17.1	3.9	24.6	5.4	2.6	3.2	7.9	6.8
South	3,653.8	32.4	42.2	20.8	12.8	3.8	19.2	4.3	2.4	2.8	7.7	5.8
Southeast	1,710.6	16.8	25.1	11.0	20.3	4.6	27.6	5.8	3.5	3.6	8.1	7.1

Source: Bracho 1998.

Participation of Six- to Fifteen-Year-Olds in School

Basic Education

It is necessary to point out the unequal regional distribution of school-age population (between six and twelve years) that attends primary school: the Center-Periphery has 30.2 percent of the primary school population, the Center has 16.2 percent, the West-Center has 13.6 percent, and the South, 12.3 percent; 7.8 percent reside in the Capital, 4.8 percent in the Southeast and 4.1 percent in the North Pacific.

Table 10.2 summarizes the educational attainment of the relevant population to the basic education system—those between six and fifteen years of age.[4] The percentages of children between six and twelve who do not attend school fluctuate between 3.5 percent in the Federal District, up to 25.7 percent in Chiapas. Among the other regions, the smallest share of students outside of school is in Nuevo León, with 4.6 percent. In the Southeast region the conditions are more variable, from 9.6 percent in Tabasco to 1.42 percent in Campeche. The Center-Periphery also shows greater regional differences from 8.3 percent in San Luis Potosí, to the state of Michoacán with 17.1 percent of children who do not attend school, slightly more than the share in Oaxaca and Guerrero.[5]

The proportion of thirteen to fifteen year olds who have not completed primary school represents almost 10 percent in the Federal District, between 15 and 17 percent in the North and Center, 22 percent in the West Center, and one-third in the Center-Periphery and the Southeast; the region with the largest gap is the South, where 42 percent of children in the age appropriate group for secondary school have not completed primary school. Within this region the figure varies between one-third in Guerrero and more than half in Chiapas.

The combination of children who have completed primary school but do not continue their education with the earlier indicators of average years of schooling completed presents an image of shortfall in basic education, even though it is required by the Constitution. The regions with the smallest gaps are in the North (especially Nuevo León, and with the least attendance in Chihuahua) and the Federal District. The Center and the West Center show intermediate rates, and in the Center-Periphery, Southeast, and South the rates of participation are low. Two cases stand out here: Veracruz, Michoacán, and Guanajuato, with high rates both of children who do not finish primary school and those who do not go to secondary school; and the South and Southeast with the largest share of children who do not finish primary school, although they have better rates of incorporation in relation to the transition between primary and secondary school—especially in Chiapas. This indicates that the process of exclusion is mainly happening in primary school. But once this proportionally smaller share of the population finishes primary school, the probability of success in completing basic education is greater.[6]

Table 10.2

Education Levels of the Population, 6 to 19 Years of Age (%)

Region	Primary aged students (6–12)		Secondary aged students (13–15)		Ages 16–19	
	Without schooling	In primary	Without primary	Not in school	In secondary	Without secondary
Pacific Northwest	6.7	93.3	17.3	12.1	70.7	37.8
North	6.5	93.5	15.6	16.1	68.3	38.2
Federal District	3.5	96.5	9.9	7.5	82.6	27.0
West	8.7	91.3	22.2	19.7	58.1	48.1
Center	7.0	93.0	16.3	11.8	71.9	37.8
Center, perifery	12.7	87.3	30.6	19.3	50.1	57.5
South	19.6	80.4	42.1	15.1	42.9	64.6
Southeast	11.3	88.7	33.4	13.3	53.3	53.4

Source: Bracho 1998.

Content and Efficiency of Primary and Secondary Education

Primary and secondary education plans and programs of study as well as the school year calendar are formulated by the Ministry of Public Education (SEP), which now stipulates 200 days of school with school days of four hours. In all the cycles art education and physical education are offered (two hours).

In the first two grades of basic education, emphasis is placed on teaching Spanish and mathematics, with nine and six hours spent per week, respectively, on these two subjects. In addition, three class hours per week are spent on the area of knowledge integrated with the environment. In the third year of primary school the time spent on Spanish and mathematics is reduced to six and five hours per week, respectively, and studies are begun in natural science (three hours), history and geography (one and a half hours each) and civic education (one hour). Throughout the total cycle, art and physical education (two hours) are offered.

The plan of secondary school study stipulates five hours per week for increasing competence in Spanish, five hours for mathematical skills, and courses are introduced in physics, chemistry, biology, history, geography, civics, and foreign languages (English or French). The plan of study also incorporates artistic, physical, and technological activities.

A distinct characteristic of primary education in Mexico is the distribution of free textbooks edited by SEP. They are compulsory and the only option for teachers to use. The most recent reforms in the basic educational system included a revision of the texts that had been used since the 1970s. The new texts are based on a national contest that called for proposals for each of the subjects. The subject content was also revised during the early 1990s. Under the new federal system, each district is in charge of producing history and geography books with specific regional content, but general books are produced nationally. Under this system, guidebooks with additional teaching aids are included to help teachers with their plans, programs, and textbooks. More recently the government has been developing similar aids for secondary education, but these efforts have not yet become widespread and are focused specifically on the most unprotected sectors.

Efficiency of the Educational System

This section evaluates the efficiency of the educational system based on the principle indicators used by SEP for basic education: the percentages of desertion, failure rates, terminal efficiency in primary school, and the transition from primary to secondary school. Information for the five years implicitly covered in the 1990–91 and 1994–95 school years is utilized. See Table 15.2 in chapter 15.

Despite the general improvements between 1991–92 and 1995–96, the comparative results are similar in each of these academic years to that of the whole period. The South shows a level of efficiency far below the rest of the nation in all the indicators.

Secondary school shows tendencies similar to those described above. That is, passing from primary school, the indices of "efficiency" and "absorption of graduates from the previous cycle," are high in the South, considering their high inefficiency in primary school. This supports the theory of a tendency toward greater differentiation and selectivity in southern educational systems (see Table 10.2).

In relation to the principal indicators of yield—such as desertion, repetition, transition, and failure—we do not have precise information at the state level for these phenomena for each grade. Therefore we present national indicators. It must be kept in mind that in the Mexican case, we do not even have tests of yield or learning that could give a more precise picture of educational quality,[7] nor do we have individualized systems of school enrollment registries that would allow the precise identification of these phenomena. For this reason we use the information available through SEP.

Estimates by the National Population Council (CONAPO) indicate that there are 21.67 million people between the ages of five and fourteen in Mexico, of whom 15.22 million are in the age group that should be in primary school (six to twelve years). With primary school enrollment of 14.66 million persons and of 2.78 million in the first grade of primary school (1995–96), the estimates of SEP about attendance of those six-year-olds has not substantially changed during the 1990s: approximately 10 percent of the children this age do not go to primary school, and the share of those above-age children (those older than six) for the period has been stable, at about one-fifth (see Table 10.3). At the national level, for the 1995–96 school year, terminal efficiency, estimated based on the enrollment in the first grade of primary school, was two-thirds,[8] which indicates an increase of a little more than 10 percentage points in comparison with 1990–91. The global desertion from the cycle shows a decrease for the period of a little more than 2 percentage points, falling from 5.3 percent for 1990–91 to 3 percent in 1995–96.

Student failure in primary school has decreased, especially in the first grade, falling from 9.8 percent in 1991–92 to 7.8 percent in 1995–96. Desertion also has fallen in these school cycles, from 4.6 percent to 3 percent, although with better results in the intermediate grades than in the first grade.

Investment in Education: Public and Private Expenditure

Analysis of educational spending in Mexico usually is difficult not only because access to original disaggregated information is limited, but also because there are modifications from year to year in the form in which categories of public spending are grouped, which at times makes it difficult to interpret the information. In this section we use SEP information at the national level and try to clarify in each case if the source of variation in public spending can be attributed to different forms of gathering information.[9]

As indicated at the beginning of this chapter, the crisis of the 1980s had very strong impacts on public spending on education.[10] With a historic maximum in

1982, the decade after that was characterized by systematic cuts in education spending, to below 10 percent of public expenditure. For 1990 the Ministry of Education accounted for 11.1 percent of public spending and in 1995 education represented 21.3 percent of federal spending, a decrease from 26.8 percent in 1994 due to the economic crisis that began in 1995.

National educational expenditures are mainly public as opposed to private expenditures. As shown in Table 10.4, public spending represents more than 90 percent of total educational expenditure and is mainly the expenditure of SEP. Although this table shows a relative decrease in the share of private spending in total educational expenditure, other studies have indicated important increases in the share of educational expenditure in the family budget, increasing from 8.5 percent of household expenses in 1984 to 10.3 percent in 1989, and reaching 12.2 percent in 1992 (Bracho 1995a). This fact is important in that it coincides with the period of relative decrease in the share of education in public expenditure, and a period where the inequality in income distribution and in the amount of relative poverty of some sectors increased (Székely 1994; 1995).

Finally, the distribution of SEP's expenditure by level and category of education reflects a greater share of spending on basic education, close to 50 percent, with a large proportion allocated to primary education (see Table 10.5). The unit cost of primary education (1,731.30 pesos in 1994) is the lowest of all the levels of formal education.

Final Comments

This chapter describes the system of basic education in Mexico and the general conditions of its evolution during the 1990s. Remembering that educational matters in Mexico were strongly affected by the crisis of the 1980s, with respect to financing, and by the perceptions of public policy that their development was satisfactory, the decade of the 1990s has brought important changes in the system, starting with the process of decentralization of administration and control. There has been a trend toward increased shares of public resources allocated to education. With respect to primary education, there have been modifications of the curriculum and the introduction of new educational materials as well as new programs that attempt to address the problem of desertion and backwardness in regions that are vulnerable because of their poverty.

The chapters on Mexican education in the following sections of this book specify the main issues that the education system is addressing in order to create a new vision of national development. It is sufficient to conclude here with some final thoughts on the evolution of the national educational system.

The expansion of education has been a central issue on the agendas of Mexican governments during the twentieth century, especially since the 1970s. At the same time, the ability of the state to invest in education has been severely affected by economic cycles, especially with the dramatic decline in public expenditures

Table 10.3
Primary Education. Principal Indicators of Output: Proportion of Population Attending, Repetition Rates, and Transition Rates

School year	Population 6 years old	% attendance 6 years old	Number enrolled 6 years old	Rate (%) desertion	First Grade new entrants	Coefficient of repetition First Grade	% transitioning from 1st to 2nd
1990–91	2,183,432	90.7	1,939,310	21.7	2,528,987	17.6	83.8
1991–92	2,185,438	90.4	1,974,855	20.6	2,487,308	17.1	85.0
1992–93	2,188,987	91.4	2,001,236	19.4	2,482,621	16.5	86.4
1993–94	2,193,513	88.6	1,943,127	20.4	2,441,849	12.6	90.9
1994–95	2,197,692	89.6	1,969,931	21.5	2,508,994	10.9	93.2
1995–96	2,197,239	90.5	1,987,749	19.7	2,475,452	10.9	92.3
1996–97	2,199,971	93.2	2,049,356	17.7	2,488,738	10.0	93.1
1997–98	2,202,544	94.8	2,088,900	15.7	2,479,145	9.0	93.9
1998–99	2,201,428	96.5	2,124,970	13.8	2,465,946	8.1	94.7
1999–00	2,197,233	98.2	2,157,978	11.9	2,449,845	7.2	95.5
2000–01	2,192,182	99.9	2,189,990	10.0	2,433,322	6.3	96.4
2001–02	2,186,499	99.9	2,184,531	9.0	2,400,584	6.3	96.4
2002–03	2,180,290	99.9	2,178,546	8.0	2,367,985	6.2	96.5
2003–04	2,167,604	99.9	2,166,087	7.0	2,329,126	6.2	96.5
2004–05	2,150,782	99.9	2,149,492	6.0	2,286,694	6.1	96.6
2005–06	2,130,485	100.0	2,129,420	5.0	2,241,495	6.1	96.7
2006–07	2,106,120	100.0	2,105,278	4.0	2,192,998	6.0	96.7
2007–08	2,079,860	100.0	2,079,236	3.0	2,143,542	6.0	96.8
2008–09	2,051,986	100.0	2,051,576	2.0	2,093,445	5.9	96.9
2009–10	2,022,525	100.0	2,022,323	1.0	2,042,751	5.9	96.9
2010–11	1,993,219	100.0	1,993,219	0.0	1,993,219	5.8	97.0
Increase with respect to 1995–96	−5,057	10.4	202,241	−49.2	−42,130	−42.2	4.4

School year	% transitioning from 2nd to 3rd	% transitioning from 3rd to 4th	% transitioning from 4th to 5th	% transitioning from 5th to 6th	Coefficient of desertion	Number deserting primary school	Total enrolled
1990–91	93.6	92.9	91.6	89.6	96.8	1,827,821	14,401,588
1991–92	95.0	93.2	92.7	90.9	97.2	1,861,838	14,396,993
1992–93	95.1	93.4	93.2	91.7	97.2	1,880,769	14,425,669
1993–94	96.0	94.2	94.0	92.7	97.4	1,917,374	14,469,450
1994–95	94.9	94.5	94.3	93.4	97.8	1,989,247	14,574,202
1995–96	96.7	94.1	95.0	94.3	97.8	2,034,400	14,623,438
1996–97	96.6	94.5	95.2	94.7	98.0	2,072,271	14,657,106
1997–98	96.6	95.0	95.5	95.1	98.2	2,146,627	
1998–99	96.5	95.4	95.8	95.5	98.3	2,134,939	
1999–00	96.4	95.9	96.1	95.9	98.5	2,159,414	
2000–01	96.4	96.4	96.4	96.4	98.6	2,174,998	
2001–02	96.4	96.4	96.4	96.4	98.7	2,201,862	
2002–03	96.5	96.5	96.5	96.5	98.8	2,203,858	
2003–04	96.5	96.5	96.5	96.5	98.9	2,193,806	
2004–05	96.6	96.6	96.6	96.6	99.0	2,184,301	
2005–06	96.7	96.7	96.7	96.7	99.1	2,157,557	
2006–07	96.7	96.7	96.7	96.7	99.1	2,136,506	
2007–08	96.8	96.8	96.8	96.8	99.2	2,115,382	
2008–09	96.9	96.9	96.9	96.9	99.3	2,088,453	
2009–10	96.9	96.9	96.9	96.9	99.4	2,058,071	
2010–11	97.0	97.0	97.0	97.0	99.5	2,024,928	
Increase with respect to 1995–96	–0.4	2.4	1.4	2.2	0.8	0	
						140,598	

Source: SEP Informe de labores 1995–1996.

Table 10.4

Educational Expenditures for Administrative Support (budget given in 1,000s of 1988 pesos)*

	Educational expenditure total**	Public expenditure (%)						Private expenditure***
		Total public	Total federal	SEP	Other sources	State	Municipal	
1988	14,009,674	91.06	88.14	91.49	8.51	11.45	0.40	8.94
1989	15,543,144	91.61	76.98	68.06	8.92	14.24	0.39	8.39
1990	18,301,053	91.92	81.74	82.25	17.75	17.89	0.36	8.08
1991	20,322,139	94.76	83.75	83.88	16.12	15.95	0.30	5.24
1992	23,264,696	93.60	85.57	84.80	15.20	14.11	0.32	6.40
1993	26,436,157	94.19	87.42	84.76	15.24	12.30	0.28	5.81
1994	28,493,229	94.77	88.74	87.01	12.99	11.01	0.25	5.23
1995	24,677,726	95.28	89.89	89.19	10.81	9.88	0.23	4.72

Source: SEP. 1997. *Compendio estadistico del gasto educative, 1996.*
*Implicit GDP deflator, base 1993.
**Total in current pesos: 1988: $14,009,674; 1990: $29,727,740; 1995: $90,113,183.
***Estimated.

Table 10.5

Distribution of SEP Expenditures on Education, Cultural, Recreation, and Administrative Services (as a proportion of the budget of that year. Annual total in 1,000s of current pesos.)

Level of service	1988	1989	1990	1991	1992	1993	1994	1995
Educational Services								
Preschool	4.7	4.4	5.0	4.9	5.3	5.8	0.7	0.7
Primary[1]	26.4	25.7	25.9	25.0	28.5	31.3	4.9	4.8
Secondary	14.7	14.6	15.4	14.5	15.1	14.9	1.8	2.1
Technical High School[2]	13.8	13.6	11.6	10.2	9.4	9.5	9.4	10.4
Normal	1.7	1.3	1.4	1.2	1.1	1.0	0.4	0.4
High School[3]	17.2	13.7	13.9	13.4	12.6	12.1	12.5	13.0
Post-Graduate	3.4	1.4	1.2	1.2	1.0	1.1	2.0	0.9
Adult Education[4]	2.0	2.5	2.0	1.7	1.9	2.2	1.5	1.5
Education Research	0.1	2.8	3.2	3.1	4.1	4.3	4.0	4.7
Construction	4.3	3.0	3.4	2.7	2.5	2.8	2.3	2.6
Aid to Basic Education	0.8	1.7	2.1	1.9	1.7	2.2	52.4	51.0
Cultural, Recreational, and Administrative Services								
Culture, Sports, and Recreation	3.4	2.4	2.3	2.4	2.6	2.7	2.1	1.7
Planning, Administration Coordination, Evaluation	7.6	12.9	12.7	17.6	14.1	9.9	6.2	6.1
Total*	10,287,100	13,389,494	18,369,800	27,056,204	36,158,000	46,241,874	56,586,960	68,836,899

Source: SEP. 1997. *Compendio estadístico del gasto educativo, 1996.*
[1]Includes Primary Education, Special Education, Indigeneous and Rural Education.
[2]Includes Techinal High School Degree, General and Professional High School Degree.
[3]Includes Advanced Technical and University.
[4]Includes training for work.
*Based on budget of that year. Total in 1,000s of current pesos.

during the 1980s. Almost independent of the political priorities that have changed with each decade, the educational system has maintained a fairly high growth rate, except at the high school level. Throughout, education has continued to be highly relevant in the perceptions of the society at large. This is demonstrated in the growth in average years of schooling, in the growing private expenditures on education, and in the decrease in dropout rates from basic education.

Despite the expansion in the supply of education, there are still a significant number of children who never enter school or dropout before finishing primary school. This is especially true in rural areas and poor urban zones. In 1996–97 the terminal efficiency rate for primary school was up to slightly over three-fifths of the children that began six years before. The secondary school absorption index showed a recent increase up to 87 percent, but still remains a long way from universal, which is implicit in extending compulsory education to include secondary school. At the other extreme in educational distribution, the growing social demand for mid-level and higher education, coupled with its high rates of return for economic output in Mexico (Bracho and Zamudio 1994; Psacharopoulos et al. 1996) will make it politically expedient to expand the supply at that level.

The problem of education is important in social research to the degree that new economic policies and the changes in the level of policy, together with the growing concentration of national income and the search for ways to increase employment, require focusing on conditions for an effective distribution of education as one of the ways of solving the problems of poverty, unemployment, and growth.

Notes

1. The data are taken from Secretaría de Educación Pública 1997.
2. The methodology and most general results of the analysis of education in the census of 1990 are found in Bracho (1998). The analysis is based on a survey of 1 percent of individuals and tries to generate an educational regionalization based on the educational distribution of the states in Mexico. In sum, the entities covered by each geographic region that is the product of that analysis are:

North Pacific: Baja California, Baja California Sur, and Sonora
North: Coahuila, Chihuahua, Nuevo León, and Tamaulipas
Capital: Federal District
West Center: Aguascalientes, Colima, Durango, Nayarit, and Sinaloa
Center: State of Mexico, Morelos, Querétaro, and Tlaxcala
Center-Periphery: Guanajuato, Hidalgo, Michoacán, Puebla, San Luis Potosí, Veracruz, and Zacatecas
South: Chiapas, Guerrero, and Oaxaca
Southeast: Campeche, Quintana Roo, Tabasco, and Yucatán

3. Guanajuato and Puebla, in the Center-Periphery; Chiapas and Guerrero in the South; and Yucatán in the Southeast.

4. The rates of participation are estimated as follows: of the population in the age group relevant to the level, it is determined if the level was completed or if it is currently attended (this defines the column "studying," and corresponds to the traditional estimation of rates of participation). The column labeled "not studying" refers to the population in the age group who completed the previous level, but are not studying now. In addition, the population in the relevant group that did not complete the preceding level is identified as an estimation that is not often made, but that in our opinion defines a very important dimension of educational backwardness.

5. A more precise calculation of these rates of exclusion from primary education should include the relative correction of the difference between the date of the census survey and the beginning of the school year, given that the rule of SEP indicates that only children who are at least six years old can enroll. The rates in the seven to twelve year group decrease, but continue the trends shown here. It was decided, however, to maintain the calculation based on the conventional national and international age groups.

6. Post-basic education shows even lower levels of distribution in the country and maintains the tendencies of regional differences shown for basic education. Only in the capital are more than half of young people attending higher middle school and around one-quarter receiving higher education, in relation to the respective age groups of between sixteen and nineteen years and between twenty and twenty-four. For a more extensive discussion of this result, see Bracho (1998).

7. Currently SEP is developing tests of educational achievement and competencies. It is known that there are achievement tests used by SEP (see the results reported in Palafox et al. 1994), as well as others that are applied to evaluating the achievement of teachers—Carrera Magisterial—however, they are not available to researchers and are only accessible to those involved in educational planning.

8. Currently, SEP estimates terminal efficiency, taking as a base only the enrollment of new entry to first grade (that is, without taking into account for the calculation those individuals that repeat the grade), with which the estimation of terminal efficiency reaches 80 percent for this cycle. Table 10.3 presents both.

9. In addition, information disaggregated to the state level can be problematic, as is shown in a recent study on educational financing within a federalist framework (Latapí and Ulloa 1997).

10. The study by Lustig (1991) is an excellent source for analyzing the economic restructuring during the decade of the 1980s and its impact on financing social needs. For a reference specifically on the impact on the educational system, see Padua (1994).

References

Bracho, Teresa. 1995a. "Gasto privado en educación. México 1984–1992." *Revista Mexicana de Sociologia* 57, no. 2 (April–June).
———. 1995b. "Distribución y desigualdad educativa. en México." *Estudios Sociológicos* 13, no. 37.
———. 1997. "La exlusión de la educación básica. Decisiones familiares sobre escolarización." Working Paper, CIDE. Centro de Investigacion y Docencia Economica.
———. 1998. "México desde la perspectiva regional. Perfil educativo de sus adultos y tendencias de escolarización de sus niños." Working Paper, no. 68 CIDE.
Bracho, Teresa, and Andrés Zamudio. 1994. "Los redimientos económicos de la escolaridad en México, 1989." *Economía Mexicana* 3, no. 2.
———. 1997. "El gasto familiar en educación. México 1992." *Revista Mexicana de Investigación Educativa* 2, no. 4, segundo semestre.

Latapí, Pablo, and Manuel Ulloa. 1997. "El financiamiento de la educación básica en el marco del federalismo." Working Paper, CESU-UNAM.

Lustig, Nora. 1991. *Mexico, the Remaking of an Economy*. Washington, DC: Brookings Institution.

México. Secretaría de Educación Pública. 1997a. "Perfil de la educación en México. 1997." México: SEP.

———. 1997b. *Compendio estadístico del gasto educativo, 1996*. México: SEP.

———. Various years. *Informe de labores*. México: SEP.

Padua, Jorge. 1994. "Tranformaciones estructurales, políticas educativas y eficiencia en el sistema escolar en México." *Estudios Sociologicos*. vol. 12, no. 36.

Palafox, Juan Carlos, J. Prawda, and E. Vélez. 1994. "Primary School Quality in México." *Comparative Educational Review* 38, no. 2.

Psacharopoulos, George, Eduardo Velez, Alex Panagides and Hung Yu Yang. 1996. "Returns to Education during the Economic Boom and Recession: Mexico 1984, 1989, and 1992." *Education Economics* 4, no. 3.

Secretaria de Educación Publica. 1997. "Perfil de la educación en México": SEP.

Székely, Miguel. 1994. "Estabilización y ajuste con desigualdad y pobreza: el caso de México." *El Trimestre Económico* 61, no. 1.

———. 1995. "Aspectos de la desigualdad en México." *El Trimestre Económico* 62, no. 2.

Part III

Repetition and Dropout: Measurement and Programs

11

RUBEN KLEIN

Repetition and Dropout in Brazil: Measurement Issues

Introduction

To plan educational policies, it is important to know how the educational system is behaving. Good and correct statistics are essential to monitor and diagnose the problems of the educational system, allowing the planners to decide which kind of actions should be implemented to improve the system and also to find out if they are being effective.

Educational planners should take into account the following information:

1. the enrollment by grade and age,
2. the percentage of an age cohort (all children born in a given year) that has access to school and at which age,
3. the transition rates between grades, that is, the promotion, repetition, and dropout rates,
4. the percentage of a school cohort (all students that enter in a school system for the first time in a given year) that concludes each grade and graduates,
5. what the students know and are able to do at each or some grades,
6. the available resources to finance the system and how they are being spent.

In this chapter, we will consider only statistics related to the flow of students along the educational system, which is related to the first four cases listed above. These statistics have been known to have problems.

In Brazil, Teixeira de Freitas (1947), using demographic arguments, showed that the number of repeaters collected by the Educational Censuses was under-reported. His work was not understood at the time and was forgotten. It is important to mention that Teixeira de Freitas was director of the statistical agency of the Ministry of Education. Schiefelbein (1975) has shown that the actual rates of repetition in fourteen countries in Latin America, including Brazil,

Research for this chapter was partially supported by a Ford Foundation grant.

were much higher than the official rates reported by the governments. Also, the repetition rates in Brazil were among the highest in the region. For this reason, he developed his own methodology based on enrollment by age and grade, the size of an age cohort and on some assumptions. He argued, correctly, that the official number of new entrants in the first grade of the educational system was much higher than the size of the modal age cohort for that grade for several years, and this is a demographic impossibility.

Fletcher and Ribeiro (1988) have shown the same in Brazil, using household survey data and their own methodology. Klein and Ribeiro (1991), using Educational Census data, show that the repetition rates are wrong on all grades and that the error is due to a conceptual error in the educational system definition of a repeater. For the educational system, a repeater is a student who is enrolled in the same grade as the year before due to having flunked the grade. In fact, the correct definition is this: a repeater is a student who is enrolled in the same grade as the year before, no matter the reason.

There are three possible kinds of repeaters:

1.   those who repeat because they flunked the grade the year before,
2.   those who repeat because they abandoned school during the year and were considered by the school neither as having passed nor as having flunked,
3.   those who repeat despite having been considered by the school as passing the grade ("approved").

Klein (1995) developed a methodology to estimate the transition rate statistics based on enrollment and number of approved students and on an assessment of dropout rates for the first and second grades. The size of the modal age cohort for the first grade is used to calibrate this assessment.

All these studies show that the repetition rates are much higher than reported and that the dropout rate in the first grade is much lower. Non-corrected dropout rates can even be negative, as in the fourth and eighth grades in Brazil. A better way to see the inconsistencies of the non-corrected data is to look at the number of approved dropouts at each grade—almost all numbers are negative.

Correction of the transition rates is very important because they change the interpretation of the results. High dropout rates may indicate lack of school and/or lack of interest of the family in having its children attend school. High repetition rates show that there are enough schools and that the families care about their children attending schools. This focuses the problem on the school, on the teaching activities, and on school attitudes. It also calls attention to the quality of the system. Are the students learning? Are the high repetition rates due to the fact that the system is too rigorous and requires too much? In fact, there can be high or low repetition with good or bad teaching and learning. This is a very important aspect of the educational system: what the students are learning and how well. The goal of the educational system should be to attain very low repetition and dropout rates and very high levels of learning.

The myth of high dropout rates is also related to an erroneous argument used both in Brazil and in the rest of the world—the argument of the "school pyramid," which relates the enrollment in all grades. By the argument, all students that reach the *kth* grade in the *kth* year were enrolled in the first grade of the year of reference and all these students are new. This model assumes that no repetition in any grade exists, only dropping out. In this way, in a system like the one in Brazil, high dropout rates are obtained. And, of course, the model assumption is strongly violated and therefore cannot be used. This model has to be purged.

The transition rates are related to the flow model as described in Thonstad (1980). For some analyses this model has to be extended as shown in Klein (1995). Flow simulations of a school cohort based on transition rates of a given year, supposed constant along the years and not depending on the age of the student and if he/she is a new student or a repeater, allow us to estimate how long, on average, a student stays in school, what is the expected number of students that will graduate and so forth. It is not reality, but it gives an idea about the behavior of the system. If the system is changing, it gives us an idea about what will be happening in the future.

Household data, based on the age of the individual, on which grade the individual is in or which was the last grade concluded successfully, on the contrary, tell us what has already happened: what proportion of an age cohort has already concluded a certain grade or has graduated, how many are entering or leaving at each grade and until what age this is happening.

Results

In this section we present and interpret results for Brazil, obtained by the methodology described in Klein (1995), using data from the educational censuses. We start with repetition rates for 1983 and 1995. Table 11.1 shows corrected and non-corrected repetition rates. It can be seen that corrected repetition rates are very high, in fact much higher than non-corrected rates in all grades, showing that repetition is a very important problem in the Brazilian educational system. From 1983 to 1995, repetition has decreased in the first grade from around 60 percent to around 45 percent and about 3 percentage points from the fifth grade on.

Repetition is higher at the beginning of each cycle of schooling, that is, first grade, fifth grade, and ninth grade. Repetition decreases during the cycle, that is from first to fourth grades, from fifth to eighth grades, and from nineth to eleventh grades.

Table 11.1 also shows corrected and non-corrected promotion rates for 1983 and 1995. It can be seen that corrected rates are lower (in some grades, much lower) than non-corrected rates. In all grades, promotion rates have increased from 1983 to 1995. For the eleventh grade (the final grade), the promotion rate is equal to the approval (passing) rate, since we are not considering any further grade. It is important to see that promotion rates in the beginning of each cycle (first, fifth, and nineth grades) are lower than 0.60, meaning that less than 60

Table 11.1

Repetition and Promotion Rates

| Grade | Repetition rates | | | | Promotion rates | | | |
| | With correction | | Without correction | | With correction | | Without correction | |
	1983	1995	1983	1995	1983	1995	1983	1995
1	0.58	0.44	0.28	0.23	0.40	0.55	0.45	0.64
2	0.31	0.31	0.22	0.20	0.63	0.66	0.69	0.74
3	0.25	0.24	0.17	0.14	0.66	0.72	0.72	0.80
4	0.21	0.20	0.14	0.11	0.66	0.75	0.80	0.91
5	0.38	0.35	0.24	0.21	0.51	0.60	0.60	0.68
6	0.33	0.28	0.20	0.17	0.57	0.67	0.67	0.75
7	0.30	0.23	0.17	0.13	0.60	0.72	0.69	0.79
8	0.23	0.18	0.12	0.10	0.61	0.70	0.92	1.01
9	0.39	0.35	0.15	0.15	0.51	0.55	0.66	0.66
10	0.28	0.24	0.10	0.10	0.66	0.69	0.72	0.75
11	0.13	0.14	0.05	0.05	0.84	0.85	0.84	0.85

Source: Author's calculations.

percent of the students in these grades pass to the following grade in the next year. We also call attention to the impossible value of 1.01 for the non-corrected promotion rate at the eighth grade in 1995.

Table 11.2 shows the total dropout rate of students (passed and non-passed). It can be seen that in the first eight grades, the corrected dropout rate has decreased considerably from 1983 to 1995. It is important to compare the corrected and non-corrected dropout rates.

The non-corrected rates are very high in the first grade (0.27 in 1983 and 0.13 in 1995), in the fifth grade (0.16 in 1983 and 0.11 in 1995), in the nineth grade (0.19 in 1983 and 0.18 in 1995), and in the tenth grade (0.18 in 1983 and 0.14 in 1995). Curiously, in the fourth and eighth grades, final grades of the first and second cycles, when these rates should be higher (due to problems of access), the dropout rates are negative in the eighth grade for both years and negative in the fourth grade for 1995. Of course these values are absurd. Although positive for the fourth grade in 1983, they are lower than the dropout rates for the previous grades.

The corrected rates show that dropout is not the "big" problem indicated by the non-corrected rates. In fact, it is very small in the first grade, only 0.02 in 1983 and 0.01 in 1995. The dropout rate between the fourth and fifth grades was high and now it is approximately at the same levels of other grades, indicating that access to the fifth grade (the former *ginásio*) has been attained. Dropout rates between eighth and nineth grades (that is between the primary and middle schools) are still high, indicating that problems remain with access. The corrected transition rates change the focus from dropout to repetition with all the consequences in interpretation and diagnostics of the educational system.

If dropout rates of approved students were computed, it would be immediately obvious that the non-corrected rates are wrong. Table 11.2 also shows the corrected and non-corrected dropout rates for the passed students. It can be seen that all non-corrected rates are negative (obviously impossible), with the exception of the first grade in 1983. This is due to the high number of "passed" repeaters in that grade in that year. Students may repeat any grade inspite of having passed due to school or parents deciding students don't have "maturity" or due to students moving from undeveloped towns to more developed towns and schools deciding that the child is not prepared for next grade and has to repeat or some other cause. But in Brazil, the big reason to repeat the first grade inspite of having passed is the subseriation (or subdivision) of this grade. In this way there are first grade A and first grade B, for instance. Students pass first grade A but stay in first grade B, so they are still in the first grade.

The flow simulations mentioned in the introduction show a worrisome but improving picture.

It is expected that with the 1983 transition rates:

1. Seventy-two percent of a school cohort finishes fourth grade, taking on average 6.5 years;

Table 11.2

Dropout Rates of Passed Students

Grade	Dropout rates				Dropout of passed students			
	With correction		Without correction		With correction		Without correction	
	1983	1995	1983	1995	1983	1995	1983	1995
1	0.02	0.01	0.27	0.13	0.01	0.005	0.10	-0.01
2	0.06	0.03	0.10	0.06	0.05	0.02	-0.01	-0.07
3	0.09	0.04	0.11	0.06	0.05	0.02	-0.01	-0.05
4	0.13	0.05	0.07	-0.02	0.09	0.03	-0.05	-0.12
5	0.11	0.05	0.16	0.11	0.05	0.03	-0.04	-0.05
6	0.11	0.05	0.13	0.08	0.06	0.03	-0.04	-0.05
7	0.10	0.04	0.14	0.07	0.05	0.02	-0.04	-0.05
8	0.15	0.11	-0.04	-0.11	0.11	0.10	-0.20	-0.21
9	0.11	0.11	0.19	0.18	0.04	0.05	-0.11	-0.07
10	0.07	0.06	0.18	0.14	0.03	0.02	-0.03	-0.04
11	0.03	0.02	0.11	0.10	0	0	0	0

Source: Author's calculations.

2. Thirty-six percent of a school cohort finishes eighth grade, taking on average 12.1 years;
3. Twenty-two percent of a school cohort finishes eleventh grade, taking on average 16.2 years.

And with the 1995 rates:

1. Eighty-eight percent of a school cohort finishes fourth grade, taking on average, 5.8 years;
2. Sixty-six percent of a school cohort finishes eighth grade, taking on average 11.2 years;
3. Forty-four percent of a school cohort finishes eleventh grade, taking on average 15.2 years.

It can be observed that the results are much better with the 1995 transition rates—more students finish and in a shorter time. Considering a different data base, a household survey, the PNAD (Pesquisa Nacional de Amostra por Domicílio) done in Brazil by IBGE, the Brazilian Statistical Office, we can obtain estimates for the percentage of an age cohort that has concluded a given grade.

Results from the 1995 PNAD tell us that up to 1994, 78 percent, 43 percent, and 27 percent of an age cohort were already finishing, respectively, fourth, eighth, and eleventh grades. These percentages are between the expected numbers, obtained from the simulations with 1983 and 1995 transition rates, for concluding these grades.

Conclusion

Repetition in Brazil is still too high. Higher repetition at the beginning of each cycle indicates that selectivity is higher at those times. This is also true in higher education. It also indicates that students entering each new cycle are ill prepared for it and that teachers are not prepared to deal with this situation. National assessment data confirm this. Students, in general, do not know what they should do at the end of each cycle, and the situation gets worse as the grades get higher.

Dropout rates in the earlier grades are low. Students drop out at later ages after repeating many years. We have seen that dropout rates are already falling. It is to be expected that if repetition rates fall, dropout rates will fall even more. Intervention therefore should be made at the beginning of each cycle, both to prevent repetition and to improve the quality of education. The first grades are especially important. Efforts should be made to improve the training of teachers, especially in math. Preparatory courses for teachers for the first four grades have very little math. New ways of teaching, with more student participation, should be developed.

What kinds of intervention should occur?

In our opinion, the school has to recognize its responsibility to teach and promote its students and learn how to deal with its clientele, no matter their socioeconomic level and cultural class. The school has to find new ways to teach and involve the students.

Traditional teaching in Brazil accepts that students do not learn in school and need tutoring at home by the parents or by hired tutors. This may work for middle class and upper class families, but it certainly does not work for lower class families.

In 1999, the teacher alone decides if a student will pass or not and usually no one can change his or her decision. There should be some rules about when a student should not pass. Which subjects can retain a student in his grade? At the present time, it can be any subject, including physical education, music, arts. What is essential in each subject for the student to know? For instance, in São Paulo State, since the beginning of the decade, there has been a decree by which a student can contest a teacher's "fail" decision. This challenge is judged by a committee which asks the teacher for an explanation. We believe the decrease in the repetition rates in São Paulo State, in all grades, is in part due to this decree. In 1999, in some places, there is the possibility of an appeal against the decision of flunking. In other places, a student who flunks in one subject can pass to the next grade, but has to attend that subject again. And some places are creating automatic promotion inside some cycles of two to four years.

In some places, there are some decisions for automatic promotion. The teachers are usually against this and find ways of avoiding it, such as recommending the student leave school during the year or recommending to the parents that the student stay in the same grade despite the automatic promotion. Even so, many more students pass and teachers tend to complain that the students are more poorly prepared. This creates another problem. Teachers are supposed to teach the grade's content and are not used to reviewing materials students need and have not mastered. Automatic promotion without continuous evaluation and monitoring of what the students are learning may be a very dangerous course.

On the other hand, repeaters tend to be stigmatized. Instead of receiving more attention and more specialized teaching, the opposite tends to happen. Repeaters get bored and feel out of place in a regular class or they are put together in a class of repeaters that is considered a "problem" class by the school and is thus neglected. Brazilian data indicate that repetition does not help.

Teachers need to be better prepared, have good books, and other classroom materials. And, of course, teachers need higher salaries. Family participation has to be encouraged in school activities. School administration is another very important factor. There is no good school without a good principal. Policymakers need information on enrollment by age, transition rates, conclusion rates, and comparable achievement data along the years so that interventions in the system can be planned and evaluated for their efficacy. (This is usually not done.) Except for the assessment data, most countries have data on the flow of students, although almost certainly, they need corrections.

In Brazil, there have been some measures that created other cycles, like the Ciclo Básico de Alfabetização (Basic Literacy Cycle, or CBA) in São Paulo State in 1984, and Minas Gerais State in 1985. The CBA replaces the first and second grades in a unique cycle without separation into grades. The student is considered automatically passed at the end of the first year and considered as continuing at the end of the second or later years. The CBA is supposed to be in modules, and the student can proceed at his/her own pace. The problem is that a lot of students take more than two years, showing that "repetition" still goes on. Considering the students in the initial year at the CBA as being in the first year and the others in the second, the result is a decrease in repetition in first grade and an increase in repetition in second grade. The repetition in first grade, although much lower, does not disappear because there is still repetition due to mid-term abandoning and despite being automatically passed.

In this decade, in some cities, the Ensino Fundamental, or primary school, was transformed into three cycles: grades 1 to 3, grades 4 to 6 and grades 7 to 8. The official retention is only at the end of each cycle. The same behavior of repetition can be observed. Repetition falls in the first years of the cycle and increases in the last year. It never ends because of the repetition by mid-term dropout and despite being automatically approved.

There is a tendency to consider these cycles as ungraded and to lose track of the repetition process. We believe that there should be a control of the number of years a student spends in each cycle. The kind of analysis we are doing provides information on what is happening.

The longer the cycle, the harder it is to maintain control of the process. This may be happening (or has happened) in Rio de Janeiro State, where automatic promotion was instituted from first to fifth grades in state schools.

Another process that was used to decrease repetition in first grade in some states was the Classe de Alfabetização (literacy class, or CA), which in fact replaced a subdivision of the first grade. The problem is that this CA still has the same defects as the regular first grade, retention of students, although there is officially no flunking. The result of this was a decrease in the number of "approved repeaters."

Since it looks like the system needs two years for the first grade, we think creating an extra grade, prior to the first grade, is a good idea. And it would be even better if children would start earlier, at age six.

The Brazilian government has made the proposal to increase the Ensino Fundamental by one year, starting at age six, at the end of 1997, as part of a national educational program. But without dealing with the essential matter of how to teach and what, it may not help very much.

References

Fletcher, P.R., and S.C. Ribeiro. 1988. *Projeto fluxo dos alunos de primeiro grau.* PRO-FLUXO (mimeo).

Klein, R. 1995. "Produção e utilização de indicadores educacionais." (2a Versão Preliminar). (mimeo).

Klein, R. and S.C. Ribeiro. 1991. "O censo educacional e o modelo de fluxo: o problema da repetência." *Revista Brasileira de Estatística* 52, no. 197/198: 5–45.

Schiefelbein, E. 1975. "Repeating: An Overlooked Problem in Latin American Education." *Comparative Education Review* 19: 468–487.

Teixeira de Freitas, M.A., 1947. "A escolaridade média no ensino primário brasileiro." *Revista Brasileira de Estatística* 8: 395–474. Republished in 1989 by *Revista Brasileira de Estatística* 50: 71–160.

Thonstad, T. 1980. *Analysing and Projecting School Enrolment in Developing Countries: A Manual of Methodology.* Paris: UNESCO, Statistical Reports and Studies 24.

12

María Celia Agudo de Córsico

Argentina: Programs for the Prevention of Repetition and Dropout and Their Results

Introduction

The nature of repetition and dropout and the implications they have for education and society are considered in this book. This chapter discusses some of the main plans, programs, and projects developed in Argentina in response to the problems of repetition and dropout in the first grades of primary school. National plans conducted by the National Ministry of Culture and Education will be presented, but some reference to provincial endeavors will also be made.

All over the world, repetition and dropout in elementary school are strongly associated with poverty. This relationship is even stronger in developing countries where, for instance, middle class children have more chances to receive preschool education although, as a group, they are not at risk of suffering repetition or dropout. The conclusions of an enormous number of national and international reports on scholastic achievement show that family background—not schooling—accounts for most of the differences in students' achievement levels (Sautu and Eichelbaum de Babini 1996). Preventive and compensatory policies have proven to be much less influential than the socioeconomic-cultural status of the children's families.

Many factors have been identified as directly influential on repetition and dropout. Some of them are in a sense exogenous to the school, for example, the economic status and/or the living conditions of the families. Other factors are really endogenous with respect to the school. These include the quality of teachers' education, teachers' competence, didactic strategies, or curriculum contents. As schools cannot directly modify the structural aspects of society, at least immediately, it is expected that the endogenous variables can be manipulated in order to attenuate the effects of the negative exogenous factors. If the school has any power to counteract the impact of negative or adverse factors, that power lies in the quality of education it offers (Psacharopoulos and Woodhall 1985, 205–243).

Toward the end of this century there is a series of well-known strategies (principles, initiatives, and proposals) applied in trying to prevent repetition and dropout. Some of them are firmly established and others are controversial. But one of the main conclusions, after studying many school systems, is that there is not a single recipe or prescription that can be applied to all countries. Another principle that must be followed is that in order to achieve at least some success in the struggle against those problems, not a single prescription but a real strategy including some fundamental lines of action must be adopted. The problem is hard to solve because in addition, the factors associated with repetition have a different impact or vary in nature depending on whether we are considering the first grades or the last ones at elementary school level.

As the problem is not new, it is not surprising to identify several common facts with respect to this topic. We shall mention only a few of them and make a brief comment about each.

1. Repetition and dropout in the school system works against democracy. In fact, there is a tremendous contradiction between the search for social equity and the type of unfair selection that repetition and dropout imply.
2. It is necessary to expand the preschool level in order to lower the number of repeaters and dropouts in the two first grades of primary school.
3. The conditions of learning must improve if it is the intention to overcome both negative phenomena. In this last sense, compensatory education has been proclaimed as a key educational resource. At the same time, the efficiency of compensatory education has been severely questioned.
4. Teaching methodology must be improved, particularly with respect to reading and writing. The problem is greater in multi-lingual and multi-cultural countries, where for the initial learning of reading and writing it is advisable to take the children's mother tongues as the starting point.
5. It is necessary to use evaluation as an integrative part of the teaching and learning process and not merely as a selection device. This statement is valid for the whole school system but it is particularly important for the first grades of primary school, where children need a better guide for their learning processes.
6. It is also necessary to improve methodology, procedures, and instruments for measuring repetition and dropout more precisely.
7. It is necessary to make schools effective: schools are effective when the proportion of low-income children demonstrating academic mastery is virtually identical to the proportion of middle class children who do so.

An attempt to reproduce the non-controversial initiatives must include :

a) elaboration within each country of a map of repetition, improving the collection and treatment of statistical information;

b)   estimation of the necessary investments;
c)   definition of priorities by establishing a hierarchical order of measures to be taken;
d)   development of programs of feeding and nutrition at schools;
e)   providing schoolchildren with the materials necessary for school work;
f)   providing schoolchildren with the best books;
g)   extension of compulsory preschool education (Lockheed and Verspoor 1992);
h)   improvement of the pedagogical process;
i)   paying special attention to cultural and linguistic differences among the school population (Agudo de Córsico and Manacorda de Rosetti 1994);
j)   improvement of the teaching of reading and writing;
k   development of appropriate standards for evaluation and promotion;
l)   improvement of teachers' education and teachers' in-service training courses (UNESCO: OIE 1996).

Repetition and Dropout in Argentina

During the last fifteen years significant progress in Argentina in terms of schooling coverage has been observed. The repetition ratio at the primary school level has decreased. However, none of the above-mentioned initiatives have been implemented at a fully satisfactory level, and there are reasons to suspect that the expansion of elementary school attendance has brought about a lower quality of education. Considering the seven grades of the traditional primary school level (before the Federal Law of Education enacted in 1993), repetition and dropout, on the average, are not extremely severe problems in Argentina. According to the 1994 National Census of Teachers and Educational Institutions, published in 1996, repetition in the public schools (80 percent of all primary school enrollment) is about 6.8 percent. But behind the average there is great diversity. In fact, there is great inequality among different school areas and even among entire different school districts, and herein lies the real problem. Table 7.2 in chapter 7 shows the repetition rates for poor and non-poor seventh grade primary school pupils for five provinces and the Federal District.

Following a categorization used by the CFI (Federal Council of Investments), Buenos Aires (the province), the Federal District of Buenos Aires, and the provinces of Córdoba, Mendoza, and Santa Fé are Advanced Provinces; Entre Ríos, Salta, San Juan, San Luis, Neuquén, and Tucumán are Intermediate Provinces; Chubut, La Pampa, Santa Cruz, and Tierra del Fuego are Low Density Provinces; and finally, Catamarca, Corrientes, Chaco, Formosa, Jujuy, La Rioja, Misiones, and Santiago del Estero are labeled as Backward Provinces.

The repetition ratios that can be read in Table 7.2 substantially correspond to the above mentioned categorization elaborated by CFI. It must be noted that the

new Federal Law of Education (since 1993) has produced an expansion of compulsory education in Argentina. Compulsory education nowadays covers one
year of pre-primary education plus nine years of general basic education (EGB).
For this reason, in the near future a main concern for the public authority will be
repetition and dropout, not only of children in the old seven-year period, but of
all those children attending compulsory school for ten years.

Structural change is not easy to implement, particularly under the present
socioeconomic circumstances (officially admitted unemployment is 17 percent in
1997). It is not unrealistic to predict new difficulties at this new promotion
bottleneck from the seventh to the eighth grade. The Federal Law of Education
(enacted in April 1993), the Federal Educational Pact (an agreement among the
national government, provincial governments, and the City of Buenos Aires
government, formerly the City of Buenos Aires Municipality, in September of
1994), and the Quinquennial National Plan have established among other objectives for non-university education for 1995–99 increasing the coverage of education service, lowering the level of the regional educational inequality, improving
the general quality of education, and increasing the educational system's internal
efficiency.

But it is not enough to formulate objectives; both the complexity of the
context within which the plans must be implemented and the quantitative magnitude of the main aspects involved in that complexity must be considered (Argentina, Ministerio de Cultura y Educación 1995).

In evaluating the present situation of the educational system in Argentina,
it is important to stress from the beginning that within the federal framework
of the political-administrative structure, the national state has retained for itself
the definition of the educational policies and in the provinces has delegated the
responsibility for the implementation of those policies.

Related to the educational situation, it is illustrative to remember that in 1978 the
process of transferring all the primary schools from the National Ministry to
the provincial educational authorities was completed. Between 1991 and 1993
all the secondary schools belonging to the national government were transferred
to the provinces. The Argentinean socio-political structure consequently assumes
that educational discussions and negotiations take place in a decentralized system
in which provinces are strongly dependent on the National Government for financial support for their schools. Another important aspect to be mentioned is that the
transfer of schools from the national government to the provinces took place at the
same time in which it was intended to introduce the above mentioned changes in
educational quality, equity, and efficiency. To make things even more complicated, there is a great diversity among the provinces in terms of financial resources and administrative structure and functioning, as well as socioeconomic,
cultural and professional levels. Simultaneously, the provinces are involved in
internal administrative changes. This influences each province's opportunity to
achieve the so-called educational transformation. Note that only factors endoge-

nous to the educational system have been pointed out in these paragraphs, and not the exogenous ones that will not be considered in this chapter.

Since the end of the last century, primary school education has been free, universal, and compulsory in Argentina. In this respect, the country is ranked among the highest in attendance at primary school in Latin America. Universal access and high retention levels have been achieved in primary education in Argentina. The gap between total school years and grades passed is mainly due to failure in the first grades of primary education. Consequently, repetition must be reduced in order to improve the system's quality and efficiency. But repeaters come from the lowest socioeconomic strata of Argentinean society. Therefore, although this chapter is mainly concerned with educational plans for the prevention of repetition and dropout, it is well known that the problem cannot be solved by appealing exclusively to internal or endogenous factors within the education system.

None of the different above mentioned measures aimed at the prevention of repetition and dropout have been neglected or omitted by either the National Educational Authorities or the vast majority of the provincial authorities in Argentina. Their responsibilities are distributed as follows: because of the educational decentralization, and according to the Federal Law of Education, the National Ministry of Education in Argentina is now a ministry without schools, but has developed plans and projects for in-service teachers' training, National Evaluation Operatives (developed in 1993), and a Social Educational Plan. The last two activities will be analyzed in this chapter, because they are especially relevant for the topic (Argentina, Ministerio de Cultura y Educación 1993).

Evaluation

These annual operations consist of a very large survey including, among many other instruments for collecting relevant information about school characteristics, school personnel, children's parents and the children themselves, and a series of achievement tests. These tests of mathematics, language, social sciences, and natural sciences are administered to a very wide national sample of children who are at the third and seventh grades of primary school and at the second and fifth years of secondary school. The results of these achievement tests are published, including references to the most difficult test items, followed by an analysis of the probable causes of failure and some pedagogical and didactic orientations.

The ministry's reports on the results of National Evaluation are useful documents. If they are appropriately used they can serve as good tools for the diagnosis and treatment of school difficulties and, in turn, for the prevention of repetition and dropout. It must be noted that the National Ministry has not published any study about explanatory variables of school achievement. No reasons are given for this omission.

Social Educational Plan

In 1993, the National Ministry of Education created the Under Secretary of Compensatory Policies, to be in charge of the Social Educational Plan. The main objective of this Plan and the mission of the Under Secretary is to develop actions in favor of more and better education for the schools functioning within less favorable socioeconomic environments. During the last four years the National Ministry of Education has invested increasing amounts of money to implement the Social Educational Plan. According to the official information, between 1993 and 1996, $552,732,378 was invested in this Social Educational Plan.

The Plan includes two Programs: "Better Education for Everybody" and "Improving School Buildings." In turn, the "Better Education" program includes three projects: "Improving the Quality of Education at Schools," "Stimulating Institutional Initiative," and "Promoting Alternative Proposals." The program "Improving School Buildings" includes the following projects: "Building Schools," "Eradicating Hut Schools" (i.e., of schools in huts), "Building School Rooms in Kindergartens," and "School Building Repair."

Official information indicates that the Social Educational Plan reaches 11,820 schools and its main objective is to contribute to the equality of educational opportunities for all children. According to the same source, the Plan serves more than 3,000,000 children. The Plan has built 1,960 new school buildings, and 2,747 school rooms, and has repaired 2,747 schools. During the same period, and as a part of the same Plan, 10,600,000 books have been distributed among schoolchildren and 16,000 schools have received didactic material. These are the main achievements after the four years of so-called compensatory policies. Information about how this Social Educational Plan in fact reaches the schools, teachers, and children was obtained by analyzing a part of the data base gathered by the National Ministry of Culture and Education about the National Evaluation Survey for this chapter (Argentina, Ministerio de Cultura y Educación 1997).

The data corresponds to primary schools in six different provinces (out of twenty-four different units for the whole country—twenty-three provinces and the Federal District of Buenos Aires). The sample size includes a primary school enrollment of 297,592 and 922 schools in the six districts.

Schools and enrollment are indicated; no distinction has been made between public or private institutions, or between urban versus rural categories. Some like Greater Buenos Aires (part of the province of the same name and the Federal District of Buenos Aires), are under-represented in the sample. On the other hand, some provinces, in particular Santiago del Estero (number 23) are over-represented in the sample. There is not enough room in this chapter to explain the reasons behind these particular sample sizes. In order to generalize from sampling data to the entire population, a weighting of the province results must be applied. With this in mind, the commentaries in this section about the sampling data will be confined only to the internal analysis.

Table 12.1

Social Education Plan: Number of Schools Incorporated to the Plan, and Years During Which the Schools Received Contributions (sample data)

	Federal District (n = 79)	Greater Buenos Aires (n = 38)	Córdoba (n = 65)	Corrientes (n = 83)	Mendoza (n=53)	Santiago del Estero (n = 116)
			Social Education Plan			
Incorporated	9	15	3	54	36	58
Not Incorporated	65	21	12	19	14	8
No Answer	5	2	50	10	3	50
		Years during which the schools received contribution*				
1993	1	10	0	9	7	16
1994	2	7	3	18	18	22
1995	2	7	3	23	23	52
1996	8	14	4	46	29	46
Program 1		"Better Education for Projects"				
1. Improving the quality of education	14	24	6	42	51	46
2. Stimulating institutional initiatives	4	5	3	38	7	25
3. Promoting alternative proposals	2	5	0	4	2	.8
Program 2		"Improving School Buildings"				
1. Building schools	16	32	0	1	2	3
2. Eradicating hut-schools	13	26	1.5	0	2	.8
3. Building school rooms in kindergartens	14	26	1.5	26	19	9
4. School building repair	15	32	1.5	11	30	14

Source: Ministerio de Cultura y Educación, 1996, and unpublished data.
*Balance between incorporation and withdrawals in each year.

The survey included an extensive questionnaire addressed to school principals (434 in the sample studied). From the long instrument, only four questions (numbers 42 to 45 in the original form filled in by school principals), directly related to the Social Educational Plan, were processed for this chapter. Table 12.1 shows the corresponding data, as well the number of schools which were incorporated into the Plan.

Although the restrictions already made prevent any attempt at a direct generalization about the school population, from each of the subsamples presented it is possible to formulate the following comments: (a) the proportion of incorporated schools, with respect to the number of schools within each of the sampled provinces, corresponds to the degree of "poverty" or presumed needs, particularly in the cases of Corrientes and Santiago del Estero; (b) it is easy to see that the Plan expanded after its creation in 1993; (c) the large numbers of non-respondents in Córdoba and Santiago del Estero make those cases hard to interpret. This lack of response may be the result of ignorance about the Plan on the part of the school principals or even the consequence of a negative attitude.

Table 12.1 contains data on the two Programs. Within the columns there are data corresponding to each of the selected provinces. Each cell contains the percentage of schools in each subsample that obtained benefits from the different projects involved in the Plan.

In Program 1 ("Better Education for Everybody"), the highest percentages correspond to the first project ("Improving the Quality of Education"). This project has to do with special in-service training courses for teachers. The National Ministry offers financial support for seminars and courses. It can be seen that the so-called backward jurisdictions, such as Corrientes and Santiago del Estero, show the highest percentage of financial support within Program 1. The two other projects do not show significant percentages with the exception of Corrientes and Santiago del Estero.

For "Improving School Buildings" (Program 2), the percentages of benefits obtained are lower. Only one province, as a matter of fact only part of the province of Buenos Aires ("Greater Buenos Aires"),[1] received much help. It is not surprising that the national authorities tried to concentrate more economic effort in this highly complex and demographically dense area.

Table 12.2 includes percentages of affirmative answers about contributions received by some of the schools and also estimation of the value of these contributions.

As readily predicted from Tables 12.1 and 12.2, Greater Buenos Aires, Corrientes, Mendoza, and Santiago del Estero have received the highest percentages of contributions through the Social Educational Plan. In these cases, books and materials for the students were the most frequently mentioned. With the exception only of Corrientes, the National Financial Support institutional initiatives have been comparatively low.

Final Comments

Undoubtedly the introduction by law of an extra year of compulsory pre-primary education counts as a positive measure toward preventing repetition and dropout in Argentina. If the political intention of the government is to reduce repetition and dropout at school, it is absolutely necessary that socioeconomic plans be congruent with educational purposes. Obviously, if the socioeconomic plans do not include an improvement of the living conditions of the popular sectors, it is

Table 12.2

**Contributions Received by the Schools Through the Social Educational Plan.
Has this help contributed to the improvement of the institutions' management?**
(in percentages of the 423 schools in the sample)

Provinces

Type of contribution	Federal District (n = 79)		Greater Buenos Aires (n = 38)		Córdoba (n = 65)		Corrientes (n = 83)		Mendoza (n = 53)		Santiago del Estero (n = 116)	
	Affirmative answers	Have contributed to managerial improvement	Affirmative answers	Have contributed to managerial improvement	Affirmative answers	Have contributed to managerial improvement	Affirmative answers	Have contributed to managerial improvement	Affirmative answers	Have contributed to managerial improvement	Affirmative answers	Have contributed to managerial improvement
Books for the students	11	7	37	37	6	6	51	49	66	60	51	46
Books for school library	11	9	18	16	6	6	51	45	62	60	50	45
Teacher's library	6	5	10	10	8	1	49	46	43	41	49	45
Resources for building improvement	6	4	33	21	1	1	14	12	36	32	12	10
Materials for school work for students	7	5	50	45	6	6	48	46	55	51	48	42
Materials for the teachers	5	4	10	8	5	5	37	37	41	40	40	37
Didactic equipment for the school	5	5	18	16	5	5	47	43	45	43	47	42
Support for institutional initiatives	4	5	5	5	3	3	41	40	15	15	22	21

almost meaningless to devote economic efforts to compensatory and preventive measures within the school system with that purpose in mind.

There is a great contradiction in claiming equal educational opportunities for everybody, on the one hand (Ministry of Education, for instance), and adopting a severely restricted economic plan affecting mostly the poorest sectors of the population, on the other. This is the case for the time being in Argentina, with the highest historical rate of unemployment and the precarious and unstable working situation of a vast sector of the lower strata of the population.

The preventive plans against repetition and dropout that have been presented in this chapter must be considered in the light of this unfavorable socioeconomic frame for the popular sectors that suffer poverty in Argentina. Of course, it must be admitted that with no preventive or compensatory plan at all the situation would be worse. Economic inequality creates or magnifies the problem, and any kind of preventive or compensatory plan may be too weak to counterbalance the unfavourable situation.

There is not enough room in this chapter to present, even in a brief overview, the provincial initiatives dealing with the prevention of repetition and dropout. Only a few of them will be mentioned in the following lines. Some provinces have paid more attention, by means of special programs, to the teaching and learning processes of initial reading and writing. In some instances, specific surveys and research studies have been developed to obtain more rigorous information about the incidence of repetition and dropout in certain schools in order to identify those children who are at risk of school failure.

Note

1. Greater Buenos Aires is the adjacent area around the Metropolitan area that, although it is not physically separated, forms part of the provincial territory of the Province of Buenos Aires. The largest province of Argentina bears the same name of the capital city. So, Province of Buenos Aires and Federal District of Buenos Aires (City of Buenos Aires) are distinguishable in terms of the political division of the country. Greater Buenos Aires includes the City of Buenos Aires, which is also known as the Federal District of Buenos Aires and also a part of the province of the same name.

References

Agudo de Córsico, C., and M. Manacorda de Rosetti. 1994. *Interacción lingüística entre maestros y alumnos y su influencia sobre el rendimiento escolar.* Buenos Aires: A-Z.

Argentina. Ministerio de Cultura y Educación. Secretaría de Programación y Evaluación Educativa. 1993. *Marco General del Sistema de Evaluación de la Calidad. Documento de Trabajo No 1.*

———. 1995. *El Financiamiento Educativo Argentino en un Contexto de Restricción de Recursos,* by A. Morduchowicz. Buenos Aires: Ministerio de Cultura y Educación.

Argentina. Ministerio de Cultura y Educación. 1996. *Censo Nacional de Docentes y Establecimientos Educativos 94.* Buenos Aires: Ministerio de Cultura y Educación.

————. 1997. *Operativo Nacional de Evaluación 1996.* Base de datos. Unpublished. Buenos Aires: Ministerio de Cultura y Educación.

Lockheed, M.E., and A. Verspoor. 1992. *Improving Primary Education in Developing Countries.* New York: Oxford University Press.

Psacharopoulos, G., and M. Woodhall. 1985. *Education for Development.* New York: Oxford University Press.

Sautu, R., and A.M. Eichelbaum de Babini. 1996. *Los pobres y la escuela. Trabajos de investigación.* Buenos Aires: La Colmena.

UNESCO: OIE. 1996. *La repetición escolar.* Geneva: UNESCO, International Education Office.

13

IVANY RODRIGUES PINO AND
MARIANE CAMPELO KOSLINSKI

Government Programs to Eliminate Repetition, School Dropout, and Exclusion in Brazil

The Problem

In the 1970s and 1980s, education in Brazil was not equally available to the nation's diverse regions and classes, which is indicated in the differing average numbers of years of schooling in the nation, shown in Table 13.1. Moreover, within schools, differing expectations about students according to their origin contributed to educational inequalities.[1]

Brazil has not yet been able to achieve its goal of eight years of education for all children. Extreme concentration of income influences school attendance: 97 percent of seven to fourteen year old children from families with income greater than two minimum salaries per capita are in school; this includes 90 percent of urban and 72 percent of rural families. Barely 75 percent of poor children attend primary school: 73 percent of children from the Northeast and 95 percent of children from the Southeast do so (PNUD/IPEA 1996). Similarly, the highest rate of failing a grade (19 percent) and lowest average amount of schooling (4.1 years) are in the Northeast, while the Southeast region has the lowest failure rate (12 percent) and the highest average schooling (6.2 years); the Federal District in the state of Goias in the Center-West region has the highest average schooling, 7.5 years, as shown in Table 13.2. Moreover, Fletcher (1997) indicates a surprising increase in the repetition rate in the third to eighth grades of basic education and in high school.

The 1988 Constitution and the 1996 Law of Directives and Bases of Educa-

---

This chapter is an abridged version by the editors of a larger text to be published elsewhere.

Table 13.1

Average Number of Years of Schooling in Brazil, 1960–1995

Region	1960	1970	1980	1990	1995
North-Center West	2.7	—	4.0	—	5.6
Northeast	1.1	1.3	2.2	3.3	4.1
Southeast	2.7	3.2	4.4	5.7	6.2
South	2.4	2.7	3.9	5.2	6.0

Source: IPEA/PNUD 1996. *Relatório sobre o desenvolvimento humano.*
Note: Figures for 1995 calculated by MEC/INEP/SEEC.

Table 13.2

Failure and Dropout in Brazil: Percentage of Students Enrolled in the First Through Eighth Grades

	Brazil	South	Southeast	Center-West	North	Northeast
Failure	15	15	12	15	18	19
Dropout	16	9	13	16	23	20

Source: MEC/INEP. 1996, *Informe estatistico.*
Note: Brazil has 34 million students enrolled in basic education. The dropout indicator includes students who left school during the year and returned for the same grade in the following year and those who permanently dropped out.

tion (LDB), which provided for decentralization and restructuring of education, gave rise to federal and state programs to control repetition and dropout. This chapter describes these programs in 1997; the recent inauguration of many of these programs results in a lack of data available to evaluate them.

Repetition and Dropout: Programs of School Reorganization

The innovative idea of school cycles within which students could not fail a grade dominated the reorganization of schools in Brazil under the 1996 LDB and the 1997 National Curriculum Parameters (PCN), which were to take effect in 1998. Beginning in the 1980s, some states and municipalities created a basic literacy cycle (CBA), comprising the first and second grades, which allowed students to learn at different rates; brief summaries of these programs are shown in Table 13.3.

São Paulo

In 1984, São Paulo created its CBA, along with reform of the curriculum, teacher training, and the educational evaluation system. These changes led to a 9.6 percent improvement in students who enrolled in 1984 and were promoted to

Table 13.3

Description of Programs to Prevent Repetition and Dropout in Brazil

Unit	Program	Type and duration of program
MEC	1. Accelerated Learning. For students in the first four grades of basic education, who have more than two years' age/grade distortion. Replacement of school failure by success with the stimulation of students' self-esteem and mastery of curriculum by special pedagogy. 2. Every Child in School. Universalization of access to and permanence in school.	1. Temporary treatment. 2. Treatment.
Maranhão	1. Program of Accelerated Learning. MEC's Pilot Program.	1. Temporary treatment.
Minas Gerais	1. Accelerated Classes. Strategy for students with multiple repetitions. 2. Basic Literacy Cycle (CBA) up to the third grade. Strategy of organizing teaching/learning as a continuous process, breaking the barrier between grades. 3. Fifth Grade Project. Modification of pedagogy used in the fifth grade.	1. Temporary treatment. 2. Permanent prevention and treatment. 3. Permanent prevention and treatment.
Paraná	1. Correction of Student Flow. End multiple repetition in the third, fifth, and seventh grades of Basic Education. 2. Summer School Program. Classes for students in the fifth through eighth grades who failed up to two subjects.	1. Temporary treatment. 2. Treatment.
Pernambuco	1. Partial Promotion. Articulated with the Program of Compartmentalized Evaluation. It is an alternative for reorganization of schooling without interruption.	1. Permanent treatment.
São Paulo	1. Accelerated Classes. End multiple repetition. 2. Reorganization of School System. Articulation of a group of programs to eliminate repetition and control dropout. 3. Continuous promotion. Organization of basic education in one or more cycles.	1. Temporary treatment. 2. Permanent treatment and prevention. 3. Permanent treatment.
Distrito Federal	1. Family School Supplement. Program of minimum income placing the school problem of children in the context of social exclusion. 2. School Saving Program. Funds credited in the Bank Savings Book of the Federal District the name of the student in the Family School Supplement Program.	1. Permanent prevention and treatment. 2. Permanent prevention and treatment.

Source: Authors.

the third grade in 1986, compared to the corresponding results in 1985.

In September 1997, the state of São Paulo instituted continuous promotion in basic education, which lasts eight years, organized into one or more cycles, based on the successful school cycles that had been introduced in the city of São Paulo's school system.

The State Secretary of Education in São Paulo provided for:

1. Physical reorganization of the school system, which reached 73 percent of the schools in the state. The reform separated schools for young children from those for adolescents. This increased the school day from four to five hours. In 1994, 254 schools had three shifts a day and 1,039 had four shifts. With the new organization, schools with only two shifts rose from 999 to 2,373. This also allowed fifth grade teachers to work forty hours in one school, which had not usually been the case before the reform.

2. Decentralization of school management and transfer of funds to schools' parent associations (ADMs) for small expenses, such as materials and computers, and for the improvement and maintenance of the school. The sums increased from R$4 million in 1994 to R$44 million in 1995 and R$170 million in 1996.

3. A school evaluation system (SARESP), which evaluated and disseminated information about the school's efficiency, as indicated by student test results. In 1996, 1.2 million third and seventh grade students were tested. In 1997, tests were extended to the fourth and eighth grades; the results were helpful to teachers in the continuing education programs.

4. A summer school program, lasting three weeks, for students who failed.

The basic cycle (CB) had 58.6 percent of enrollments in the school reorganization program, but the lowest pass rate (31.7 percent). Promotion rates increased in higher grades. In the fifth through eighth grades, 59.3 percent of the students who enrolled in the program had failed four or five subjects. The largest share (39.5 percent) were fifth grade students.

The summer school program was organized in two cycles: grades 1 to 4 and grades 5 to 8, achieving the greatest success in the higher grades. Differing from the Paraná program, which was restricted to students who failed no more than two subjects, this program allowed students who had failed all eight subjects to participate, which was important for the great impact of São Paulo's program, because 85 percent of the students in the program had failed more than two subjects. However, pass rates in the program fell as the number of subjects studied increased, from 77.7 percent for students enrolled in one subject to 40.3 percent for those enrolled in eight subjects. Success was greatest in those subjects that could be studied as a unit and did not depend on cumulative learning. Classes that made the greatest demands for study had the highest success rate.

In 1995–96 the São Paulo programs saw a decline in the failure rate from 11.7 percent to 8.6 percent, and dropout fell from 9.1 percent to 7.6 percent. This improvement saved R$134.4 million, since each student cost $R600.

Minas Gerais

In 1995, after CBAs were not very successful in Minas Gerais, the government reformed them, taking advantage of the schools' new financial autonomy, evaluation system and teacher training. (See chapter 17 in this volume.) In this new phase, the CBA was conceived of as giving a student enough time to learn to read and write, breaking the bottleneck in the flow from the first to the second grade. The success of this program resulted in its extension to the third grade in 1996.

In 1995, the city of Belo Horizonte in Minas Gerais introduced the idea of a "standard school" with three cycles; for six to eight year olds; nine to eleven year olds; and twelve to fourteen year olds.

In 1995, Minas Gerais created a program focusing on the fifth grade, because it had been a bottleneck in student progress. In 1994, fifth grade dropout and repetition rates were 20.75 percent and 22.98 percent, respectively, compared to average rates for basic education of 12.48 percent and 19.32 percent. The program began with surveys in state schools of students who had repeated grades many times, and diagnoses of actions needed to improve fifth grade education. Teachers were trained and the State Secretariat of Education provided systematic monitoring.

The next step was the selection of pilot schools in Belo Horizonte as experimental laboratories for the project, which was to be extended to all fifth grade classes in state schools with the goal of achieving a 91 percent promotion rate for fifth grade students at the end of 1999. Faculty, staff, students, and their families are to be involved in the project.

North and Northeast

São Paulo's experience was applied in other cities and states. In the Northeast, literacy classes were introduced in the last year of kindergarten for seven and eight year old children. The state of Pernambuco (in the Northeast) allowed schools to voluntarily adhere to a partial progress system, offering various options. Depending on how rapidly they learned, students would be promoted before or at the end of the school year. Students who did not meet standards in up to two subjects would be promoted and given extra instruction outside of regular school hours. If the student had learned 50 percent of the basic subject matter in any discipline, the extra instruction would cease and the student would be returned to a normal status. As a result of the program, student behavior improved: students went to the library to study; there was greater attendance by students who failed in one subject but who knew that they could continue their studies; there was increased self-esteem; and approximately 40 percent of students were promoted at the first exam.

Paraná

In Paraná (South region), a pilot summer school program let fifth to eighth grade and high school students who failed in one or two subjects have a new chance of promotion. Students would have thirty classroom hours of personalized attention in classes of no more than thirty students. Students who mastered 50 percent of the curriculum would be promoted and guaranteed a place in their original school. Teachers from their school would be given materials aiding group work and individual attention. Evaluation would be continuous, and not restricted to tests and grades. Adhesion to the program depended on meetings of teachers and parents of children who failed; teachers would be trained and time provided for educational planning.

Repetition, Dropout, and Age/Grade Distortion: Accelerated Learning Programs

High repetition rates lead to age/grade distortion that can result in dropout. There is great variation in the age of students in the grades surveyed.[2] Only 42 percent of basic education students and 38 percent of middle school students in 1995 were in the grade appropriate for their age. Enrollment therefore was concentrated in grades with the highest failure rates—the first, second, and fifth grades—and there was a possible deficit of enrollment in other grades.

The age/grade distortion transformed the eight years of required basic education to 11.2 years. This implies three grade repetitions, which are a cause of dropping out. Moreover, in each grade, average proficiency in reading and mathematics decreases with the age of the student. The greatest age/grade distortion among seven to fourteen year olds is in the Northeast, with 52.52 percent, and the lowest rate is in the state of São Paulo, with 16.31 percent. The problems encountered in basic education led the Ministry of Education to undertake a program to improve promotion rates, beginning with a pilot project in Maranhão (Northeast) in 1995, and extended in that year and 1996 to São Paulo (Southeast), Mato Grosso do Sul (Center West), Paraná (South), and Minas Gerais (Southeast).

In 1997, the Ministry of Education and Sport (MEC) formalized its Accelerated Learning Program, designed to increase students' self-esteem and exercise of citizenship. MEC proposed aiding the education ministries of the states, cities, and the federal district, monitoring projects for students in the first four grades who exhibited more than two years of age/grade distortion.

At the beginning of the program, accelerated learning classes would have no more than fifteen students. The program would expand until age/grade distortion disappeared, hopefully in four years. Adhesion to the program was free, and states and municipalities had to present detailed plans to join. MEC would provide teaching materials developed by the state of São Paulo and the Brasília Education Technology Center (CETEB), which provided management and didactic information, as well as modules for self-esteem, social identity, citizenship, and environment, based on an interdisciplinary approach of Portuguese language, mathematics, natural science, and social studies. MEC guaranteed financial support for duplicating teaching materials, teacher training, supervising the program, and evaluation of its results. The states and municipalities had to facilitate the adoption of the program and monitor it. It was hoped that the program would improve classroom conditions by having students of the same age in classes, and increase the number of places available for new students. The Accelerated Learning Program was used in several states. For example, in 1995 Maranhão used the programs in the second and third grades. Promotion rates rose from 83 percent to 88 percent in 1996. In Minas Gerais, an accelerated learning program was to enable third and fourth grade students to complete both grades in one year. São Paulo focused attention on the fourth grade. The program placed attention on developing student abilities rather than on completing a curriculum. The teacher was to diagnose students' specific needs, provide continuous assessment of their progress, and receive training, books, and materials. School administrators, teachers, and the students' families were to be involved.

Classes of twenty to twenty-five students were organized into two levels: (1) for those at least ten years old from the basic cycle going into the fourth or fifth grade, and (2) for those eleven years old, from the third or fourth grade, going into the fifth grade. They met five hours a day (one hour more than regular school). Teachers received training every two months, and reports of progress were given to municipalities.

Paraná initiated an accelerated learning program in 1997, designed for students in the third to seventh grades. Classes of twenty-five to thirty students were for two or more grades, preferably grouped by age. The program included teacher training to favor interaction with students in order to develop their sense of security. The program emphasized basic areas in the curriculum and provided time to teachers for continuous evaluation of students. The summer school program was expected to reduce the 10 percent repetition rate of fifth to eighth grade students to 2 to 3 percent in 1998.

Repetition, Dropout, and Exclusion: The "Every Child in School" Program

Students are excluded from school when they do not have access to a school or dropout of school. Approximately 2.7 million—10 percent of Brazil's school-age children—were not in school in 1996. The Ministry of Education and Culture created the "every child in school" program in October 1997, to be implemented in 1998, in order to assure that all children would attend and remain in school. The program is designed to aid school-age children and adolescents who (1) lack access to school at an appropriate age; (2) had been in school but no longer attend; (3) have an age/grade distortion of more than two years; (4) are members of high-risk groups; and (5) are more than fourteen years old and have had little schooling.

Specific strategies are provided for each group using accelerated learning programs and multi-grade rural schools. Teaching is organized in modules, rather than grades, in rural schools with only one teacher. Students will be promoted when they master the curriculum, so that they can adapt their schedule of learning to agricultural and weather conditions, as provided by Article 39 of the 1996 LDB. Four states have begun to install this program, whose teacher training and instructional manuals are financed by MEC. The program also includes continuous promotion by dividing basic education into cycles. In 1997, São Paulo accepted this in both its state and municipal school systems. Literacy (in the Comunidade Solidaria program) for twelve to eighteen year olds, is applied to productive activity. Education to improve quality of work, begun in 1996, for youths and adults is designed to provide them with the equivalent of four years of basic education. Businesses will give classes at the work site; MEC will furnish teaching materials for teachers and students.

These programs will involve articulation with state and municipal programs and mobilization of civil society, including work with non-governmental organizations and actions to eliminate child labor. MEC also will provide resources to complement those of FUNDEF, distribute textbooks, and attend to provision of food in school.

Repetition, Dropout, and School and Social Exclusion: The Federal District Program

The Family Educational Supplement program began in the Federal District in 1995. There are proportionately fewer poor in the Federal District (16.7 percent) than the Brazilian average (20.6 percent). The program assures monthly payments during a year of one minimum salary to each family below the poverty level that has all their seven to fourteen year old children enrolled in and regularly attending public school. The family must have lived in the Federal District for five consecutive years. Criteria for selection of families to receive this payment include income, type of housing, employment, and amount of schooling of family members. A school savings program, tied to the educational supplement program, guarantees each student from a family in this program one minimum salary yearly credited to a bank savings account, which can be partly withdrawn after the fourth and eighth grades and entirely withdrawn in high school. This was accompanied by better teaching conditions, improved school libraries, and the introduction of school councils. Evaluation of the program is carried out with the aid of UNICEF and UNESCO. The program cost less than 1 percent of the Federal District's budget and covered 65 percent of the 35,000 families that were eligible for the program. Students whose families received income supplements had lower dropout rates and a rate of promotion 10 percent higher than students whose families did not receive these supplements. Dropout rates fell from 6.2 percent in 1994 to 5.2 percent in 1996, and promotion rates increased from 70.1 percent to 74.5 percent.

In 1997, the marginal cost of a student was R$915.56 per year. The economic benefits of the program were 2.1 million reais (1 reais = 1 dollar), a saving of more than 10 percent of the investment in the program in 1996 (R$19.6 million).

Future Outlook

The several programs spoken of here are characterized by decentralization and supervision. However, they should take into account both teacher training and the social function of a school. The programs' success should increase the ability of the poorest citizens to earn a living and consequently should improve Brazil's highly unequal income distribution. This concept underlies the government's strong commitment to four-year financing of the programs and its multiple strategies to publicize and implement them, which is a strong element favoring their success.

Notes

1. Data presented here should be examined in conjunction with those presented in chapter 8 in this book.
2. The survey SAEB/95 included 2,289 public and 511 private schools, 90,500 students in the fourth and eighth grades of basic education and the third year of high school.

References

Fletcher, Philip R. 1997. "As dimensões transversal e longitudinal do modelo profluxo." Rio de Janeiro, UNESCO, 1997.
Pino, Ivany R., and Angel Pino. 1992. "Educação escolar, desigualdade social e cidadania." In *A educação e os trabalhadores*. São Paulo: Página Aberta.
Ribeiro, Sergio Costa. 1990. "A pedagogia da repetência." *Tecnologia Educacional: Rio de Janeiro* 19, no. 97 (November/December).

Documents

Assoacação de Professores do Estado de São Paulo, APEOESP, 1997. As Inovações Introduzidas pela Secretaria de Educasão do Estado, São Paulo, Novembro.
———. 1996. *Informe Estatístico*. Brasília .
———. 1997. *Aceleração de Aprendizagem*. Programa e Subsídios para Implantação.
———. 1997. *Evolução da Educação Básica no Brasil 1991-1997*. Brasília.
———. 1997. *Programa de Aceleração da Aprendizagem—Orientação para Implantaçao*. Brasília.
———. 1997. *Programa Toda Criança na Escola*. Brasília.
———. 1998. *Relatório Final SAEB/95*. Brasília.
Programa das Naçes Unidas paro o Desenvolvimento Instituto de Pesquisa Econômica Aplicada Secretaria do Estado de Educaço. Governo do Distrito Federal. PNUD/IPEA. 1996. *Relatório sobre o Desenvolvimento Humano no Brasil 1996*. Brasília.

Avaliação a Partir do Estudo do Programa Bolsa Familiar para a Educação no Distrito Federal. Brasília. IPEA.

Sant'Ana, Sílvio Rocha, and Andréa Moraes. 1997. *Avaliação do Programa Bolsa Escola do GDF.* Brasília. Fundaçao Grupo Esquel Brasil.

SEE-GDF. 1995. *Bolsa-Escola Poupança-Escola.* Brasília.

———. 1997. *Apresentação dos Programas Bolsa-Escola e Poupança-Escola.* Brasília (September).

Secretaria do Estado de Educaço-Governo do Estado do. SEE-GE Pernambuco. 1997. *Programa "Progressão Parcial."* Recife.

SEE-GE Minas Gerais. 1996. *Conheça o Ciclo Básico de Alfabetização.*

———. 1997. *Educação de Qualidade para Todos.* Belo Horizonte.

———. *Reflexões: Projeto 5a Série em Destaque.* Belo Horizonte.

SEE - GE Paraná. 1997. *Projeto de Correção de Fluxo.* Curitiba.

———. 1997. *Estudos Complementares de Férias.* Curitiba.

SEE - GE São Paulo. 1995. *Mudar para Melhorar: Uma Escola para a Criança, Outra para o Adolescente.* São Paulo.

———. 1996. *ACTA 293.* São Paulo.

———. 1996. *Relatório das Atividades da Secretaria de Educação.* de São Paulo. São Paulo.

———. 1997. *O Que Mudou na Escola Pública Paulista?* São Paulo: Fevereiro.

———. 1997. *Relatório de Resultados Projeto Escola nas Férias.* São Paulo: Julho.

———. 1997. *Reorganização da Trajetória Escolar no Ensino Fundamental: Classes de Aceleração.* São Paulo.

14

Cecilia Cardemil O.

Prevention of Repetition and Dropout: Quality and Equity in the First Years of Primary Education in Chile— Two Programs to Achieve Them

Challenges, Principles, and Measures of Chilean Educational Policy from 1990 to 1997

Challenges: Sufficient Coverage, Inadequate Quality

When democracy arrived in Chile in 1990, the access to primary and secondary school was satisfactory. The coverage of basic education (between six and thirteen years of age) was 95 percent, and that of middle school (secondary, between fourteen and seventeen years of age) was 81.77 percent (MINEDUC, cited in Cox and Jara 1989). The problem with education is rooted in quality. Standardized tests are applied every two years to fourth and eighth grade classes in all primary schools in Chile. They measure the achievement of the minimal educational objectives in reading–writing, mathematics, natural, and social sciences. During the 1980-90 decade, the average quality of basic education in the nation reached 58.6 percent of these objectives. These results are surprisingly low in free schools, which have yields between 45 and 50 percent, while the tuition-based schools reached an average between 75 and 80 percent of the minimum objectives (MINEDUC, cited in Cox and Jara 1989). This low quality may result from the neoliberal policy decisions that installed competitive financing mechanisms accompanied by the drastic reduction of public spending, forcing schools to function under very precarious material conditions; and from the conditions of the teaching profession: its salaries were very low; it was subjected to harassing policies during the military regime; and it lacked incentives for professional development.

Principal Policy Guidelines

To remedy this situation, from 1990 through 1997 policy decisions were guided by three fundamental principals: (1) improving education qualitatively, guaranteeing to all children effective learning of basic abilities; (2) implementing greater equity and positive discrimination in the distribution of education, offering more opportunities to achieve acceptable levels of learning to the neediest children who have the greatest risk of not acquiring basic learning; (3) making education a task of all: people, communities, and local and national institutions. From this perspective, the state promotes the investment in education by nongovernmental organizations, including businesses.

Measures for Attending to Educational Needs

Educational policy is directed to:

Improving conditions and inputs. This refers to substantially raising the minimum conditions encountered in subsidized education, from the physical spaces to the quality and availability of books and teaching materials; improving health; and providing significant salary increases and the professional updating of teachers. In 1991 a Teaching Statute established a national regulation of teachers' conditions of employment, providing a common structure and improvement in remunerations, rewards for improvement, work experience, and work in difficult conditions, and high job stability. With an amendment of this statute carried out in 1995, the remunerations have grown 80 percent since 1990, approaching $640 per month for a thirty-hour week (Cox 1997).

Executing and promoting innovations to enrich processes. Educational policy was designed to improve learning processes in language, mathematics, and understanding of the social and material world.

Educational decentralization. This consists of measures to induce schools to design and execute their own educational improvement projects with government resources. The policy includes: generation of an Educational Improvement Project (PME), the existence of a fund of resources for carrying out projects, and a system of aid and supervision by the Ministry to endorse the schools in carrying out these projects.

Equity. Programs are focused on taking care of poor schools, offering equality of educational opportunities to groups with very distinct cultural backgrounds, assigning more resources and paying special attention to the poorest groups of the nation. The Rural MECE Program[1] establishes measures to improve the quality of rural schools, especially those furthest from urban centers. It also redefines the curriculum and teaching practices, making the linguistic and cultural codes of rural children a necessary point of departure for the work of the school and not an obstacle. Both the government-sponsored 900 Schools and the private Learning Is Sweet programs are directed to poor urban or rural municipalities and are described in the following sections.

The 900 Schools Program

From its inception in 1990, the democratic government implemented a program for the improvement of primary schools in poor sectors at the national level. It is focused on the 10 percent of schools (900) with the worst record and the greatest urban and rural poverty. Through 1997, 2,100 schools have participated for one or more years (MINEDUC 1997). The program is basically centered in the first through fourth grades. In order to improve the quality of learning in language and mathematics, and to increase self-esteem and basic conditions for learning, the program grants materials and prepares human resources.

Improvement of Material Resources

Priority is given in the first three years to repair of schools, including student furniture. Open shelves for classrooms are supplied. Grants are made for teaching materials and libraries for classrooms. Schools are given materials, teaching games, and notebooks for individual and group practice of reading and writing, arithmetic operations, and the discovery of the environment. The materials are modified according to the needs observed by the supervisors and specialists. Today, all schools and grades receive libraries and some of these materials.

Schools also receive study guides, tape recorders, and mimeograph machines, other equipment and documents. During the two first years schools in the program received study guides in basic areas. Today these texts are given to all primary school students in Chile. Supervisors, who are the agents from the Ministry responsible for training teachers and directors of the schools in the program, are also given technical and research documents to aid the improvement of teaching.

Preparation of Human Resources: Training Strategies

Teams of experts are in charge of the development of theoretical and educational approaches to be used, and the production of teaching materials and the guides for their use. The areas included are:

Language. Teachers are given incentives to place greater value on students' language and experience, immersion in written language, the development of systematic activities for knowing, and dominating the structure and function of language. They promote the practice of silent reading to stimulate the taste for and the sense of reading and writing as an area of personal and group communication.

Mathematics. The importance of oral calculation is emphasized for the development of logical thought. Incentive is given to increasing the value of experience of a cultural and fantasy world as a means of approaching the development of logico-mathematical language and thought. The creation and solution of problems whose difficulties are adapted to the children's abilities is promoted, as well as the use of mathematical language using varied materials and objects, forms, and numbers.

Social-affective development. Learning Workshops are directed to groups of students of the third and fourth grades who have the most precarious family conditions. For this activity, older children of both sexes are incorporated as monitors, selected by the schools themselves, considering their importance to the community that surrounds the school, their training (post-secondary studies related to education and their job situation), and their interest in the younger students.

Transfer of Teaching Methods to School Agents

The central teams intensively prepare the supervisors responsible for training in the schools. These in turn meet with teachers in the schools every fifteen days for two hours in a workshop on focuses and educational methods for specialties and use of educational materials in the classroom. They also train the monitors intensively, meeting with groups of twenty students of the third and fourth grades for two hours, twice a week, outside of normal class hours. They also plan their relationship with the teachers, following up with them on the progress of these students and visiting the families, in order to guarantee the children's attendance at the workshop, whose activities include games and group dynamics, stimulation of spoken language, calculations needed for the development of their daily life, manual and artistic activities related to motor development, imagination, and creativity, and visits to social organizations in the community.

Initial Program Evaluations and Adjustments That Are Occurring

The 900 Schools Program (P.900) was evaluated in its first two years of implementation (Gajardo 1994; Cardemil and Latorre 1992) with respect to:

Infrastructure and educational materials. These actions produced a positive climate in the schools due to the fulfillment of the promises and the quality of the products distributed.

Teachers, classroom practices of language and mathematics, and perception of the Learning Workshops. Bases were developed at the school level for an exchange between teachers in themes related to their teaching practices and experimentation with educational suggestions to facilitate children's learning. Teaching practices were modified in the classroom. Teachers' attitudes and styles became more interactive, producing greater confidence and the expectation of positive achievements in the children. The use of time in the class was shifted from discipline to instruction. Class time was used to explore the experiences of children. Mathematics problems that took daily life into account were emphasized, such as the need to make arithmetic calculations without writing materials.

From the beginning, examples from daily life and exercises of arithmetic calculation without writing were introduced. Also, strategies differing from the mechanical response of students were selected, although old strategies and mechanical response persisted in the notions of and operations with numbers. Teachers had conceptual and methodological gaps that required specialists to produce guides, workbooks, and documents to meet their training needs. In the first stage they noticed an underutilization of the teaching materials in the schools, for fear of their loss or deterioration. Today the materials are more frequently used, above all outside of the classes. The proposal of Learning Workshops at first engendered a lack of confidence in the teachers and directors, but the work of the young people with children and the effects on their development that were achieved with the activities and the interpersonal relations overcame the reticence of the different actors.

Directors. During the first stage, directors saw the program more as a possibility of obtaining resources for the school than as an educational process that would give incentives to changing teaching practices. The corrections made in the way the program was carried out led many of them to participate in the workshops for teachers during the second year and to enforce the use of practices that demanded teaching and learning in the classroom. From 1993 to 1995 the program was a pilot project, an improvement in school management that after 1998 will be extended to all the schools in the program (MINEDUC 1998).

Supervisors. They were accepted by the teachers and directors as advisers who facilitated the teaching process, bringing them closer to the individualized learning needs of the students. They facilitated acceptance of the Learning Workshops, playing a key role by facilitating communications between directors, teachers, and young people, training them in acceptable behavior for the social development of the children and relationships with their families.

Students. The program awakened their interest and a positive attitude toward the challenges of learning. Interviews carried out with the children who attended the Learning Workshops revealed their progress in basic conditions for learning, in their self-esteem, in the broadening of language, in the desire to attend school, and improve their results. Their families appreciated the changes in these children. This reinforced their ties to the school and increased the expectation of completion of primary school (Cardemil et al. 1994). Today, the program delineates specific work with families in meetings with the school to strengthen the socio-affective conditions of the children (MINEDUC 1998).

There were two evaluations of learning, an external one applied by the Center for Research and Development of Education (CIDE), and one of the system itself, performed by the System of Measurement of National Educational Quality (SIMCE). CIDE's evaluation measured levels of ability in the areas of language and mathematics, while SIMCE's measured the achievement of minimal learning objectives in the same areas. The number of courses that increased in both language and mathematics achievements is greater than those that decreased. Also, in the second year of primary school, a little more than half of the schools significantly improved. In the second use of the 900 Schools Program, which began in 1990, the advances in fourth grade experienced in language have a range of variation of 3.09 to 10.7 points, with an average of 5.071 points. Declines in language averaged 4.50 points varying from 3.36 to 6.66 points, indicating problems both in the population that attended these schools and in school management, mobility of teachers, and other aspects that caused resistances or difficulties in the face of the changes that the program proposed (Filp 1994). The courses that had the lowest achievements in 1990 advanced most with respect to those that had the highest percentages at the beginning. This would suggest that from its beginning the program has been achieving a positive result. The smaller advances in this measurement were in the fourth grade, because these courses had less time for exposure to the program. Nevertheless, the average in all the courses including the fourth year showed improvements by the students participating in the program (Latorre 1992–93).

Follow-up of the results of the evaluation of the System of Measurement of National Educational Quality, SIMCE. The Ministry and those who conducted the P.900 Program followed up the results with the use of tests that were applied to all the students in the educational system every two years.

A comparison of the sustained increase in the weighted averages of test scores obtained by these schools since the beginning of the program with the weighted averages of the free schools (total of municipal and subsidized private schools) measured by SIMCE that are not in the program indicates that although there are significant advances that show the effects of positive discrimination, these achievements do not assure a real equality of opportunity. These measurements and advances refer to the minimal cultural abilities in the fourth grade of primary school, indispensable for the rest of learning. There are 119 schools that have not improved enough in the entire period of the program to conclude the program and 114 schools that have re-entered it in the current year (MINEDUC 1997). In the opinion of those who conduct the program, these schools require clarification of criteria about their situation and specific focuses (MINEDUC 1998).

While 10 percent of schools with the best results today achieve 86.7 percent of the minimum objectives, the 10 percent of schools most vulnerable achieve 53.6 percent of the objectives. Moreover, a higher socioeconomic level is associated with better results, "which could indicate that school at the 4th year reproduces inequality of cultural capital" (García Huidobro 1997, 15). Similarly, there are one and a half million young people that have not completed grade school and are not in any part of the system. This indicates that the resources destined to policies focused on positive discrimination are very scarce. The P.900 program

incurred a cost of $16.7 million in the first year and a half of implementation—
$26 yearly per student. In 1996–97 the expenditure of the program was reduced
to less than half of that spent in 1992.

The decentralization and utilization of market tools (financing through subsidies and competitive funds) generate undesirable effects: those who have greater
economic and cultural capital rapidly obtain the available benefits, the poorest
remain subject to a more limited supply. Private schools can choose their population: while 25.8 percent of their enrollment belongs to the lowest one-fifth
socioeconomically, 42 percent of the municipal school population is in this quin-
tile. Private schools tend to avoid admitting the poorest students, so that they
show better results with fewer resources and they select families with greater
abilities of financing school activities.

Sixty percent of the differential school achievement is explained by factors
external to the school, for example, the family atmosphere, and educational
policies have not been designed to modify them. The educational climate of the
family explains between 40 and 50 percent of the impact the socioeconomic and
family characteristics exercise on the achievements (García Huidobro 1997).
What happens to learning when the family is included in the goals and activities
related to learning will be shown in the description of the second program.

The Learning Is Sweet Program: Improvement of Learning
Quality, a Challenge for the Family and the School

From 1990, the family has been incorporated as a basic educational agent in the
processes of continuous increase of capacity and training that are offered to
teachers from the free schools by CIDE. In 1995 the beet sugar producing firm
IANSA became involved in the financing and implementing of a pilot program
designed to prepare as a group the parents, teachers, and directors of sixteen
municipal schools. The program, known as Learning Is Sweet, has the aim of
increasing the essential educational conditions for improving the achievements
of students in primary schools located in geographic zones and communes of low
socioeconomic development.

The program was carried out during 1995 and 1996, organized around three
days each year of improvement with school teams and three follow-up visits each
year to all the schools. The program was executed with 242 participants. Indirect
beneficiaries were estimated at 114 teachers, 5,583 families, and 6,329 students.

The core focus of the program was made up of a set of factors related to the
equality of education and learning from preschool to the end of basic education:

1. a stimulating and affectionate atmosphere for learning in the home and in
    the school;
2. interactions and educational resources that broaden the initial conditions and
    favor successful and significant learning by the children;

3. management of strategies of mediation by the family and teachers;
4. methodologies adapted to the development of competencies in the domain of language and of logical-mathematical thought;
5. strengthening of educational management within the schools.

Program Content Lines Developed with School Teams

Affective development, social abilities, and formation of values. Parents and teachers used attitudes and educational resources to generate a social-affective climate adapted to the needs of children and adolescents, to the exercise of social ability, and to the acquisition of principles of respect, autonomy, and cooperation with others.

Development of language and of logical-mathematical thought. Teams worked on the revision of educational practices, teaching materials, and programs. Skills were related to the need to understand and interpret the world in order to act efficaciously, using previous experiences and formal knowledge.

Work coordinated with the family. Provisions were made to incorporate the family into the actions to improve the conditions in which their children learn.

Educational management. The directors and technical heads of the schools were trained regarding the management, monitoring, and evaluation of the school's educational project, the use of educational resources and relations with the family in order to improve the students' achievements.

Educational Resources for Training and the Schools

The program contributed manuals and guides on language, mathematics, and social-affective relations for teachers to use with their students in the classroom. Books were provided for the development of techniques of participation in school and in the classroom, simulation games for the training and broadening of school teams and for conducting the educational project. Folders and guides were supplied to families for their educational work in the home and their participation in the class meetings.

Results of Intervention

Teachers and classroom practices. Feelings of competence and self-esteem in teachers increased significantly because they felt able to generate cordial and stimulating climates for their students. They created learning guides and elaborated classroom projects for language and mathematics in the various grades. They incorporated the daily life of their students, and utilized the educational materials that they had received from other learning programs (P.900, PME, MECE). Nonetheless, the changes were slow. As with the former programs, teachers also followed traditional practices of teaching, resulting in confusion and gaps in the achievement and authoritarian styles of relationship between the teacher and students.

School–family relations. There was an increased disposition to incorporate the families of pupils in school activities. In some schools, teachers and administrators began to perceive parents as having a role as educators, to recognize their knowledge and to attend to their educational needs. However, in others, the lack of confidence and fear of the controlling role that parents could acquire over educational processes persisted.

Mothers and educational practices. The majority of participating mothers tried to stimulate and aid their children in their homework and school activities. They took initiatives in order to help the teachers in their work, and they dared to conduct some parent meetings that included the teachers, extending these activities to those of other organizations outside of the schools.

Achievements of the students in the fourth year of primary school. At the end of two years, of the sixteen schools, eleven showed advances in the results of SIMCE exams of the fourth grade students. Eight of the schools achieved advances greater than the average of schools in the region. One of these schools stood out because it was classified in the highest national percentages, reaching the level of achievement of the private schools. Two schools with less vulnerable populations increased their achievement an average of 10 points and one of them also approached the results of the private schools. Taking into account that it is more difficult to increase achievement significantly with higher initial conditions, this result becomes significant.

What factors acted on the three schools that fell in their percentages and in the two that maintained low scores? The most significant advances took place when a director assumed educational leadership and administered educational resources as a function of the students' achievements. In these schools teachers frequently met to exchange educational experiences. Directors and teachers were not afraid to incorporate parents into the process. In the schools that improved at the average rate of the region, the director delegated actions with an attentive but distant style of supervision. The teaching teams met occasionally. The times and style of relations with the family depended on each teacher, and were focused on the repair of the infrastructure or acquisition/reproduction of educational materials. Finally, the schools that had declining results (three schools) and no advances (two schools) appeared to be characterized by directors playing a bureaucratic role. They were more interested in public relations with the town and more preoccupied with the maintenance of order and control inside the school, emphasizing administrative requirements, and ignoring the possible collaboration of the mothers.

Items for Reflection

The programs presented make the importance of equity in educational quality visible, and require strong and sustained financing to make possible the advances in the learning of the least favored students. In the case of Learning Is Sweet, the average unit direct cost per year per beneficiary in this program is $514.70. If the direct and indirect population of children impacted by the program is taken into account, the average unit cost per child is around $20 per year.[2]

The decision of investing to reduce inequity requires understanding that the change occurs slowly, because it is a change of cultural models, of governing principles.

In the Learning Is Sweet program, the poor sector families showed not only their sensitivity to assuming their educational responsibilities, but also their capacity to carry them out. Nevertheless, it was the schools that decided the areas in which they could develop their educational capacities. It is therefore necessary to ligitimate the families' educational role and therefore their rights and responsibilities in the formal education of their children.

Moreover, the directors' management of the schools with difficult conditions in both programs shows that in addition to continuous training of teachers, a specific high level training of school directors is required.

The policy decisions to approach equity also must consider the importance of making visible the role of ethical principles and values in the distinct levels of society. The educational system has a fundamental place, stimulating the learning of ethical attitudes and behaviors related to respect for differences, non-discrimination, autonomy, and solidary cooperation. It is this that could re-situate its relevance in the interrelation with the achievement of cognitive, affective and social competencies and contribute to making equity a motor of society's development.

Notes

1. The Rural MECE Program is the comprehensive program implemented by the central Ministry to attend to the needs of the rural schools with one, two, or three teachers. The program includes training and technical assistance by Ministry supervisors, specialized assistance in curricular areas, improvement of school infrastructure, provision of educational resources (libraries and textbooks), and the organization of meetings among teachers of different schools in order to break the isolation experienced by rural teachers.

2. In the program there were twenty-five indirect beneficiaries for each direct beneficiary or participant. Learning Is Sweet was implemented among 242 adults (teachers and parents) who are considered the direct beneficiaries. All of the students are considered as indirect beneficiaries, as well as the teachers and parents who attended the activities in the different schools without having participated in the training sessions of the program itself.

References

Cardemil, C., and M. Latorre. 1992. *El programa de las 900 escuelas: ejes de la gestión y evaluación de su impacto.* UNESCO: Santiago de Chile. Marzo.
———. 1997. *Informe final. Procesos y resultados del programa mejorando la calidad de los aprendizajes: Un desafío para la familia y la escuela. Aprender es Dulce.* Santiago de Chile: CIDE.

————, et al. 1994. "Evaluación de lo no formal en el programa de las 900 escuelas." In *Cooperación internacional y desarrollo de la educación*, ed. M. Gajardo. Santiago de Chile: ASDI, AGCI, CIDE.

Cox, C. 1997. *La reforma de la educación chilena: contextos, contenidos, implementación.* Santiago de Chile: Ministerio de Educación, MECE.

Cox, C., and C. Jara. 1989. *Datos básicos para la discusión de políticas en educación (1977–1988)* Santiago de Chile: CIDE-FLACSO.

Filp, J. 1994. "Todos los niños aprenden. Evaluaciones del P-900." In *Cooperación internacional y desarrollo de la educación*, ed. M. Gajardo.

Gajardo, M. 1994. Cooperacion internacional y desarrollo de la educacion. Santiago de Chile: ASDI, AGCI, CIDE.

García Huidobro, J.E. 1997. "Perspectivas de la educación escolar." In *Educación escolar 2000.*

García Huidobro, J.E., and C. Jara. 1994. "El programa de las 900 escuelas." In *Cooperación y desarrollo de la educación*, ed. M. Gajardo.

Latorre, M. 1992–93. *Evaluación de rendimiento escolar de los alumnos del programa de las 900 escuelas.* Santiago de Chile: CIDE.

MINEDUC. 1997. *Programa de mejoramiento de la calidad de las escuelas básicas de sectores pobres. Programa de las 900 escuelas. Datos de estadistica.*

MINEDUC, División de Educación General. Orientaciones. 1998. *Rediseño y metas del P-900.* Enero.

15

Sylvia Schmelkes

Policies Against School Failure in Mexico—An Overview

The Context

Basic education in Mexico has been structurally reformed in the last few years. In 1992, the National Agreement for the Modernization of Basic and Normal Education decentralized basic and normal education, reformed the curriculum, and upgraded teaching conditions. In 1993, the General Law of Education obligated the government to provide one year of preschool education and extended compulsory education from six years of primary education (ages six to fourteen at the most) to nine years of basic education, including three years of lower secondary school.

In decentralization, the federal government has retained the definition of national norms for basic and normal education (mainly, but not exclusively, in curriculum), evaluation, and compensation among the states. The latter means that the federal government must invest more and develop special programs in the states that lag behind the national mean in the various indicators of educational development at the basic level.

In primary education curriculum, a "back to basics" approach probably best defines the direction of the reform, with a much stronger emphasis being placed in reading, writing, and arithmetic. Perhaps the most notable activity of the Ministry of Education during the last few years has been the publication of a considerable number of high-quality free textbooks for all children at the primary level (free textbooks have been available since 1961—but these constitute a completely new version). There are materials for activities in mathematics, didactic guides for teachers, books for classroom libraries, and so forth.

In teaching conditions, the government upgraded teachers' working conditions and salaries, reformed initial training institutions and curriculum, and emphasized in-service training. The first important modification was the establishment of a horizontal teaching career, which allows for both economic improvement and professional recognition of teachers who have an adequate to good performance (as measured through classroom planning, pupil assignment, peda-gogical knowledge, and student achievement) while remaining as classroom teachers. In 1996, 300 Teacher Centers, supplied with computers, the Inter-net, library, educational videos, televisions, and videocassette recorders, were opened all over the nation as a mechanism for making in-service training opportunities more accessible to teachers in the different regions. The ur-gently needed reform of initial training (normal schools) was launched in September 1997. In this chapter, I describe persisting problems in basic edu-cation and three programs that have been carried out during the last nine years, from 1990 to date.

Persisting Problems

Mexico has suffered two main problems in the development of its basic educa-tion, and those problems still persist. They are the quality of education and the distribution of educational opportunities.

Quality of Education

Direct measures of quality—what children learn in school—are unavailable on a national basis. Nevertheless, several partial studies consistently turn up alarming results: on average, children always fail whatever they are tested on (40 percent is the median of these results) (Guevara 1991; Tirado 1997; Martínez Rizo and Escalera 1990; Schmelkes 1996; among many others).

Indirect measures of quality offer us a nationwide picture of the problem:

1. According to census information of 1995, 8 percent of Mexican children between six and fourteen years of age (primary school age) are not in school. The great majority of these 1.5 million children inhabit very small rural communities (under 100 inhabitants) or belong to families of migrant agricultural workers and travel with their parents during a large part of the year. (The number of small, rural communities without schools is growing.) Nevertheless, for a system that has established nine years of compulsory education, primary school coverage still represents a serious challenge.

2. The national rate of repetition for the primary level is not high when com-pared to that of other Latin American countries: 7.8 percent in 1994–95, and it has remained stable for the last three years. Repetition in the first grade—traditionally double the primary level average—has been brought down from 17.6 percent in 1990–91 to 11.1 percent in 1996–97.

3. Inter-cycle dropout rates in primary school are also low when compared to those of other similar countries: 5.3 percent in 1990–91, and an estimate of 2.9 percent in 1996–97. Nevertheless, when one adds repetition to inter-cycle drop-outs and considers the intra-cycle dropouts, one arrives at the following.

4. Terminal efficiency rates (percentage of sixth grade graduates with respect to newly enrolled first grade students six years before—an indicator based on apparent cohorts) are still very low: 80 percent in 1995–96. This means that twenty out of every one hundred students do not finish their six grades of primary education in six years.

Inequality in the Distribution

Opportunities differ for students with different socioeconomic characteristics. The system is responsible for this inequality in at least three aspects:

1. Educational opportunities have traditionally expanded following the trickle-down model (from the richer to the poorer areas, from the urban to the rural, from the mestizo to the Indian, and so on);
2. There are evident and alarming differences in the quality of school buildings, learning materials, training of teachers, supervision, communication of the individual school with the system as a whole;
3. Even when the material aspects are similar, schools operate less satisfactorily when the community of reference is poorer—supply conforms to the characteristics of the demand.

Unequal primary school efficiency is shown in Table 15.1. Similarly, student achievement in urban middle class schools differs significantly from that in schools located in urban marginal areas, in rural developed areas, in rural marginal areas, and in indigenous communities. The difference is so large that sixth grade students in the poor urban, rural, and indigenous schools achieve lower, and sometimes much lower, scores on average than fourth grade students of urban middle class schools (Schmelkes 1996).

Uneven quality of the training of teachers and of their performance in the classroom has contributed to inadequate and unequally distributed educational opportunities, and has been getting worse during the last few years because of:

1. The deterioration of teacher salaries, which became an acute problem during the years of the economic crisis (1982–1990). Even though important efforts have been made to restore the buying power of teachers' salaries, the fact is that they are only just regaining their 1982 levels. During those long years, many teachers abandoned the profession. Many of those that stayed had to get another job within or outside the teaching profession. Many of them have no time to plan their classes.

2. The transformation of normal education into a third-level profession in 1994, requiring a full six-year high school education and four years of higher education. This happened precisely in the middle of the economic crisis, when

Table 15.1

Indirect Measures of Quality—National Average, a Rich and a Poor State, 1995–1996 (%)

	A richer state: Nuevo León	National average	A poorer state: Chiapas
Average repeticion	3.8	7.8	14.7
Repetition in first grade	7.0	10.9	15.1
Intra-cycle dropouts	1.4	2.9	4.9
Terminal efficiency	89.6	80.0	48.2

Source: Secretaría de Educación Pública. 1997. *Informe de labores 1996–97.* México: Secretaría de Educación Pública.

teaching salaries lost their competitiveness with respect to other occupations. Enrollment in normal schools decreased drastically after this reform, and many lay teachers have had to be hired for the more remote rural areas. Besides, those entering the teaching profession are increasingly those who have been rejected by their first choice, which is a university education.

Recent Policies and Programs for Combating Failure and Improving Quality in Primary Schools

A "solidarity" program to help poor children begun in 1990, a 1991 program to aid education in the poorest regions in Mexico, and a 1993–94 recommendation for automatic promotion from the first to the second grade have been in effect to permit their tentative evaluation. A new intersectorial program, Programa de Educación, Salud y Alimentación (PROGRESA) for combating poverty, which includes education, has just been launched, but will not be analyzed here.

Programa "Niños de Solidaridad"

In 1990 the president directly set up a program, called Solidaridad, aimed at combating extreme poverty. One of the projects within this program was the Programa Escuela Digna (Respectable School Program), which established community committees of parents and teachers who administered new resources and contributed labor and materials to improve the village or neighborhood school. (During the crisis decade—the 1980s—capital investment in education was practically canceled.) In 1990, 22,365 schools were rehabilitated in this manner. Mexico then had around 90,000 primary schools.

Immediately following this program, the Programa Niños de Solidaridad (Children in Solidarity Program) was established. The aim of this program was to help the poorest children finish their primary education. The program operated with almost complete independence from the Ministry of Education. It consisted of the following components:

1. Very poor communities were selected. These communities had to have a Committee for Escuela Digna that would also operate this program, and the schools had to be complete public primary schools.
2. The children of grades 1, 2, and 3 elected between twelve and twenty-four children who, according to them, needed the benefits of the program. This election was reviewed by the Committee. Only one child per family was allowed.
3. The families of children thus elected were given each month both $118 Mexican pesos—then the equivalent of US$40—per child, and a basket of basic foodstuffs for the family.
4. The elected children had to attend the nearest clinic for vaccinations and nutrition checking at least once every three months. The program also asked the elected children to maintain average grades of 8 on a scale of 1 to 10. This, however, created many problems for the teachers, who felt responsible for taking the scholarship away from a child who needed it if they graded low. At its peak, the program aided approximately 600,000 children.

Two studies were carried out to evaluate this program. The first (Rosas, Martínez, and Fortoul 1992) evaluated its operation. The second (Carasco 1994) also evaluated its operation, but in addition analyzed effects on permanence and achievement. They found certain flaws in the distribution of both the scholarships and the baskets of basic foodstuffs, and in the operation of the health clinics, which are generally understaffed and lack both equipment and medicines, and can therefore not provide an adequate service. Nevertheless, the problems of the actual distribution of the benefits of the program are no greater than could be expected in such a complex arrangement. The main problems are found more in the conception of the program than in its actual operation. For example, limiting the benefits to at most twenty-four children in the school is a mistake. In fact, the program seems to assume that poverty is something relative in nature, not absolute, when it is very well known that small rural communities in mountainous rain-fed districts live in poverty, and that the difference between families is so small that it does not justify such a selection. Whole communities should be selected, not individual children. In spite of this, the second study finds that children that receive the scholarship always perform lower on the tests applied than the rest of the groups involved. The differences are not large and no significant tests were carried out. Nevertheless, in Puebla, children with scholarships scored 5.88 on average (on a scale of 10), while children without scholarships scored 6.81. In Oaxaca—the other state studied—the differences are much smaller (6.34 vs. 6.43), but nevertheless in favor of the children who did not receive the scholarship. This study concludes that in fact the program selects the poorest children, but that it does not benefit all of the children in extreme poverty in the community. In some cases the study found that the children who received the scholarships were teased by other children. (The new program, called PRO-GRESA, is selecting whole communities and eliminating individual families who do not need the benefits.)

The Solidaridad program does seem to have an effect on the permanence of the children in school. The second study (Carrasco 1994) finds that the children are scared of losing the scholarship. Unfortunately, no hard data are available on the Program's impact on perseverance.

But perhaps the more important critical conclusion drawn from the study of the operation of this program (Rosas, Martínez, and Fortoul 1992) is the fact that this is a program aimed at attacking factors on the demand side of the educational equation. The schools, the principals, the teachers, and the ordinary functioning of the primary school system are left untouched. The situation is so absurd that, instead of completing incomplete primary schools—schools that do not offer the six grades of primary education and which are found in some of the poorest rural communities in the country—in order to ensure that primary school completion is possible, the program simply erases them from the list of eligible communities. Rosas et al. found serious operation problems—mainly acute teacher absenteeism—in many of the primary schools where Solidaridad operates. A program that only attacks the demand side of the educational equation and does not improve the capacity of the educational system to offer an attractive, relevant, and quality school program will only be "buying" the children's attendance without ensuring that they will learn in school. The new intersectorial program, PROGRESA, is in the main repeating this one-sided strategy. (Although some resources for strengthening the supply side are foreseen, this is not the focus of the program.)

Programa de Atención al Rezago Educativo (PARE)

Mexico received a loan from the World Bank in 1991 in order to combat school failure in the four poorest states of the country, establishing the Program for Remedying Educational Deficits (PARE). The program was to spend $352 million over a period of five years. It was designed to benefit all primary schools—except middle-class urban schools—in the states of Chiapas, Oaxaca, Guerrero, and Hidalgo (a poor state, but not the poorest; for political reasons, Michoacán, which should have been the fourth state, was not included).

PARE was aimed at improving the supply side of the educational equation. Several different components were gradually put into effect over a period of four years of operation. These were:

Educational materials. The program defined packages of educational materials aimed at aiding the teaching process (dictionaries, maps, globes, balls, typewriters, duplicators, overhead projectors, and such). The schools located in the extreme poverty areas should receive three times as much material as other schools.

Educational supplies for the children. Children received notebooks, pencils, rulers, also according to the degree of poverty of the community; the program gave more to the poorest.

Texts for education in indigenous languages. The bank financed the writing of books for learning to read and write in eight indigenous languages: the two most important in each state. Due to the time it took for the in-site supervised authoring of these books by indigenous teachers, the books were not made available until 1994.

School libraries. The program extended a previously existing project for school libraries and distributed 159 books (90 for children and the rest for parents and teachers) to multigrade schools and 295 to complete schools which offer six grades of primary education.

Distribution infrastructure. Forty-three storage rooms were built in strategic places in order to make the distribution of education supplies and textbooks more efficient.

Teacher training. Courses were designed for regular primary school teachers and for indigenous primary school teachers. Using the cascade method, the courses offered had a total of 198,000 attendees. The program included a small stipend for transportation costs.

School infrastructure and equipment. An amount was designated to build new classrooms and to equip them, as well as to rehabilitate schools and to fortify those in dangerous sites (against earthquakes, mainly).

Strengthening of school supervision. Supervisors were given a stipend to cover traveling costs to schools, conditional on proof of the signature of the school principal and the community authority, that the school had been visited three times a year. The sector supervisors (one level up) were given two vehicles that were meant to facilitate supervisor visits to schools. Supervision offices were built and equipped. And courses were given for supervisors and school principals.

Incentives for teachers. Teachers working in very remote communities with no services were given an incentive consisting of a 100 percent increase in their salaries. This incentive, however, belongs to the school, not to the teacher. When the teacher leaves the school, for whatever reason, the extra salary incentive stays with the school. Teachers had to demonstrate good attendance by having the community authorities testify in writing to their statement in order to receive the incentive. Teachers were asked to work in the afternoon with children who were falling behind, with adults, or to divide their groups between morning and afternoon in the case of multigrade schools.

Evaluation. The project included an evaluation of impact and a cost-effectiveness study, to which we will refer.

The project was complex and faced several operational difficulties. A new structure had to be set up for administering the project both at the central level and in each of the states. Some of the main operational difficulties are: (1) Administration of the project (and particularly the acquisition and distribution of the goods and services the project included) took precedence over the educational aspects. In fact, the academic coordination of the project, which should have been in the ordinary structure of the Ministry of Education, was practically lost during the four years of operation. (2) The different components actually operated as separate projects, with very little coordination between them. Thus, teachers were not trained to use the educational materials that were given to the schools; the incentive for teachers had very little to do with their teaching performance as such; the supervisors had very superficial information on the scope of the project, and so forth.

Moreover, the context in which the schools operate, and the way they operate, are not taken into account by the project. In rural schools teachers are often absent and their mobility is high, though incentives for teachers have helped to remedy this situation. The communities in general do not know their rights with respect to education or how to enforce them. Teachers who are sent to these communities have probably just finished their training and have no experience. Actual teaching time is between two and a half and three hours (instead of the official four hours), and the number of days on which children have classes in a year is between 80 and 150 (instead of the official 200). In multigrade schools (the majority of rural schools are multigrade), this time is distributed among the different grades, though more time is allotted to the first two grades. The program was not designed with these pressing problems in mind (Troncoso 1996; Ezpeleta and Weiss 1994).

An analysis of repetition, dropout, and terminal efficiency rates for the states in which the program operated between 1991–92 and 1995–96 does not allow us to conclude that the program had a particular impact. In Table 15.2, data for the four states that participated in the program, as well as the state of Michoacán, which is similar in poverty levels and educational development to the other four, are given.

A greater rate of improvement in the less developed states is natural, since low rates are more sensitive to any type of policy or reform in education, even at the national level, so we cannot attribute the higher rates of improvement in the PARE states, with respect to the national average, to the program itself. When we compare the PARE states with Michoacán, however, we discover greater improvements in Chiapas and Guerrero in first grade repetition rates, and improvements in all the states with the exception of Michoacán in dropout rates. Nevertheless, the absence of significant differences in average repetition rates and in terminal efficiency rates between Michoacán and the PARE states leads us to state that, at best, four years of operation of a program such as this are not enough to impact these indicators of educational development.

Muñoz Izquierdo (1996) analyzed the effects of PARE on educational attainment. Base line information is statistically equivalent, both in Spanish and in mathematics, for the PARE states and for Michoacán (control state), with the exception of the indigenous schools, where Michoacán is higher in both cases. He

Table 15.2

Evolution of Education Development Indicators in the Four PARE States, in Michoacán and in México as a Whole, 1991–1992, 1995–1996 (%)

	1st grade repetition 1991–92	1st grade repetition 1995–96	Average repetition 1991–92	Average repetition 1995–96	Dropout rate 1991–92	Dropout rate 1995–96	Terminal efficiency 1991–92	Terminal efficiency 1995–96
Chiapas	24.8	15.1	15.2	14.7	13.9	4.9	40.3	48.2
Guerrero	24.3	16.4	12.8	13.3	8.1	4.4	52.0	61.1
Hidalgo	19.3	11.5	11.3	8.3	3.1	2.1	79.4	90.3
Oaxaca	22.1	17.3	17.1	13.5	6.4	3.6	58.4	70.4
Michoacán	19.9	13.3	12.3	9.7	3.7	4.8	66.1	77.8
National Average	17.1	10.9	9.8	7.8	4.6	3.0	71.6	80.0

Sources: Secretaría de Educación Pública. 1997. *Informe de labores 1996–97.* México: Secretaría de Educación Pública. Troncoso, E. (ed). 1996. *Programa para abatir el rezago educativo: operatividad y efectos educativos.* México: Secretaría de Educación Pública.

found that the poorest schools—indigenous, rural, and community courses, and one-teacher schools in very small, dispersed rural communities—improved their achievement over the three years, whereas this does not occur in Michoacán. In some of these cases, differences become significant in favor of the four PARE states. Nevertheless, the results of the test never go above 50 percent, with the exception of the second grade, which achieved 60 percent in Spanish and mathematics from the beginning. Thus, it can be said that PARE impacts educational attainment in the poorer schools, but not enough as to achieve average passing grades among the PARE students.

Agreement Number 165

For the 1993–94 school year, an agreement recommended that children should not be allowed to fail the first grade and should be promoted to the second grade of primary school. Teachers were asked to give the children two years for learning to read and write, not one, as is traditional. Thus, the concomitant suggestion to principals was that they should allow the same teacher in charge of the children in grade one to follow them on to grade two.

As we have seen, repetition in the first grade has always been much higher than the average repetition in primary school. This is due to the fact that the only grade in which there is a perfectly clear and measurable terminal objective is grade one, where children are supposed to learn to read and write. Children who had not achieved this aim by the month of May (the school year runs from mid-August to mid-July) were failed in the first grade and made to repeat it.

This traditional practice is unsound because children learn at different speeds and many children who do not learn to read and write in one year will most surely do so in two. Children who come from a non-literate environment are most likely to take longer to learn the basic skills of reading and writing.

Moreover, repetition leads to dropping out. Repetition makes children feel ill at ease with their younger classmates, and this increases the possibility of repeated failures, so that the problem, instead of being solved, is aggravated. Opportunity costs of attending school are greater for the parents, the older the child is. So there is a greater probability that repeaters—especially multiple repeaters—will abandon school when they are twelve to thirteen years old without having completed their primary education (Muñoz Izquierdo et al. 1979).

An automatic promotion policy can be considered successful if repetition rates in the first grade decrease and do not increase in the second grade. Available information seems to demonstrate, however, that even though there is a tendency for schools in certain states to fall back again into traditional practices, the policy was in fact successful and should be more forcefully applied. Table 15.3 illustrates this.

Data corresponding to states where the problem is considerably larger than the national average show a similar reduction of rates of second grade repetition

Table 15.3

National Average—First Grade and Second Grade Repetition Rates Before and After the Recommendation Not to Fail Children in First Grade

School year	First grade repetition rate (%)	Second grade repetition rate (%)
1991–92	17.1	11.2
1992–93	16.5	10.2
1993–94	12.6	11.2
1994–95	10.9	10.8
1995–96	10.9	10.3

Sources: Secretaría de Educación Púlbica. 1997. *Informe de labores: 1996–97.* México: Secretaría de Educación Pública. Secretaría de Educación Pública. 1996. *Informe de labores: 1995–96.* México: Secretaría de Educación Pública.

in the 1993–94 school year, and in some cases in the 1994–95 school year. However, Chiapas, for example, reduced its rate from 24 percent in the year before the agreement to 17.4 percent and then again to 12.8 percent, but brought it up again in 1995–96 to 15.1 percent. Nevertheless, the rate never reached its original level, and second grade repetition rates did not increase.

Final Remarks

I have reviewed three very different attempts to combat school failure. The first has to do with a policy measure that recommends teachers not to fail students between first and second grades. This is absolutely costless, and is paradoxically the one that shows the highest results.

The second is a program (Solidaridad) aimed at combating the factors on the demand side that affect access and permanence in school, but that does not address the quality of educational supply. Thus, children may be motivated to go to school, but if the quality of rural education remains the same, these children will face a situation where teachers are often absent, where the school is closed because the teacher has left and has not been replaced, and where in general teaching is teacher-centered, repetitive, uninteresting, and irrelevant to these children.

Extreme poverty in Mexico has been growing during the last two decades. Undoubtedly, measures aimed at ensuring that students are well fed and that they do not have to work are needed for a significant number of both rural and urban communities. However, the unit chosen should be the community (given that poverty can be defined in absolute terms), and steps should be taken to significantly improve the widely documented appalling quality of educational supply in poor communities.

The third program reviewed (PARE) is a very ambitious, complex, and expensive program that addresses many of the known factors on the supply side that affect the quality of educational results without addressing the problems of the population. This program has been revised and expanded and is now operating in all the marginal municipalities in the country, financed by additional loans from the World Bank and the Inter-American Development Bank. In more recent versions, it has incorporated early childhood education (a non-formal program aimed at parents) and adult education (literacy and basic education). Nevertheless, though we can say that some effects are visible in educational achievement, particularly for children attending the poorest schools, four years seems not to have been enough to impact repetition and dropout rates in the four poorest states of the country.

In general, school failure among children living in poor rural and indigenous regions in poor states has proven to be a more difficult problem to solve than was originally imagined by the designers of the programs.

Mexico wishes to combat failure. The main objectives for the primary school level of the 1995 educational program that now orients educational policy (Poder Ejecutivo Federal 1995) are the improvement of quality, equity, and relevance. Clearly, the achievement of universal basic education has to do with our capacity for dealing with failure in very well defined sectors of the population: the indigenous communities, the very small dispersed rural communities, the urban-marginal settlements, and the rural migrant workers. These groups probably represent around 90 percent of coverage problems and a similar percentage of school failure.

We are learning to combat failure. The educational ingredient of these programs should have priority over the administrative one. Closer follow-up mechanisms including community and classroom observation should be an integral part of evaluation procedures. But perhaps the most important question to consider has to do with the appropriation of the program on the part of principals, teachers, and communities. Greater participation of both teachers and community members in the identification of the problems of each school and in the definition of what they need in order to solve them would perhaps make implementation of programs aimed at combating school failure more complex, but would probably lead to faster and more lasting results.

Bibliography

Carrasco Altamirano, Alma, ed. 1994. *Evaluación de aprendizajes escolares. Programa Niños de Solidaridad.* Puebla: Benemérita Universidad Autónoma de Puebla. Mimeo.

Ezpeleta, J., and E. Weiss. 1994. *Programa para abatir el rezago educativo. Evaluación cualitativa de impacto. Informe final.* Mexico: Departamento de Investigaciones Educativas del Centro de Investigación y Estudios Avanzados del Instituto Politécnico Nacional.

Guevara N.G. 1991. "México: ¿Un País de Reprobados?" *Nexos* 14: 162.

Martínez Rizo, F., and M.E. Escalera. 1990. *La educación básica en México: Diagnóstico de la educación básica en Aguascalientes 1983.* Mexico: Secretaría de

Educación Pública, Consejo Nacional Técnico de la Educación.

Mexico. Secretaría de Educación Pública. 1997. *Informe de Labores: 1996–97.* Mexico: Secretaría de Educación Pública.

Muñoz Izquierdo, C., ed. 1996. *Principales resultados y recomendaciones de la evaluación del PARE.* Mexico: Centro de Estudios Educativos. Mimeo.

Muñoz Izquierdo, C., P.G. Rodriguez, M.P. Restrepo, and C. Borrani. 1979. "El síndrome del fracaso escolar y el abandono del sistema educativo." *Revista Latinoamericana de Estudios Educativos* 9, no. 3.

Poder Ejecutivo Federal. 1995. *Programa de Desarrollo Educativo 1995–2000.* Mexico: Poder Ejecutivo Federal.

Poder Legislativo Federal. 1993. *Ley General de Educación.* Mexico: Secretaría de Educación Pública.

Rosas, L., S. Martínez, and B. Fortoul. 1992. *Los efectos y el funcionamiento del Programa Niños de Solidaridad: Estudio exploratorio sobre la primera etapa del programa.* Mexico: Centro de Estudios Educativos. Mimeo.

Schmelkes, S., ed. 1996. *The Quality of Primary Education: A Case Study of Puebla, Mexico.* Paris: International Institute for Educational Planning, Centro de Estudios Educativos.

Tirado, F. 1997. *El modelo histórico: Un ejercicio didáctico para su aplicación.* Ph.d. dissertation for Doctorate in Education. Aguascalientes: Universidad Autónoma de Aguascalientes.

Troncoso, E., ed. 1996. *Programa para abatir el Rezago Educativo PARE: Operatividad y efectos educativos.* Mexico: Secretaría de Educación Pública. Mimeo.

Part IV
Decentralization

16

ANA MARÍA BRIGIDO

Decentralization of Primary Education in Argentina

Introduction

Argentina operates under a federal system of government. The Constitution grants the provinces a broad political, economic, and cultural autonomy. In education, however, there exists a long-standing tradition of central government hegemony. Among the frequent attempts to decentralize the educational system there are two key events to be considered in this chapter: (1) the transfer of the primary schools to the provinces from the National Ministry of Education in 1978, and (2) the passing of the Federal Education Act in 1993.

Our starting point is a strict definition of decentralization, which goes beyond the simple decentralization of education functions. It implies the shift of authority over financial, administrative, and pedagogical matters to lower levels of government (Fiske 1996). Its main advantages are: (a) the reduction of public spending; (b) a more efficient decision-making process; (c) improvement in the quality of education; and (d) the democratization of the system.

In fact, the relationship between decentralization and the advantages attributed to it is not obvious. On the contrary, in those countries with strong regional disparities, dysfunctional effects may arise, such as the danger of disarticulation, segmentation, and fewer financial resources for the system (Sánchez Martínez 1992). This is especially true for Argentina, which has different levels of regional development. There are densely populated areas, like the Federal District (Buenos Aires) and the Pampas region where 70 percent of the population lives; and there are sparsely inhabited areas, like the South of the country (Patagonia). The two former regions enjoy greater fiscal autonomy since it is there that most of the Argentine wealth is concentrated. The Northeastern and Northwestern areas, instead, are poorly developed; they lack economic resources to finance the education system as well as trained personnel to manage it. Consequently, the quality of education deteriorates. In these regions there are few possibilities of adjusting education to regional needs, and democratic participation in managing the system is difficult to accomplish.

Development of the Decentralization Process

Relationship Between the Federal Government and the Provinces

In Argentina the relationships between the central and the provincial governments are complex and difficult. In educational matters the powers of the federal government and provinces are ambiguously defined in the Constitution. This ambiguity has led to overlapping of functions between the two levels of government as to the setting of a national system and a provincial system with full powers to manage primary, secondary, and higher education. Even though the Constitution grants the provinces autonomy to manage primary education, some of them were, and still are, unable to do so due to lack of technical and financial resources. This forces the National Government to permanently assist the most needy provinces through subsidies and the creation of schools (Kisilevsky 1990). In this way, the central power exerts strong control over education throughout the country. A centralized system thus developed, dominated by the National Ministry of Education with provincial governments playing a minor role.

Transfer of Education Service to the Provinces

The demands of the provinces for the full enforcement of the federal system in education dates back to last century. After several unsuccessful attempts, all primary schools depending on the National Ministry of Education were finally transferred to the provinces and to the Federal District in 1978. Even though the military regime justified this measure as the need to adjust primary education to the characteristics and requirements of each region, most analysts agree that the only aim was financial: to reduce spending and to balance the accounts of the central government. Despite this mainly economic reason, the measure was the first step toward putting decentralization principles into operation. The provinces had to undertake the control of all primary education and to incorporate a significant number of schools and teachers.

The second transfer of educational services run by central government took place between 1992 and 1994, when the provinces took over secondary schools and higher non-university institutions. As in 1978, the need to balance fiscal accounts played an important role, but in this instance the legitimacy of the measure was respected since it was undertaken by a democratic government and accepted by all the districts.

The Current Institutional Framework

The Federal Education Act passed in 1993 defines a new structure for the educational system, regulates the functioning of all the levels except the university level, and clearly establishes the roles of central and district governments to rule and manage education.

Provisions of the Federal Education Act

The Federal Education Act defines the Argentine educational system as: (a) Preschool Education, comprising kindergarten for children between three and five years old; attendance of five-year-old children is compulsory; (b) compulsory Basic General Education (EGB), lasting nine years with three cycles; (c) Multi-Track High School Education, which follows EGB and lasts a minimum of three years and has various technical and academic tracks; (d) Higher (University) Education, which grants first professional and academic degrees; and (e) Post-Graduate Education. The governance and administration of the educational system is concurrently the responsibility of central and local powers. Such administration must be organized following these criteria: national unity, democratization, decentralization and federalization, participation, equity, articulation, transformation and innovation. In addition to other functions, the central government must: (a) set the common basic contents of curricula for different levels; (b) promote the decentralization of educational service and provide the support required by local governments; (c) develop technical and financial cooperation programs to foster educational quality and get equivalent achievements in the different regions; (d) promote and organize a teacher training network; (e) assess the operation of the system in all districts through a special evaluation system and periodic quality control. The district authorities must plan, organize, and manage the system in their territories, approve curricula, organize and run public schools, and also evaluate the system.

The Federal Act gives a relative autonomy to the "school unit" to prepare its own plan (known as an "institutional project") and acknowledges the right of the "educational community" to participate in the management of the "school unit" and in the drafting of its project. The existence of these regulations, however, does not guarantee their enforcement.

The new law states that central government investment in the education system is a priority that must be carried out with the resources designated in the national and local budgets. This investment must be increased during five years at a rate of 20 percent per year as from the 1993 budget. The difference between this target and the available resources must be financed with direct taxes imposed on the wealthiest taxpayers and specifically allotted to education. The Act further states that the central power must finance special educational development programs undertaken by districts in order to overcome educational emergencies—such as insufficient number of teachers to satisfy demand; deterioration of school buildings; and high rates of failures and/or dropouts—to make up for regional educational disparities, to face the problems of underprivileged areas, and/or to put into practice educational experiences of national interest. These programs must be financed with budgetary funds, or with special allocations to be used for this purpose.

Legal Provisions at District Level

Because they are autonomous, the provinces and the Federal District have passed their own laws to govern the educational systems in their districts. In most cases, these laws have been modified to adjust to Federal Act provisions and emphasize decentralization. However, there are some noticeable differences among them. In some districts decentralization is broad, giving some autonomy at the school level to modify the curriculum and to purchase and manage property, if so stated in its "institutional project." In other districts, instead, the laws recommend that decentralization be applied only if it is "convenient or possible," or that it be adopted to define some operative issues, but keeping centralization in legal matters. The bodies that govern the systems vary from province to province. In some districts the structure is dual-headed, with overlapping of functions among the Ministry and the Local Councils of Education. These councils may have consultative or executive functions, and in some cases they are the top governing bodies of the system.

In order to make decentralization effective, most of the districts have established special provisions, which have been unevenly implemented. These provisions are: (a) creation of local or regional school boards accountable for managing education, with different degrees of autonomy depending on the province; (b) establishment of school or institutional boards that have consultation functions or some decision-making power, depending on the province; (c) empowerment of schools to formulate their "institutional project," which must include a proposed curriculum, standards of operation, and school rules; (d) participation of the "educational community" in the different kinds of boards through its representatives, who may be elected by direct or indirect voting.

Coordination of the System

The Federal Council of Culture and Education, which is in charge of unifying the national education system, increased in importance after the transfer carried out in 1978. It is composed of the minister of Education, who is the president of the Federal Council; the highest educational authority of each district; and two representatives from the Council of Universities. Its main functions are: (a) to advise on policies to ensure the harmonious cultural development of the country, the improvement of education as a whole, and the setting of priorities; (b) to coordinate and implement measures to put into effect the policies adopted in the different districts; (c) to set the basic standards for each level of education and the acknowledgement of courses of study, certificates, and degrees. The Federal Act confers new functions to the Federal Council, giving it a main role in the implementation and coordination of the education system.

Financing of the System

Resources for Education

The district governments have two types of resources for the funding of education: those provided by the district's own tax-collection and those coming from the federal sharing of taxes. The central government, in turn, has funds to finance compensatory policies, the provision of school equipment, and the training of teachers. Except for four districts—namely Federal District, Buenos Aires, Córdoba, and Santa Fe—which collect more money in taxes, the other districts have scarce resources and depend almost entirely on federal revenue sharing to finance their expenditure.

The funds provided through federal revenue sharing in a federal principle belong to the provinces but are collected by the central government. The centralized administration of those funds aims at profiting from economies of scale to compensate for the differences between districts. The revenue is distributed between the central government and the provinces (primary distribution); in turn, the sum corresponding to the districts is automatically distributed among them (secondary distribution) without a previous budget allocation. The operation of this mechanism of federal revenue sharing is a perpetual source of conflict, mainly because the secondary distribution coefficients are not established on the basis of clearly objective criteria and because there is a strong incentive to increase expenditure when the political costs of tax-collection are not borne by the provinces (FIEL 1993). In recent years, the revenue sharing system has been affected by the macroeconomic and social security crisis of the 1980s as well as by the degree of political kinship between the central and the local governments. Since in most provinces resources come from federal revenue sharing, the provision of the educational service is affected by the dispute between the central power and the districts about the right share on those resources. However, the funds coming from federal revenue sharing can be freely used by the provinces; the specific funds for education are determined by the budget laws of each district and frequently the programming of expenditures does not meet the educational demands.

An additional source of revenue for education is provided by the private sector, basically through Parents' Associations and private schools. There are no official statistics to estimate the total amount contributed by Parents' Associations, but in general it is not very significant.

The amount provided to the system by privately run schools has not been accurately estimated, although it is known that in some districts it is important. Some estimates show that the private expenditure on education at the primary and secondary school levels, in the Federal District, for instance, raised the public resources for the sector 82 percent; for Córdoba, the increase was 18 percent (Morduchowicz 1996a). In a poor district like Chaco, instead, there is almost no contribution from the private sector.

Expenditure on Education and Its Effectiveness

Expenditure on education must be placed within the frame of the general spending of each district. A characteristic of these expenditures is the lack of programming. On the other hand, the provinces show constant fiscal deficits, whereby they must constantly request assistance from the central government.

Table 16.1 shows that for all the districts as a whole, educational expenditures

Table 16.1

Selected Indicators of Spending on Education per District, 1993–1994 (%)

Regions and Districts	Total spending on education/ Total public spending	Total spending on education/ GDP	Spending on personnel/ Total spending on education	Spending on real investment/ Total spending on education	Spending on preschool and primary school level/Total spending on education	Current spending per student in primary school level (in US$)	Effective spending per student in primary school level (in US$)	Provincial own-resources/ Total spending
Total	25.4	3.0	80.6	2.5	50.7	—	—	625.8
Federal Capital	29.8	2.5	75.1	2.1	33.8	967.5	699.5	81.0
Pampas Region								
Buenos Aires	25.3	1.8	81.1	1.1	45.3	368.1	222.3	47.0
Córdoba	28.6	3.5	70.6	2.8	39.4	568.7	326.2	36.0
Entre Ríos	21.1	3.1	82.2	4.2	74.2	710.1	367.1	27.0
La Pampa	25.9	6.0	81.6	1.0	58.4	1,252.1	587.5	36.0
Santa Fe	30.2	3.4	76.6	0.0	59.2	693.2	403.3	41.0
Cuyo Region								
Mendoza	22.5	2.9	82.2	2.5	67.4	641.0	316.0	27.0
San Juan	29.4	5.3	88.5	0.3	61.2	869.2	349.4	9.0
San Luis	27.6	6.2	78.2	11.0	50.4	886.7	322.7	19.0
Northeastern Region								
Corrientes	31.0	4.6	95.9	1.6	56.3	595.8	264.2	8.0
Chaco	33.5	5.0	94.8	0.2	61.0	665.1	239.5	11.0
Formosa	18.9	5.8	94.6	0.6	56.9	675.1	227.9	5.0
Misiones	26.2	3.7	71.1	3.4	51.1	481.9	216.5	14.0

Northwestern Region							
Jujuy	21.2	4.8	92.2	3.1	53.4	565.9	255.4	23.0
Salta	21.8	3.4	88.3	3.0	56.9	531.1	168.9	20.0
Catamarca	25.5	7.2	96.5	0.3	57.1	1,056.9	341.9	7.0
La Rioja	20.1	7.2	97.2	0.7	46.4	927.0	326.2	4.0
Tucumán	21.5	3.1	70.7	4.9	71.0	670.2	328.4	26.0
Santiago del Estero	24.8	4.9	98.5	0.9	71.8	774.2	217.4	7.0
Patagonia Region							
Chubut	16.4	4.0	93.2	0.1	70.2	1,292.9	575.5	23.0
Neuquén	20.3	6.9	84.9	3.5	48.1	1,190.7	570.4	28.0
Río Negro	21.9	5.9	86.1	0.9	52.6	869.2	314.0	25.0
Santa Cruz	23.4	7.0	73.7	6.6	41.6	1,017.9	406.9	9.0
Tierra del Fuego	21.9	7.5	69.5	15.6	36.6	1,412.6	667.0	n/d

Source: Morduchowicz (1996a, Table 3), columns (1)–(8); FIEL (1993), p. 171, column (9).

are 25 percent of the total expenses of the provinces. Adding expenditures linked to the sector but carried out by other areas of government, which are not included as spending on education (school lunches, some school buildings, science and technology, etc.), the total expenditure on education would increase about 10 percent. However, if the expenditure on education is considered as a percentage of GDP for each district, it is only 3 percent. Considering the total spending, the amount for payment of salaries is very high. In contrast, investment expenditure is trifling, if any.

Expenditure per pupil is generally used as the indicator of the effort made by the state to provide education, but its value is limited. Higher expenditure per pupil does not guarantee higher educational quality. Morduchowicz (1996b) estimated the effectiveness of the expenditure per pupil on student achievement by including the population growth rate, the percentage of pupils who repeat a school grade, and the pupils' results in the National Quality Evaluation Tests implemented yearly by the Ministry of Education. He indicates that part of the effort made by the provinces to provide education is wasted. The greater ineffectiveness is observed in poorer districts.

Teachers' Salaries

The district governments are free to decide on teachers' salaries and they are responsible for personnel hiring, supervision, evaluation, and promotion. In addition, each district has its own Teacher By-Laws, which set teachers' rights and duties. There is a great disparity among districts regarding not only the amount and composition of salaries but also the norms that regulate labor relations in this sector. Both aspects are closely related.

The main rights granted by the teacher by-laws in almost all the provinces are the following: (a) the right to stability in their job; (b) paid leave of absence; (c) reassignment of tasks in case of illness or impairment, with no reduction in salary; (d) acknowledgement of the family members' needs; (e) fair and updated pension benefits upon retirement. These rights often clash with the objectives of the system, increase labor costs, and are usually the main stumbling block to introducing changes in education (FIEL 1993).

There are large variances in teacher salaries among districts, making an "average" salary less meaningful. Salaries are paid in cash. If there are fringe benefits, there is no information about them. Table 16.2 shows the results of a comparative study of the monthly salaries in several districts. In some districts, the difference between gross and net salary is higher than 20 percent, because most of the salary components are subject to deductions for the social security system. Consequently, in these cases labor cost is higher.

Another difference between districts concerns seniority. In some cases, the salary is increased 75 percent when the teacher has worked for fifteen years.

Table 16.2

Gross and Net Salary Per Month of a Primary School Teacher, Single Shift, 1995 (in $US)

District	Beginning of career (1)		Middle of career (2)		End of career (3)	
	Gross salary (4)	Net salary (5)	Gross salary (4)	Net salary (5)	Gross salary (4)	Net salary (5)
Federal Capital	358.12	319.81	626.16	550.32	760.17	665.58
Buenos Aires	346.67	287.59	498.33	408.17	606.67	494.29
Chaco	339.39	263.03	507.76	393.51	628.02	486.72
Chubut	449.71	350.78	696.4	543.19	837.36	653.14
Entre Rios	333.57	273.48	498.74	403.58	616.72	496.52
La Rioja	444.20	359.32	694.53	557.08	873.89	873.33
Mendoza	460.93	387.38	616.85	519.04	728.22	613.08
Misiones	332.33	275.82	484.58	400.05	593.33	488.79
Neuquén	693.12	n/data	909.27	n/data	1,063.66	n/data
Rio Negro	473.39	403.69	697.78	548.39	873.54	680.21
Santa Cruz	867.68	756.50	1,014.28	876.71	1,098.06	945.41
Santa Fe	489.11	393.86	575.52	456.30	654.06	522.28
Tierra del Fuego	916.33	772.12	1,094.00	921.36	1,205.04	1,014.63

Source: Gurman (1996).

(1) Beginning of career: no seniority.
(2) Middle of career: fifteen-year-seniority.
(3) End of career: twenty-three-year seniorty or more.
(4) Basic salary, ordinary components, frequent non-ordinary components, and annual bonus.
Ordinary components include basic salary, function, teacher conditions, and specific activities. They are associated with the post, not the person who holds it. Frequent non-ordinary components include seniority, unfavorable area, and perfect attendance. It does not include family allowances, or unfavorable area bonus, except in Chaco, Tierra del Fuego, and Santa Cruz, where this bonus is considered as an ordinary component.
(5) Gross salary minus personal contributions imposed by law.

Salary components vary from province to province. These components are associated with the local educational background characteristics, the government's salary policy, and its relationship with the unions. There are no rules to coordinate district decisions on this issue.

Giacometti and Lumi (1995) have noticed that teachers' salaries are 8 percent lower than the average salary of the economy. It should be pointed out that teachers do not spend more than twenty-five hours per week in the classroom—although this does not include preparation time—and that their leave of absence system is more flexible than that for other workers.

Decentralization Results

On balance, what are the effects of the 1978 transfer? As mentioned before, it had only economic aims, ignoring technical-pedagogical considerations, so that its results have been somewhat negative for educational quality, equity, and effectiveness (Filmus 1995). Census data show some improvement in the population's overall educational level in the 1980s, but this improvement can hardly be attributed directly to the decentralization of education.

And what about the transformation of education undertaken by the Federal Act? At the moment, it is not possible to assess the real impact of this provision on the schools. This transformation started only four years ago, under the leadership of the National Ministry of Education. It was undertaken in a framework of serious budget restrictions and is strongly opposed by the teachers' unions. Teachers' claims for better salaries are perennial. Besides, it is not easy to change long-standing behavior. Educational centralism, which has prevailed in Argentina for over a century, has developed a large bureaucracy that perpetuates itself and hinders the development of autonomous strategies of education.

The achievement of the goals set forth by the Federal Act—quality and equity, democratization of the system, and institutional autonomy, among others—can only be evaluated in the long term. The National Ministry of Education has already started some programs and activities with that purpose: Educational Social Plan, National Teaching Training Program, National Program for Educational Quality Evaluation, Educational Information Federal Network, strengthening of the Federal Council of Culture and Education as a coordinating and concertating body for educational policy, preparation of the common basic contents for all the schools nationwide, technical assistance to the provinces to implement the reforms. The short-term aim—to guarantee the financing of the system through budget previsions—has been only partly accomplished, and with some delay: but it appears to be insufficient to reach the main objectives posed by the Federal Education Act.

Conclusions

Although in Argentina the institutional conditions for the decentralized operation of educational system exist, as defined in this chapter, we are still in the first stages of the process. Several steps are required for its definitive consolidation:

1. Ensure the effective fulfillment of the Federal Act as well as the education local rules. Because there are no formal mechanisms in Argentina to enforce them, effective policies and strategies to reach the objectives are required.
2. Keep the debates and decisions about the educational system away from partisan disputes. This spirit could facilitate the relationship between the National Ministry of Education and the local governments, and the application of decisions could be easier.
3. Take steps to achieve an effective engagement of the local actors with the government of education. Without actions aimed at encouraging the participation and promoting the responsibility of those actors in the system, it will be hard to change the attitudes generated by decades of centralism in the governance of education.
4. Increase the resources to finance the system. However, if the increment does not go with a set of actions to get a better distribution of resources to the provinces, as well as to prevent the deflection of the budget items devoted to education to other purposes, any increment will be insufficient.
5. Improve the status of teachers, who now have little professional status. As we have said, actions to reverse the situation have been taken, but if they do not go along with a substantial increase of teachers' salaries, it will be very hard to improve the quality of education and to have the benefits of a decentralized system.
6. Develop technical skills to implement educational reform in the provinces. The scarcity and in some cases the lack of trained human resources at the local level is a real obstacle to reform.

The National Ministry of Education is currently compensating the local needs with specialized staff from the nation. However, that aid cannot be a definitive solution because it could undermine the principle of decentralization adopted by the Federal Act.

Bibliography

FIEL. 1993. *Hacia una nueva organización del federalismo fiscal en la Argentina.* Buenos Aires.

Filmus, Daniel. 1995. *Estado, educación y sociedad en la Argentina de fin de siglo.* Buenos Aires: Academia Nacional de Educación.

Fiske, Edward. 1996. *Decentralization of Education. Politics and Consensus.* Washington, DC: World Bank.

Giacometti, A. and Lumi, P. 1995. "Análisis sobre la estructura salarial y el gasto educativo." Buenos Aires: Ministerio de Cultura y Educación.

Gurman and Otros. 1996. "Análisis interjurisdiccional del salario docente." Buenos Aires: Ministerio de Cultura y Educación.

Kisilevsky, Marta. 1992."La relación entre la nación y las provincias a partir de la trans-
ferencia de escuelas primarias." Buenos Aires: Documento del CFI.
Morduchowicz, Alejandro. 1996a. "El gasto público provincial en educación y los
mecanismos de asignación de recursos en el sector." Buenos Aires: Ministerio de
Cultura y Educación.
————. 1996b. "El financiamiento educativo: Argentina en un contexto de restricciones
de recursos." Buenos Aires: Ministerio de Cultura y Educación.
Sánchez Martínez. 1992."La descentralización federal como criterio estratégico de la
política educacional." *Revista de la Universidad Blas Pascal* 2: 143–152. Córdoba.

17

MARIA LIGIA DE OLIVEIRA BARBOSA

School Organization: Centralization/Decentralization for Primary School

The literature on decentralization defines it as a process that produces "attempts at redistribution of resources, decision making spaces, jurisdictions, required activities and responsibilities, finally, political-economic power, in each specific social formation, faced with the crisis of the central Nation-states and the developing peripherical States. This redistribution can occur between government agencies, between state powers and between the State and society" (Silva 1995, 17). This concept requires an appropriate historic and social context in order to be useful in solving problems.

The implementation of policies to decentralize education began to occur in Brazil in the context of the battle for redemocratization of the nation that led both to the election of state governors who opposed the military regime in 1982, as well as to important changes in the political system that culminated in the direct election of the president of the republic in 1989. Its origin in this context brought the political/institutional dimension to the forefront of educational policy: a major emphasis was placed on participation, especially through the creation of democratizing mechanisms such as the election of principals or the participation of school councils (composed of representatives of teachers and other school employees, parents, and students over sixteen years of age). In Minas Gerais, councils are presided over by the principal. The councils are responsible for management, from transfer of state funds to quality of teaching. However, this is true just in the case of Minas Gerais; they are not installed in all the states in Brazil. In the early 1980s the federal government was almost completely absent in educational matters. Meanwhile, the debate about the collection and distribution of public resources had begun at the end of the 1970s, when the profoundly centralized legislation elaborated by the military governments still was in force. This was also an important facet of the democratization process.

The context in which decentralization originated favored an immense diversity of proposals and policies. This is one of the most important distinctive characteristics of the decentralization process in Brazil, compared to other Latin American nations: there was no clear federal government policy favoring it. According to Lobo (1995), only the administration of Fernando Henrique Cardoso (1995–) has made any effort in this direction. But when compared to other countries, "Brazil still lacks a consistent and organic path that leads toward decentralization" (Lobo 1995, 33).

The Constitution of 1988, despite the expectations of change, maintained the ambiguity of attributions with all their unfortunate results such as the dispersion of power and resources, the lack of attention to really needy groups, and the failure to hold public agents responsible. Given the enormous amount of pressure from the most diverse segments of the nation, it was decided to only attack the most visible aspect: the centralization of resources. The impact of decentralization varies among the states. In this chapter, we will analyze one of the most systematic and far-reaching proposals for decentralization. This is the policy carried out by the government of Minas Gerais for public education. It is important to note that from here on our analysis cannot be extended to the country as a whole, neither for its results nor for its significance.

In the strictly educational area, the two most common forms of decentralization are the transfer of administration of schools from the federal government to the states and cities and the cession of greater autonomy in school management. The aim of these procedures would be the search for greater community participation and greater adaptation of educational services to the desires of users. In addition, one cannot forget the necessity of rationalizing public expenditure.

As we noted above, there is a fundamental need to place decentralizing policies in context because the advantages of these are not unequivocal. Alberto Mello E. Souza points out the principal risks in this area: "Economies of scale could justify greater centralization of purchases, but the greater costs of distribution (storage and transport) attenuate them. Educational innovations, by having been stimulated by a climate in which diversity and initiative are rewarded, should occur more intensely in decentralized systems. On the other hand, given the inequality of income and of tax capacity among cities, decentralization negatively effects equity, in the sense of equality of opportunities for access to quality education" (Mello 1995b, 149–150). Here we encounter the major challenge of these policies: guaranteeing the necessary equilibrium of public accounts and the equity of expenditures. Equity, being a multi-dimensional concept, is a source of intense debate, especially when education is discussed.

With respect to resources to be spent on education, in the beginning of the 1980s there already were two important modifications, in spite of the negative effects that they had:

> In the first, there was the consolidation of financial transfers to the states in the Convênio Único. [The Convênio Único is a resolution made by MEC concern-

ing the allocation of money in a more systematic way. Before it, money was given to the states for each project they sent to the Ministry. The existence of the Convênio Único signified the institution of a systematic criterion: each state would receive money according to its economic status. The richer states would receive less than the poorer.] The Convênio Único at the beginning of the fiscal year established the sums to be transferred to the states within the four or five programs that it included. The upper limit that would belong to each State was furnished by MEC (the national Ministry of Education and Sports), and the states presented their Annual Plans, which contained projections of their main actions and resources for each program. (Mello 1995b, 160)

In 1984, the Ministry of Education introduced another change, granting direct contact with the municipalities, without the interference of state governments. In this way, the municipality was to present projects that, when approved, would guaranty the transfer of at least 25 percent of the federal share of the "educational salary," which is a tax that each enterprise pays: 2.5 percent of all the wages in the firm. The enterprise can pay it to the government or use it in the education of its employees.

The Constitution of 1988 maintained ambiguities which respect to obligations, which is particularly important in education. In the new legal situation, the federal government was made responsible for higher education, the states for secondary education, and the municipalities for basic education. These parameters, meanwhile, were not made obligatory. Thus, we have federal and state universities, middle school under both federal and state authorities (and also a few cases of municipal middle schools) and basic education still is, for the most part, maintained by state governments. The national Ministry of Education became responsible for the afternoon school meal and for textbooks for basic education. On taking charge of these tasks of executing policy, the Ministry ended up by leaving aside its function of formulating policies and evaluating school systems during the 1980s.

The existence of two systems that were in charge of basic education from the first to the eighth grade (city and state) generated one of the biggest problems for management of educational policies. Meanwhile, until the beginning of 1995 the Ministry of Education had not made any effort to mitigate the ill effects of this duality. The changes that occurred until that year, such as the transfer to two states (Minas Gerais and São Paulo) of management of purchase and distribution of textbooks, were the result of the claims of the states themselves and not a policy of the Ministry.

Another problem generated by the existence of two systems arose from the greater participation of the municipalities in public receipts, established by the Constitution of 1988, which also benefited the states but on a smaller scale. Due to this difference, in some states there was an alteration of the situation of the two systems in favor of that of the municipalities. The reasons for this are quite varied and range from the smaller indebtedness of the municipalities (which made them more able to invest considerable funds in the improvement or even the creation of their own teaching systems) to the implementation in the local systems of legislation (which did not exist earlier) governing the conditions of teachers' work, indicating a significant reduction of the use of clientelistic methods for the selection and employment of teachers.

In addition to this, some state governments—Paraná is a good example—gave incentives for sharing technical and pedagogical assistance with the municipalities. Another important reason was that, with the grave financial situation of the states, the teachers of the state system had losses in salaries that led to long and wasteful strike movements that implied a loss of quality of teaching in the state system. Finally (and this point is controversial), some analysts have suggested that the municipal plans were more conducive to innovations. As a new instance of this case, Paraná offered an important example: the municipalities of Maringá and Jaboatão achieved good results by permitting public schools to be managed by groups of teachers and by the community (Mello 1995b).

Within this complex picture, doubts remained as much in regard to the competence of each institutional level (which resulted from the ambiguities of the law) as in regard to the improvements in the municipal school systems. Where the state government invested in the process of decentralization, guaranteeing the centralized maintenance of controls over the functioning of the two systems, that are indications of a certain success. This is the case in Minas Gerais, Ceará, Santa Catarina, São Paulo, and Paraná. According to studies of decentralization, the existence of a central agent that originates and manages policy, and is responsible for orienting and establishing rules, forms, and limits of decentralization is one of the key elements for its success. Our analysis of the case of Minas Gerais covers the implementation of a model of decentralized educational policy and of the role that the state government played in this process. This model has two aspects: the municipalization of the schools and the transfer of power to state schools.

The Educational Program of the Minas Gerais Government

Beginning in 1991 State Secretary of Education of Minas Gerais (SEE) decided it would be better to systematize work that had been going on for several years in diverse forms. In this period a single policy began to be produced that became autonomous by the creation of a Coordinating Unit of the Project and an Advisory Committee, both part of a loan agreement made with the World Bank in 1994 to improve the state's educational system. The state's behavior is measured in terms of the possible (and necessary) increase in learning of students and in the completion of primary school.

A disastrous situation was encountered in the evaluation of student achievement in the public school system. João Batista Araujo Oliveira indicates that only 54 percent of the students in the first year of primary school arrived at the third year, in 1990. And this contingent knew only 50 percent of the language curriculum and 30 percent of mathematics curriculum. The State Secretary of Education proposed a project for improving the quality of primary school education in Minas Gerais, Pro-Quality (Pro-Qualidade), which made use of some ongoing experiments such as the basic literacy cycle, introduction of tests designed to measure student achievement, competitive selection of school principals, transfer of non-salary resources to the schools, strengthening of student associations, planning and school management, and campaign to make people aware of the importance of education. The project organized to assist improvements in five principle areas: (1) strengthening of the management of the educational system; (2) improvement of school infrastructure and management; (3) development of teaching; (4) supplying teaching and learning material; and (5) reorganizing school aid.

These topics were conceived as specific sub-projects in "the search for school autonomy, in its pedagogical, administrative and financial aspects; the strengthening of school management, principally by means of changing the process of naming of school principals, of instituting school councils; the development and professionalization of teachers, specialists and other educational workers; the evaluation of school achievement, as a way of searching for improving teaching quality; and the promotion of the articulation of the state with the municipalities" (Mello and Wey 1994, 137).

The Process of Municipalization

The Constitution of 1988 established that 25 percent of municipality and state resources should be spent on education. Of these resources, 60 percent should be applied to basic education. Primary education refers to the first four years of Basic Education, which is defined in the Brazilian Constitution as the eight years of compulsory education. The limits of organizational responsibilities are not clear. Moreover, some municipalities had a system of only minimally acceptable schools, but in order to comply with the constitutional mandate it was nonetheless necessary that the states transfer schools to them. In Minas Gerais, this process started under the government of Hélio Garcia, in 1983–87. From 1995, with the establishment of the Fund for Maintenance and Development of Basic Teaching (FUNDEF), which was composed of earmarked funds obtained from 15 percent of the most income-yielding municipal taxes, a strong incentive was created for the teaching systems to come under the control of municipalities because the resources were transferred to them independently of the number of students in them. As the resources no longer went to the states, at least in the case of the richest municipalities, the local system was in better operating condition. It should be added that 60 percent of these resources were to be spent on teaching. Another important fact is that the state government had always spent more on education than the percentage stipulated by the Constitution (25 percent of its income), reaching 45.48 percent of its receipts in 1996, averaging 36 percent during the 1990s, and falling to 33.2 percent in 1997.

The transfer of schools to municipal control was made difficult by the poor conditions in some municipalities in the interior of the state. Most important was the lack of qualified technical personnel to manage the local school system, and to evaluate and demand solutions. An additional problem was that various educational authorities had totally different conceptions of the municipality's obligations.

The policy developed by the SEE had been to transfer schools to municipal control whenever possible and to guarantee equal treatment to students and teachers in the two educational systems in the state. The integration of the state and the municipalities increased greatly, especially in the 1994–98 government. For example, teachers and principals from both municipal and state schools can attend the programs for qualification of teachers and principals offered by the state. The municipalities that wish to participate in the evaluation exams to which the students of the state system are subjected (exams of the state itself, of the national government [SAEB] and also those of UNESCO, Latin American and Caribbean Region—UNESCO/OREALC) can do so together with the state system, with the costs covered by the state. In addition to this, a book fair is to be held for the organization of school libraries and for the "reading corners" where literature books appropriate for the students' age are placed at their disposition in each classroom. This fair will be held exclusively for the municipal systems and be entirely financed by the state.

With regard to the situation of teachers, there are differences between the two systems, which are autonomous regarding contracting, formulation of career plans, salary levels, and retirement systems. The legislation that regulates the teachers' work situation is federal and merely establishes that the states and municipalities should formulate their own plans and rules. Before the end of 1998, Minas Gerais should complete its definitions of the state teaching career, and the teachers' union has been consulted regarding this.

Another indicator of integration between the state and municipalities is that the school curriculum defined by the SEE remains the main reference for the municipal systems in the state and even for the private school system. The teachers from both systems are invited to participate in systematic discussions to evaluate the form and content of teaching the various disciplines.

School Autonomy or the Transfer of Powers to State Schools

In Brazil there are no institutionalized mechanisms for measuring the parents' demand for education, nor evaluating any legal institution that would respond to this demand. Parents are at liberty to select the school in which they wish to matriculate their child. Mello and Wey (1994) and Castro and Carnoy (1997), among others, indicate that decisive democratizing elements of the Minas Gerais policy include (1) attempting to guarantee that the students study in the public schools closest to their home, although this is not a legal requirement; (2) creating school councils; (3) giving the school decision-making powers for administering specific funds; (4) selecting principals by competition; and (5) bringing the parents into school management and listening to their claims and criticisms. The establishment of decentralization in 1991 required intense preparatory work, principally together with the legislature. The Constituent Assembly in Minas Gerais had already foreseen the competitive selection of principals in 1988, but the ordinary law required to implement this constitutional provision had not yet been passed because of the resistance by the professional unions of the educational sector, principally the School Principals' Association (Mello 1995a). The process became increasingly institutionalized despite some problems. It had the visible merits of mobilization of communities using mass communication; immense credibility of the process, resulting, perhaps, from the transparency of the rules; and political maintenance of a process that was opposed to party interests (political naming of principals) or corporate interests (the existing principals, who were organized). However, the form of selection through tests provoked resistance by the teachers' union. In the first phases the participation of the parents was intense; apparently, it became a routine procedure. But studies like that of Gomes (1994) point to the fact that, despite the election process having increased the influence exercised by the school's teachers, "parents and students, in part because of their level of schooling did not know how to fulfill their role, [and now] seem timid clients who are not very demanding" (Gomes 1994, 38).

The school councils—or *colegidos**—grew in Minas Gerais in the first government of Hélio Garcia (1983–87) but were deactivated in the following governing period, to be re-instituted beginning in 1991.

The central idea for the creation of the councils was to broaden the participation of parents, teachers, and specialists in school management. They were used to promote greater integration of the school with the community, as well as to establish teaching, financial, and administrative and pedagogical autonomy, as well as a more democratic school management. Each year parents (50 percent) and school employees and teachers (50 percent) are elected to each council, which has at least six and no more than twelve members (Albano and Junho 1995). The role of the council is to propose and evaluate.

In her evaluation of the process of implanting the councils, Mello (1995a) indicates two groups of problems: establishment of rules for activities of the school council and the definition of the different competencies of the principal

---

*Colegiado is a kind of school council, created in some states in Brazil, to allow more participation of parents, teachers, and administrative staff in the way the schools work. Its competence for deciding is wide-ranging: from administrative problems to pedagogical questions, although, in real life, they have not managed to carry out these responsibilities.

and of the *colegiado*; and difficulties regarding legal impediments. In a later study, Albano and Junho wrote,

> [T]he school council is understood as a democratic conquest, bringing the State and civil society together. The value that the school council adds to school functioning is greater in small communities than in large urban centers. Parents and principals are those most enthusiastic about the school councils, while teachers are those least interested. Teachers do not perceive with clarity that the school council has been a mechanism bringing them closer to the parents and a space to give greater value to their role. The parents, knowing school environment better through the school councils, are increasingly more aware of the daily efforts of the teachers. Principals felt that a weight was lifted from their shoulders by the possibility of sharing administration of their schools with the school councils. The capacity of the principal is central to its mobilization. This works better or worse when the principal is more or less dynamic ... the functions of the school councils are not sufficiently clarified, which makes its autonomy a frustrating factor in some cases. (Albana and Pena, n.d.)

One of the decisive elements for the justification of this project of financial decentralization was the idea that scale economies made by the central administration are totally lost because of the additional transport and storage costs, deterioration and embezzlement, delays in delivery and ignorance of local needs. Minas Gerais tried to supply the schools' daily needs as rapidly as possible. Using a series of legal and banking mechanisms, the Caixa Escolar (School Fund) was created under the new government proposals to receive transferred resources from the central government; it is responsible for planning, management, and lending of the funds, but the school principals and school councils participate actively in this process. According to 1993 data, these resources were used principally for the maintenance of buildings and equipment. From 1995, the educational expenditures of the School Funds were concentrated in the purchase of teaching and didactic material (Administration and Execution of Pro-Qualidade). This signifies a change in the use of the school funds that previously had gone to support some needy students. The SEE is trying, increasingly, to improve both the criteria for transfer of resources, including the possibility that members of the *colegiado* and principals obtain the necessary knowledge for a more efficient management of the transferred resources. According to the administration and execution of Pro-Qualidade, the financial gains from this type of proceeding greatly surpassed the losses from corruption and, more often, errors that always occurred. In order to have an idea of the size of transfers to the School Funds, in 1997 Pro-Qualidade invested R$174,892,219.75 (US$ 162,237,470.00 [R$ 1.00 = US$1.078]) for around 2.8 million students in state schools. But Pro-Qualidade is just a small piece in the secretariat budget, in its various parts. Of this total, R$48,017,304.00 (US$ 51,762,653.00) was transferred to schools that spent more than 50 percent of the funds in the organization of libraries.

The financial dimension was extremely important, but the other components of autonomy in state schools form a new profile of educational management that encompasses certain legal and pedagogical parameters that are compatible with innovations (Mello 1995a). Finally, and perhaps the most important item: decentralization strongly invested in giving the school the capability to function effectively in autonomous and democratic ways. This investment includes activities ranging from training courses to advice for elaborating project management. Unhappily, we have not yet found the mechanisms more capable of producing the same effect of competent participation by the members of the school community. The community includes not only the school council but also all the students, parents, teachers, and employees of the school.

No less important, the SEE established permanent auditing systems that function both for programs and for specific components of the programs, as is the case of the process of decentralized purchasing. In addition to the General Audit of public accounts, carried out by the Tribunal de Contas, the programs of the Secretariat of Education undergo three kinds of evaluation: an accounting audit by an independent auditor, a qualitative evaluation by groups of specialized consultants, and a series of opinion research surveys carried out particularly in the programs of teacher training. At the suggestion of the Secretariat itself, the most important indicator of adequate realization of its initiatives is the improvement of the index of student achievement obtained in the state and national tests.

The most significant factor in the decentralization process conducted by the state government is the existence of a sufficiently clear and defined project, looking toward the transfer of resources and the democratization of decisions without losing effective control over the content of education supplied, the rules of school system functioning and correct procedures. It is the SEE itself that defines goals and programs, establishing the levels of quality and knowledge to which the student should have access. Permanent assistance to and integration with the municipalities guarantees that the decentralizing process would not be barely a reduction of costs but a real attempt to bring public school closer to the community that it serves.

Bibliography

Albano, Celina, and Valéria Pena. n.d. "Educação—Colegiado"—Relatório de Pesquisa. Unpublished research report.

Albano, Celina, and Valéria Junho. 1995. "Colegiado: a comunidade dentro da escola." Mimeo.

Castro, Cláudio Moura, and Martin Carnoy. 1997. *Como anda a reforma da educação na América Latina?* Rio de Janeiro: Editora da FGV.

Fundação João Pinheira, M.G. 1995. *Autonomia escolar: uma estratégia de avaliação.* Belo Horizonte: Relatório final, Mimeo.

Gomes, Cândido Alberto. 1994: "Gestão participativa nas escolas: resultados e incógnitas." In *Gestão escolar: desafios e tendências,* Série IPEA, 145. Edited by José Amaral Sobrinho, Antônio Xavier, and Fátima Marra. Brasília: IPEA.

Jornal Do Brasil. Special edition for November 2, 1997. encarte especial em 02 de novembro de 1997.

Lobo, Thereza. 1995: "Políticas sociais no Brasil: descentralização para mais eficiência e eqüidade." In *Descentralização, eficiência e eqüidade,* ed. João P.R. Velloso, Roberto C. Albuquerque, and Joachim Knoop. Rio de Janeiro: Instituto Nacional de Altos Estudos.

Mello, Guiomar Namo. 1995a: "Escolas eficazes: Um tema revisitado." In *Gestão educacional: Experiências inovadoras.* Série IPEA, 147, ed. José Amaral Sobrinho, Antônio Xavier, Guiomar Mello, and Rose Silva. Brasília: IPEA.

Mello, E. Souza. 1995b: "Gestão da escola e qualidade da educação." In *Descentralização, Eficiência e Eqüidade.*

Mello, Guiomar, and Vera Lúcia Wey. 1994. "Estado de Minas Gerais: em busca de um novo padrão educacional." In *Gestão educacional: experiências inovadoras.*

Silva, Pedro L.B. 1995: "Descentralização de políticas sociais: marco teórico e experiências internacional e brasileira." In *Descentralização, Eficiência e Eqüidade.*

Sobrino, José Amaral, Antônio Xavier, and Fátima Marra, eds. "Gestão da escola fundamental: situação atual e tendências." In *Gestão escolar: desafios e tendências.* Brasília: Série IPEA, 145, Brasília, 1994.

18

Jaime Vargas S.

Educational Decentralization in Chile

Introduction

This article describes and analyzes the principal aspects of the reform that began in 1981 under the military regime and sought to decentralize education in Chile. It also covers the process of decentralization of teaching and curriculum begun in 1991 under the elected democratic government.

Context

The process of decentralization of the Chilean educational system took place within the context of major reforms based on the principles of a market economy. Beginning in 1974, a broad restructuring of the economy and the state made the market the principal allocator of resources and limited the role of the state. Decentralization in education was an extension of the transformations and decentralization carried out in many sectors of national life. The maximum reduction of state intervention was desired to open a broad space for private participation and competition in the management of educational service.

Justification and Central Aspects of the Reform

When the reforms were implemented in 1981, the Chilean educational system provided basic education to more than 90 percent of children between the ages of six and thirteen years, the average number of years of schooling (7.8) was among the highest in Latin America, and the illiteracy rate (8.9 percent) among the lowest in the region (Prawda 1992). Despite this, those who urged the reform focused on profound inefficiencies in the system. The public schools were centrally administered, with problems of bureaucracy, inefficiency, and ineffectiveness in achieving an acceptable quality of education.

The stated objectives of decentralization were: (1) improving the efficiency of the management of education and maximizing the use of the public resources that were assigned to it; (2) contribution to the improvement of the quality of education; (3) increasing the equality of educational opportunities; (4) favoring the participation of parents in educational matters; and (5) improving the working conditions of teachers.

The levels of the educational system that were affected by decentralization were, principally, preschool education, basic education (eight grades), and middle school education (four grades), with its two tracks: humanistic-scientific and technical-professional.

The process of decentralization was based on a combination of legal rules and regulations, and not on a basic decentralization law. Decentralization fundamentally consisted of: (1) the transfer of primary and secondary schools to the 335 municipalities of the nation; (2) the transfer of a portion of secondary vocational schools to private non-profit organizations, known as "corporations," created by associations of employers, and (3) the transfer of resources to municipal and privatly subsidized schools on the basis of a per student subsidy.

Thus, the decentralization was based on three basic principles: (1) the resources assigned by the state to education would be distributed among the subsidized private and municipal schools on the same basis: a subsidy per student actually attending; (2) the administration of these schools would be carried out by decentralized bodies, both municipal and private organizations; and (3) the schools would compete for students under equal conditions, and those that could successfully compete would obtain a larger quantity of monetary resources than those that were unsuccessful (Jofré 1988).

At the same time, the Ministry of Education would no longer administer schools; it would not contract teachers, public schools would become the property of the municipalities, and these would be completely free in their administration, with the sole exception of their need to follow "technical pedagogic" norms (Jofré 1988). This entire process was assumed to be consistent with free labor relations between municipalities and teachers, subject only to general labor laws.

The decentralization was carried out after a previous effort of deconcentration by the Ministry of Education, through the creation of Regional Secretaries of the Ministry of Education, in 1974, and of Provincial Administrations of Education, in 1980.

Decentralization did not cover aspects relating to teaching and technical supervision of educational establishments, given that these activities remained centralized at the Ministry of Education. On the other hand, teachers received economic incentives when their transfer, and the consequent change in their work situation, took place and they began to be governed by the regular labor system.

Institutional Organization Before Decentralization

Until 1974, Chilean education had an institutional organization in which centralization and some aspects of functional and territorial decentralization were combined. This organization corresponded to that of a unitary and strongly centralized state.

Consistent with this, the financing of public education, as well as subsidies to private education, were fixed within the yearly budget debate (Nuñez 1994).

Until the decentralization reform, almost all the teachers were state or public employees, governed by an administrative statute. The exception was constituted by teachers in private education.

Institutional Organization After Decentralization

At present (in 1998) the main functions of the Ministry of Education are those of: (1) proposing and evaluating educational policies and educational and cultural development plans; (2) assigning the necessary resources for the development of educational activities; (3) evaluating the development of education as an integral process and informing the community of the results; and (4) authorizing the official recognition of educational establishments, when appropriate.

At the local level the Ministry maintains only functions of technico-educational supervision and inspection of compliance with the requirements for receiving state subsidies. Since 1981, public primary and middle school educational establishments have maintained administrative independence from the Ministry; this function belongs to the jurisdiction of communities within the municipalities. Financing of the establishments continues to be public, but by means of the direct transfer of resources through the subsidy system, which is the same as that which governs private establishments. Today, the nation's existing communities (335) are in charge of public basic and middle school education.

With the goal of carrying out its educational administrative activities, the municipalities can create autonomous non-profit private law organizations called Municipal Corporations, presided over by the mayor (the highest community official), and can directly administer the schools through the creation of a specific unit integrated in its organizational structure: the Department of Administration of Municipal Education.

Among the principal duties of the municipalities are: (1) the hiring of teachers, by public examination, and the determination and payment of salaries and benefits to which they are entitled according to the law, after 1991 dictated by the regulations of the Teaching Statute; (2) the improvement of the school infrastructure and its maintenance; and (3) the administration of the state subsidy for education and of other resources for this purpose.

The educational institutions can be classified according to their juridical-administrative characteristics as:

Municipal: public institutions administered by the municipalities and financed by the State through the per student payments system;

Private subsidized: private institutions, administered by private parties and receiving financing from the State through the per student payments system;

Private paid: private institutions, administered by private parties, which receive no state financing.

Corporations: public institutions, administered by private non-profit organizations that receive state financing in the form of a contribution which is paid yearly, and which corresponds to the operating cost existing when they were taken over; this payment is readjusted according to the price index.

Aspects Related to Financing

After the transfer of the administration of public schools from the Ministry of Education to the municipalities, the financing of these institutions now depending on the municipalities continues to be regulated by the regimen of subsidies.

In order to obtain the state subsidy, in addition to accrediting a "sustainer" (the owner or person responsible for the school), institutions must comply with the requirements of official recognition by the Ministry of Education, consistency of plans and programs, and effective availability of human resources and infrastructure.

The Ministry of Education is in charge of making the subsidy payments. The government contribution is paid monthly to the schools in accordance with the average aid to classes registered by course in the semester preceding the payment. It is the responsibility of the Ministry of Education to oversee the financing of aid to students in order to proceed with granting the corresponding subsidy.

From the point of view of finance, private education can be divided into two sub-sectors: private tuition schools and private schools that receive subsidies. The private tuition schools are financed with resources coming from the students' families, who pay tuition and monthly fees for education. Private subsidized schools were financed exclusively with the state per-student subsidy, until 1988, when privately subsidized institutions for primary and middle school and municipal middle school institutions could use a system of shared financing, which in practice means that they can charge students' parents a given amount (much lower than that charged by private tuition schools). In the case of these establishments there is a discount (lower than the subsidy from the state). This additional funding may be used freely by schools.

Aspects Related to Teaching Personnel

Public school teachers in preschool, primary, and middle education have gone from a regimen of state officials under the centralized Ministry of Education, to a mixture between a private and a special labor regimen. Between 1981 and 1991 educational personnel were governed by common labor laws, even though in the case of the municipal sector there were some special labor rules.

In 1991 the Statute of Education Professionals was approved, better known as the Teaching Statute. This rule applies to teaching, administration, and technical personnel of preschool, primary, and middle schools, both in the municipal and privately subsidized institutions, as well as the corporations of administration designated for technical education.

The new statute defined teaching as a profession. Although the state unified teachers in the professional dimension, it separated them in contractual matters. Thus, the professionals who found themselves under the municipal administration remained subject to a career regime of public service, while the professionals in the private establishments remained subject to a type of private labor contract that up to a certain point was distinct from the current labor contract. It establishes a minimum remuneration for all, and leaves the determination of remunerations above the basic minimum to individual or collective negotiation (Nuñez 1994).

The combination of a decentralized educational management structure and statutes governing teachers leads to different duties for the distinct levels of administration. Unlike the arrangements when educational administration was centralized, the Ministry of Education does not deal with the initial formation of teachers, which was delegated to the Autonomous Universities to deal with, nor does it have a role as employer of teaching personnel. Its responsibilities were reduced to assuring that teaching personnel had a legal regimen.

The provincial level of the Ministry of Education intervenes by: (1) authorizing or vetoing planned number of teachers proposed yearly by each municipality; (2) proposing to the respective regional secretaries a prioritized list of private subsidized schools or high schools that request a special assignment of funds because of difficult conditions; and (3) the department chief or supervisor who represents him, can act as authorizing officer, without the right to a vote, in the commissions that make decisions in public exams to select teaching personnel in the municipal sector.

At the local level the municipalities are legally the employers of the teaching personnel and are charged with their administration. Without undercutting the responsibilities of the Ministry of Education, and within the margins of the Statute of Educational Professionals, they have autonomy of decision making in hiring teachers (by means of national public competition); in assigning directors', teachers', or technical staffs' positions to their establishment and personnel within the municipality (local unit); in setting salaries beyond those fixed by the Statute; in terminating the services of professionals, according the specifications of the Statute, and, in general, in carrying out the obligations of an employer. In practice, in the municipal schools, the directors lack important authority regarding personnel management.

In contrast to the public schools, supporters of private subsidized schools have autonomous responsibility for personnel management. There is freedom of hiring, with the sole limitation of the requirements of the corresponding professional degree. There is freedom to create or eliminate jobs, as well as to set salaries, always relating to the base of the minimum salary established by the Teaching Statute and respecting the legislation governing individual and collective bargaining. They can terminate contracts, even though legislation tends to limit this freedom through strong indemnifications in favor of teachers fired during the school year.

Other Aspects

Although the municipalities had and continue to have a legal identity and their own property, between 1973 and 1988, the municipalities were directly under the Ministry of Interior. The mayors were designated and there were no organs elected by the community. The municipalities began to be able to democratically elect their officials in 1992.

Regarding the tax system for financing education, there was only one tax system, whose collections went to the general budget of the nation. The municipalities had the right to receive a portion of some taxes such as the territorial tax, those on commercial patents, and annual permits for motor vehicles, but the largest share of taxes went to the national treasury. There were no special taxes for education.

There is a Common Municipal Fund, which collects part of the taxes destined for common purposes and redistributes them according to a formula that combines demographic and social components, so that the communities with the highest incomes receive proportionally less than those with low incomes, as a form of progressive redistribution between rich and poor communities. There is also a National Fund for Regional Development, administered by the national government, that assigns resources to the regions to invest in infrastructure, including the construction, repair, and equipping of school buildings. The allocation is made based on the presentation of projects prepared by municipalities and prioritized at the regional level.

Educational Decentralization 1981–1990: From Institutional Decentralization to Pedagogic Decentralization

In 1980 Chile enjoyed a period of economic prosperity, which influenced aspects of the decentralization process. In a context of abundance of resources it was decided to link the subsidy per student to the consumer price index. Additionally, the system gave the majority of the municipalities a one-time monetary incentive allocated according to the speed with which the transfer was effected. The subsidy was established at a level 30 percent greater than the implicit subvention level at this time, and 61 percent above the subventions that the private subsidized schools were receiving (Jofré 1988).

The subsidy to the private subsidized schools increased, making it equal to that of the municipal schools. This led to the increase of privately subsidized schools from 1,674 in 1980 to 2,643 in 1985. By 1983 the transfer process was highly advanced: 5,692 schools had been transferred, representing 87 percent of the number of schools initially belonging to the government. Also transferred were 65,234 teachers, equal to 78 percent of the total, and 1,618,904 students, representing 83 percent (Jofré 1988).

However, a deep financial crisis in 1982 forced a major restriction of public spending on education and a modification of the terms of per-student subsidies of education, whose adjustment mechanisms could not be maintained. The value of subsidies was frozen and their real value fell substantially. The private subsidized school sector lost its initial dynamism. Financing of the municipal schools became increasingly difficult, because of the deterioration of the subsidies and the loss of students. On the other hand, teachers began to express their opposition to a system that was affecting their collective interests. In this context, the government had to dictate the first specific legislation for teachers. Additionally, transfers were suspended in 1983, so that more than 800 institutions, and more than 19,000 teachers and 331,000 students, remained under the centralized jurisdiction of the Ministry of Education.

This crisis led to the first financial difficulties of the municipalities in financing education. Until the 1982 crisis, the municipalities had been administering their schools in relatively favorable conditions. When indexation was suspended, the first deficits appeared. Before this, the mayors asked for aid from the central government, and the deficit was covered. (In 1983, the deficits were already 450 million pesos. They returned to being covered by the central government, and in 1984 they rose to 1,143 million, increasing to 1,705 million pesos in 1985.)

In 1982, sixty-eight municipalities asked for and received contributions from the central government to cover their deficits. In 1985, 205 municipalities received these contributions. The eighty-five municipalities that showed a deficit in 1982 were an important share of rural schools in their systems. In 1985, forty-seven clearly urban municipalities were showing a deficit (Jofré 1988).

A second problem that arose in this period was a strong pressure to equalize the incomes of the teachers. The municipal teachers demanded treatment equal to that of central government employees. Faced with this, an allocation of resources was created that was parallel to the resources for subsidies that the Treasury was paying to teachers in municipal and private subsidized schools. Despite these difficulties, in 1986 the transfer to the municipalities of all the schools that remained in the central government was completed.

When the democratically elected government assumed power in 1990, the authorities decided to continue with decentralization of education in opposition to an important group of teachers and educators who, in the hope of regaining traditional privileges, wanted to return to the old centralized system. The structure of subsidized education was maintained, with the central government assuming a more active role than before 1990 in setting curricular and labor policies. The educational policy priorities shifted to focus on the improvement of quality and educational equity. Additionally, attempts were made to improve the work situation of teachers, assuring stability in their jobs and improving salaries

Table 18.1

Evolution of National Enrollment by Type of School, (%), 1981–1995

Year	City	Private, subsudized	Private, tuition-based
1981	78.0	15.1	6.9
1982	75.2	19.7	5.1
1983	71.2	22.4	6.4
1984	68.2	26.3	5.5
1985	65.3	28.1	6.6
1986	63.1	30.8	6.1
1987	60.7	32.7	6.6
1988	59.0	33.4	7.0
1989	58.7	34.4	7.3
1990	58.0	34.4	7.7
1991	57.8	34.0	8.0
1992	57.7	34.1	8.2
1993	57.4	34.1	8.5
1994	57.3	34.0	8.7
1995	57.1	33.8	9.1

Source: Ministry of Education.

by means of applying the Teaching Statute. In terms of pedagogical decentraliza-tion, the Ministry of Education decided to set up a portion of the curriculum, leaving schools to design about 50 percent of it.

Beginning in 1990 the Ministry of Education was preoccupied with the qual-ity of teaching processes and of the work conditions of teachers, and the Minis-tries of Interior and the Treasury were preoccupied with aiding the municipalities, trying to brake the economic drainage that municipal education represented (Espinola 1994).

Conclusions

The decentralizing reforms carried out in the Chilean educational system during the 1980–90 period could be characterized by three types of interventions: (1) administrative decentralization; (2) financing via subsidy per student; and (3) making the curriculum more flexible. Administrative decentralization was manifested in the transfer of educational administration from the central govern-ment to the municipalities. The subsidy, for its part, introduced elements of market competition into the system. Finally, the increased flexibility of rules on the application of the curriculum are based on the expectation that they will be adapted to local characteristics and resources and will make the work of teachers easier (Espinola 1994).

Pedagogic and curricular decentralization after 1990 appears as a government response to the problems of quality and equity in the educational system. In turn, the government perceived these problems to be a consequence of an institutional decentralization concentrated only in administrative and financial aspects.

The profound effect generated by the financial mechanism of the subsidy per student introduced competition among educational institutions. According to Espinola (1991) the need to obtain resources through student attendance "required the directors, and also the teachers, to look outside the school and to pay attention to what the parents wanted in it." Thus, the need of responding to "the clients," trying to satisfy them with the educational services offered, would be a new element that has generated changes within the schools. Finally, one must also point out the impact of competition on demand for educational services (see Table 18.1), which caused the sustained and massive transfer of students from the municipal schools to private subsidized schools over a ten-year period.

Thus, according to the stated objectives, it is possible to conclude that the decentralization reform led to better opportunities to improve the efficiency of the system as well as to greater parental participation. On the other hand, teachers' working conditions got worse, at least regarding their salaries. Finally, a strong controversy surrounds the effect of the decentralization reform on quality and equity of education.

General References

Aedo, Cristián, and Osvaldo Larrañaga. 1993. *Política social: Un marco analítico.* Washington, DC: ILADES/Georgetown University, Serie Investigación. Programa de postgrado en economía.

Arriagada, Patricio, Juan Matulic, and Cristián Trucco. 1979. *Descentralización de la gestión educacional en Chile.* Santiago. Mimeo.

Cerda, Ana María, María de la Luz Silva, and Iván Núñez. 1991. *El sistema escolar y la profesión docente.* Santiago: PIIE.

Chile. Ministerio de Educación. 1991. *Estatuto de los Profesionales de la Educación.* Law no. 19.070. Santiago.

———. 1992. "Informe Nacional." In OEI, *II Conferencia Iberoamericana de Educación: "La descentralización educativa,"* ed. OEI, pp. 173–181. Santa Fe de Bogotá (Colombia), November 4–6.

Jofré, Gerardo. 1988. *El sistema de subvenciones en educación: La experiencia Chilena.* Santiago: Centros de Estudios Públicos, Doc. de trabajo no. 99.

Latorre, Luis, Iván Nuñez, Luis Eduardo González, and Ricardo Hevia. 1991. *La municipalización de la educación: una mirada desde los administradores del sistema.* Santiago: PIIE.

Pérez, Andrés. 1996. *El marco normativo de la descentralización educativa en América Latina: comentario a las presentaciones de Silvia Novick de Senen González, Juan Casassus y Elizabeth King.* London, ON: University of Western Ontario.

Tünnermann, Carlos. 1996. *Panel: "Condiciones para el éxito de la descentralización en países con diferentes niveles de desarrollo. Sumario."* n.p. Universidad Centroamericana, July 25–26.

Works Cited

Espinola, Viola. 1991. *Descentralización del sistema escolar en Chile.* Santiago: CIDE.
———. 1994. *La descentralización de la educación en Chile: Continuidad y cambio de un proceso de modernización.* Santiago: CIDE, Doc. no. 2/94.
Nuñez, Iván. 1994. "El caso de Chile." In *Descentralización y planificación de la educación: experiencias recientes en países de América Latina,* Capítulo 5, Malpica C. París: UNESCO, Informe de Investigación no. 102.
Prawda, Juan. 1992. *Educational Descentralization in Latin America: Lessons Learned.* World Bank, a view from LATHR no. 27.

19

Alec Ian Gershberg

Dropout Rates and Preschooling in a "Decentralizing" System: The Case of Mexico, 1992–1996

Introduction

Mexico has recently implemented a reform process aimed at transferring some aspects of basic education finance, administration, and governance from the central government to sub-national jurisdictions.[1] The aim of such reforms is primarily to improve educational outcomes. This chapter will briefly describe the decentralization reform process in Mexico and describe and attempt to explain trends in outcomes during the reform process. The time span of assessment is only four years, which makes asserting a definitive causal link between the reform process and outcomes unfeasible; nevertheless, we can connect the reform process with the development of certain policies and programs that appear likely to have a positive affect on outcomes. In particular, we highlight how state-level bureaucrats have used the new powers transferred to them to invest more heavily in preschool education—a strategy that is widely believed to improve dropout rates in primary and secondary education.

Mexican Education Reforms and Decentralization

The Mexican system of primary and secondary education underwent two major reforms from 1978 to 1997 that it labeled "decentralization."[2] The first, 1978–92, involved the deconcentration of the federal government's Public Education Secretariat (Secretaría de Educatión Pública, or SEP). Thirty-one federal delegations (Servicios Coordinadós de Educación Pública, or SCEPs) were established in each state in an effort to move federal administration out of the capital and closer to the populations served. The most recent major reform, explored in this study, began in 1992 and transferred responsibility for direct service provision from the federal government to the states.

Historically, the federal government dominated the financing of education, providing about 80 percent of funds for basic education nationally through a budgeting process requiring each of the thirty-one delegations to compete for a national pool of resources allocated annually by the federal government. Most of the approximately 1 million primary and secondary school teachers remained federal employees.

Since mid-century, states could establish their own education systems financed through their own revenues. These systems remained virtually independent of the federal system, with their own teachers and administrators (both state employees) and their own infrastructure, and accounted for about 20 percent of basic education funds nationally (Gershberg 1995). The degree to which states chose to do this varied widely, with some states, like Nuevo León, actually spending more of their own resources on the state system than the federal government spent on the federal system in their state. On the other hand, some states, such as Hidalgo, relied almost entirely on the federal government's system of primary and secondary schools and had no basic education system of their own prior to 1992.

The National Agreement for the Modernization of Basic Education (NAMBE), signed by the governors of all thirty-one states in 1992, legally transferred the previously federal system (teachers, administrative personnel, and infrastructure) to the states, which had to establish their own state ministries of education (State Education Entity, or SEE), if they had not already done so.[3] The 1993 General Education Law (Ley General de Educación, or LGE) solidified the 1992 NAMBE, and gave it more legal muscle. We will refer to the 1992 NAMBE and the 1993 LGE together as "the decentralization legislation." Federal and state-level shares of education finance have not, however, changed significantly since 1992 (Gershberg 1996b). In fact, many aspects of education finance and administration remained as centralized after 1992 as they did before. Tables 19.1 and 19.2 show that, at least officially, only the aspect of civil service and management systems exhibit a significant transfer of central authority to states. Nevertheless, as this chapter argues, state-level officials both managed to innovate within these constraints and went farther in implementing reforms than the legislation officially allowed them to do.

State-level officials made preschool education a priority in the years after the 1992 reform. In some cases, this emphasis began prior to the reform, but both state and federal officials agreed that the 1992 reforms allowed for greater progress to be made in preschool education.

Trends in Outcome Measures Before and After 1992 Reforms

This section presents a preliminary exploration of educational outcomes before and after the 1992 NAMBE. Tables 19.3 and 19.4 present basic outcomes for the period 1988 to 1994, all of which are presented in percentage terms.[4] Note that

Table 19.1

Framework for Analyzing Accountability in Mexican Reforms, 1992–1996

Framework aspect	Comment/summary judgment
I. Finance Revenues Expenditures Salary Scales	**Relatively unchanged authority for central and sub-national governments.** No change at all on the revenue side. Very little change on the expenditure side: Federal government continues to determine transfers to states based on yearly budget negotiations, although states do literally spend the money, which they did not do before. States have only slightly more control over *how* to spend than before 1992. Some recentralization of salary negotiations since the federal government now determines salaries for all teachers, not just those in the formerly separate federal system. States have, thus, lost some of the power to negotiate with those teachers that were in the previously separate state systems.
II. Auditing & Evaluation (Financial, Performance, Operational and Program)	**Central government transferred only financial auditing responsibility.** The Ministry no longer does very much due to state autonomy. Little change in quantitative evaluation systems. Some states are developing some evaluation geared toward creating qualitative complements to the Ministry evaluation. States have the same responsibility to provide basic data, but the Ministry may have less ability to verify, due to state autonomy.
III. Regulation and Policy Development, including curriculim and textbooks	**Officially, central authority is unchanged.** States are, however, finding more room to maneuver developing programs officially against Ministry norms. This is explored in detail in this chapter.
IV. Demand-driven Mechanisms (Expressions of Demand)	**No change.** No vouchers or other traditional demand-driven reforms. Some increased datate interes in polling stakeholder priorities through qualitative evaluations and survey.
V. Democratic Mechanisms (Voting, Citizen Particiaption and Conflict Resolution)	**Officially, no change. Perhaps** *some* **democratic impact:** state governors are (arguably) closer to the electorate than central officials and have more control over the sector: they now appoint the state's education secretary, who has the few increased powers described in aspects III and VII. Official support of citizen participation, but not many successful examples of its taking root.
VI. Service Provider Choice/Mix (Public,Private and NGO Provision)	**No change.** No inclusion of private sector. Very little parental choice to pick schools. Little change in the differentiation between formerly separate federal and state school systems. Little or no involvement of NGOs and other civil associations compared to other countries in the region.
VII. Civil Service and Management Systems	

Source: Adapted from Gershberg (1996b).

Table 19.2

Distribution of Functions for Basic Education Before and After 1992 NAMBE for Federal and State Systems (Before) and Unified System (After), Mexico

Function and framework aspects	Before 1992 NAMBE	After 1992 NAMBE
Educational Policy and Regulation (Normatividad)	FEDERAL: Central under SEP STATE: State under State Secretariats of Education (SEEs),	UNIFIED: Central under SEP with some increased flexibility (implicit and explicit) for states (SEEs)
Financial Resource Mobilization I. Finance	FEDERAL: Resources centralized, based on historical budget trends and yearly federal-state negotiations, and allocated by SEP to SEP's State Delegations (SCEPs) with final approval from Ministry of Finance (MOF). STATE: State decision based on state priorities, determined by governor. Own-source funds established largely by federal revenue-sharing formula.	UNIFIED: Federal Financial Resources centralized, based on historical budget trends and yearly federal-state negotiations, and allocated by SEP, with final approval from MOF, to (1) State Treasury, Finance Secretary, or SEE, and (2) small administrative budget to SCEPs. Additional state contributions based on state priorities, determined by governor. Own-source funds established largely by federal revenue-sharing formula.
Sources of Funding I. Finance	FEDERAL: Entirely central through SEP. STATE: Entirely state from own-source funds. Great variety in the level of state contributions from 0% to 54% See Gershberg (1995) for more details.	UNIFIED: Mostly federal to finance formerly federal system. States continue to provide funds at levels similar to pre-1992 levels to finance formerly state systems. All funds, including federal, transferred to state governments. Some states maintain separation of funds for two former systems; others consolidate funds into single education budget.

215

	FEDERAL/STATE	UNIFIED
Auditing II. Auditing	FEDERAL: Central through both central SEP and SCEPs. STATE: States through SEEs and other agencies under executive and legislative control.	UNIFIED: Largely state through SEEs and other agencies under executive and legislative control. Central involvement only if egregious misuse suspected, due to state autonomy in federal system.
Curriculum Development III. Regulation	FEDERAL: Central. One curriculum for entire country complemented with regional and ethnic teaching materials developed largely by SEP. STATE: State approved, largely based on central guidelines, with some development of state-specific programs.	UNIFIED: Central. One curriculum for entire country complemented with regional and ethnic teaching materials developed largely by SEP. States establishing some increased input to formerly federal curriculum.
Teacher Hiring, Firing, and Creation of *Plazas* I. Finance III. Regulation VII. Civil Service	FEDERAL: Central. Combined procedures between SEP and SCEPs. National teacher's union (SNTE) greatly influences outcome. STATE: SEEs with influence from state-level sections of SNTE.	UNIFIED: Wide variation across states. Largely central for *plazas* created with federal funds; SNTE greatly influences outcome. States have control over federal *plazas* not filled by SEP or national section of SNTE, but also negotiate with state-level sections of SNTE.
Teacher Salaries and Benefits I. Finance; III. Regulation; VII. Civil Service	FEDERAL: National scale fixed by central government and negotiated with unions. Allowed for pay differences based on regional factors such as hard working conditions. STATE: Officially negotiated by states with state-level sections of SNTE. Salaries, however, were largely in line with national scale, with some differences. Benefits did differ across states.	UNIFIED: Salaries for *all* teachers still largely negotiated in center based on previous national scale. Most states, thus, have lost whatever power they had to negotiate salaries at the state level. States have more power to affect benefit packages than salary levels, but still come under central pressure to provide benefits packages that arise from SEP-SNTE national level negotiations.
Pre-service and In-service Training and Upgrading VII. Civil Service	Special teacher training schools (Normal Schools) operated separately by SCEPs and state governments. Federal normal graduates placed in formerly federal schools; state normal graduates placed in formerly state schools. Separate ongoing training efforts.	Special teacher training schools (Normal Schools) operated together by SCEPs and state governments. Federal normal graduates placed in formerly federal schools; state normal graduates placed in formerly state schools. States taking on more responsibility for ongoing training efforts.

(continued)

Table 19.2 (continued)

	FEDERAL / STATE	UNIFIED
Textbooks I. Finance; III. Regulation	FEDERAL: Designed by SEP and published and distributed free of charge by SEP. STATE: Federal government provided SEP texts free of charge providing strong incentive to use SEP texts.	UNIFIED: Designed by SEP and published and distributed free of charge by SEP. States free to choose alternative texts which for which they must pay.
School Calendar Setting III. Regulation	FEDERAL: SEP (180 days) STATE: Set by state, but no states had different calendar.	UNIFIED: SEP initially kept 180-day valandar, which states were free to extend. Some states established 200-day calandar, which was subsequently adopted by SEP, with some flexibility built in.
Information System II. Auditing VII. Civil Service & Management	FEDERAL: Integrated by SEP through the gathering of information by SCEPs. STATE: Under state control, which largely relied upon SEP's system.	UNIFIED: Integrated by SEP through the gathering of information by SCEPs and supplemented by nascent state-level systems. States tend to rely on SEP system for quantitative information gathering, and supplementary information they provide is more qualitative
School Building & Maintenance I. Finance; VII. Civil Service & Management	FEDERAL: State representatives of the federal parastatal building agency (CAPFCE) in compliance with SCEPs under broad regulations by SEP and CAPFCE. Locations chosen by state-level CAPFCE officials. Some involvement by Parent Associations, especially in rural areas. STATE: States built own school infrastructure and chose locations.	UNIFIED: States choose building agency which must be in compliance with CAPFCE and SEP regulations. States negotiate locations with CAPFCE. More involvement of Parent Associations, especially in rural areas. Plans are in place to give states greater control over CAPFCE and school construction locations.

these tables refer to school years, not calendar years. Thus, the tables refer to the 1988–89 to 1994–95 school years. The fact that the 1992 NAMBE was signed at the end of the school year in May facilitates analyzing these outcome data: 1991 (or the 1991–92 school year) represented the last year of the pre-decentralization regime, while 1992 is the first full year of the post-decentralization regime. Tables 19.1 and 19.2 present the raw outcomes, while Tables 19.3 and 19.4 present the absolute and percentage changes in these outcome indicators. Since all the raw outcome measures are rates, the absolute change is simply the difference in the given rate over the time period expressed in percentage points. The percentage change is the percentage change in those same rates over the time period, and is the measure of most importance for the discussion that follows. Data are presented for three states and for the country as a whole. The three states are Aguascalientes, which is included because it is generally considered the state that made the most rapid progress after the decentralization, Guanajuato, and Hidalgo. In this section, we concentrate on analyzing national outcomes and the State of Aguascalientes as a means for establishing a benchmark for national trends and one particularly successful state.

Tables 19.3 and 19.4 compare time periods of two different lengths. First, we examine the 1988–91 and 1991–94 time periods. Since 1991–92 was the last year before the decentralization, and the two periods are of the same length (three school years), the comparison is valid; including 1991 in the second time period captures the changes since the last year before the reform. Second, we examine the 1990–91 time period; this was the year before the decentralization,[5] and we present these data to capture the trend in outcomes in the year immediately prior to the decentralization. Note that in some cases the trend in an outcome measure is negative for the three-year period before decentralization but turned positive in the year before the decentralization. For instance, in Aguascalientes the percentage change in the enrollment rates for secondary schools (Table 19.3) was negative from 1988 to 1991, –0.1 percent, but positive for the 1991–92 period, 2.3 percent. In such cases two points must be made: (1) the negative trend in enrollment rates in the state turned positive the year *before* the decentralization, making it more difficult to attribute the positive post-decentralization outcome to the decentralization itself, and (2) we must compare the rate of growth in the year before and the years after; for instance in Aguascalientes, the 8.3 percent change from 1991 to 1994 represents an annual rate of growth of 2.7 percent (not presented in the table), which is quite similar to the pre-decentralization annual rate of 2.3 percent. Finally, we examine the 1992–93 time period because it is the one-year period (thus comparable to the 1991–92 period) immediately after the 1992 NAMBE.

Naturally, the reliability of these data could be called into question. States would have had an incentive to present particularly good results in the year

Table 19.3

Absolute and Percentage Changes in Enrollment Rates and in Terminal Efficiency Rates

State	Education level		Enrollment rates (%)				Terminal efficiency Rates (%)			
			1988–91	1991–94	1990–91	1992–93	1988–91	1991–94	1990–91	1992–93
Aguascalientes	Preschool	Absolute Δ	-2.8	13.8	1.0	9.0	—	—	—	—
		Percentage Δ	-4.1	20.9	1.5	12.7	—	—	—	—
	Primary	Absolute Δ	-0.1	1.8	2.8	1.1	7.5	2.5	2.4	0.2
		Percentage Δ	-0.1	1.9	3.0	1.1	11.2	5.6	3.3	0.3
	Secondary	Absolute Δ	-0.1	7.0	1.9	6.6	-2.4—	5.6	1.9	3.3
		Percentage Δ	-0.1	8.3	2.3	7.7	-3.1-	7.6	2.6	4.3
Guanajuato	Preschool	Absolute Δ	-9.0	11.9	2.2	6.3	—	—	—	—
		Percentage Δ	-13.9	21.4	4.1	10.3	—	—	—	—
	Primary	Absolute Δ	-16.5	0.2	0	0.2	3.1	3.0	1.4	1.6
		Percentage Δ	-14.4	0.2	0	0.2	5.5	5.0	2.4	2.7
	Secondary	Absolute Δ	0.3	4.0	0.8	-0.7	0.2	3.3	2.0	0.6
		Percentage Δ	0.4	5.2	1.0	-0.9	0.3	4.7	3.0	0.8
Hidalgo	Preschool	Absolute Δ	-7.5	19.4	2.8	10.5	—	—	—	—
		Percentage Δ	-11.9	3.5	5.3	16.3	—	—	—	—
	Primary	Absolute Δ	-8.2	1.3	0	1.6	9.2	7.6	1.2	2.3
		Percentage Δ	-7.7	1.3	0	1.6	16.8	12.9	2.0	3.4
	Secondary	Absolute Δ	-0.6	2.0	-0.2-	0.3	0.9	3.0	1.2	2.0
		Percentage Δ	0.7	2.4	-0.2	0.3	1.2	3.9	1.6	2.6
Mexican Republic	Preschool	Absolute Δ	-0.4	11.9	1.8	6.9	—	—	—	—
		Percentage Δ	-0.6	18.6	2.9	10.0	—	—	—	—
	Primary	Absolute Δ	0	0	0	0	3.1	3.8	1.7	1.2
		Percentage Δ	0	0	0	0	5.6	6.5	3.0	2.0
	Secondary	Absolute Δ	0	2.3	0.8	1.0	0.1	2.6	1.3	1.2
		Percentage Δ	0	2.7	0.9	1.2	0.1	3.5	1.8	1.6

Source: SEP, adapted by Gerhsberg.

Δ= change

219

Table 19.4
Absolute and Percentage Change in School Dropout and in Absorption Rates

State	Education Level	In school dropout rates (%)				In school absorption rates (%)			
		1988–91	1991–94	1990–91	1992–93	1988–91	1991–94	1990–91	1992–93
Aguascalientes	Primary								
	Absolute Δ	−2.2	−0.9	−2.6	−1.9	—	—	—	—
	Percentage Δ	−66.7	−82	−70.3	−79.2	—	—	—	—
	Secondary								
	Absolute Δ	−1.0	−2.5	−1.5	−2.	−1.8	11.9	1.7	7.5
	Percentage Δ	−10.5	−29.4	−15.0	−24.1	−2.2	15.2	2.2	9.2
Guanajuato	Primary								
	Absolute Δ	−0.8	−1.6	−1.0	−0.9	—	—	—	—
	Percentage Δ	−0.1	−34	−17.5	−20.5	—	—	—	—
	Secondary								
	Absolute Δ	−0.4	−1.7	−0.8	−0.3	−0.1	5.2	0.7	2.1
	Percentage Δ	−3.6	−16	−7.0	−3.2	−0.1	7.7	1.1	3.0
Hidalgo	Primary								
	Absolute Δ	−0.9	−1.6	−0.1	−0.4	—	—	—	—
	Percentage Δ	−22.5	−51.6	−3.1	−18.2	—	—	—	—
	Secondary								
	Absolute Δ	−0.1	−1.3	−0.1	0	−0.7	1.8	−0.3	1.4
	Percentage Δ	−1.2	−15.9	−1.2	0	−0.9	2.3	−0.54	1.7
Mexican Republic	Primary								
	Absolute Δ	−0.7	−1.3	−0.7	−0.5	—	—	—	—
	Percentage Δ	−13.2	−28.3	−13.2	−12.2	—	—	—	—
	Secondary								
	Absolute Δ	−0.3	−1.5	−0.7	−1.0	−0.3	2.2	0.6	1.7
	Percentage Δ	−3.3	−17.0	−7.4	−11.9	−0.4	2.7	0.7	2.0

Source: SEP, adapted by Gershberg.
Δ= change

following the decentralization, in order to show that they were making progress with their new responsibilities. However, given auditing and budgeting practices of the federal government, it is more difficult for states to alter these rates over longer periods of time, so examining the three-year periods before and after the 1992 decentralization should serve to mitigate some data manipulation.[6]

Table 19.3 shows that enrollment rates nationally differed quite substantially for the three different levels of schooling included in basic education. Preschool enrollment rates show the most dramatic improvement. Preschool enrollment rates fell slightly in the 1988–91 period, but rose 11.9 percentage points from 1991 to 1994, a rise that represents an 18.6 percent improvement from the year before the decentralization to the 1994–95 academic year. True, preschool enrollment began to improve, by 2.9 percent, the year before the decentralization, but the 10.0 percent improvement in 1992–93 is striking. In Aguascalientes preschool enrollment showed even more impressive improvement. It fell 4.1 percent in 1988–91 and rose 20.9 percent in 1991–94. Again, while the trend began improving the year before the decentralization, 1.5 percent, the 12.7 percent jump 1992–93 is a testament to the effectiveness of efforts by the state to target preschool programs in the years immediately following the decentralization. However, we cannot attribute such improvement exclusively to the decentralization reforms.

National primary school enrollment rates showed no change over the time period. Likewise, secondary school enrollment rates showed little change nationally in the pre- and post-decentralization periods. However, to the extent that increased preschool enrollment might eventually improve primary school enrollment, the trends presented above foster guarded optimism for the medium and long term.

Terminal efficiency rates are perhaps the most important educational outcome measure. Table 19.3 shows that nationally the number of students finishing primary school on time hovers around 60 percent from 1991 to 1994. On the other hand, secondary school absorption rates (the percentage of students finishing primary school who subsequently enroll in secondary school, shown in Table 19.3 are high, over 80 percent from 1988 to 1994). If one sets completing secondary school as an important goal for competing in a global economy, the main problem seems to be getting students to finish primary school. Table 19.3 shows that in the nation as a whole, primary school terminal efficiency improved steadily both before (5.6 percent) and after decentralization (6.5 percent), and that the fastest improvement actually occurred in the 1990–91 period. Thus, we do not have sufficient evidence to say that the reforms have had a significant effect to date on this important outcome measure. The same holds true for secondary terminal efficiency and primary and secondary school dropout rates (Table 19.4). In Aguascalientes, primary terminal efficiency rates showed more improvement before decentralization than after, and secondary terminal efficiency rates improved at approximately the same rate in 1991–94 as they did in

1990–91, so that we cannot say that the decentralization positively affected this important outcome measure. The same can be said at the national level regarding absorption rates, though Aguascalientes did show improvement in this measure after decentralization (Table 19.4).

Preschool Education in the States of Hidalgo and Guanajuato

It is clear that many state administrators emphasized preschool education in the years immediately following the 1992 reforms. While their powers to implement change were officially very small, we found two important outcomes from the decentralization legislation regarding preschool and other policies to improve dropout rates: (1) There appears to have been a reserve of good ideas at the state level that had been previously suppressed by the overly centralized bureaucracy; this supports a common notion of the benefits of decentralization, that sub-national officials are closer to the populations they serve and more able to discern both their needs and demand (see for instance IDB 1994). (2) The fact that decentralization was officially being promoted by the central government, even if the official transfer of power was significantly smaller than the central rhetoric, prompted state officials to go farther than before in their defiance of federal norms and rules in order to effect changes in which they believed. This fact appears to have bolstered reforms likely to impact positively on dropout rates in the long run due to improved preschooling.

Preschool Education in the State of Hidalgo

A widely recognized outcome of the decentralization legislation is the State of Hidalgo's innovative preschool program developed shortly after 1992 and based on the implementation of a new pedagogy called "Lectura y Escritura" (Reading and Writing) that departed from SEP guidelines. The idea to target preschool education sprang from the first-ever state secretary of education's knowledge of the efficacy of preschool education, and he coordinated a team of education scholars who developed the pedagogical guidelines by drawing from preschool research in Mexico and the United States. In particular, having achieved nearly 100 percent enrollment rates in primary school, education officials decided to concentrate on reforms that would both reduce failure rates and increase terminal efficiency, and decrease the need for compensatory programs. In addition, state officials recognized the political incentive to present the governor with a program that would prove popular and have a quick impact in as many communities across the state as possible. Since the governor had never before involved himself "profoundly" in educational policy, he gave the secretary of education significant independence in the development of the program.

Interestingly, federal officials recognized the program's success but insisted that it is in violation of federal regulations because it teaches children to read and write in preschool—for as little as ten minutes per day. According to federal regulations, this should not happen until primary school, and federal officials expressed concerns that these children would be "bored" in primary school. State-level officials admitted that this is true, but said that they decided to implement the reform despite knowing that it was against federal rules. The state secretary of education was an able lawyer (now the state attorney general) and found a loop-hole in SEP regulations upon which to base the legal claim for the program's permissibility. The details of the legal defense reveal interesting lessons: the state admitted that the program went against an internal SEP regulation, but that it was in conformity with the letter, if not the spirit, of the decentralization legislation. As a sovereign state, they claimed they were not bound by an intra-agency federal memorandum. It was a full year before state officials were confronted by SEP. They eventually defended the program successfully in front of President Zedillo, who had served previously as the nation's secretary of education. There is no indication that the SEP will dismantle the program, though they have tried to discredit it, first through the national teachers' union (Sindicato Nacional de Trabajadores de la Educación, or SNTE) and then through public statements by SEP officials. The SNTE, however, provided little resistance. With the exception of some older teachers, most preschool teachers exhibit enthusiasm for a program that makes their schools more than day-care centers.

Having fallen 11.9 percent from 1988 to 1991, preschool enrollment rates increased by 35 percent, from 55.5 percent in 1991–92 to 74.9 percent in 1994–95 (Table 19.3). While it is true that enrollment improved by 2.8 percentage points in the year before the reform (1990–91), the rate of improvement in the years after the reform is dramatic (10.5 and 19.4 percentage points in 1992–93 and 1991–94, respectively; see Table 19.3).

This improvement is only due in part to the pedagogical innovations outlined above. While state officials were fighting their battle over "Lectura y Escritura," they worked closely with the National Council for Educational Development (Consejo Nacional de Fomento Educativo, or CONAFE, the federal compensa-tory program targeting isolated communities) to send preschool teachers to many unserved communities. From 1992–93 to 1995–96, the state and CONAFE col-laborated to create almost 400 new preschool programs. CONAFE was responsi-ble for 75 percent of these new programs, and the state created the remainder with a CONAFE-styled program of its own. The source of this initiative was the state education secretary, who effectively proposed a matching financial arrange-ment to CONAFE. State officials also used their increased budget flexibility to prioritize preschool education within the funding they received in their yearly budgets from SEP, primarily through the allocation of new teachers to preschool. CONAFE responded favorably and proved supportive, despite some resistance to the new pedagogy.

Terminal efficiency rates for both primary and secondary schools showed steady improvement both before and after 1992 (Table 19.3), and there was only a slight improvement in secondary school absorption rates (Table 19.4). On the other hand, both primary and secondary school dropout rates showed more rapid improvement after 1992 than before (Table 19.4).

Preschool Education in the State of Guanajuato

Guanajuato has made significant progress in preschool education in the 1990s, primarily in terms of increased enrollment rates. As shown in Table 19.3, the three years before the 1992 NAMBE saw preschool enrollment rates drop by 13.9 percent. This trend reversed in the year before the 1992 decentralization, 1990–91, when enrollment rates increased by 4.1 percent. In the years after the NAMBE, however, enrollment rates increased even more dramatically—10.3 percent in 1992–93, the first year after the agreement, and 21.4 percent in the period from 1991 through the 1994–95 school year. State education officials attribute this improvement in part to efforts to improve preschool coverage that began before the most recent decentralization, as well as to changes effected by the NAMBE.

The initiative for the focus on preschool education had several sources. First, primary school enrollment rates were strong, near 100 percent (Table 19.3), while primary school terminal efficiency and failure rates left significant room for improvement. A state review of both Mexican and international education literature, along with consultation with academics in the education field, led planning officials to conclude that enhanced preschool enrollment held the highest potential for increased primary school efficiency and other improvements in retention. Interestingly, state officials contend that focusing on secondary school enrollments would have proven more politically popular among constituents (particularly urban parents), especially given that the decentralization legislation made secondary school obligatory but not preschool. Second, the governor, who was a member of an opposition political party, was aware that increasing preschool coverage would provide a presence for his government in many rural and indigenous communities across the state.

The 1992 decentralization gave state education officials some meaningful new powers that aided the preschool efforts. First, state administrators were able to place new teachers in preschools at rates greater than before the NAMBE. Thus, while salaries for teachers continue to be negotiated centrally, the state could exercise greater control over the distribution of teachers across the different levels of basic education. Second, the newly formed State Department of Education (Secretaría de Educación de Guanajuato, or SEG) began to recruit secondary school graduates and other non-normal school graduates of postsecondary schools as preschool teachers, called *para-maestros*. Recruitment efforts concentrated in particular on enlisting young women from the targeted communities, based on the assumption that they were more likely to live and remain in their home towns.

While this practice began before 1992, it increased afterward for several reasons. State officials encountered less resistance from central SEP officials against this alternative method of staffing preschools. Also, the SEG was able to negotiate more effectively with the union, which originally lobbied against the practice of using the *para-maestros* for the obvious reason that they were non-union. These successful negotiations with the union rested on the SEG's demonstrating that the *para-maestros* were not receiving teaching posts considered favorable to most normal school graduates and union members. They were placed in precisely the areas from which most union members tried to escape as soon as possible after being placed in them. State officials attribute this SEG–union dialogue to the 1992 NAMBE, which increased the number of issues for negotiation (e.g., benefits packages) and thus disarmed the union's opposition to this particular practice.

Another innovation of the preschool program in Guanajuato was the eligibility of three to five year olds. This practice, directly in violation of SEP regulations, also began before 1992. But state officials claim that before 1992 the practice was both clandestine and actively opposed by SEP. Since 1992, SEG has actually developed and published its own criteria and regulations for preschool as a complement to SEP's general guidelines and has gained more confidence to defy the SEP in this regard.

Enrollment rates for primary and secondary schools, terminal efficiency rates for primary and secondary schools, and absorption rates for secondary schools all showed some improvement after 1992 (Table 19.4), and dropout rates improved both before and after decentralization (Table 19.4), although we cannot attribute these trends to decentralization.

In both Guanajuato and Hidalgo, the case study evidence regarding preschool improvement provides some indication the state is headed in the right direction and that decentralization has played at least some supporting role.

Conclusions and Lessons Learned

Capacity and effective ideas exist at the sub-national level.

- We found consistent evidence of capable state administrators ready to develop and implement effective policies—often with a clearer focus on clients, a more effective use of resources, and/or innovative programs. This finding is significant because lack of sub-national administrative capacity is often cited as a major concern regarding transferring control from central government bureaucracies (Peterson 1994; Gershberg 1995). While the lack of experience at the sub-national level is by no means a trivial issue, we did not find it as critical as might be expected: for example, the State of Hidalgo in Mexico handled its new educational responsibilities very well, even with little previous state-level experience. We believe that sub-national administrators have effective ideas (and the ability to implement them) that have been stymied by lack of control over the requisite policy levers.

• We find some evidence that states use increased programmatic flexibility to develop pedagogical innovations in areas with high returns, such as preschool. The cases show that sub-national administrators are crafty at eking out more power and control than they are officially given. Through scrutinizing legal codes or simply gaining confidence to defy central norms, sub-national authorities seemed to take "decentralization" reforms, however limited *de jure*, as signals that they should do more, *de facto*. This is particularly true for regulation and policy development. The state-level SEP delegations (SCEPs) previously had little incentive to pursue such innovation, since they would have been violating norms established by their superiors in their own bureaucracy.

Central government continues to have critical responsibilities particularly for compensatory financing; so-called "decentralization" may alter but not actually reduce the central role.

• Well-targeted central compensatory resources and policies are needed to alleviate inequity. Sub-national administrators immediately lobbied central compensatory programs to effectively support their own innovations.

• It is also clear that non-decentralized federal compensatory programs (such as CONAFE in this case) continue to have a key impact and supporting role in programs developed by the state. We find some evidence that states have used the decentralization legislation and their increased flexibility in program design to lobby and involve federal compensatory programs effectively. Part of this cooperation stems from the willingness of states to commit resources under their control and combine them with federal funds.

Given these preliminary findings, we can tentatively assert that decentralizing the traditionally highly centralized educational bureaucracies in Latin America can free up sub-national officials to pursue reform strategies that can positively impact the problems of dropout and retention rates. Naturally, the ultimate success in this area is a long-term process and will depend on the precise nature of the decentralization reform and the specific powers actually transferred from the center. Nevertheless, the Mexican results allow for guarded optimism.

Notes

This chapter grew out of the research project for the Inter-American Development Bank (IDB) entitled "Decentralization and Recentralization: Lessons from the Social Sectors in Mexico and Central America." The research assistance of Norma Mogrovejo and Melissa O'Brien was invaluable. Comments from Michael Jacobs, Steve Doherty, and Bill Savedoff are gratefully acknowledged. The opinions expressed do not reflect those of the IDB or its board of directors. The author is solely responsible for all statements, interpretations, and errors.

1. Mexico is a federal country with thirty-one states and one Federal District (Mexico City, the national capital). Within the states, there are over 2,500 municipalities.

2. This chapter is based on case study work in Gershberg (1996b), which provides details on the methodology used to formulate many of the insights and assertions made below.

3. Basic education refers to preschool, primary, and secondary school levels. The NAMBE also included initial, indigenous, and normal schooling. Only teachers and administrators in the National Council for Educational Development (CONAFE, the federal compensatory program targeting isolated communities) and the Federal District remained officially employed by the federal Government.

4. The source for Tables 19.3 and 19.4 is SEP (1994).

5. Remember that the 1990–91 time period is really a comparison between the 1990–91 and 1991–92 school years; therefore it is the time period immediately before the May 1992 NAMBE.

6. In addition, all these data have computation problems because neither the SEP nor the SEEs can track individual students. For instance, one could see enrollment rates of over 100 percent (because of students being left back or migrating between states); the terminal efficiency rate suffers similarly.

General References

Gershberg, A.I. 1998a. "Decentralization and Recentralization: Lessons from the Social Sectors in Mexico and Nicaragua," OCE Working Paper Series, WP-379. Washington, DC: Inter-American Development Bank. August 1998.

———. 1998b. "Decentralization, Recentralization and Performance Accountability: Building an Operationally Useful Framework for Analysis," *Development Policy Review*, vol. 16, no. 4: pp. 405–431.

Inter-American Development Bank (IDB). 1994. *Economic and Social Progress in Latin America: 1994 Report*. Washington, DC: Inter-American Development Bank, October.

SEP. 1994 *Indicadores Educativos: 1988–1989 a 1994–1995*. Mexico, D.F.: SEP.

———. 1996. *Compendio Estadistico del Gasto Educativo, 1995*. Mexico City: SEP, March.

Works Cited

Gershberg, Alec Ian. 1995. "Fiscal Decentralization and Intergovernmental Relations: An Analysis of Federal Versus State Education Finance in Mexico." *Review of Urban and Regional Development Studies* 7, no. 2 (July).

———. 1996b. "Case Study Report: Mexican Educational Decentralization 1992–1996." Washington, DC: Inter-American Development Bank, RE2/SO2. October 20. Mimeo.

Peterson, George E. 1994. "Decentralization in Latin America: An Overview of Lessons and Issues." Washington, DC: World Bank, LATAD, May. Mimeo.

Part V
Curriculum

20

Edith Litwin

Curricular Ideologies: Prescriptions and Normative Traditions in Teaching, Theories, and Practices

From the pioneering treaties by Bobitt at the turn of the century to the current debates, there have been different trends and principles for analyzing the curriculum, its reforms, and changes. The curriculum states the essential principles, purposes and features of education approaches, so that they may be implemented or guide classroom activities.

As regards tendencies in curriculum design, we can distinguish three different approaches: (1) A normative tradition that broadly covers the academic, humanistic, or field currents which emphasized the purpose of education, the distinction among academic disciplines, fields of knowledge and the settlement of structures around fields or areas, and the assignment of time to each of them. (2) Prescriptive designs that set the objectives of teaching, their design, and the appropriate ways of carrying them out, independently of the actual conditions or contexts. (3) Different curriculum analyses, all of them based on research processes.

When designing a curriculum, teachers' research about their actual work is fundamental. The importance of a curriculum that discloses its implicit aspects is recognized, an analysis is made of the teachers' representations or of their thought processes. In our view, what keeps these approaches apart is their prescriptive or non-prescriptive nature in analyzing actual teaching. In analyzing a curriculum, we may either distinguish its tendencies and nature from pedagogic and teaching concepts or understand its structure in terms of the political and administrative environment in which it was formed.

Background: The Past Twenty Years in Curriculum Design and Its Application in Argentina

Theory

When analyzing the curricula in the past twenty years, we believe it is highly relevant to consider the political contexts in which they were designed and implemented. This will show how the discussions that arose as to the reforms reflected the political project of which they were a part and the nation's political instability, rather than recognize styles, tendencies or structures. It must be taken into account that until December 1983, the curriculum introduced into Argentina originated in the period of military dictatorships.

In 1972, the Ministry of Education implemented Curricular Guidelines from the first to seventh grades in primary school. This document put forward a division by fields of knowledge: language, mathematics, social, and natural sciences. For each field it stated its objectives, contents, activities, and methodological suggestions. This proposal had no theoretical-epistemological framework, no analyses of approaches to science or technology, no basic concepts, no current issues, no links to reality. It just consisted of a synthetic document drawn with different criteria by fields of knowledge.

In 1978 the National Education Council, which was in charge of the guidelines for the whole of the education system, was dismantled, and primary education was decentralized to the respective districts. Therefore, for the period between 1978 and 1994 we can only analyze documents for the provinces or for the Federal District. Thus, in 1980 the Secretary of Education of the City of Buenos Aires designed a new curriculum which was clearly seen as a political proposal of the military dictatorship. Unlike the preceding synthetic curriculum, this one was analytic and covered over one thousand pages. The antagonism with former guidelines was expressed in the development of a theoretical framework explaining infant learning, concepts of discipline and teaching implications, guiding axes, extensive bibliography for teachers, and so forth. This prescriptive model generated strong closed and dogmatic structures for reflecting on learning and on the development of scientific knowledge. Besides, during the dictatorship other curricular documents were generated which, in spite of putting forward the latest advances in research in psychology, still kept their prescriptive nature. A long-distance training program was also implemented with theoretical bases and examples similar to those of the curricular design.

With the advent of democracy in Argentina in 1986, a new design for primary education was generated for the city of Buenos Aires, which was preceded by research done for the previous proposal. In this proposal there is an attempt to promote the integration of fields and to leave the design of implementation open. It represents a tendency or option for contents, even though it includes a research process.

On April 14, 1993, the Federal Education Law No. 24,195 was passed, which modified the structure of the educational system, increasing compulsory schooling from 7 to 10 years. This includes a compulsory initial level at age five plus nine years of basic education in three 3-year-long cycles. Thus, the structure of the five- or six-year-long non-compulsory secondary school was broken up: the first two years were integrated in the third cycle of general education, and a cycle was created (called polimodal) for the last three years of schooling before college.

In 1994 the Common Basic Contents (CBCs) were regulated for the initial and basic levels for the whole of the country. This document replaced all the preceding ones and it was distributed (one per school) for the teachers' reference and orientation. This document establishes the development of the CBCs at the national level, but it also attempts the formulation of a curricular design at the district level and the formulation of plans for each school.

Application of Curriculum Design

An important aspect of curriculum design is how it determines the use of time in the classroom. Typically, the school year is 260 days per year, four hours per day, although in some schools the school day is seven hours. Each day, approximately 80 percent of the time is spent on teaching, and the remainder is spent on taking attendance or other tasks. From 1980 to 1986 in Buenos Aires, teaching time was distributed, approximately, 19 percent on language, 19 percent on mathematics, 17 percent on social sciences, 15 percent on natural sciences, and 30 percent on other topics. From 1994 on, under the CBCs, approximately 18 percent of the time was spent on teaching language, 18 percent on mathematics, 17.5 percent on social sciences, 17.5 percent on natural sciences, and 29 percent on other topics. These statistics represent general trends: the different school districts determine the use of teaching time in the classroom. Thus, there are no definitive national statistics on these aspects of teaching in Argentina.

Innovations and Current Reforms

In practice, in 1997 schools used the Common Basic Contents as if they had been the established curricular designs. Relatively few institutional projects have been developed and some district designs are under way, but this has not prevented the implementation of the CBCs. The main feature of the CBCs is the organization of the fields of knowledge: language, mathematics, natural sciences, social sciences, technology, art, physical education, ethics, and civics. In each field, the contents are formulated per cycle and per unit. The units refer, in general, to large areas in a field of knowledge, to teaching and learning strategies specific of each field and to attitudes related to such fields or procedures. This exhaustive list of contents has resulted in their division into conceptual, procedural, and attitudinal contents. The units include explanatory syntheses and they suggest the possible connections between topics.

Theoretical-explanatory frameworks regarding knowledge and fields have been put aside. As a design, the new document is framed in an academic tradition and has a closed structure. In a curriculum, the distinction between conceptual, procedural, and attitudinal contents has resulted in a fragmentation and denaturalization of the fields of knowledge. Due to the obstacles that its production has created, a new document has appeared called The CBCs in the School, which is a simplified version of the preceding document and has examples.

A main characteristic of this document is the fact that it has been drawn up by well-known scholars from the academic community. This means that the reform under way has assigned priority to the updating of the contents of and approaches to teaching. The discussions during the choice of contents were related to thematic organization and selection. New curricular spaces have been created: those of integration of fields through the creation of fields of knowledge, the development of cross-sectional contents, and the inclusion of new fields. An instance of field integration was the change in the contents of the teaching of history and geography by creating the field of the social sciences, which also includes sociological, economic, political, and anthropological issues. We are concerned here with the implementation of these teaching proposals by the teachers themselves, since these new fields were not part of their training, and the implementation of this approach must be preceded by a deep treatment of the subjects involved. If this step is omitted, really important issues of the fields involved may be overlooked or false relationships may be established among the fields.

Other creations of new areas or subjects include, for example, the teaching of civics or of technology. In the former case, ethics and civics have been proposed in three important districts with large numbers of students as cross-sectional contents: in the provinces of Buenos Aires, Misiones, and Santa Fe. The cross-sectional contents are those that reflect social, community and labor demands, and issues related to topics, procedures, and attitudes of common interest; therefore, they are not merely characterized by their social significance, but they keep the division in the curriculum into conceptual, procedural, and attitudinal contents. They will be approached at different levels of complexity, according to the grade level. The cross-sectioning requires time and space in the design, and accounts for two different curricular views: a globalized or integrated one, and one by areas and fields. It poses the need to change the organizing context in the classroom. If these points are not analyzed, ethics and civics may weaken as teaching spaces.

The teaching of technology introduces a totally new field into schools in Argentina. However, most teachers are not familiar with this field, and there is very little methodology developed for its teaching.

Analyzing teaching with regard to the implementation of designs leads to a study of diversity in the educational context of the different districts. The schools in the city of Buenos Aires, the schools in the city of Resistencia (capital of the province of Chaco), or the rural schools of the province of Chubut reflect different needs and demands. These differences, expressed in actual teaching, have had the curriculum as a homogenizing factor through time. It is true that in 1995 the CBCs were a nationwide proposal on which the design had to be created and that the design of each district had to consider diversity. However, to the extent that the designs per district have not been elaborated yet, the CBCs continue acting as that homogenizing factor against the announced diversity. Thus, the reform generates a strong recentralizing movement as it cancels all previous designs and puts forward a base document on which the curricular designs for each district must be elaborated. As a result of this re-centralizing movement, by the end of 1997, one-half of these designs had been elaborated with similar formats, categorizations, and developments. Some districts, such as the city of Buenos Aires, have not presented their designs yet, even though they have elaborated many documents for the educational institutions. Other districts have generated very significant movements of shared and of cooperative work.

The changes in the structure of the school system and the introduction of the CBCs reflect the concern with a reform of the educational system. A highly significant aspect of the contents is that they have become the orienting curricular document for classroom work. The reform policy in Argentina is, then, a curricular policy without a curriculum. The introduction of the new contents, however, is not random. All the people involved—teachers, school principals, and supervisors—must attend courses in a system of Continuing Teacher Education. They get credits for these courses, and they must add up a certain number of credits by the year 2000 to be able to remain in the system. The courses are taught by level and by cycle in the first levels of the system. Thus, teachers attend only the courses for their level and get the same number of credits for courses on psychology, teaching of mathematics, and physical education, since they are all the same length. Each course must offer thirty credits, which means thirty class hours. Before the year 2000, a teacher must have 180 credits, a principal 200 credits, and a supervisor between 240 and 250 credits. The idea of an optional series of courses chosen according to levels and equivalent credits could form a coherent package if the teachers choose it as such, but it may not do so if they choose courses because of number of hours, distance, friendship, or obligation rather than subject matter.

The introduction of innovations and the promotion of quality in teaching are also the aims of two co-existing projects of the Ministry of Education with autonomous financing. One of them is called Proyecto Nueva Escuela (New School Project, which differs from the one in Colombia although it has the same name) and is made up of a nationwide net of schools that receive special training, high-level academic and professional counseling, and a specially equipped infrastructure, which includes computers, school libraries, and supplies. It is a pilot experience with head schools, satellite schools, and border schools in each region with a special set of tasks. The other project is called Plan Social and it has the aim of stimulating and giving financial support to educational experiments in schools. The members of the institutions make the request for financial aid for the projects that are evaluated by the district officials and then by the Ministry of Education.

As part of the Social Plan, there is a project of support to rural teaching that affects most repeaters and dropouts from the system. It consists of a program through which material is distributed free to the students; this is very high quality material that has already proven successful in keeping enrollment high. The project is just going through its early stages and there are no statistics on it.

These changes, however, have not affected the number of students per course, which varies widely for the whole of the country: from twenty to up to fifty students in 1997; nor have the changes affected the time distribution or the institutional program of the schools, since no new channels have been opened nor have new work programs been created for the identification of the various institutions.

Teaching Materials

The cost of materials, typically, was $40 for books, $30 for other supplies, US$20 for uniforms. This would require 15 to 20 percent of a minimum wage (paid every month) if acquired new. As a result, perhaps many students did not have textbooks and other materials. Books were not available in school libraries until 1997, handicapping students' ability to learn. Yet, we believe that educational reform in Argentina has been mainly organized through a curricular program and its implementation is secured through the training of teachers. In this context, practical matters have been greatly distorted. There are teachers who based their teaching on pupils' textbooks instead of working with other materials to provide a new perspective on the topic. Further, both teachers and students received materials intended mainly for the students. These are textbooks published by private firms and, thus, not distributed free, except to those students covered by the Social Plan.

By materials we mean the resources used by teachers in order to guide and motivate students, and to provide them with situations that make learning possible. They influence content through the selection of topics and of their treatments; they are, therefore, cultural vehicles and make up the curriculum in that they themselves constitute what is taught and what is learned. By becoming the school curriculum, the chosen materials contribute to a closed structure by crystallizing contents and deciding in all cases what is the best activity for building up knowledge.

In the case of Argentina, textbooks and manuals for the different courses of the cycles of General Basic Education develop the new contents and suggest activities supporting the learning processes. In general, the activities offer a great variety of programs. They try to establish links with knowledge from previous cycles and from daily life. They foster the development of analogies and they approach students' comprehension problems. Some publishers distribute books free to teachers. Even though there is a wide variety of books available to students, our research shows that a single publishing house has monopolized the market, with a new growing firm trying to displace it. In general, teachers adopt the publishers' proposals, which are really valuable, and have made the manual the new curricular document guiding their teaching. Thus, if the reform option was curricular through the formulation of new contents, then the methodological approaches have been prescriptive, to the extent that the reform has become the application of the manuals or textbooks.

Furthermore, the use of other materials in the classroom is rare. The introduction of computers as a technological aid has brought about some controversy. In some cases where not enough hardware was available, teachers and students were encouraged to practice with cardboard models of computers. In other cases, computers were sent to schools that had no electricity. However, the most serious problems are that teachers do not know how to use them and that they lack the adequate software.

Another proposal implemented by the Ministry of Education was the creation of school libraries in 1997 equipped with a score of educational texts. The fact that this project is in its early stages makes it impossible to evaluate its effects.

Perspectives and Proposals

A curriculum that in a democratic way attends to the needs of the economically disadvantaged sectors of society must be approached from the standpoint of social justice; it must also be a space open to the contributions of research on fields of knowledge and on teaching. Such a curriculum should take into account the conditions for and against its introduction. It should consider the process of teachers' training and not that of recycling.

Argentine curriculum lacks a design. When it is designed, perhaps textbooks will no longer play a prescriptive role. Curriculum designs should start in the classroom; organizing schools as centers of inquiry into the teaching and learning processes and into the structures that support them in the contemporary historical context. Achieving this implies a long process in which discussion about reform begins during teacher training. Reforms should not be imposed on teachers. We must consider the process of restructuring schools and teacher training and professional conditions. One of the priorities in these working conditions should be an increase in salary. Once again, reforms should not be imposed on professionals, threatening their working conditions: salary, stability, autonomy of decision making, rewards, etc. Changing schools and their practices is not just a matter of mandating changes or instituting programs; rather, it requires a joining together of such complex and varied things as teachers' opportunities to learn new ideas, to discuss and plan with other teachers, and also to develop a supportive culture for teachers' continuous learning and understanding of the process of change.

General Bibliography

Apple, Michael. 1986. *Ideología y currículo*. Madrid: Akal.
———. 1997. *Teoría crítica y educación*. Buenos Aires: Miño y Dávila Editores.
Argentina. 1995. *Contenidos Básicos Comunes para la Educación General Básica*. Ministerio de Cultura y Educación de la Nación. Consejo General de Cultura y Educación. Buenos Aires.

Bernstein, Basil. 1988. *Clases, códigos y control. Hacia una teoría de las transmisiones educativas.* Madrid: Akal.

Bolívar, Antonio. 1996. *"Non scholae sed vitae discimus*: límites y problemas de la transversalidad." *Revista de Educación* no. 309: 23–65. Madrid: Ministerio de Educación y Ciencia.

Contreras, Domingo José. 1990. *Enseñanza, curriculum y profesorado.* Madrid: Akal.

de Alba, Alicia. 1991. *Currículum: crisis, mito y perspectivas.* México: Centro de Estudios sobre la Universidad, UNAM.

Eisner, Elliot. 1992. "Curriculum Ideologies." In *Handbook of Research on Curriculum,* ed. Philip Jackson. American Educational Research Association. Chicago: Rand McNally.

Feldman, Daniel. 1994. *Curriculum, maestros y especialistas.* Buenos Aires: Libros del Quirquincho.

Gimeno Sacristán, José. 1997. *Docencia y cultura escolar. Reformas y modelo educativo.* Buenos Aires: Lugar Editorial.

Stenhouse, Lawrence. 1984. *Investigación y desarrollo del curriculum.* Madrid: Morata.

Terigi, Flavia. 1997. "Reflexiones sobre el nivel jurisdiccional de especificación curricular." *Novedades Educativas* 9, no. 84 (December).

Torres, Jurjo. 1994. *Globalización e interdisciplinariedad: el curriculum integrado.* Madrid: Morata.

21

Ana Lúcia Amaral

Curriculum and Teaching in Brazil: Current Conditions and Outlook

Introduction

The purpose of this chapter is to discuss questions related to curriculum and teaching in the current Brazilian education system and their role in the high rates of repetition and dropout, which stain its educational record. Above all, we wish to link educational problems with the current Brazilian situation.

Brazil is a nation characterized, above all, by its high levels of inequality. In order to characterize national disparities, we will utilize the Human Development Index (HDI), which works with the basic concept that three essential conditions are present in all levels of development: longevity, educational level, and access to resources. We use the HDI to delineate the three large groups into which Brazil is divided, assigning the states and Federal District as follows (IPEA 1996, 11–16):

1. High Human Development—Rio Grande do Sul, the Federal District, São Paulo, Santa Catarina, Rio de Janeiro, Paraná, Mato Grosso do Sul, and Espírito Santo;
2. Medium Human Development—Minas Gerais, Goiás, Mato Grosso, Rondônia, Amazonas, Roraima, and Amapá;
3. Low Human Development—Pará, Acre, Sergipe, Maranhão, Tocantins, Piauí, Ceará, Rio Grande do Norte, Pernambuco, Paraíba, Alagoas, and Bahia.

In this chapter, we explore curriculum and teaching both nationally and regionally, referring to three states from the three different regions: São Paulo, Minas Gerais, and Pernambuco, representing areas of high, medium, and low human development, respectively, according to the criteria of the HDI.

Curriculum and Teaching

The "Portrait" of Our Schools in Recent Decades

Brazil was always able to take pride in some "islands of excellence," that is, some schools that could be readily compared to good schools in the first world.

There also existed some significant innovative programs in certain cities, but the vast majority of our schools were characterized by poor installations, teaching, and material resources: the few materials were restricted to textbooks in basic areas (Portuguese and mathematics) supplied by the government; other materials, such as books, notebooks, and writing materials, were supplied by families. This absence of material resources, associated with the lack of preparation and even disinterest by the teachers (remuneration and incentives were minimal), led to low quality of teaching: traditional methods of exposition and copying; uncoordinated contents; irrelevant curricula unrelated to children's conditions and interests.

Due to the poor condition and small size of some school buildings, some schools have to operate three shifts per day of three and a half hours each—an insufficient amount of time for satisfactory results by the children. To save costs, official recommendations are to make the maximum use of available space. The result is that, in inadequate schools, an average of forty students are in a class-room with only one teacher, which prevents any modification of the placement of school desks, and any activity that is different from exposition or copying texts written on the blackboard. Exposition is carried out with an average student in mind; different individuals, whether in terms of speed of learning or interests, cannot be considered (one size fits all).

The low remuneration of teachers obliges them to double their workday in either the same or another school, keeping them from meeting their colleagues and attempting any kind of group work. A monotonous and insipid routine is imposed.

Evaluation, even though new references are being incorporated into the teachers' discourse, is still processed in very traditional ways. Different evaluation methods and instruments are being used (exercises, works, observation), but the "tests"—objective or not—continue as the main indicators of proficiency, linked to very a premature judgment that the teacher makes of students, in a national version of the "self-fulfilling prophecy" (Amaral and Santos 1998). There are no incentives for promotion and the great number of failures does not inconvenience anyone, because failing students has been incorporated into school culture. Above all, the "gap" between school culture and that of the new students from the lower classes made it impossible for them to succeed, generating successive repetitions and, finally, dropping out from school.

Changes in Curriculum and Teaching: A National Proposal

In 1990, Brazil participated in the World Conference on Education for All in Jomtien, Thailand, and agreed to provide present and future generations with quality primary school education. After this meeting, a movement was initiated to make the states sensitive to providing quality education.

In 1996, after a long trajectory of amendments and alterations, Law no. 9394/96 was approved. This law (LDB—Lei de Diretrizes e Bases da Educaçao

Nacional) established the bases and guidelines governing national education, replacing the 1971 law (Brasil, MEC 1996). Its curricular provisions were characterized by great flexibility. A common national base is recommended for basic and middle school education, to be complemented in each teaching system and school by a diversified part, in order to respond to the regional and local characteristics of society. The required part should include the study of Portuguese and mathematics; knowledge of the physical and natural world and current social and political conditions; art and physical education. The teaching of history should take into account the contributions of different cultures and ethnic groups in the formation of the Brazilian people. The diversified part requires teaching of a modern foreign language starting with the fifth grade. The curricular content of basic education should observe, then, the diffusion of basic values of social interest, citizens' rights and obligations, respect for the common good and democratic order, as well as the special characteristics of life in each region.

The law made it possible to organize school into yearly series, by semesters and cycles, and ungraded classes organized on the basis of age, competence, and other criteria. It increased the minimum required annual school hours from 180 to 200 hours of schoolwork. Regarding evaluation, continuous, and cumulative evaluation of students' behavior and achievements should be made, emphasizing qualitative over quantitative aspects. This makes it possible to advance in courses and grades by means of verification of what has been learned.

Continuing its policy of improving education, formulated in 1997, the Ministry of Education and Sports, through its Secretary of Basic Education, initiated National Curriculum Parameters (PCN) for the first four grades of basic education (Brasil, MEC, SEF 1997). There was a great debate about the PCN, seen by many as a step backward in the discussion of decentralization, regionalization, and contextualization of teaching. Meanwhile, Minister Paulo Renato Souza declared that the object of the PCN is "indicating qualitative goals that would help the student confront the real world as a participative, thoughtful and autonomous citizen, knowledgeable about his rights and duties."

The parameters of the PCN, organized after consulting specialists in various fields of knowledge, incorporating successful educational experiences, were to furnish basic general and specific orientations in Portuguese language, mathematics, natural sciences, history and geography, art, physical education, and areas known as "transversal themes": ethics, health, environment, sex education, and cultural pluralism. It gave great importance to the culture of the student, considering it as a starting point in the acquisition of technical-scientific and cultural ideas, which are human patrimony, without losing sight of the importance of the contents learned. As a support to this policy, the Ministry of Education has been revitalizing the "School Books Program" through which the federal government provides basic books and supporting writing materials free of charge to all students enrolled in the basic cycle of public schools.

Aside from this, more than suggesting contents to be covered, the PCN advanced methodological orientations. Without falling into dogmatism, it incorporated the most important contributions that pedagogy had offered and provided options. It recommended active methods, with clear preference for what today is called constructivism, emphasizing the role of the teacher as the facilitator of learning. Teaching orientations highlighted: (a) autonomy, as a capacity to be developed by students and as a general teaching principle guiding pedagogical practices; (b) diversity, understood as attending to the specific needs of individual students, to the specific individual; (c) interaction and cooperation, comprehended as the need to incorporate students' understanding and use of the spoken word so that they would be capable of living together productively and cooperatively in a group; (d) disposition to learn, which is understood as significant learning; (e) organization of time as an important factor in the construction of autonomy; (f) organization of space, allowing the adoption of active teaching practices; and (g) selection of material taking into account diversity as a relevant factor.

It is suggested that schooling be organized by cycles, rather than school grades, because they are more flexible, more consistent with the rhythms of learning, effectively contributing to overcoming the problems of student development. School organization by cycles is supposed to be up to each school system (state, district, and so on). Elementary schools can comprise two or three cycles lasting two, three, or even four years each. At the end of each cycle, students are submitted to formal and quantitative evaluation. If necessary, they are given special support in whatever matter they might need. Evaluation, intrinsically linked to the question of school organization, is treated as a "combination of actions that have the function of nourishing, sustaining, and guiding pedagogic intervention." The PCN recommended continuous and systematic evaluation, giving priority to qualitative aspects and comprising different dimensions of learning. The results should be conceived of as indicators for the reorientation of educational practice and never as a means of stigmatizing students.

The next section presents how the two most important expressions of government policy in relation to curriculum and teaching in basic education—the LDB and PCN—were applied in the three Brazilian states that we selected as representative of the "three Brazils": São Paulo, Minas Gerais, and Pernambuco. Due to the recent implementation of these policies, the proposals have been carried out for only a brief time, but they already have positive results to show.

The State Proposals

São Paulo. São Paulo is selected to represent a region with a high level of human development because it is the richest and most industrialized state in the nation. Beginning with projects such as the "Pattern Schools" and the "School with a New Face," the Secretariat of Education of the State of São Paulo was, progressively, introducing innovations that were very much in agreement with the proposals of the LDB and the PCN. Initially, it promoted a restructuring of the state school network as a way of rationalizing its oversight of schools. This was soon followed by a series of proposed innovations (APEOESP 1997; Governo do Estado de São Paulo 1997).

In 1997, it instituted the regime of continuous progression in basic education, with a duration of eight years that could be organized in one or more cycles. The organization by cycles has begun, in a pioneer initiative, with the creation of the Basic Cycle of Literacy that, later, was extended to other states. The Basic Cycle of Literacy was the first initiative to lower the unacceptable rates of repetition after the first school year. It gave students a longer time to learn the basic skills of reading, writing, and speaking. The notion of cycles was extended beyond the limits of literacy and achieved greater curricular flexibility and better attention to the students' different rhythms of learning.

With the aim of correcting the flow of students—the age of 30 percent of students in basic education differed by two or more years from the normal age of students in the grades they attended—the Secretariat created the Project for Accelerated Classes. The project was to make the curriculum more flexible, provide special teaching material, and give specific preparation to teachers to correct the problem of overage students. It is a "surgical" program that should self-destruct once continuous promotion takes place.

The Sala-Ambiente Project was inspired by innovations by the "New School" movement, transforming the classroom environment, changing the professor from an instructor to a facilitator of learning and giving students the opportunity of "learning to learn." The classrooms are transformed into true learning laboratories.

In this context of innovations, evaluation acquires new dimensions, such that:

1. Internal evaluation at school is transformed to aid student learning throughout this process. It is hoped that evaluation's punitive and exclusionary character will be transformed into a multi-dimensioned group of facts about the progress and development of learning.
2. External evaluation seeks to evaluate the student, institution, or system by means of national tests. The practice of group pedagogy has been emphasized and used in the process of teacher training. There is a great effort at sensitizing the school in the sense of incorporating parents and families into the school community.

Minas Gerais. This state was selected as a representative of medium development. Minas is a very peculiar state: it is, in truth, a mixture of the "three Brazils," because its southern region is equivalent to the richest regions of São Paulo. It possesses regions of intermediate development and part of its northwest region is classified as one of the poorest of the nation. Thus, although it has some good indicators, it is registered as a region of medium development.

Its pedagogical proposal, which it delineated in 1991 and was able to carry out thanks to the continuity of government, closely resembles the São Paulo proposal: having begun with the Basic Cycle of Literacy, it ends up by instituting two four-year cycles in primary school, and inaugurating the process of continuous promotion (SEEMG 1997). In addition to the project of Accelerated Classes, which are required but provisional, pilot projects were conducted that envisioned the constant transformation of the school: one of them, inspired by the successful New School (Escuela Nueva) project in Colombia, brought New School methods to rural schools, dynamizing the curriculum and practices of multi-grade schools; another, inspired by the Accelerated Schools project created by Henry Levin of the University of Stanford, CA, collectivized school management and dynamized teaching practices, incorporating concepts of Dewey, Piaget, Vygotsky, and Freire, among others (SEEMG, SSDE, SDE, DNPC 1996).

Just as in São Paulo, in Minas there was an attempt to change the way evaluation was carried out, restructuring internal evaluation and since 1992 carrying out external evaluation of the school system (SEEMG 1994). In Minas, the Sala-Ambiente Project was not launched.

The Minas proposal emphasizes, above all, school autonomy and group work. The school was to incorporate the family into the school community. Each school was expected to have group development of its own—a PDE (Plan of School Development)—approved by the School Governing Council, an organ in which various segments of the school community are represented.

Pernambuco. This state was selected as representative of regions of low economic development. Pernambuco is situated in one of the poorest regions of the nation—the Northeast—and has rich cultural traditions and activities; it is a major tourist attraction. The data referring to this state were gathered from a State Report—1995/96 (Pernambuco 1997) and a Four Year Educational Plan—1996–99 (Pernambuco 1996). In the Report, one can see that many important actions have been already carried out, such as: 25,000 state teachers and 8,000 district teachers have been trained in service; incentives have been give to the development of pedagogical projects; a *Handbook on Shared Pedagogy* was elaborated and sent to the schools to help teachers and students on curricular problems. In addition, many cultural programs have been developed: vacation at school, children's art saloon, Winter Festival carrying out many workshops dealing with several arts, Music at School Program in 30 metropolitan region schools (City of Recife, capital of the state), creation of 262 Centers for Technology at state schools, and so on.

However, according to the Pernambuco's "Report on Education—1995–96," in 1995, there were still 120,000 children between seven and fourteen years of age (approximately 10 percent of school-age children) who did not attend school (Pernambuco 1997).

Like Minas Gerais, the State of Pernambuco benefited from political continuity, which gave permanence and consistency to its pedagogical proposal. Its State Four Year Education Plan (1996–99), inspired by the Federal Constitution and Federal Ten Year Plan of Education for All, proposed to (a) universalize basic education with quality and progressive extension of middle school;

(b) enhance the value of teachers; and (c) democratize educational management, above all, management of students. It tried to make school a competent, flexible, agile, creative, pleasurable place, that takes account of the students' potentialities, a place characterized by curiosity to understand the complexity of the world and disposed to propose changes. School is understood as a place of teaching, learning and cultural enrichment, but above all, as a basic social right: it is necessary that its contents and attitudes favor the consolidation of humanity's conquests and advances. It praises a democratic standard of collective management, emphasizing the responsibility of the school for the success of the student.

Methodologies point toward a teacher who is a coordinator of the teaching process and mediator in the learning process, adopting a constructivist pedagogy based on Emília Ferrero and Paulo Freire. Evaluation is already treated in its two dimensions: internal (as a process of evaluation used to identify teaching situations favoring the improvement of teaching and learning), and external (as periodic tests in stratified samples of the state school network). Despite making clear its preoccupation with changing the exclusionary character of evaluation (traditional views ignored the diagnostic dimension of evaluation; more recent trends also see evaluation as a means of evaluating both the quality of learning and the quality of teaching), the state of Pernambuco has not yet been able to put proposals of continuous promotion, or of organizational structure in cycles into practice.

Pernambuco's Four Year Education Plan argues that the curriculum should be included in the current debate and take into account the cognitive capacities and sociocultural background of the student, adapting its contents to the daily life of the student, and leading to scientific and cultural knowledge that is the patrimony of humanity. In addition, the adoption of "transversal" themes is suggested.

Conclusions

Governmental organs seem to be convinced of the necessity for great change in the Brazilian educational panorama. At least, that is what appears in official documents. We explore here, although superficially, the Law of Directives and Bases of National Education (LDB) and the National Curricular Parameters (PCN), in which, despite the great they flexibility provide, there will be control of educational products via external evaluation. We do not yet know the repercussions that these evaluations bring.

Analysis of the educational proposals of the states of São Paulo, Minas Gerais and Pernambuco indicates that there are not great differences among these and the national policies. The educational field today carries on advanced, modern discussion in tune with the most significant national and international educational experiences. The common curricular base is in part diversified, attending to regional and local needs. It is characterized by great autonomy of school systems and of the school; organization by cycles and continuous promotion; evaluation emphasized in its qualitative aspects; active and constructivist methodologies; contents that are significant and placed in an appropriate context; continuous training of teachers; emphasis on collective teacher and student work; and incorporation of the family and community into the school community. These are some of the pillars that sustain the new proposals, with the aim of providing quality education for all. It seems that the country has taken account, finally, of the fact that the place of children is in school and that unlimited efforts should be made in order to turn the school into a competent and agreeable institution that is attractive to its clientele.

We know that educational reforms do not take place on paper, but in the classroom. It is indispensable that changes take place, primarily, in the minds of both educators and the community itself. Above all, it is necessary that conditions of greater relevancy be guaranteed: the establishment of teaching careers and adequate salaries, in order to give incentive to current teachers and attract new and good teachers; an agreeable and healthy school environment, with a reasonable number of students in the classroom; libraries and teaching equipment and technology brought up to date and present in sufficient quantity; an increase in the length of the school day for students and teachers (little can be done with shifts of three and a half hours). Without this, no proposal of teaching and/or curricular modification will give a good account, truly, of promoting quality education.

Bibliography

Amaral, Ana L., and Lucíola L.C.P. Santos. 1995–98. *A avaliação escolar: perspectiva sócio-antropológica*. Faculdade de Educação, Universidade Federal de Minas Gerais, Conselho Nacional de Desenvolvimento Científico e Tecnológico. Ongoing research.

Althusser, L. 1971. "Ideology and Ideological State Apparatuses." In *Lenin and Philosophy and Other Essays*, pp. 172–186. New York: Monthly Review Press.

APEOESP (Sindicato dos Professores do Ensino Oficial do Estado de São Paulo). 1997. "As inovações introduzidas pela Secretaria de Educação do Estado de São Paulo." *Caderno de Formação* no. 5 (November).

Baudelot, C., and Roger Establet. 1971. *L'École capitaliste en France*. Paris: Maspero.

Bourdieu, P., and J.C. Passeron. 1977. *Reproduction*. Beverly Hills: Sage.

Bowles, S., and H. Gintis. 1976. *Schooling in Capitalist America*. New York: Basic Books.

Brasil, Ministério da Educação e Cultura (MEC). 1996. *Lei no. 9394/96; Lei de Diretrizes e Bases da Educação Nacional de 20/12/96*.

———. Secretaria de Ensino Fundamental (SEF). 1997. *Parâmetros Curriculares Nacionais (1a à 4a série)*. Brasília.

Freire, Paulo. 1986. *Pedagogy of the Oppressed*. New York: Continuum.

Governo do Estado de São Paulo. Secretaria de Estado da Educação. 1997. *A escola de cara nova*. São Paulo.

Instituto de Pesquisa Econômica Aplicada. 1996. Relatório sobre o desenvolvimento humano no Brasil. Rio de Janeiro, RJ: PNVD. Brasília, D.F. IPEA.

Pernambuco. 1997. *Plano Estadual de Educação—Secretaria de Educação e Esportes. Relatório 1995–1996*, January.

———. Secretaria de Educação e Esportes. *Plano Estadual de Educação 1996–99*.

Rodrigues, Neidson. 1984. *Estado, Educação e Desenvolvimento.* São Paulo: Cortez.
Salgado, Maria Umbelina C. 1981. "O papel da didática na formação do professor." *Revista da ANDE* 4: 9–18.
Saviani, Dermeval. 1985. *Escola e democracia.* São Paulo: Cortez.
Secretaria de Estado da Educação de Minas Gerais (SEEMG). 1994. *A política educacional de Minas Gerais: prioridades, compromissos, ações,* Belo Horizonte, March.
———. 1996. *Projeto de experiências pedagógicas inovadoras de regime não seriado no Ensino Fundamental, (CBA à 4a série).* Belo Horizonte, December.
———. 1997. *A implantação do sistema de ciclos no Ensino Fundamental: características, fundamentos e estratégias.* Belo Horizonte, November.

22

Francisco Álvarez

Curriculum and Educational Materials in Chile

Introduction

Chile's educational curriculum in primary school does not assume that students have attended preschool, since national coverage in 1995 was 34 percent, with an average annual growth rate in coverage of 7.5 percent since 1990. The structure of the curriculum is that in the first grade, 20 percent of time is devoted to the area of language (both reading and writing), and 17 percent to mathematics. Other subjects included are science, and its share of the curriculum is around 8 percent. By the eighth grade, basic literacy, ability to write, and numeracy are expected to have been achieved; class time devoted to language and mathematics is maintained, but the skill level is raised. For example, in the area of language, students study grammar and Spanish literature in the later years of primary school.

Yet the implicit transformation of students and their culture is viewed by some as a rejection of the student as a human being; moreover, a different view of the human being and group relationship than that of successful memorization and submissive deportment is sought. Thus, curriculum and educational material developments are planned to work together to inculcate more active and autonomous behavior by students in a situation that both helps them learn how to learn and provides a curriculum suited to their daily lives as well as to advancing their academic skills.

The curriculum for primary education was subjected to a comprehensive revision in which not only were the subject contents updated, but the entire notion of what counts as pertinent learning was debated and redefined. The 1996 "Curriculum Reform in Primary Education" is based on "Fundamental Objectives and Minimum Contents." The organization of the entire curriculum is now based on "learning sectors." This concept refers to the different categories of homogeneous grouping of types of knowledge and experiences that children should cultivate during their primary education. The learning sectors include the following sub-sectors: language and communication; mathematics; science; technology; art; physical education; orientation; religion; language and communication; foreign language; mathematics education; comprehension of the natural, social and cultural environment (see Table 22.1).

An important part of curriculum design is the development of educational materials. Thus, within educational policy in Chile there has been a major thrust toward improving the educational resources available for the classroom, especially the provision of teaching materials in the first through fourth years of primary school, since the official ministerial focus on children's school future has been at these levels.

This policy is based on the conviction that children's learning improves quantitatively and qualitatively when teachers have at their disposal educational materials that facilitate more interactive teaching practices. It is vital to know what kinds of materials allow teachers to modify the relationship that they establish with their students, changing it from a "frontal" approach, in which the teacher deposits knowledge in the student, to a more interactive approach.

The education policies of the two Concertation governments (1990–) encouraged an interactive style of education through the promulgation of the Organic Constitutional Law of Teaching (LOCE) in Chile in 1990. It established the "minimum requirements which should be met by primary and secondary education" (Article 1) with the aim of developing cognitive capacities, values, and attitudes (Article 2). In the LOCE, the basis for the development of a more flexible and decentralized curriculum begins to appear (Article 11). It includes programs for broadening educational strategies aimed at improving the quality of teaching and of language and mathematics learning in the first years of primary school. These programs incorporate the use of materials that favor conditions for the development of oral and written language, calculations, the capacity of listening, observing, questioning, and cooperation with others in daily life. The materials also help teachers to interact with their students differently than the way that has traditionally been favored by the school system.

Educational Materials and Participative Pedagogy

Educational material ranges from the table or desk which the student uses in the classroom, to the instruction guide for the development of exercises in the computer, as well as the blackboard, textbook, audio-visual aids, and so forth. Some of these materials are well known. The use of computers, through the Ministry-financed *enlaces* (networks) has been effective in bringing knowledge to people in isolated rural communities. But since it is knowledge that is the focus, rather than the computer that is used to obtain it, the use of computers is less important in urban neighborhoods. The high cost and limited number of computers and other "hardware," compared to the universal use of printed materials, has led to a focus on "educational material," which in this chapter refers to printed teaching

Table 22.1

Curriculum Reform in Primary Education: Fundamental Objectives and Minimum Contents (1996)

Learning sectors	Learning subsectors
Language	Language and communication Foreign Language
Mathematics	Mathematics education Comprehension of the natural, social, and cultural environment
Science	Study and comprehension of nature Study and comprehension of society
Technology	Technological education
Art	Artistic education
Physical education	Physical education
Orientation	Orientation
Religion	Religion

Source: Author.

material used directly by students to orient, stimulate, and facilitate learning. It includes textbooks as well as books that form the classroom library, printed guides, and games.

Significance and Use of Materials

What and how do educational materials contribute to learning? What characteristics do they need to possess to be considered as useful and convenient, or even necessary? In dictionaries like that of Santillana, two aims of educational materials are established: (1) facilitating communication between teacher and student, and (2) bringing ideas closer to feelings. But in spite of these interesting theoretical distinctions, school practice has long been dominated by the very restricted aim of controlling what students retain or memorize. At times mechanisms to "entertain" are incorporated to make less unpleasant the task of memorizing facts, formulas, or concepts whose meaning has not been understood.

Popular or Informal Education has made a significant contribution in showing the schools the meaning and use of educational material. In Chile during the 1980s some space was opened for social participation within the context of the dictatorship, based on the principles of communication and critical reflection proposed by Paulo Freire. The development of educational materials is very important in allowing persons involved in an educational situation to express their vision of the world, integrating it to global culture, and developing an evaluation of social practices. Insights into learning, based on the experience in popular education, have led small groups of education professionals to "transfer" that experience to the development of educational materials for primary education. This development led to the production of educational materials based on games from daily life—cards, dominoes, and others—through which the method of active participation works efficiently for educating participating adults. This strategy was re-created in order to be used in the training of teachers and parents in helping children learn. Educational materials are an effective resource for experiencing interchanges that generate an adequate context for learning. The materials are classified as: (1) material reconstructing realities, which seek to convert individual and subjective knowledge into shared knowledge and objectives; (2) material enabling competencies, which produce knowledge that emphasizes conduct (Corvalán 1991).

Educational materials have:

1. A motivating function. The simple fact that they appear in the classroom as a novelty makes them interesting. In addition, because the material invites the students to do something, it contributes to their becoming an active protagonist in their own learning.
2. A cognitive function. To the extent that educational materials are directed to students as individuals and as members of a group, and invite them to solve situations that use their cognitive abilities, they contribute to the development of such abilities and to the development of new knowledge in the group and individually.
3. A function of development of autonomy and creativity. To the degree that the teachers stop being the center of activity and this passes to the students, who must investigate, summarize, analyze, observe, and compare, the students gain security and self-confidence. Each time, the student feels more capable of accomplishment, and the teacher is more able to assume the role of guide in the learning process with more authority.

Nonetheless, UNESCO's studies indicate that educational materials do not replace the importance of people (UNESCO 1988).

Pedagogic Concepts That Support Different Uses of Educational Materials

The distinct functions assigned to educational materials are not intrinsic to the materials themselves, but are linked to the intention of the educator who makes use of them. It is asserted that there are three large concepts of "education" that lead to different meanings with respect to the use of educational material. These concepts are (1) the transmission of knowledge; (2) teaching/learning techniques; and (3) the development of thought and the elaboration of knowledge. Three elements are distinguished in each of these foci: the needs of those who learn, materials or resources specialized for learning, and the role of the educator.

The Transmission of Knowledge Approach

The transmission of knowledge approach corresponds to traditional teaching practice. It is characterized by a person on a platform speaking to an audience who keeps quiet while listening. Many of the characterizations of this approach, above all the graphic ones, have descended to the grotesque. For example, on the cover of a review dedicated to the analysis of teaching, a teacher appears, opening the heads of students and depositing in them a series of mathematical formulas.

This approach centers all pedagogic tasks on the teacher, who teaches in an authoritarian manner (within the limits set by the authority) what he/she considers to be knowledge. What the students should learn is what others have established as knowledge, requiring the student to adapt to an established social order. The authority not only establishes what is knowledge, but also what is needed. This focus has penetrated all the pores of society: it is the mother or father who knows when the boy or girl is cold, hungry, or needs to play or to sleep. In school it is the teachers who determine how much time of continued work or how much recreation or physical exercise out of doors the children and young people need. In the work centers it is the bosses who give instructions about how to do things and the workers have only to carry out orders.

For the child, this way of behaving does not correspond to what actually is known and to his or her social and cognitive development. This behavior conceives of children and young people as not yet able to have opinions, emit judgments, and make decisions. For this reason many teachers in the classroom listen to children, find what they say agreeable and amusing, but do not believe that they really are people yet, and they do not take their opinions into account when they make decisions.

The good teacher is one who transmits contents well, makes a good "deposit" of them in his or her students. For this reason, this kind of pedagogy has also been called the "banking method" (a term coined by Paulo Freire and incorporated into contemporary pedagogic and didactic thought). Good teacher training consists of providing the teacher with clear and precise knowledge, and in training him/her so that he/she can transfer this knowledge to others. There is little variation in lectures and few resources are needed, given that students as well as teachers always are doing the same things: expounding a theme, copying what the teacher says, memorizing for the examination. In summary, (1) the learning needs are pre-established by the adult's authority; (2) the educational materials are limited to structured textbooks; and (3) the educator's role is centered on being a good transmitter.

The Mechanistic Approach, Centered on Techniques

There is a great emphasis on organizing the teaching system around the latest techniques. In Latin America this focus was a pillar of the great educational reforms that began in almost all the nations during the 1950s and 1960s. Courses on educational technology, programmed instruction, exposition of operational objectives, and so on appeared everywhere. Teacher training was centered on the use of programmed instruction, operative teaching modules, multiple choice tests as an instrument of evaluation. The teachers became experts in these methods, but the students' learning processes did not change much. Even worse, after some years of euphoria over new techniques, people began to speak of the deterioration of the quality of learning. In summary, the mechanistic approach can be described as a variant of the transmission approach, where: (1) learning needs are predetermined by authorities and are not always related to the students' interests; (2) there is a major development of educational materials and techniques, with a marked accent on individual effort and success—technique is made holy; and (3) the teacher continues to maintain the role of transmitter of knowledge, only now aided by techniques that make him/her more adept at transmitting.

Approach Centered on the Development of Thought and the Expansion of Knowledge

This approach is characterized by focusing on the persons who are learning and on the relationship that they establish with their environment, especially with adult mediators, in order to learn effectively. Without a doubt, psychology and sociology help us to understand peoples' needs, but it is the people who best express their learning needs, in accordance with their interactions and experiences. Above all, learning occurs when one has faith that a person is capable and can by his own actions form and develop his character (García Huidobro 1982).

Teachers who use this focus ask their students to join them in developing learning goals, establishing commitments about what they wish to achieve together. The students are active participants in learning. Their ideas are taken into account, their knowledge and experiences help them to obtain new knowledge. The initial question in a class no longer is "what will I teach them?" but "what do they wish to learn and for what reason?"

Knowledge is an instrument that allows people to grow, insofar as it enables them to develop abilities for their integration, participation, and development in the society in which they live (Riviére 1984). Knowledge is not understood as something completed. It is constructed in the interaction and dialogue with the others and with the world.

What place do educational materials play in this approach? They are the supports or resources that allow students to become aware of their knowledge and help them, through the development of linguistic, logical, or social abilities and capacities, to acquire or develop new knowledge. A teacher turns to the educational materials to the extent that they are necessary to help the students in their learning and not as mere entertainment to make the task of learning or studying more pleasant. In this approach teaching is dedicated to clarifying the criteria that should guide the behavior of people involved in the learning and teaching process, and a teacher is someone who aids people involved in the learning process, in a relationship that is not "person to person," but "person to person in group." The function of a teacher thus is to present students with cognitive challenges and provide or suggest resources (actions, materials, abilities, etc.) that lead them to exercise their abilities and cognitive skills for their enrichment and development.

Educational Materials for the Renovation of Teaching

Research and analysis about the use of educational materials in popular education asserts that the use of these materials creates the basic conditions for learning. One example is the use of games. The game as educational instrument is very similar to any other parlor game that uses game boards, cards, dominos, dice, play money, or any other element, and at times uses competition or confrontation, to create a stimulating situation that attracts participation. In our culture the game is essentially a means of entertainment, where people put aside the problems of their daily lives. A game is a simulation when it reproduces situations from the daily lives of persons who are going to use it, allowing them to discuss the problems which they normally confront and the ways they usually use to resolve or overcome them. This provides the opportunity for imagining more organized alternative solutions based on the players' common interests. Thematic games are those based on problematic areas of real life, such as health, drivers' training, housing, relations of couples, popular myths and beliefs, and so forth. These simulation games provide an opportunity for subjects as a group to search for different possible solutions by means of conversation and dialogue, exercises in the use of language, communication, and problem solving, creating cognitive and social skills that permit the players to grasp and develop new ideas, allowing them to begin new activities.

Characteristics of Education Materials

The principal characteristics of education materials can be summarized as follows:

Enjoyable: Educational materials should have an enjoyable character which invites the student to participate and to interact with the materials in such a way that those who use them are motivated to express ideas and opinions or to refer to possible solutions to a problem that must be resolved.

Group-based: Education materials are designed for group use, and, at the same time, include, and often require, periods of individual work during their use in the classroom.

Applied learning: Education materials are organized around objectives related both to school learning and, at the same time, to concrete situations in the daily lives of the students where that learning is exercised and applied.

We shall now examine two examples of educational materials.

Example 1: The "Even-Uneven" card game is a game, inspired by dominoes, composed of ninety cards that represent the numbers 1 through 10 according to how they are presented (see Table 22.2). The students can work with them in order to place them in increasing or decreasing order, place pieces in a position that will enable them to win the game, but they also play with the aim of adding to obtain the total, or subtracting to obtain the remainder. Once they have been permitted to play and use the material that represents numbers in all possible ways, they can be asked to carry out operations of arithmetic that they are able to do with the aid of this material.

Table 22.2

The "Even-Uneven" Card Game

Form of the card	Number represented	Number of cards
⊗	1	30
⊗⊗	2	15
⊗⊗⊗	3	10
⊗⊗	4	8
⊗⊗	5	6
⊗⊗⊗	6	5
⊗⊗⊗	7	5
⊗⊗⊗⊗	8	4
⊗⊗⊗⊗⊗	9	4
⊗⊗⊗⊗⊗	10	3

Source: Author.

Example 2: Improving School Discipline. In this material the use of games is mixed with writing. It consists of twenty cards; on each one is written a possible factor that would help or hinder a class group to have a better work or study environment. Students are faced with the question of how they could improve their studies in class; they discuss various ways, according to the cards that each student selects, until they agree on one or several that will constitute a group promise of how to behave. The game facilitates dialogue among students, and requires them to understand what is written on each of the cards and to relate it to their own situation and problems in class. This is oriented to the development of learning socio-affective skills and abilities.

It is interesting to note that teacher training in Chile incorporates educational games. In the 1980s the use of educational materials allowed teachers to question, discuss, and change their teaching practices. For example, with a game of cards replicating situations of teacher–student interactions, only one appears to be speaking. The teachers must complete what the other person would say in this situation. Then, once they have responded to all the cards, each one of the responses is analyzed and classified as "those responses that facilitate learning and why" and "those that do not facilitate it." In this way the participants express and question their practices, constructing theoretical bases of how to act. Thus they experience and conceptualize learning, with the aid of the coordinator-facilitator.

Teachers who have undergone this type of learning experience are motivated to provide experiences of the same nature in their classrooms, creating materials based on games from daily life, such as dominoes and others, and they claim that the children use them to exercise the cognitive and social skills that they must develop to achieve learning, such as using language naturally (redaction, orthography) or calculating costs and budgets with precision (addition, tables, and so on).

Educational material by itself may not help students to learn if a teacher brings students such materials without presenting an interesting challenge, or without providing precise instruction that guides them in the purpose of the game. Nonetheless, educational materials facilitate the creation of conditions in which learning becomes possible because they embody the characteristics that create conditions of a participative pedagogy and favor the development of thought. What are these characteristics?

1. Educational material for students should be created taking into account their characteristics and interests, so that the invitation to learn is related to their lives, aspirations, and expectations. It cannot be centered on the mere explication or development of contents. Materials for children should be structured recognizing that the game is one of their most serious activities (Álvarez et al. 1995).
2. Good educational material has to be characterized by requiring an action, a cognitive act, such as resolving a problematic situation, proving certain hypotheses, elaborating a proposition, and so on. For example, a board game such as "The School Career" allows players to relate to situations and information in order to solve the problems posed in the game. Students have to synthesize and express actions that they themselves carry out, in writing (CIDE 1990).
3. Educational material should invite the student to combine his personal efforts with those of the group in order to resolve situations in a cooperative manner. Educational material does not ignore that personal and individual work is necessary for any learning. The majority of such materials for work with teachers and students is developed to be carried out in groups, even though many of them have parts that include other prior individual tasks as a condition for accomplishing the collective work.
4. Educational material, ultimately, must assure a process of integrating the development of and search for knowledge. It should aid students to discover the interrelations that are given between different kinds of knowledge, and this should be done explicitly. One material used in the training workshops

for teachers in P.900 schools was the "development of a newspaper about school life." This activity made it possible to develop knowledge in diverse areas. It was necessary to make calculations of costs and measurement of paper (arithmetic and geometry); to discuss and reach agreement about topics, news, and information that would be considered for the newspaper (knowing how to listen, respect other opinions, tolerate, decide as a group—civic education and values); to interview; edit commentaries and news; invent jokes (language, spelling), and to find interrelationships, since they could not create the newspaper if they did not integrate these different areas of knowledge.

In recent years there has been an increase in learning guides, a type of educational material that has begun to be developed and has awakened interest of teachers (Schiefelbein et al. 1993). The guides organize curriculum as a function of the teacher's aim and the children's interests and learning needs. The guides facilitate group work in the classroom and also, in some cases, the participation of the family at home, given that children and their families are invited to investigate aspects from daily life related to their family environment and cultural tradition.

The development of guides encourages the teachers' redesign of the curriculum and introduces elements of belonging and relevance for students' learning. The guides are an inexpensive teaching resource that stimulates teachers' creativity and motivates students. Nevertheless, their implementation demands time for work and coordination from the teachers in order that they be adopted as a permanent teaching resource in the school. In this respect, it would be interesting to investigate the requirements of teaching time and space for this kind of material to be incorporated into systematic classroom practice. Experience shows that the guides allow the teacher to retake his real place as generator of knowledge, of evaluator and facilitator of learning.

Conclusion

This chapter has sought to underscore the relevance of alternative non-formal education materials which enhance as much as or even more than textbooks, the stimulation of fundamental learning. Policy decision makers should consider the importance of these materials, especially as a strategy to develop independent reflection by classroom teachers.

Bibliography

Álvarez, F., C. Cardemil, B. Icaza, and L. Mayorga. 1995. "Familia y centros educativos." Santiago, Chile: Teleduc U.C.

CIDE. 1990 . "Materiales educativos 1." Santiago, Chile: CIDE.

Corvalán, Javier. 1991. "Material pedagógico y programas educativos. Análisis de tres experiencias." Santiago, Chile: Santiago, CIDE.

García Huidobro, J.E. 1982. "Paulo Freire y la educación de adultos como acción cultural." Santiago, Chile: CIDE.

Narro, L. 1987. "El cuaderno guía y la educación bilingüe bicultural en México." Santiago, Chile: UNESCO-OREALC.

Riviére, A. 1984. "La psicología de Vigotsky: sobre la larga proyección de una biografía." *Infancia y Aprendizaje* 27–28.

Schielfebein, Colbert, and Sotomayor. 1993. "Adaptación de guías de aprendizaje: dos casos exitosos." Santiago, Chile: UNESCO-UNICEF-CIDE.

———. 1988. "Guías para el desarrollo de materiales de capacitación para la educación inicial." Santiago, Chile: UNESCO.

23

MARGARITA GÓMEZ PALACIO

Prevention of School Failure in Basic Education in Mexico

The school, as every institution with precise objectives, tries to have its students reach a minimum desired level. Not reaching these objectives constitutes a failure. In the case that concerns us, it is school failure. By school failure we understand a low, unacceptable performance by the students who, because of this, cannot be promoted from their grade.

Despite the term "school failure," it is not possible to specify if it is the school or the students who fail. A widely held view is that the school cannot fail, given that it is the school that has defined its own objectives; therefore it is students who fail. It is necessary to search for the origin of student failure. Others think that given the magnitude of school failure, it is the school that has failed because it has not been able to make students achieve the desired objectives. It is necessary to question the school about the relevance of its programs and of its curricular contents, about the preparation and quality of its teachers, and about the school materials offered, both to teachers and students, and so forth. As in all problems that concern a large population, it is not possible to take sides because there are multiple elements that determine school failure, and surely each student's failure responds to irremediably differing combinations of these elements. However, the analysis of simple statistics around the entire world shows us that generally the students who fail are in the first grades of primary school, and that this determined by the failure to adequately learn to read and write. In Mexico this problem has been one of our preoccupations for more than twenty-five years.

At the request of the government of Nuevo León we began a study of the causes of failure and dropout in basic education at the end of 1973. Educational authorities were disturbed by the high indices of failure shown by educational statistics, despite the fact that the state of Nuevo León had always been distinguished by having one of the highest levels of education in Mexico.

We knew that failure and dropout led to school failure. In Mexico in 1973, only 38 percent of primary school students finished primary school on time; that is to say that 62 of every 100 students repeated the same grade 1, 2, or 3 times, which indicates that if students did not ultimately drop out, it took them up to ten years to finish the sixth grade.

In our first study in Nuevo León we found that independent of whether or not students attended preschool by the time they were six years old, the age at which primary school begins in Mexico, there was an enormous difference among the students in their cognitive development, which depended more on their cultural environment than on other factors such as health. Trying to understand the origins of this difference, we thought that because reading and writing were the most important topic in the first grades, it could be useful to measure the students' levels of conceptualization when they began the first grade in rural areas, as well as in marginal urban areas and in middle class urban areas. Table 23.1 gives the percentages of students in each of these groups of schools in each of the differing levels of reading and writing ability. Level 1 (the highest) indicates children who almost knew how to read, and level 5 (the lowest) indicates students who did not know where reading took place, if reading is of drawings or of writing, if a student could read a text without drawings, and so on.

At the end of the school year we found a large correspondence between the levels of conceptualization that the students had at the beginning of the school year and the level of failure at the end of the school year, which reached almost 40 percent. Moreover, we found that of students who failed the first grade, 80 percent came from the marginal urban or rural zones and only 20 percent came from the urban middle class. With these data at hand it was decided to create a program to meet the needs of the children who had failed. This program was called the "Nuevo León Plan," and it was considered to be a remedial program. The "Nuevo León Plan" created a center, composed of specialists, where teachers were trained for the first grade following a methodology that focused on increasing students' comprehension and adapted to the needs of each child. Seven centers were formed in the poorest regions. Each center aided twenty groups that functioned within regular schools; students returned to their schools once they overcame their problems. At the same time, the pilot center continued to carry out research on the topic of language acquisition. This was how the "Proposal for Learning Reading and Writing" was formulated.

These special groups were called "integrated groups"; their use was extended to the entire nation. However, we saw that a preventive program with the aim of helping students at risk was not the best way of reducing school failure and we decided to broaden the program to include regular students, using the proposal that was conceived for this program, which we called IPALE, which is the acronym in Spanish for "Implementation of the Proposal for Learning Reading and Writing." This program was installed throughout the nation but with only a limited number of groups.

Table 23.1

Levels of Language Conceptualization

	Rural population	Poor urban population	Urban population
Levels	6 Years	6 Years	6 Years
1	—	—	32
2	—	5	35
3	32	36	23
4	58	59	10
5	10	—	—
Total	100	100	100

Source: Author.

Preliminary Results of IPALE

Given that during the first ten years of operation of the program of integrated groups and then of IPALE only a minimal share of the population benefited and the character of the intervention was more therapeutic than preventive, the results could only be estimated for the recovery or success of the students who were part of the program. In the case of the integrated groups, there was a good recovery level: 80 percent, if we take into account that we are describing a population with difficulties whose students had repeated the first grade one or more times, or had been diagnosed as having learning problems.

Broadening the program to normal student populations led to an increase in the level of success: 92 percent of students were promoted from the first to the second grade. When we presented this evaluation to the Secretary of Education, we were invited to broaden the program, which then was called "PALEM," whose acronym in Spanish stands for "Proposal for Learning Reading, Writing and Mathematics." PALEM was gradually extended to the thirty-two states of Mexico, and included students in both the first and second grades, but could not include all students in these grades in all schools. Although this program was successful, it could not be implemented everywhere because there were insufficient funds for training and advising all teachers. On the other hand, because the program only covered the first two grades of basic education, it could not guarantee that the rest of primary education would maintain the quality of education we demanded, not to mention the fact the material distributed by the Secretariat of Education distributed did not provide the communication and functional focus that we wanted to give to the program.

What has been the evolution of the nation's education, based on statistics? Mexico's terminal efficiency of education (80 percent) has grown slowly and is at a level well below that obtained by the leading first world nations (98 percent) (see Table 23.2).

Table 23.2

Desertion and Failure Rates, 1985, 1995

Year	Desertion rate (%)	Failure rate (%)
1985: 1st to 3rd grade	14.4	40.2
4th to 6th grade	12.8	18.9
1995: 1st to 3rd grade	16.1	31.8
4th to 6th grade	11.5	19.2

Source: Author.

We find that if the failure rate fell in the first three grades between 1985 and 1995, dropout increased, especially in the first three grades, which is especially troubling. Moreover, if we not only take account of the quantity but also a surface evaluation of the quality of education of students when they finish the sixth grade of primary school, we find that only 4 percent of the students have a reading and writing level greater than that of the sixth grade; 16 percent are at their grade level and the remaining 80 percent are at the fifth, fourth, third, and even second grade levels, which indicates that even though the level of terminal efficiency has improved, the level of quality continues to be very much below that desired, which in part determines the high percentage of students who graduate from primary school but do not continue their education by enrolling in secondary school, even when this is required. This, along with a very high share of students who fail the first grade of secondary school, determines the low number of students who complete basic education.

PRONALEES

At the beginning of the current presidential term in 1995, the Secretariat of Public Education established the goal of strengthening programs for reading and writing and, being aware of the preponderant role played by the adequate management of oral and written language in education, created the National Program for Strengthening Reading and Writing in Basic Education (PRONALEES). PRONALEES, utilizing the human resources already existing that had had experience in IPALE and in PALEM, created a group of a limited number of experts to improve the quality of teaching, with the aim of (1) formulating a program of teaching language that reflected the results of research and work undertaken during the last twenty-five years; (2) elaborating free textbooks that are given to children, and providing corresponding teachers' guides; (3) creating a national network of advisers that would be placed in updating programs for teachers, helping them to improve the quality of their educational practices; (4) collaborating with all the programs and institutions that directly or indirectly strengthen reading, for example, the programs of Public libraries, of Reading Corners in

Schools, Adult Education; the exposition of writers' workshops; an increase of book fairs; (5) continuing research programs in reading and writing; (6) publishing works that aid teachers in their job of teaching reading and writing; (7) establishing pre-reading programs at the preschool level, to improve the level of students' preparation upon entering primary school; and (8) aiding and training teachers who will teach handicapped students or those with learning disabilities, so that they will truly benefit from entering normal classes.

Advances

It can be said that during these three and a half years of intensive work, PRO-NALEES, with the aid of the government, has achieved the following:

1. The formation and consolidation of the program's structure has occurred. There is a central office in Mexico City and a coordinator in each of the nation's entities.
2. Creation of a network of advisers who are trained and responsible to the state coordinator, who program and facilitate courses, consultancy, seminars, and workshops for teachers. Currently there are around 5,500 consultants who have been trained, but three times as many are needed to meet students' needs.
3. The revision of the Spanish program and the elaboration of a new program for the first to sixth grades of primary school took place. This new program assures the coherence and continuity of communication and functional focus proposed from the beginning of the efforts to improve reading and writing. The program covers the four indispensable elements of oral language, reading, writing, and thinking about language. The program was drawn up in consultation with very experienced teachers and applied as a pilot project with a significant group of students.
4. The completion of free textbooks that respond to the program's requirements for first and second grade primary school students. They are being prepared for third and fourth grade students, and we hope that they will be distributed in September 1999. Each grade has a book of reading, a book of activities, and a book of cut-outs. Three and a half million copies of each of the books have been printed and distributed throughout the nation, to students and teachers, principals, supervisors and those in charge of technical teams. The books have had an excellent reception by students, teachers and parents.
5. The preparation of books for teachers. These include: (a) The teachers' book, which follows each of the readings in the students' book. It explains simply to the teacher the aims of the lesson, the theoretical limits it invokes, the proposed activities, and the way of evaluating students' progress. (b) The file of activities. These have been elaborated for first to sixth grade

teachers; they propose complementary activities that the teacher can undertake not only in Spanish but also in other areas. (c) The Program Advance. This is simply a guide that allows the teacher to evaluate the degree of improvement that his/her group has achieved, and to verify that it has included all the proposed points of the program. (d) A large number of teachers have been given three books that form part of the "Teachers' Library" program. These three books explain different psychological, sociological and linguistic theories that could aid teachers' educational practices.

Conclusion

School failure and educational quality have been the "neuralgic" themes of all governments and especially of the Mexican government. We are aware that the efforts that we are making will take a long time and that only time will allow us to see to what degree we have achieved our aims. We count on the great aid given by the Secretariat of Education and by the thousands of teachers who have adopted our programs, and we hope that the effort we are making will promote the arrival of a better Mexico.

Part VI

Teaching Conditions: Training and Salaries

24

EMILIO TENTI FANFANI

Teachers' Training, Work Conditions, and Salary in Argentina

Introduction

Over the last fifteen years starting with the restoration of the constitutional regime in 1983, primary education in Argentina has shown both growth in enrollment and problems with respect to yield and quality. The latter include an increase in the rate of repetition, especially in the first two years both of primary and secondary school. More than 1 million children and adolescents repeat the school year, and another million children between five and seventeen years of age are not in school.

Grade repetition and educational achievement constitute complex phenomena provoked by a combination of factors related to demand (characteristics of children and their families, social and cultural environment, etc.) and supply. Among the latter, teachers play a basic role. All the other elements—textbooks, teaching resources, time spent on task, physical infrastructure, and so on—are efficacious and influence school processes and products based on how the teachers use them. In turn, teachers' quality is the product of a mix of factors, including their initial and total training, work conditions, and salary. The educational system's inadequate quality and yield are accompanied by strong malaise among the teachers.[1] This is related to the "reform of the state" which has led to a deterioration of working conditions in essential public services—health, justice, security, and education—and the practical disappearance of the "impresarial state" as an effect of privatization. Teachers now constitute the largest component of the public sector. In the mid-1990s, the number of teachers greatly exceeded the combined total of public workers in security, justice and health in the main Argentine provinces.

In this chapter I present a synthesis of the condition of three of the most important dimensions of the teaching profession: initial and total training available to teachers, regulations that govern access to and conditions of work, and material pay and benefits.

Teachers' Training

Argentina has a complete network of more than 700 institutions that train teachers for all levels of the school system. Given the decentralized structure of Argentine education, public and private teachers' training institutions depend on provincial educational administrations.[2] According to a 1994 study by Diker and Terigi, this system is characterized by its "heterogeneity, diversity and lack of specificity." In principle, heterogeneity is not necessarily bad, and may be necessary to meet the diverse demands of the system. There are training schools oriented toward the various levels of the educational system and to specialties within it; there are public and private institutes, higher education teacher training, national higher teaching institutes, and also national higher schools of business and national higher schools that among other things offer some kind of teacher training. In addition, training is offered by the universities.

Eighty percent of these schools are public institutions so that the state, through the provinces rather than through the central government, has a determining presence in teachers' training. All national teachers' training policy must be negotiated within the Federal Council of Education, which is composed of the provincial Ministers of Education and coordinated by the national Minister of Education. Moreover, almost 20 percent of the institutions that train teachers also offer training for other careers. The expansion of other, non-university-level technical areas into these old traditional teacher-training institutions has changed their atmosphere, causing them to lose their original specialized nature. Sixty-eight universities (thirty-one government and thirty-seven private) offer teacher training courses, and a high proportion of teachers who work in teachers training institutions have university degrees.

This diversity of training institutions has led to uneven preparation of teachers in primary education institutions. In 1994, 88 percent had pedagogical training. A little more than half of them (52.8 percent) had completed non-university higher education; almost one-third (31.1 percent) had a teacher's degree at high school level (which requires five more years after primary school). Finally, 7.3 percent of teachers have not received any pedagogical training. Yet there is not any systematic evidence that demonstrates a given relationship between type and level of teacher training and student yield.

Critiques of Teacher Training

Critics of teacher training point out the same defects: general obsolescence; anachronistic routinization; isolation; obsolescence of the contents of teacher training leading to unsuitability of teachers, aggravated by the current deficient working conditions so that the most talented young people are not recruited. Moreover, there is an enormous gap between initial teacher training and current methodological and epistemological developments. Current training does not take account of the problems and needs of students from different social groups; there is no coherence between the teaching methods by which new teachers are taught and those they should apply to behave in a creative and participative manner; they are not motivated to work in a team nor to produce knowledge from their daily practices; and their training favors a unidimensional vision of current conditions and an ahistorical view of knowledge (Bonder 1997). As distinct from universities where students can plan their own academic life, teacher training schools have little democracy, which does not contribute to flexibility (Cardelli 1997). In addition, as a result of the precarious level of general education of many teachers and administrators, which is associated with low levels of reading comprehension, dependence on the textbook, and a tendency toward extremely utilitarian visions of teaching, most teachers are alienated and remain outside of the information and debate about the great themes of education, national and international policies that define their role and their present and future outlook (Torres 1995). In contrast to the shortcomings of teacher training, it nonetheless is hoped that teachers would carry out new tasks, such as ecological education for daily life, peace and tolerance, solidarity and democracy, health, an esthetic education and so forth.

Working Conditions

Fragmentation

The quality of teachers' work is related to continuity on the job. In 1994, a little more than half of the teachers in primary school had a regular appointed position. The rest worked in temporary positions as interns or aides; this led to high teacher turnover in these jobs, which has harmful effects on the functioning of educational institutions, such as a low sense of identity and belonging, difficulties in carrying out the school mission, low degree of cooperation with the community, and absence of future outlook, which probably makes it harder for students to learn. One-quarter of primary school teachers work in more than one school, and almost one out of ten primary school teachers has another non-teaching job (Braslavsky and Birgin 1994).

Regulations

Although the teacher has some autonomy to carry out his/her work, the major decisions on selection of curriculum, teaching methods, use of time and space, the technical criteria of evaluation, and the definitions of educational goals, among others, are not made by educators, but by administrators who are outside of the classroom. In general, these decisions are contained in a series of formal rules that often limit what it is possible to do even though the conditions that gave rise to these rules have disappeared. In this sense, it is common to find rules being followed without anyone, neither those with oversight nor those who execute the rules, having any true interest in doing so.

Our examination of the rules that determine the entry into and progress in the teachers' career in public schools is limited to the National Teaching Statute of 1958, a statute that established a series of institutions for the corporative participation of teachers in entering and progressing in the teaching career and that served for many years as a model for the teaching statues approved by the provinces, and the Teaching Classification Councils that regulate the evaluation, classification and qualification of teaching that apply in the autonomous city of Buenos Aires, analogous to teaching councils in the majority of Argentine provinces.

In the city of Buenos Aires a 1985 statute governs teachers' careers. The Teaching Classification Councils are central to this. There is a Council for each level of the school system (preschool, primary, and so on), which is composed of nine members of whom six are elected by the teachers themselves or by labor unions. The other three members are designated by the city's Secretary of Education. The Councils have strategic functions, given that they assign teachers to their jobs in "order of merit," which is assessed by the Council itself.

How are teachers evaluated? Criteria include: degrees obtained; length of service in teaching; other degrees and courses; cultural, teaching and other "valid antecedents." These are supplemented with the annual evaluation of the teacher by the school principal. The system of qualification and evaluation does not necessarily improve teaching because the only mobility in the job is leaving teaching for management and principal's positions (Morduchowicz and Marcón 1996, 50). In turn, this unique set of advancement priorities, including length of service and a system of credits from courses, induces teachers to take courses and short classes that do not necessarily relate to the content of teaching, solely in order to obtain points toward promotion. This system has little to do with rewarding quality.

Evolution of Teachers' Salaries

The level of Argentine teachers' salaries has suffered a marked deterioration. From 1980 to 1995 the number of classroom teachers increased 65 percent; the number of students increased 55 percent; and public investment in education increased only 13 percent. The difference between these shares is much more significant if we take into account that 80 percent of the budget is allocated to personnel. The data in Table 24.1 indicate the continued fall in teachers' real salaries since the mid-1980s for classroom teachers in the 32.4 percent of schools that were under national jurisdiction through 1991. These data are considered typical of all primary school teachers' salaries.

The loss of teachers' position relative to the salaries received by workers who are not self-employed and employees in many cases was the result of explicit

Table 24.1

Trends in Teachers' Real Wages by Experience, National Jurisdiction Years: 1976–1991. Base Year 1976 = 100

| Year | Index | Seniority | |
		15 Years	Maximum
1976	100.0	100.0	100.0
1977	92.6	92.6	92.6
1978	121.9	122.0	122.0
1979	128.0	128.0	128.0
1980	151.6	151.6	151.6
1981	160.0	146.2	146.6
1982	89.0	88.6	88.6
1983	121.9	127.0	131.9
1984	191.9	146.5	168.5
1985	114.9	140.2	161.5
1986	85.8	104.9	120.5
1987	85.0	103.6	114.9
1988	76.8	91.8	104.8
1989	66.0	67.0	74.1
1990	59.6	60.8	65.5
1991	66.4	61.8	63.9

Source: Fernández, Lemos, and D.L. Wiñar (1977), p. 66.

policies of reducing teacher salaries, such as delay in payments, replacement of pay in money by provincial bonds in at least five provinces, reduction of teaching hours worked and the reduction of salaries paid—in some cases to almost one-third of the 1976 level. This was the case in thirteen provinces during the 1990s (Birgin 1997).

In order to interpret the data on 1996 salaries from Table 24.2 it is necessary to take account of the fact that while teachers' salary corresponds to an average day of four to five hours of work in the school, average salaries in the economy refer to workers who work an average of eight hours per day. Despite this difference, teachers' salary generally is low compared to the national average gross salaries. The most obvious case is the city of Buenos Aires. In this important district, teachers' salaries are equal to slightly more than half the income of salaried workers. This difference is significant because Buenos Aires, along with Tierra del Fuego and Santa Cruz, is a district where the highest salaries in the nation occur. Another fact to keep in mind is the extreme disparity among teachers' salaries in the nation. For the same task with the same length of service, teachers receive very different pay (see Table 24.3).

There are inequalities of salary both for the carrying out of equivalent tasks in each of the provinces and for the level of qualification. In some provinces (Misiones, Santa Cruz, and Rio Negro) the differences in pay among teachers in

Table 24.2

Gross Salary of Primary School Teachers (10 Years' Experience) and Average Gross Salaries in the Formal Economic Sector, by Province
(in 1996 pesos)

Province	Gross salary, Primary school teacher	Average gross salary in formal sector	Ratio of gross teachers' salary to gross average Salary
Average	527	853	0.62
Santa Cruz	920	1,209	0.76
Tierra del Fuego*	879	1,147	0.77
Neuquén	744	960	0.78
Santiago del Estero	631	636	0.99
Catamarca	610	726	0.84
La Rioja	578	660	0.88
Rio Negro*	555	693	0.80
Mendoza	531	628	0.85
Federal Capital	528	1,128	0.47
La Pampa	522	603	0.87
Santa Fé	510	665	0.77
Chubut	499	991	0.50
Córdoba	499	687	0.73
San Luis	490	715	0.69
Jujuy	455	574	0.79
San Juan*	448	585	0.77
Tucumán	446	652	0.68
Buenos Aires	430	747	0.58
Misiones	430	594	0.72
Chaco	424	555	0.76
Entre Ríos	409	580	0.71
Formosa	380	572	0.66
Corrientes	378	588	0.64
Salta	353	604	0.58

Source: Based on data of the Ministry of Culture and Education, Ministry of Economy. Works and Public Services and Municipality of the City of Buenos Aires. Cited in Lumi, S., 1997, p. 103.
*There were salary reductions in fixed sum or percentage. The resulting figures were distributed among the various salary components.

the different educational levels is relatively small. In others (Buenos Aires and Chaco) salaries for teachers in secondary school are 33 percent higher than those of their colleagues who teach primary school. The same differences are observed when salaries are analyzed according to province and level of responsibility or length of time in job. These inequalities in large part are the result of the decentralization of primary education and have no rationale other than the availability of resources and the autonomy of spending them by each provincial administration. However, there is a national trend of a prolonged decline

Table 24.3

Salary Differentials by Level and Jurisdiction, Basic Monthly Wage, Minimum Seniority, 1995

Province	Teacher's wage	Average basic wage, based on teachers' usual number of hours	Percentage difference
	in $		in %
Buenos Aires	346.7	462.2	33.3
Chaco	339.4	452.6	33.3
Chubut	449.7	452.4	20.6
Entre Ríos	333.6	393.6	18.0
La Rioja	444.2	549.4	23.7
Federal Capital	358.1	447.0	24.8
Mendoza	460.9	614.8	33.4
Misiones	332.3	340.4	2.5
Río Negro	473.4	515.2	8.8
Santa Cruz	867.7	905.2	4.3
Santa Fe	489.1	553.8	13.2

Source: Morduchowicz and Alejandro (1997), 4.

in the real salaries of teachers from the mid-1970s to the beginning of the 1990s. The best years with regard to salary were during the first half of the 1980s, and a loss in the relative position of teachers' salary compared to that of salaries obtained by the average salaried workers in the formal sector of the economy has occurred.

This sharp fall led to a "social redefinition of the teaching profession, with a profound impact . . . on level of living, professional respectability, cultural formation and social origin of the new teachers, as well as strong transformation in the subjective perception of teaching and the social position of teachers. For the first time they saw themselves treated as any salaried worker and responded to this new situation in various ways. Teaching can be said to have been lowered to the level of the laity, in the sense that the teacher was completely separated from his 'aura' " (Paiva, Junqueira, and Muls 1997, 114).

The Current Debate

In recent years teachers have lost control over the determination of classroom content. And improvements in teacher training have not been forthcoming. This loss is closely related to salary conflicts between the unions and their employers, and evidence indicates a notorious decrease in teachers' salaries all over the country, stagnant conditions of work, initial training that shows no substantial change, and in-service training that, despite a certain increase in the amount and coverage, appears to have effected changes in language more than effective modifications of the means of doing things in the classroom (Tenti Fanfani 1998).

Salaries and Conditions of Work

Although everyone seems to agree that it is necessary to improve teachers' salaries, there is no consensus about how to do it and 1997 and 1998 proposals regarding teachers' salaries have not been adopted. Teachers' unions urged an immediate increase without conditions; the government offered a strategy of improvement that tied salary improvements to a modification of the work regime. In 1997 it proposed a law to create a Teachers' Professionalization Fund that was to be obtained from loans by international organizations of up to 660 million pesos. In order to obtain these resources, the provinces and the city of Buenos Aires were to establish new teaching statutes which give preponderance to professional qualification, capacitation and teaching evaluation for determinating salary levels and promotions, using criteria to be set by the Federal Investment Council. They also were to promise to install management systems for administration and physical, financial and human resources, including a unique computerized archive with complete labor information about each employee, which makes functional plans transparent in each educational establishment; to install a system of Health and Safety, including a private physician's certification of illness, for use at the work site; a budget system organized according to programs; and the computerization of all administrative processes. Finally, the proposed law established that the provinces and the city of Buenos Aires were to assign matching resources to those supplied by the National Fund. In general this proposed law applied the general criteria of the Law of Work Contracts to teachers and incorporated the dominant trends toward more flexibility in the labor force. As expected, this government proposal was strongly rejected by teachers' unions and opposition parties.

The lack of consensus about the proposed law led the Ministry of Education and Culture to modify it in April 1998. It rejected a proposed loan for the project from the World Bank and instead proposed an emergency tax of 1 percent on automotive vehicles. The Ministry agreed to let the provinces use the fund without renegotiating working conditions with teachers' unions. The resources to be obtained—around 750 million pesos—would be used to increase the salaries of teachers and administrators by 100 pesos per month. This would be paid in two annual installments. Although Congress passed the proposed law, President Memom announced that he would veto it in December 1998.

Changes in Teacher Training

In 1997 the Federal Education Council approved a document that establishes profound changes that will be progressively applied in teacher training. In Argentina, teacher training began with normal schools at the secondary school level. This was transformed into preparation with higher-level studies, and now it will be converted into a "mix" with university-level contents and the possibility of establishing the teaching career with a corresponding bachelor's degree.

The document indicates the functions that teachers' training institutes will carry out, establishes the organization of curriculum for teachers' careers and determines the degrees that will be authorized in the future. Moreover, it defines a provincial development plan and establishes the parameters for complying with accreditation criteria. In September 1997 the provincial ministers of education had already approved a document establishing that, faced with the saturation of teacher training institutes, there would be two types of institutions: those that assumed all training functions and those that carry out research and additional training. Moreover, they require that 75 percent of the faculty in the institutes should have higher education and they request that universities compete to be included in the Program of Teaching Excellence. The selected institutions also should receive academic and financial assistance for the postgraduate training of their faculties.

Teacher training will include three fields and the degrees will be adjusted to indicate them. The fields are general education, common to all teachers; education specialization, referring to the characteristics of psychological and cultural development of students and the characteristics of the schools at each level; and a specialized field, which will include the disciplinary contents of each level. Each district will create its development plan, which will include institutions accredited beginning in 1998. The plans should include the formation of all future teachers, access to training for all active teachers and the mechanisms for assuring the functions of promotion, research and development. Beginning in December 1997, all the districts should have begun their own process of accrediting non-university teaching institutions. Accreditation will have a limited time and will be renewed, for the first time, in four years.

Teachers' Unions

According to UNESCO, the majority of the 50 million teachers in the world are union members. Its report (Delors 1996) suggests that unions are partners that cannot be excluded from the debate between school and society, recommending that the educational debate on the conception and practice of reforms go beyond questions of salary and work conditions to include the central role of teachers. It is probable that unions consider decentralization—especially privatization of the contract between the teacher and the school—to be a direct threat to the security of employment. The principal point that has to be negotiated with teachers' unions is that additional funds should not be exclusively allocated to teachers' salaries, but that they could also be used for school supplies, free textbooks for students, improvement of schools and free lunch for children from low-income families (Carnoy and De Moura Castro 1995).

Many Argentine institutions claim to be union representatives for teachers.

However, the majority of teachers are represented by a series of provincial unions that form a national confederation, the CTERA (Confederación de Trabajadores de Educación de la República Argentina), whose presence in the political scene is manifested both through strikes and through newer forms of public expression, such as the teaching tent installed in front of the National Congress building since April 1997. Everything seems to indicate that the force of unions is a factor to take into account to explain the government's relative inability to introduce reforms in teachers' working conditions.

New Forms of Student and Teacher Management

For some time the voices of those who wish for a greater professional role for teachers have become stronger as a result both of the incorporation of new scientific and technological knowledge in teaching and of the transformations in the organizational context in which teachers' jobs are developed (Tenti Fanfani 1995a). Teachers' work is defined within the context of a network of relations with other jobs—director, vice-director and so forth. The new styles of organization and management introduce modifications in the job profile and in the relationships with principals, students and parents. The educational reforms that give rise to more participative and group-based management models also modify the role of the teacher. These structural changes require new abilities and attitudes of educational professionals, which should be taken into account when professional training strategies are designed. The new school management models require teachers to be able to carry out dialogues, negotiate, recognize differences and produce and maintain agreements.

At least in some nations, the institutional transformation of basic education has implied the introduction of greater complexity in the division of labor among teachers. The observable consequence in some cases is a tendency to dilute the difference between the principal and the classroom teachers by the introduction of new figures such as coordinators of areas or cycles, assistants and directors of functional departments. In synthesis, the introduction of new roles and professional responsibilities in schools contributes to producing a greater differentiation in teaching that breaks with the tendency toward homogeneity typical of the first stages of development of the national educational systems.

Students from Families with the Lowest Income Have the Least Qualified Teachers

Resources that are invested in basic education not only are insufficient but are distributed regressively. The best material, human and technological resources, are not allocated to generate equality of learning opportunity. According to experts, "research has produced considerable evidence that not having access to well qualified teachers has significant effects on students' achievements" (Whitmire 1997).

In Argentina, the data from the first national evaluation of educational quality indicate that teachers obtain the best working conditions and highest salaries in schools for middle and upper middle class students, both in the public and private system. They have greater possibilities for training and developing life-long skills than their colleagues from schools serving poor children (Cervini and Tenti Fanani 1996). The low initial abilities of the teachers and fewer chances for in-service training in schools for poor children lead to the obvious result is that the best teachers are found where there are the best students, those who come from social groups that have the most economic and cultural capital. This perverse assignment of material and human resources contributes to a vicious circle of poverty (Tenti Fanfani 1995b), in which the poverty of families leads to the poverty of educational attainments, indicated by inadequate learning leading to grade repetition and dropout.

Notes

1. In response to a 1993 survey, almost 40 percent of primary school teachers said that they would choose another profession, indicating the great crisis in the profession (Braslavsky and Birgin 1994).
2. Toward the end of 1992, the bulk of the teacher training system depended on DIFOCAD (Dirección de Formación y Capacitación Docente del Ministerio de Cultura y Educación de la Nación).

References

Birgin, A. 1997. *Las regulaciones del trabajo de enseñar. Vocación, estado y mercado en la configuración de la docencia.* Tesis de Maestría. FLACSO (Facultad Latinoameric-ana de Ciencias Sociales). Buenos Aires.
Bonder, G. 1997. *La formación docente como clave de la reforma educativa: qué, cómo y hacia dónde orientarla.* Inédito. Buenos Aires.
Braslavsky, C., and A. Birgin. 1994. "Quiénes enseñan hoy en la Argentina." In *Proyecto principal de educación en América Latina y el Caribe.* Santiago de Chile: OREALC/UNESCO: Bulletin no. 34, August.
Carnoy, M., and C. De Moura Castro. 1995. Reforma educativas en América latina, *Documento presentado al seminario sobre reformas educativas, organizado por el BID en Buenos Aires. Buenos Aires.*
Cervini, R., and E. Tenti Fanfani. 1996. *Características del maestro y rendimiento escolar de los alumnos.* Inédito. Buenos Aires: UNICEF.
Delors, J. 1996. Learning: The Treasure Within. Report to UNESCO of the International Commission on Education for the Twenty-First Century. Paris: UNESCO Publishing.
Diario Clarín. 1997. July 27.
Diker, G., and F. Terigi. 1994. *Panorama de la formación docente en la Argentina.* Buenos Aires: Ministerio de Cultura y Educación (Dirección Nacional de Cooperación Internacional)/Organización de los Estados Americanos.
Fernandez, M.A., M.L. Lemos, and D.L. Wiñar. 1997. *La Argentina Fragmentada: El caso de la education.* Buenos Aires: Mino y Davila Editores.
Lumi, S. 1997. El Sistema educativo en la ciudad autónoma de Buenos Aires. Serie estudios No. 20 (julio) CECE, Buenos Aires.

Morduchowicz, A. 1997. *La estructura salarial docente en la Argentina: Conceptos, dificultades y evidencia empirica.* Buenos Aires: Ministerio de Cultura y Educacíon, Secretaria de Programación y Evaluación Educativo. Programma estudios de Costos del Sistema Educativo.

Morduchowicz, A., and A. Marcón. 1996. *La carrera profesional docente o "la estrategia de una ilusión."* Buenos Aires: Ministerio de Cultura y Educación, Secretaría de Programación y Evaluación Educativa, Programa Estudio de Costos del Sistema Educativo.

Tenti Fanfani, E. 1995a. "Una carrera con obstáculos: la profesionalización docente." In IICE, *Revista del Instituto de Investigaciones en Ciencias de la Educación* (Facultad de Filosofia y Letras de la Universidad de Buenos Aires) 4, no. 7 (December): 17–25.

———. 1995b. *La escuela vacía. Deberes del estado y responsabilidades de la sociedad civil.* Buenos Aires: Losada/UNICEF.

———. 1998. "Las palabras y las cosas de la educación." In *Zona Educativa. Revista del Ministerio de Cultura y Educación de la Nación.* Marzo.

Torres, R.M. 1995. "Formación docente: clave de la reforma educativa." Paper presented in the seminar *Nuevas formas de aprender y de enseñar: demandas a la formación inicial del docente.* Santiago de Chile: CIDE/UNESCO-OREALC/UNICEF. November 6–8.

Whitmire R. 1997. "Poor Students More Likely to Have Less Qualified Teachers." *Detroit News,* August 1.

25

María Umbelina Caiafa Salgado

Training, Salaries, and Work Conditions of Teachers of the First Grades of Primary School

Note on the Brazilian School System and Changes in It, 1961–1996

Brazilian education consists of public and private school systems, organized in collaboration with the federal government, states, municipalities, and Federal District. The expressions "state systems" and "municipal systems" are used to refer to public schools of the states and municipalities, respectively, and "private systems" to refer to private schools. Brazilian laws are identified by listing the number of the law, followed by an up-slash, followed by the year in which it was passed. For example, Law 4024/61 is Law number 4024, enacted in 1961.

1961–1970. During the time Law 4024/61 was in effect, the Brazilian school system was composed of the following levels: primary, mandatory, which lasted for four years; middle, which lasted seven years; and higher education. The middle level divided itself in two cycles: *ginásio* (four years) and high school (three years). Both mid-level cycles contained the secondary, academic track as well as technical courses and the professional normal school track.

1971–1981. With the publication of Law 5692/71, mandatory school came to be called *Primeiro Grau* (primary level), which lasted eight years and incorporated the former primary and *ginásio* levels. High school was required for professional formation and its name was changed to *segundo grau* (secondary level), eliminating the division between secondary, technical, and normal school.

1982–1995. In 1982, Law 7,044 revoked the requirement for professional formation, but had little influence on the *habilitação magisterio* (teaching degree) that exists up to now, since the implementation of Law 9493/96 has not been carried out.

1996–1998. Beginning with the new LDB (Law of Directives and Bases of National Education), Brazil's school system has two levels: basic and higher.

Higher education is sometimes referred to as post-secondary education, a term that includes both universities and other educational institutions. The basic level is divided into fundamental and middle school. The first lasts eight years, and corresponds to mandatory schooling. It is now an indivisible whole. Fundamental education assumes special characteristics in the first four grades: in order to be more adequate for the special needs of the age groups of its respective students, the contents are more integrated by a single teacher who is responsible for the class.

Introduction

In Brazil, the training of teachers of the first four grades of primary school, as well as the definition of the respective salaries and careers, is now undergoing a major reformulation that is governed by the Law of Directives and Bases of National Education and by the Fund for Maintenance and Development of Basic Education and Improvement of Teaching (FUNDEF). Many of the provisions of this legislation are still being implemented, which makes it difficult to evaluate their effectiveness. Thus, for a balanced evaluation of the current situation, it is important to keep in mind the model that governed teaching before, implanted in the 1970s and still partially in effect at this time of transition in 1998.

The point of departure of this chapter is the conviction that effective teaching action is aided by initial and continuing training, salaries and career possibilities, and teachers' work conditions. This chapter presents and evaluates these three topics, which form a crucial element in the educational system's behavior.

Teachers' Qualifications and Training

According to the new LDB, the teachers of the initial grades of basic education could be trained either in secondary or post-secondary schools; in the 1990s, teacher training has increasingly taken place in post-secondary schools. Secondary education, in the form of normal school, is accepted as a minimal training but full graduation is preferred, that is, a four-year course, since in other times it was possible to have two-year courses, as a remedial form. In 2006, all teachers will be required to have training in post-secondary level institutions or to have in-service training (Art. 87 Para. 40). In the meantime, this ideal is far from being attained.

Distribution and Levels of Qualification

In Brazil, data are collected for teaching position, and are not corrected for teachers working in two or more shifts or holding more than one job. The Ministry of Education reports that there are 743,345 teaching positions in the first grades of primary school. In 1996, the state and municipal systems, taken together, included 87.70 percent of the total. The federal system accounted for less than 1 percent and the private school system for 12 percent of the total.

The regions differed in respect to the relative weight of state and municipal school systems. In 1996, the municipal systems dominated the Northeast and South, with 55 percent of the teaching positions. In the Southeast and in the Center West, the state systems dominated, reaching almost 60 percent in the Southeast. In the North region, there is a relative equilibrium between the number of positions in the state and in the municipal systems. This distribution is changing rapidly, because in 1996 the municipalities were made responsible for education.

The qualification of teaching personnel working in different regions of the country can be analyzed on the basis of the data presented in Table 25.1, which allows us to identify the different conditions for fully qualified teachers and for *leigos,* who are partly qualified teachers. The majority have "complete or incomplete basic education'; other *leigos* "have high school without a diploma," or "higher education, without a B.A. or high school diploma." They occupy 170,731 teaching positions. The *leigos* category is heterogeneous, including professionals with very diverse levels of schooling, whose training requires differentiated treatment.

Initial Teacher Training

Until the new LDB was published in December 1996, the initial training of teachers of the first grades of basic education was regulated by the Federal Laws 4024/61, 5540/68, and 5692/71.

Law 4024/61 provided that training of professionals for the initial grades of basic education be carried out in institutions that were specific for this purpose: the normal school regional courses, the normal schools and the education institutes. The normal regional courses offered a four-year training program at the high school level. The normal school offered a three-year program in high school after earlier training in technical, professional, or normal school tracks. Technical personnel—"teacher trainers, supervisors and school administrators" for primary school—were trained in education institutes (Art. 52). Meanwhile, the state educational systems restricted the graduates of the normal regional courses regarding the area in which they could work. Only the normal high schools provided access to the post–middle school courses of specialization and improvement for the formation of technical personnel. The legislature recognized Brazil's diversities, allowing both the alternative formation of primary school teachers and in the possibility of regularizing temporary teaching licenses.

The 1968 university reform (Law 5540/68) created the Faculties of Education and introduced the specialist category. The link between the teachers and technicians of primary school was broken because teachers' training was separated from that of teaching support personnel. The latter were responsible for educational orientation and school administration, supervision and inspection. They were previously trained in a specific post-secondary institution, in education courses. Once access to the Faculties of Education were open to those who completed any of the forms of middle school, the pedagogical assistance personnel were no longer recruited in the primary school system.

Table 25.1

Number of Teachers in the First Four Years of the Basic Cycle and Literary Classes by Level of Education

| Level of education | Basic education | | Secondary | | Post-secondary | | | Total |
| | | | | | With Bachelor's Degree | Without Bachelor's | | |
Region	Incomplete	Complete	With high school	Without high school		With high school	Without high school	
North	13,911	15,211	46,369	2,967	1,684	233	75	80,450
Northeast	60,765	38,417	189,255	9,672	20,365	2,429	503	321,406
South Southeast Central-West	2,584	3,938	31,626	2,317	12,389	1,182	203	54,239
Total	77,260	57,566	267,250	14,956	34,438	3,844	781	456,095

Source: MEC/INEP/SEEC.

Under Law 5692/71, teacher and specialist training for teaching in primary school were treated together with that of professionals destined to any job area requiring secondary education. The Law declared, in Article 29, that this training will be made in levels that progressively increase, adjusting to the cultural differences of each region of the nation, meeting the specific objectives of each level, the characteristics of the disciplines, areas of study or activities, and the phases of development of those being educated. The minimum training required for teaching in the first four grades of the first level (corresponding to the former primary school) is "graduation from secondary school" (Article 30). Meanwhile, faced with a high percentage of less qualified teachers working at that time, the Law made provision for intensive courses for pedagogical preparation for those who completed primary school and competence exams to be administered by the State Education Councils.

Law 5692/71 transformed the normal course into the "Teaching Qualification," which could be offered by any secondary school and gave access to any higher level course. The normal schools, whose institutional culture was characterized by the strict relation with primary school, underwent significant transformation. Some started offering training for high school. Others deteriorated and disappeared. The specialty of elementary school training was lost. Specific Centers of Training and Updating of Teachers (CEFAM) were created in 1988, with the aim of regaining the specificity of training of teachers for the first grades of primary school, but their results were not impressive.

To improve this situation, the LDB in 1996 incorporated the initiatives of the educators themselves, carrying out teacher training for the initial grades of basic education in a normal post-secondary course offered by universities or by post-secondary education institutes. It requires: (1) at least 300 hours of practice teaching, and (2) teaching experience as a condition for the exercise of any other technical-pedagogic functions within the school, such as coordination of teaching and school administration. Although isolated initiatives have inspired the current legislation, it is too early to evaluate its results, since there is not a complete cohort formed under such law.

Continuing Training

Law 5692/71 did not discuss continuing training, barely mentioning the stimulation of "improvement and constant updating of teachers and educational specialists" as a responsibility of school systems (Art. 38). Thus, the 1996 LDB is innovative when it refers to "continuing professional improvement" as a way of increasing the value of teaching, establishing periodic licensing with remuneration based on such improvement (Article 67). The training may be carried out by means of correspondence courses (Article 87). In addition, the 1996 law that created FUNDEF provided financial resources for the training of inadequately trained classroom teachers (Articles 7 and 9). Earlier continuing training programs had had little benefit for students because they lacked continuity, were of limited duration, and interrupted teaching while the teacher studied specific items for the training course. Thus, greater emphasis is now placed on the school's initiative in developing actions tied to its educational mission and the teachers' daily activities. Participation in continuing training was not required, but was stimulated by a propitious institutional climate.

Salaries and Careers

Decisions about careers and salaries of teachers in the initial grades of basic education depend on the administrative sphere of the school system to which they belong. However, most municipalities and private school systems have neither any organized career plan nor criteria for setting salaries. Only recently were legal instruments created that make it possible to establish a national policy of career and teachers' salary in public teaching systems. In the case of private school systems, the subject continues without any regulation. It is resolved at the level of relations between unions and employers.

Teaching Careers

The 1996 LDB requires that the teaching career statutes and plans of the states and municipalities assure educational professionals (1) entrance into the teaching career exclusively by public competition; (2) a professional salary floor; and (3) functional promotion based on degrees or increased qualification and on the evaluation of job performance (Article 67). This last topic is still generating debate on strategies of implementation.

FUNDEF transfers resources to the municipalities if they present career and salary plans, elaborated according to the directives established by the CNE (National Education Council). They (a) establish annual holidays of forty-five days, as well as a work week of up to forty hours, with 20 percent to 25 percent of active teaching hours for class preparation and pedagogical meetings; (b) limit increases in salary for obtaining a post-secondary degree to 50 percent of the salary obtained by teachers holding a secondary school degree; (c) create incentives for promotion by qualifications that are tied to the exclusive dedication to the job, to the length of service and to evaluation, which includes teaching, as well as knowledge of pedagogy and of subjects taught. This was done to limit the payment of very unequal salaries for the same work based on the teacher's secondary or post-secondary degree.

None of these legal instruments addresses the question of teachers' retirement, which occurs at the end of twenty-five years of service for women, and thirty years for men, at full pay. There is an attempt to study the creation of funds to guarantee teachers' retirement with full pay, without using funds allocated to finance education.

Table 25.2

Starting Monthly Salaries of First Through Fourth Grade Teachers by Average Level of Training

| | High school | | | | Higher education | | | |
| Region/State | Initial salary | | Final salary | | Initial salary | | Final salary | |
	R$	US$	R$	US$	R$	US$	R$	US$
Acre	63	0	113	0	112	0	201	0
R.G. do Norte*	85	0	140	0	137	0	231	0
Ceará	173	0	204	0	311	0	366	0
Piauí	143	0	220	0	170	0	262	0
Alagoas	192	0	222	0	349	0	404	0
Goiás	129	0	232	0	189	0	340	0
Pará	152	0	238	0	350	0	660	0
Mato Grosso do Sul	168	0	274	0	266	0	478	0
Sergipe*	184	0	315	0	377	0	621	0
R.G. do Sul	237	0	360	0	251	0	449	0
Rio de Janeiro	227	0	371	0	241	0	436	0
Amazonas	354	0	418	0	544	0	639	0
Amapá	223	0	458	0	338	0	693	0
Pernambuco*	209	0	475	0	337	0	475	0
São Paulo*	286	0	475	0	335	0	564	0
Paraná	253	0	515	0	385	0	783	0
Espírito Santo	222	0	578	0	315	0	825	0
Minas Gerais	255	0	589	0	458	0	1083	0
Distrito Federal*	398	0	714	0	497	0	1010	0

Sources: SINEPE. MED/SEF/DIEAP/CGAAI 1996. Oliveira, J.B.A. et al., 1997.
Notes: U.S.$ on 12/13/96 = R$ 1.0381.
*In the states of Sergipe, Pernambuco, and São Paulo and the Federal District, the workweek is forty hours. In the other states it is twenty to twenty-five hours per week.

Salaries

The analysis of teachers' salaries is problematic because each government sphere uses different formats for the presentation of information. There is no clear information for distinguishing between basic salary and fringe benefits, so that, in this chapter, the term *salary* indicates total monthly remuneration received by an occupant of a teaching position.

The data presented in Table 25.2 refer to nineteen of twenty-seven Brazilian states. The majority of them have regimes of twenty to twenty-five hours of work per week, except the states indicated by an asterisk (*), which have a forty-hour work week. In some cases, in addition to classroom hours, teachers receive pay for work outside of class. In some cases this additional pay is included in the total, but in others it is not, preventing an in-depth analysis of the data.

Table 25.2 shows that, in two of nineteen states focused, the initial salary for teachers with secondary school training is less than R$120.00 per month, which was the national minimum salary for a forty-hour week. In two others, it is greater than R$250.00 (US$1.00 = R$1.038). All the others fall between R$120.00 and R$ 249.00 per month.

The analysis of final salaries for teachers with secondary school training shows the lowest pay in the same two states. The relation between initial and final salaries is variable. In five states, final salaries were more than double the initial salaries. These salaries are relatively high and, in all cases, the workweek is from twenty to twenty-five hours.

Regarding teachers with post-secondary school training, we see that in twelve out of nineteen states, initial salaries range between R$200.00 and R$399.00. In four others, they are below R$200.00 and in three are greater than R$400.00. The figures for final salaries are quite diverse: five states paid between R$200.00 and R$399.00, six between R$400.00 and R$599.00, four between R$600.00 and R$799.00, one between R$800.00 and R$999.00 and two more than R$1,000.00.

The differences among salaries of teachers with high school and those with post-secondary education varies greatly among the states. Thus, while five states are characterized by similar pay for these two levels of training, seven have high salaries for teachers with post-secondary education compared to those for teachers with only secondary school education.

The comparison between the salaries of teachers in state systems and those in private systems is difficult because the base of calculation of private school salaries is hours in the classroom, not monthly salary. Thus, Table 25.3 is based on the following calculation: salary per classroom hours multiplied by twenty hours multiplied by 4.5 weeks (including payment due to weekends and holidays) multiplied by 1.20 (percentage paid for class preparation and pedagogical meetings).

With the exception of Paraná, salaries in the private school system are higher than those in the state system, and in three states the difference is greater than 50 percent. This difference should be evaluated carefully, when the salaries compared are the starting levels in public and private schools, since there is no structured career ladder in private schools.

There are no significant differences between the average and median wages per hour of teachers and other categories of workers with similar levels of schooling. Teachers have a slight advantage at the lower end of the salary scales but, at the highest levels of pay, the salaries of teachers are consistently below the median of salaries of other groups with similar schooling (Oliveira et al. 1997). Teachers' salaries in the municipal school system range from less than half the minimum wage to salaries that are higher than those in the state schools (Gatti 1997).

The 1996 legislation establishing FUNDEF governs all public schools (Law 9495/96); to implement it, Resolution no. 8 of the CNE states "The average monthly remuneration of teachers will be the equivalent of the average cost per

Table 25.3

Starting Monthly Salaries of Teachers of First Through Fourth Grades with Average Level of Education

Region/State	Public system		Private systems	
	R$	U.S.$	R$	U.S.$
Pará	152	158	189	196
R.G. do Sul	237	246	459	476
Rio de Janeiro	227	236	316	328
Pernambuco*	209	217	302	314
Paraná	253	263	224	233
Espírito Santo	222	230	346	359
Minas Gerais	255	265	452	469
Distrito Federal*	398	413	229	238

Source: Data from SINEPE MEC/SEF/DIEAP/CGAAI 1996.
Note: U.S.$ on 12/13/96 = R$ 1.038.
*Based on a forty-hour workweek.

student per year, for a job of twenty classroom hours and five hours of activities, for an average student/teacher ratio of twenty-five students per teacher, in the teaching system" (Resolution no. 8/97—CNE).

However, these rules have been strongly criticized because the average salary does not incorporate the national salary floor that has been demanded by teachers, and the value of R$315.00, adopted as the average cost per student per year, is believed to be underestimated because it does not include factors such as the number of students enrolled in literacy classes, which are the responsibility of municipalities (Monlevade and Ferreira 1997).

Working Conditions

In the following sections, specific examples are given to illustrate work conditions, but they cannot be generalized because no systematic survey of teachers' working conditions in the initial grades of basic education has been carried out.

Personal Characteristics of Teachers

Teachers of basic education tend to come from the middle and lower ranks of society (Mello 1982; Weber 1996), but the share of each segment varies among the states, reflecting their socioeconomic conditions. In general, teaching basic education is a means of upward social mobility (Gatti et al. 1994; Weber 1996).

Traditionally, teaching in the first grades of basic education is viewed as women's work, which contributes to defining some aspects of their working conditions. Teachers commonly have to assume a third job, making it compatible with domestic and professional activities (Rosemberg et al. 1982; Madeira 1982; CNTE 1998a), bringing complaints of exhaustion and of difficulties in complying with the requirement of a forty-hour week (Andaló 1995), and provoking a feeling of guilt regarding fulfillment of family obligations. This leads to "burnout" of workers who lose the sense of their relation to their job, so that things do not matter to them and any effort seems useless, leading to a low level of involvement in their activities. A recent study diagnosed symptoms of this syndrome in more than half of all basic education teachers (CNTE 1998a).

The social prestige of the teaching career is quite low, as evidenced by low salaries (Gatti 1997), by the arbitrariness and lack of respect with which teachers are treated (Gatti et al. 1994), and by the personal and social lack of self-esteem shown by the teachers themselves (Weber 1996). This low prestige may be due to the lack of definition of minimal levels of competence for teaching, so that it tends to be perceived by the population as an activity that does not require specific training.

Institutional Aspects

The institutional aspects of teachers' working conditions include some elements related to the school as a whole and others that relate specifically to teaching. In relation to school, the problems include small sites that are inadequate, badly ventilated, poorly maintained and lack security, marked by episodes of drug use, robbery and vandalism (CNTE 1998b). Teachers complain about the lack of basic resources for teaching, including books and reference materials.

It is not uncommon to find difficulties in the relationship between principals and their colleagues. Competition and rivalry between colleagues is frequent, as well as the absence of participation within the schools and in professional associations. These difficulties in relationships are a source of "burnout" among teachers (CNTE 1998a).

Meanwhile, the democratization of school management is one of the notable aspects of new practices in various states that adopted selection of principals by vote of the school community (e.g., Minas Gerais), created school councils and required the school to define its own educational goals. Some of these strategies for democratization of school management were incorporated in the 1996 LDB and are rapidly spreading to other states and municipalities.

Institutional aspects of teaching include the number of hours of work, the student/teacher ratio, the division of work among teachers and specialists, the perception of their own competence by teachers and the availability of basic resources for teaching. Hours of work vary from twenty to forty hours per week. Moreover, teachers frequently work a second shift in their own or another school.

Of the teachers interviewed by Gatti et al., 44 percent declared that they had a second activity, mainly in those Minas Gerais and São Paulo. Only 6 percent of these activities are outside of the educational field. Besides, "extra-curricular" activities listed by the teachers are not always paid. According to Gatti, there is a big difference regarding this matter among the states surveyed. In São Paulo, 77 percent of the teachers declared that they received pay for extra-curricular activity hours, against 42 percent in Minas Gerais and barely 27 percent in Maranhão (Gatti et al. 1994).

The student/teacher ratio varies from 25.4 to 27.2 in the initial grades of basic education (MEC/INEP 1997). However, these indices represent average values; the average number of students per teacher interviewed was thirty-eight in Maranhão, thirty-one in Minas Gerais and thirty-three in São Paulo. In rural zones it is not uncommon to find only one teacher, unprepared for this, responsible for multi-grade classes and attending to the needs of students from the first to the fourth grades.

The division of labor between specialists and teachers has been one of the most debated aspects of teachers' job conditions during the last two decades. Several studies focused on the transformations in teaching practice and teachers' loss of control of their sphere of work, stemming from the separation between teachers and specialists in the educational reforms of 1968–71 (Salgado 1982; Novaes 1984). Teachers argued that the central and regional administrative bodies for education have transformed themselves into mere supervising bureaucracies, distant from daily practice, that gradually impoverished teaching programs and imposed teaching methods. To remedy this situation, for the first time in Brazilian education, the 1996 LDB refers explicitly to improving the status of educational professionals, requiring teaching systems to guarantee adequate work conditions for these professionals.

Organization and Representation

Beginning in the 1970s, there was an intense movement toward organizing teachers' unions both through revitalization of existing organizations and by the creation of new ones. Among the revitalized is the Confederação Nacional dos Trabalhadores em Educaçao (CNTE), formerly Confederação dos Professores do Brasil (CPB), which brings together twenty-nine unions of public school teachers in twenty-seven states, with about 700,000 members. The private school teachers' unions are tied to the Confederação Nacional dos Trabalhadores em Estabelecimento de Ensino (CONTEE), which unites forty-seven organizations. Both the confederations are affiliated with the Central Única dos Trabalhadores (CUT), which includes workers' unions in all fields of activity.

There also were other organizations of educational professionals, such as the National Association of Post-Graduates and Researchers in Education (ANPED), the Center of Studies of Education and Society (CEDES), the National Association for Education (ANDE) and, most recently, the National Association of the Training of Educational Professionals (ANFOPE). These associations are more closely linked to higher education; however, some of them admitted teachers of basic education and were playing an important role in the re-democratization process of the nation and in the definition of the educational policies formalized in the 1988 Constitution, as well as in the application of the LDB.

Finally, there are temporary movements that unite teachers' and other groups for specific aims. An example is the National Forum in Defense of Public School, which was active during the processes of elaborating the 1988 Constitution and the LDB.

Conclusion: Teaching Action and Student School Behavior

One of the most important issues related to teachers' training, career and salaries, and conditions of work is the perverse process that links teachers with the greatest professional and personal difficulties to the neediest students who most require guidance (Mello 1982; Gatti et al. 1994; Andaló 1995; Gatti 1997; CNTE 1998a). In these circumstance, teachers tend to attribute school failure either to the students themselves, who are accused of apathy, disinterest and absenteeism, or to their respective families, who are seen as disintegrated and not in contact with the school. Few mention problems of the school itself or teaching conditions. Teachers in the neediest schools tend to assume a fatalistic attitude, seeing repetition and dropout as inevitable; in this way, they contribute to the students' failure. In a study by Gatti and others, when teachers were asked how many of their students would repeat the year, they stated on average that there would be eleven failures—that is, one-third of the class. The implication is that today there is a "culture of repetition" that marks the institutional climate of many schools and school systems.

Brazil today has a set of education laws that are advanced in many respects, but it is known that the law itself is not enough to solve education problems. On the other hand, although it is true that laws do not change reality, it is important to remember that in the Brazilian case teachers had a large role in the formulation of the laws that are being implemented today and that many successful experiences were incorporated into them. These laws are now being carried out. An example of this is the case of continuing training being placed under the responsibility of the school itself.

There now seems to be some progress in terms of social recognition of the education profession. Weber (1996) pointed out that part of the academic and social debate was transformed into educational policy and/or legislation. These changes include: public examination as the required means of access to a teaching career; the constitutional guarantee of a standard of teaching quality, which raises the value of the educator's performance in the eyes of the public; and the recognition of the teacher as a professional who masters his/her own field of knowledge.

General References

Brasil. 1961. *Lei No. 4024, 20 de dezembro de 1961. Fixa às Diretrizes e Bases da Educação Nacional.*
———. 1971. *Lei No. 5692, 11 de agosto de 1971. Fixa às Diretrizes e Bases para o Ensino de 1o. e 2o. Graus.*
———. 1996. *Lei No. 9394, 20 de dezembro de 1996. Fixa às Diretrizes e Bases da Educação Nacional.*
———. 1996. *Lei No. 9424, 24 de dezembro de 1996. Dispõe Sobre o Fundo de Manutenção e Desenvolvimento do Ensino Fundamental e de Valorização do Magistério.*
———. Conselho Nacional de Educação. 1997. *Resolução No. 3, 8 outubro de 1997. Fixa Diretrizes para os Novos Planos de Carreira e de Remuneração para o Magistério dos Estados, do Distrito Federal e dos Municípios.*
———. Ministerio da Educação e do Desporto. Instituto Nacional de Estudos e Pesquisas Educacionais. 1996. Censo Escolar, 1996.
———. Ministerio da Educação e do Despurto. Instituto Nacional de Estudos e Pesquisas Educacionous. 1997. *Sinopse Estatistica, 1996: Brasil*, Reqioes, Unidadesda Federação. Brasília: DNEP.
Brzezinski, I. 1996. *Pedagogia, pedagogos e formação de professores: busca e movimento.* Campinas, SP: Papirus. Coleção Magisterio: Formação e Trabalho Pedagógico.
Instituto de Pesquisa Econômica Aplicada (IPEA). 1996. *Relatório sobre o desenvolvimento humano no Brasil.* Rio de Janeiro, RJ PNUD; Brasília, DF: IPEA.
Romanelli, O.O. 1987. *História da educação no Brasil.* Petrópolis, RJ: Vozes.

Works Cited

Andaló, C.S.A. 1995. *Fala, Professora!: repensando o aperfeiçoamento docente.* Petrópolis, RJ: Vozes.
Confederação Nacional dos Trabalhadores em Educação (CNTE). 1988a. *A construção de uma escola pública segura no Brasil.* Brasília. Mimeo.
Confederação Nacional dos Trabalhadores em Educação/Universidade de Brasília (CNTE). 1988b. *Burnout em professores.* Brasília. Mimeo.
Gatti, B.A. 1997. *Formação de professores e carreira: problemas e movimentos de renovação.* Campinas, SP: Autores Associados. Coleção Formação de Professores.
Gatti, B.A., Y.L. Sposito, and R.N. Silva. 1994. "Características de professores(as) de 1t grau no Brasil: perfil e expectativas." *Educação e Sociedade* 5 (August): 248–260.
Madeira, F.R.A. 1982. "A esposa professora e sua terceira ou quarta jornada de trabalho." *ANDE* 4: 22-25.
Mello, G.N. 1982. *Magistério de 1t grau: da competência técnica ao compromisso político.* São Paulo, SP: Cortez.
Monlevade, J.A.C., and E.B. Ferreira. 1997. *O FUNDEF e seus pecados capitais.* Brasília, DF: Idéa.
Novaes, M.E. 1982. "Professor não é parente postiço." *ANDE* 4: 60-62.

Oliveira, J.B.A., Antônio Carlos da Ressuriçâon Xavier, José Amaral Sobrintho, Carlos Alberto Ramos, Eduardo Gonçalves Rios Neto, Maria Cristina Moreiva Barbosa, and José Teixeira Lopes Ribeiro. 1997. *Salário dos professores. Relatório apresentado ao CONSED.* Brasília, DF. Mimeo.

Rosemberg, L., M.C. Campos, and M.P. Mermelstein. 1982. "24 horas na vida de uma mulher." *ANDE* 4: 18–21.

Salgado, M.U.C. 1982. "O papel da didática na formação do professor." *ANDE* 4 (1982): 2–17.

Weber, S. 1996. *O professorado e o papel da educação na sociedade.* Campinas, SP: Papirus. Coleção Prática Pedagógica.

26

Gabriel Castillo Inzulza

Experiences in Training Good Teachers in Work Places

Introduction

Initial Training System

The system of training educational professionals in Chile during the last twenty years has been characterized by traditional frontal methods and by students who accept this; they usually come from the middle and lower middle class, with low school achievement, since the slight social prestige of the profession and the salaries that it offers impedes the recruiting of students with better expectations.

Toward the beginning of the 1970s, teachers' training depended, in large part, on the state through its normal schools. When these disappeared, training was transferred to public and private universities and professional institutes that offered a broad range of training options with respect to their orientation, duration and pedagogical concept; the requirements applicants had to fulfill; and plans and programs of study. This great variety of autonomous institutions did not permit, however, changing the traditional manner—centered on frontal education—and it was not possible to prepare the kind of teachers that the nation required. In any case, at least four years of initial training were required to receive the degree of basic education (primary school) teacher, even though the exact number of years depended on the curriculum of the higher education institution granting the degree. In 1996, only 1.4 percent of teachers (mainly in rural areas) did not have a professional degree to carry out their work (UNESCO-OREALC 1996).

Although there were not common objectives, contents, and styles for teacher training, teaching methods used in the various higher education establishments corresponded, generally, to a traditional frontal pedagogical focus, that is to say, the teacher is the protagonist and the student is passive. An analysis of the characteristics of the professors who train teachers showed that these were not greatly different from those of teachers in other careers. The problem would be

292 GABRIEL CASTILLO INZULZA

rooted, more, in that in education teachers were not offered chances to practice and apply the methods that they taught, especially those which referred to individual differences (Schiefelbein and Tedesco 1992). This is seen as much in the small number of teachers who stated that their main professional objective is that students *learn,* as in teachers' expectations of *teaching* students (Schiefelbein et al. 1994).

The low social status of the teaching profession had repercussions as far as the quality of the student body that entered teaching careers. Studies on the socioeconomic condition of students of education have demonstrated certain constants, among others: (1) a larger enrollment of women than of men—since men had greater economic expectations in other activities; (2) an important percentage had an irregular family situation—separated parents, single mothers; (3) family income was less than the minimum wage for 50 percent of the students; (4) the average achievement was not greater than a standard deviation with respect to the normal distribution of grades.

The Continuing Teacher Training System

Continuing teacher training can be offered in public or private universities or professional institutes that are accredited by the Ministry of Education though its Center of Continuing Educational Training, Experiments and Research (CPEIP). The characteristics of the courses given depends on each school, just as in the case of initial teacher training. If the system of continuing training in Chile is voluntary, there are economic incentives for teachers that have greater continuing training: they receive higher salaries.

Continuing training is concentrated in large cities. In the first half of 1998 around 360 courses were offered, of which 65 percent were in the capital (Santiago with 40 percent) and the two next most important cities of the nation (Valparaíso with 19 percent and Concepción with 6 percent [CPEIP 1998]). Continuing training was offered according to potential capacity and economic incentives, but was unattractive to teachers. Its contents usually did not respond to the needs and challenges of education, and not all those eligible for economic incentives for training used them (Comisión 1993).

Teachers' Work

The beginning salary level is $1,704,636 (US$3,788)—and is twice as high when teachers reach thirty years of experience with 40 percent increase for in-service training. On average, a teacher with fifteen years of experience and 20 percent for in-service training has a salary of $2,841,964—(the mid-year exchange rate is US$1=$450). There are no salaries in kind or fringe benefits. Teachers' average salary is similar to the GNP per capita and to the salary of secretaries. A school principal with thirty years of service and a maximum credit for teaching (40 percent) earns $4,432,053—which is equal to a little more than four minimum salaries. On average, teachers work for twenty-five years in their profession. The low salaries have had the result that 30 percent of the teachers have a second job and this has resulted in a low quality of education.

The low salaries did not motivate many men to study for teaching careers, which is reflected in the fact that 70 percent of teachers are women. Discrimination exists, however, given that less than half of the school principals are women (Chile, Ministerio de Educación 1996).

Beginning in 1991, teachers in public schools were granted job stability, which they had had up to 1973. Teachers in private schools do not have it, so that about 50 percent of the nation's teachers have this right. Teachers have the option of belonging to the Chilean Teachers' Union, which has around 81,000 members, about 60 percent of the teachers in the nation. One percent of the members' salaries are deducted as union dues. The levels of absenteeism of teachers in urban areas is not very great, however there is no control of teachers' attendance in rural areas, where absenteeism is thought to be high. An average of five school days per year are lost because of strikes.

As administrators and society in general perceive that educational quality is not good, since children do not learn enough, the social prestige of the teaching profession continues to be low. This generates a vicious circle, since it impedes the recruiting of good new students of education, as mentioned above, who would become excellent teachers and break this cycle. On the other hand, if the only action taken is to increase salaries, this would not assure an improvement in the academic achievement of education students, since they would continue to be taught by the same teachers. Improving teaching quality requires adequate pedagogical materials—such as self-study guides—that allow teachers to learn new methods and, thus, elevate the social prestige and salaries of the teaching profession (Schiefelbein et al. 1994).

In Chile, teachers' careers and effectiveness depend on their formal preparation, their informal training, work conditions and the way in which they teach. This chapter is in two parts. The first has described the formal qualifications required of primary school teachers, the actual amount of training they have had, and their salary and other job conditions. The second focuses on innovations in teacher training and methods of teaching that may have wide applicability to other nations.

Innovations in Teacher Training

This section describes both the training of good teachers in individual schools, and their training by the distribution of guides for teachers.

The Experience of San Enrique: The School for Learning

In 1971, the government primary school of San Enrique, a suburb of Santiago, requested aid from the Department of Education of the Center of Educational Improvement, Experiment and Research (CPEIP) of the Ministry of Education to improve its students' achievement. When they went to the school, the educators from this Department explained to the teachers that although they were going to help them to improve their work within the existing school system, the only way they would obtain significant learning by all their students was to adopt a distinct school mission. This distinct mission expressed itself in the dichotomy: "School for Teaching" or "School for Learning."

The "School for Teaching" was designed as a school where it was important to set out the school program in as clear and ordered a manner as possible in order to then find out which students knew the material and which did not.

The "School for Learning" was defined as a school for which learning was important and thus its preoccupation was in finding ways of getting the students to advance in their learning of various types and to increase their human development. This would occur when teachers learned to plan for success, to share with parents and neighbors, and above all to talk periodically among themselves about their information, preoccupations, successes and difficulties in the children's learning.

The school was established in the first year of the Popular Unity government of President Salvador Allende, a period in which those living in San Enrique and neighboring areas had a high conception of their power and a strong belief in the necessity of changing the customs that hindered the access of the poorest segments of society to the entitlements to which they had the right, including that of education.

For those living close to it, it seemed that the School for Learning would not be preoccupied so much with what it wished to teach as with what the students could learn. In this way, if some teachers thought that the expression School for Learning was a tautology because the school had no other aim than generating learning, those involved indicated that, if this were true, then the school had not until then fulfilled its mission and the moment had arrived to begin to fulfill it.

The teachers of the school had a meeting to make a decision. They had many times heard talk of a school distinct from those that existed, but they never had seen it. They said that teachers were not guilty of failing to generate learning in all the students. The system in which they worked did not require this of them. For the system, learning was the task of the students. The mission of the teachers was to develop programs and evaluation criteria.

The idea of a School for Learning was discussed with the parents and those living in the neighborhood until their approval was obtained. The educators of CPEIP taught the teachers who were responsible for the first grade courses how to implement it. One of the members of the Department of Education of CPEIP habitually worked with the teachers, parents, administrators and those living in the neighborhood.

The complete success of the experience came to be so well known that many teachers from other classes in the school and directors of neighboring schools began to ask for help in order to initiate similar experiences. Some researchers who learned about the experience thought that the real reasons for the success were difficult to determine because the participation of the neighbors—a determinant in the results—was more attributable to the social mobilization characteristic of the period than to the new approach in the school.

The School for Learning in Lo Barnechea and the Case of Room "G"

The methodology used in San Enrique was repeated in Lo Barnechea: in the first year the Department of Education of CPEIP aided the school in the way in which it asked for aid, but also indicated that instead of trying to adapt all of the students to the goals of the school it was necessary for the school to adapt its goals to those that the students wanted to and could achieve.

Assistance from the community was not intended in the program, except from the health clinic. All children in the first school grades received aid because community members aided not only their own children but also aided children who could not count on backing from their homes.

In 1975 the government school of Lo Barnechea put into practice "School for Learning," this time in the first to fourth grade courses. And the success of San Enrique was again repeated. Curiously, the experience of Lo Barnechea has been better known for a specific case—that of Room G—than for the broader program in which the school participated.

The Case of Room G

Room G was composed of twenty-two students in the fourth grade that the administration of the school had separated from their usual groups and placed in a new class, "Room G," with the sole aim that they finish the school year and that they leave school without obstructing the learning of the other students. They had failed repeatedly and could still neither read nor write, and there was not any expectation that, in the two months remaining until the end of the school year, they could reverse their history of failure. However, in these two final months of the school year, these students were able to learn that which they had not learned in four to eight years.

What happened? The teachers reached an agreement with the students to develop four activities: story telling; soccer or another sport; bookkeeping and other office skills; and learning some manual or technical job. A curate from a neighboring parish was put in charge of story telling. A local sports club named someone to take charge of soccer and sports; bookkeeping and other business skills as well as technological work were placed in the charge of two electricians who had a repair shop in the town. A teacher who had recently arrived at the school and two educators from CPEIP coordinated these activities.

Reading and writing began because of story telling. The curate told stories without writing anything on the blackboard because the students did not know how to read; but one day the story teller found himself obliged to write the word "hypnotizing" on the blackboard because the children asked him to. The word had stood out in the story; the students saw the possibility of "hypnotizing" younger children in the next recreation period and they insisted on learning the word well and in recognizing it in its written form. From there, without intending to, they began to enter into written texts. At the end of the year, the students of "Room G" had made such astonishing progress that the school decided to keep them in its classes. However, the Ministry of Education dropped its support of the programs at San Enrique and Lo Barnechea.

The Anticipation School y Grupo Generador

Despite the success of the School for Learning projects, researchers said that their success had occurred because of the use of a motivated and qualified team, and that it would be more important to find a strategy of innovation that could be carried out on a broad scale and that would be possible to carry out with teachers who normally worked in schools.

This reaction disenchanted the orientors who had conducted the experiment of San Enrique and Lo Barnechea; but, later, this observation led them to two very important discoveries: the strategy of the "Generating Group" and the concept of Anticipation Education and Anticipation School. The Generating Group strategy overturned the objection of the researchers who believed that to have a school centered on the student and not on programs of study required teachers who would accept this distinct school, who pledged themselves to it and were qualified to put the system in practice. The new strategy indicated that to change one or many schools one must have, above all, a highly motivated and qualified leading group to show society the advantages of the new school and the practical ways in which it can be put into operation.

The second discovery was the concept of Anticipation Education and Anticipation School. One of the most frequent objections to the idea of a School for All or of a School for Human Growth or for Peoples' Learning is the objection that the current selective school is the natural manifestation of a selective society. In this way, trying to change a school based on persons is to remain outside of current society; it is confounding good intentions with possibilities that do not exist in reality. The response usually is "We agree with this distinct school, not to create it now, but in another society that we hope will be created. Only when we can count on this new society will we also have the benefit of such a desirable school."

Before this difficulty, those who had experienced the School for Learning of San Enrique and Lo Barnechea had no other way than understanding that they, living for several years in a non-selective school, had anticipated the desired society.

Soon it was said, moreover, that all true education is *anticipatory* since it consists of following our ideal of a being, a vocation and a dignity whose real height cannot be known in advance. Self-education consists of following the ideal of the being that we will become, and when we act this way, in some way, we live in anticipation of this being that we will become.

Society wishes school to teach students to construct a more just and fraternal social relation than now exists, and school will not be able to teach the construction of this society unless the school itself acts as an example of the desired society.

This conceptualization inspired the publication in 1984 of the book *Anticipation Education* and the thesis of an anticipation school, that is, a school that *anticipates the values of a desired society*. This thesis maintains that only a school that brings into the present the values of the desired society will be capable of changing the current school in which only students learn, in which learning is more memorization than significance, in which knowledge is encyclopedic and where what is basic for students' formation is taken from instructional material. The new school should, on the contrary, be based on four themes:

1. learning by all;
2. significant learning;
3. learning of basics;
4. unity of progress in knowledge and in ethical growth.

The thesis of the Anticipation School shares the same basic thesis of the School for Learning. It adds the identification of the themes of the ideal school. What is more important, the ideal school is not proposed as a goal, but as a requirement that has to be realized now. We are not discussing looking to the desired society, but prefiguring it in the present, advancing it now in daily life, every day, and, especially, within school.

The Lo Gallardo School

The Lo Gallardo School is a primary school in San Antonio on the central coast of Chile. In 1990, every time the river that flowed at its edge rose, water flooded the school and required the teachers and students to go to other schools. This situation not only disturbed school work but also impeded both fixing the school as was wished and preserving costly materials in it.

The school's teachers asked if it would be possible to have an "Anticipation School" in these inhospitable conditions. The promoters of the Anticipation School promised to try to get the authorities to improve the physical situation of the school. In exchange, a teacher who taught music in all the school classes promised to carry out the four themes of the Anticipation School in her classes.

The teacher delayed in carrying out her proposal for six months, then did it thoroughly, so much so that her example ignited the enthusiasm of her colleagues and now the school of Lo Gallardo is an Anticipation School in all its subjects. The authorities made the improvements requested, and a strong barrier now protects the school from the river.

Lo Gallardo is accepted in all of Chile as a model of a desirable school, but its example is followed only by some teachers; others maintain the system of a selective school.

Work in the Municipalities

Anticipation Schools are also being implemented in communes in Valparaíso and Maule. The first attempt to establish them was made in 1993. In 1998 in Quilpué and Viña del Mar, which adopted Anticipation Schools, there will no longer be students who fail or repeat, at least in the first four grades. It is not that failure or repeating are abolished but that in these cases, in this new way of providing schooling, they do not make sense.

The Experiences of Dissemination: Teaching Guides for an "Anticipation School"

The Anticipation School distances itself from selective requirements and, in ex-change, foresees the values that society hopes for the future and applies them in school. Just as St. Francis of Assisi loved plants and animals and treated all as brothers, independently of the society of his time, the Anticipation School advances existing society and generates learning conforming to the values and ideals that are desired for it.

In Chile, an effort was made to spread the use of this vision of the ideal school to a larger community both by sending teachers to classes and by providing teaching/study guides for primary school. In 1993 and 1994, UNESCO published two texts with materials for primary school students, using the Anticipation School concept. In Chile, this effort of dissemination was completed in 1994, with CPEIP preparing study guides—workbooks for students—specifically indicating how to provide an Anticipation School. It was necessary to provide special training for the supervisors who gave technical help to the schools in order to teach the directors and teachers the pertinent use of the guides. The guides have been modified by incorporating the observations made by the classroom teachers, administrators, and students. The guides have improved the educational process in the classroom, and teachers say that they provide effective aid.

The other important change has been in the selection of schools that receive the guides. In the beginning, schools were selected that were not interested in working with the guides while at their sides there were schools that had not been selected but wanted them. Therefore, there was a reassignment of the materials. In some cases, schools that had not been able to receive the requested guides were able to convince their communal authorities to request the program from which the books are generated and they then proceed to publish and distribute them.

Among the characteristics of the guides for an Anticipation School, it is worth the trouble to underscore one that has allowed their use in other nations of the region. In effect, these guides do not have as a context a zone of Chile or the history of the country. They try to be materials that produce brotherhood among people, that do not speak of good international relations but that put them into practice. Thus, teachers have come from abroad to visit the nation, and joint action among teachers from the Southern Cone is planned for March 1998.

Some Conclusions About Teacher Training

Teachers' or educators' training schools provide a context in which these professionals can increase their preparation to carry out their teaching mission. Teachers' training schools include both those that use this name and those that do not.

We refer to as "good educators" or "good professionals" those who, in their work with the students, are engaged in following these criteria:

1. Students learn. The students' skills do not remain limited to memorization and book knowledge; the students advance in knowledge, they apply knowledge, they establish a dialogue between daily life and books and between the outside world and their internal essence.
2. What they learn is fundamental.
3. They include all learning in the first knowledge that is growth in humanity.
4. All students learn. Certainly not all learn the same things in the same period of time, but all advance in learning to the extent to which their capacity to learn permits them and in response to the assistance that they receive in the school.

The experiences described above allow us to obtain some inferences, useful for any instance of training:

1. Those teachers who leave a training school without being good educators can acquire this qualification in work places that provide an opportunity to achieve this learning.
2. In training teachers, it first has to be decided if they will be trained in the best way possible in the existing school system or if they should be taught to construct a different school.
3. To train valuable teachers for the existing system, trainers who are knowledgeable and enthusiastic about the current school system are needed. To train teachers for a different school system, trainers who are knowledgeable and enthusiastic about this other type of school are needed.

Note

I thank Dr. Ernesto Schiefelbein for reading this document and for the many valuable suggestions he made for its organization, and Paulina Schiefelbein for her invaluable work on the profile of teacher training in Chile.

General References

Castillo, Gabriel. 1975. "Primer Informe Escuela para Aprender." Santiago: CPEIP.

———. 1978. "Currículum universalista en la enseñanza básica: una estrategia de cambio." Santiago: Universidad Católica.

———. 1984. "Educación de Anticipación." Santiago: Universidad Católica.

———. 1993. "EL PIEMSA: Una experiencia de innovación educativa." Santiago: CPEIP.

———. 1994. *Guías de aprendizaje para una escuela deseable: indicaciones para su uso.* Santiago: CPEIP.

Chile. Ministerio de Educación. 1993. "Bases para la formulación de políticas públicas de formación y perfeccionamiento docente."

Schiefelbein, Ernesto, Gabriel Castillo, and Vicky Colbert. 1993. "Guías de aprendizaje para una escuela deseable." Santiago: UNESCO.

Schiefelbein, Ernesto, and Gabriel Castillo. 1994. "Nuevas guías de aprendizaje para una escuela deseable." Santiago: UNESCO.

Works Cited

CPEIP. 1998. "Listado Nacional de Cursos de Perfeccionamiento. Primer Semestre 1998."

Chile. Ministerio de Educación. 1996. "Compendio de información estadística." Santiago: República de Chile. Oficina Registro Público Nacional de Perfeccionamiento

Schiefelbein, E., and J.C. Tedesco. 1992. "Características de los académicos de las facultades de educación de Chile." Santiago: UNESCO-OREALC.

Schiefelbein, E., et al. 1994. "Las características de la profesión maestro y la calidad de la educación en América Latina." Bulletin no. 34, *Proyecto Principal de Educación en América Latina y el Caribe.* Santiago: UNESCO-OREALC.

UNESCO-OREALC. 1996. "Situación educativa de América Latina y el Caribe, 1980–1994." Santiago: UNESCO/OREALC.

27

Regina Cortina

The Training and Employment of Teachers in Mexico

Since the economic crisis began in the early 1980s in Mexico, there has been a reduction of public funds devoted to education and a dramatic reduction in teachers' wages. The teaching profession today is in serious social and academic crisis mainly because it is no longer a profession to which young people are attracted. During the recession that followed the economic crisis of the 1980s, the government cut wages rather than employment in the public sector. Teachers suffered the brunt of this reduction: in 1988, salaries in the public sector had fallen 55 percent, compared to 78 percent for teachers (International Labor Organization 1995, 51). The average monthly salary of Mexican teachers in 1995 was less than half in constant dollars than it had been in 1981. This was an improvement over their low in 1988, which represented 22 percent of what teaching salaries had been in 1981 (Ibarrola 1996).

Teachers are a main ingredient of success in schooling and its daily practices. The erosion of real wages impels teachers to look for complementary forms of employment. Declining compensation increases their absenteeism. Falling income diminishes their opportunities and their motivation for professional improvement. As they lose professional power and status, teachers are less able to make a difference in providing greater opportunity to those who begin life with fewer advantages.

Unfortunately, decentralization is accompanied by reduced bargaining power of teachers and their unions and the consequent decline in teachers' salaries. The World Bank is one of the main promoters and supporters of decentralization across the region. Of all World Bank projects funded in Latin America during 1990–94, 80 percent included support for decentralization (Lockheed 1996).

A recent study conducted in Mexico found that increasing the monthly salary of teachers in rural areas between 60 and 70 percent had a direct effect on decreasing the frequent switching of teachers from one school to another. Such an improvement in compensation reduced absenteeism, reversed teachers' lack of commitment to the school and its community, and stopped their flight from the teaching profession (Weiss and Ezpeleta 1995).

When the Mexican system of public education was created in 1921, it was closely associated with the agenda of the new Mexican state. The purpose of education was to help build the new nation, to create a consciousness of nationality, to foster nationwide loyalty to the central government, and to homogenize the use of Spanish as the primary language of the country. For most Mexicans, the schools are still controlled by the government for its own purposes, and for this reason most people in Mexico are not particularly interested in the schools as a community concern, even though they strongly believe in schooling and its promises of social mobility. One problem in reforming Mexican education, therefore, is that the schools are seen as part of the central government agenda. The schools are not controlled locally, even though that was the intent of the law that reformed education in 1992. By design, public education still does not serve pluralistic cultural and economic demands and is not closely connected with local communities.

During the period between 1960 and 1982 when the system of public education took form on a national scale, its remarkable expansion and growth created a highly centralized system and powerful teachers' union, the Sindicato Nacional de Trabajadores de la Educación (SNTE). Deriving its political power from the grass-roots organizational work it did for the ruling party, the PRI, the union strongly influenced the management of public schools, the direction of education policy, the conditions of employment, and professional training opportunities for teachers in Mexico.

Beginning in the early 1980s, successive administrations in the Ministry of Education initiated reforms to manage education in a more decentralized fashion and to improve the education and professional life of teachers. Most of those reforms were blocked by the group in control of the teachers' union, Vanguardia Revolucionaria, which recognized that decentralization of education would reduce the national power in the hands of the teacher's union. Reform legislation was finally passed in 1992, and it represented a new turning point in the professional life of teachers in Mexico, which is described based on a 1994–95 survey of elementary school teachers (Ibarrola et al. 1997).[1]

Teaching has been the most typical profession for both urban and rural women in Mexico. As in the past, women form the majority of employees in the field of education (Cortina 1989). In Mexico City today, women represent 80 percent of elementary school teachers. Overall, the city has an aging teaching force with only 1.2 percent of teachers younger than age twenty-four, 60 percent between the ages of twenty-five to thirty-nine and almost 40 percent older than forty. Only 3.5 percent of the teachers have the equivalent of a higher education degree (Ibarrola et al. 1997) because of the political context of national teacher training policies.

Teacher Training

In Mexico the teaching profession is closely aligned with the politics of the national regime and it is therefore not a profession encouraged and supported to improve the teaching craft and the quality of education for children in Mexico. For many years scholars have asserted the need to incorporate the training of teachers into the universities. But the training of teachers in Mexico continues to be isolated in second-tier institutions for teacher training or normal schools. Even though at present there are 160,000 students in teacher education programs, representing approximately 12 percent of higher education enrollment in the country, too often teacher training institutions are controlled by political and union interests that do not give high priority to improving the academic capacity and performance of their schools.

For more than forty years, the Mexican government has been promising to initiate reforms in teacher education. For economic as well as political reasons, the Mexican government has not invested the financial resources needed for incorporating the training of teachers into higher education, nor is it willing to train faculty to carry out this function. The initial logic of the system, one of continual expansion of public education with little emphasis on quality of the services provided, still dominates public policy for education. In 1992, an attempt was made to change this situation. The intent of the 1992 education reform law was to promote parent and community interest in the schools, creating bottom-up forces for change. However, to be effective in the long run, more active participation in schools must be linked to more active participation in political life, a change that will favor the states and the communities against the authority and centralism of the present system. In many states within Mexico, it is evident that a political transition is taking place, a complex effort to dismantle the single-party state dominated by the PRI. The states within Mexico are in the process of negotiating and trying to create alternatives that attempt to include a political venue as well as a change in mentality. Public schooling and teacher education stand at the center of this debate.

Contrary to stated aims, policy decisions in Mexico have tended to downgrade the status of teacher education because normal schools were defined as equivalent to high school, attracting males from lower socioeconomic status and women. With only one additional year of schooling in the normal school, a student could get a professional degree in addition to a secondary school diploma. Having obtained the degree, a teacher could hold a part-time teaching job while also continuing post-secondary education. But at the same time, teacher training became the lower tier of a two-tier educational system through the high school years, since the high schools remained more exclusive, more academically oriented, more male, and more affluent. Policymakers have been slow to address this institutionalized form of subordination.

In March of 1984, the administration of President Miguel de la Madrid decided to upgrade teacher education by demanding a high school diploma. As an immediate result, the training of new teachers was delayed at a moment when the government argued there were thousands of unemployed teachers. When this policy was enacted no decision was made, as mentioned earlier, to incorporate the normal schools into the higher education system. As a result, the training of new teachers sharply declined, primarily in the private normal schools, which had trained the majority of teachers. The main reason that women choose these institutions is that they are able to gain access to them more easily because most female teachers in Mexico are from an urban middle-class backgrounds and can therefore pay for their education. The high proportion of women in private normal schools is also influenced by the tradition of private normal schools run by religious organizations that are for women only. These schools used to represent the largest group of private institutions within Mexican education (Cortina 1989). Even though the majority of teachers were trained in private institutions, they prefer the jobs offered by the government due to better working conditions. This explains why now among employed teachers in Mexico City, half were trained in the public normal schools and the other half in private schools (Ibarrola et al. 1997).

The 1992 legislation provides salary incentives for teachers to seek further training beyond their initial degree. Before then, in-service teacher training was for the most part voluntary, unless the government requested a specific group of teachers to participate in a two-week program to implement a new initiative. In fact, in-service training of Mexican teachers contrasts with the way the term is understood and used in other countries. It is the most important type of training since, through the years of rapid expansion of the educational system, teachers were continuously hired without the required training, which was instead provided during their professional life. For example, during the summer of 1997, six weeks in the summer were used to explain the basic changes to the curriculum of the normal school that was taking effect at the beginning of September, and two public television channels were used to provide the in-service training for teachers.[2] The changes in the academic plan of the normal schools shows an initial commitment of the federal government to strengthen these institutions. The way the curriculum changes have been implemented, however, reveals that little has changed in the relationship between the Ministry of Education and the teachers, owing to the fact that recognition of knowledge gained through teaching experience was not important in curriculum reform.

Teachers' Careers

Once within the public school system, a typical career path for teachers has been to progress through the hierarchy to mid-level positions in the Ministry of Education or the national teachers' union. Ever since the 1930s, the seniority system has provided incentives for teachers as they moved to administrative positions in the schools and at the district level. Almost no monetary or other incentives existed for teachers to remain in the classroom. Incentives generally coincided with advancing from the classroom to administrative positions; from there to union leadership; and finally to positions in the PRI—the dominant party in national politics—which has been the traditional domain of men.

The 1992 legislation, included in the Acuerdo Nacional para la Moderni-zación Educativa, devotes a whole section to the reevaluation of the teaching profession. A critical part of that reevaluation is breaking the highly concentrated link between politics and the profession by decentralizing governmental author-ity and union control. An equally important part is strengthening the professional work and compensation for teachers at the classroom level. The latter develop-ment is a breakthrough in Mexican public life by showing a real commitment to the function of teachers as educators of children in the classroom, rather than as public employees and union members.

Two aspects of this new legislation are crucial to the improvement of teaching as a profession: the training of teachers and the *carrera magisterial,* or teaching career. Regarding teacher training, the new law gives the states responsibility for training their own teachers, and gives them control of all teacher training institu-tions, thus ending the centralization of teacher training and reducing the tradi-tional prerogatives of the national union leaders who might try to control the assignment of jobs and promotion of teachers to middle-level positions, such as school principals and district supervisors.

To provide incentives for teachers to remain in the classroom, the "teaching career" was created as a legal category and defined as a horizontal promotion mechanism. By giving teachers better salaries (their salary level linked to their level of education, performance, years of service, and an examination of their knowledge), the legislators aimed to retain teachers. This measure should benefit women, who have tended to remain as classroom teachers, while men in greater numbers ad-vanced to administrative positions or political positions within the union. More importantly, this new legislation was designed to provide stronger incentives and assign greater value to the work of teachers inside the classroom.

All teachers are required to take a multiple-choice exam as part of the process of placing them within the different categories of the "teaching career." At the elementary school level, many teachers were unable to answer even one of the questions on the multiple-choice questionnaire. Only 45 percent provided the right answers. Among preschool teachers, 70 percent gave the right answers. The preliminary results of these exams show that the states face a daunting challenge in working to retrain currently employed teachers.[3]

The new law redistributes the responsibility of public education so that states and the community play a more important role. This reallocation of the adminis-tration of education is creating many changes at the state level. For one thing, the top administrator for education at this level often manages a larger budget than the governor. The responsibilities given to the states are enormous since they have not previously had direct control of their resources, or effective decision-making powers over education. The states are working to build up the capacity to provide training for their teachers. The size of the state and the school system, in addition to regional and political differences, explain the great variance in the way the resources given to the states are used as well as the impact of the new legislation on teachers' careers and opportunities. One exemplary case of reform is in the state of Aguascalientes, which is providing in-service courses and opportunities for bachelor's and master's degrees to all teachers in their system (Gobierno del Estado de Aguascalientes, 1997). In many other states, the process of education reform, (initiated by the central government) took longer to be worked out. Some states are still in the process of learning to manage the system and bring together the different political interests that will influence the governance of education in the state.

One contrasting example is the state of Chihuahua, were the political conflict between the SNTE and the party known as PAN delayed needed reforms in the governance of education. As a result, almost no change took place and Chihuahua dropped from being fifthteenth in terms of education indicators in the country to the twenty-second, while other states have risen.[4] The modernization of the education sector in Mexico has entailed a reorganization of administrative and political forces across the country and in some cases its effects are still not visible for many teachers and their schools.

Teachers' Employment and Labor Relations

Teachers need the intervention of the teachers' union, SNTE, to negotiate with the Ministry of Education for their salaries and fringe benefits, including loans, pensions, job transfers, housing subsidies, retirement plans, day care, life insurance and health care. The basic wage of teachers is defined by their job category, and overall the wages within the profession are not highly stratified. There are not substantial wage differences, for example, between the preschool and elementary school teachers, and the junior high and normal school teachers. Wage stratification within the profession comes from past union victories, specifically the "double job." In Mexico City today, approximately half of the teachers hold two jobs (Ibarrola et al. 1997). This union victory entitled teachers and administrators to have a double salary. Economic benefits derived from double jobs are not distributed equally throughout the country. They have mostly gone to urban teachers, particularly teachers in Mexico City, the power base of the former power block in SNTE, Vanguardia Revolucionaria.

Teachers' wages have other indirect components, such as an additional monthly compensation provided for each five years of service, a compensation for teachers who live in areas with a high cost of living, and monthly compensations given to teachers for the training they receive. In addition, the newly established "teaching career" that took effect in 1993 provides monetary incentives for teachers to improve their training and to comply with in-service training.

The "teaching career" has five levels; access to each level provides additional monetary incentives in monthly salaries. For those at level A, the salary increase equals an additional one-fourth of their wages. For those at level E, the last level, the increase represents an additional one-half of their salary (Blanco Lerín et al. 1996, 23). The importance of the "teaching career" in teachers' overall compensation package is becoming increasingly important since wages have not kept pace with inflation since 1994. In spite of these economic incentives, only one-third of teachers presently working in Mexico City have registered themselves in a "teaching career." Among those, mostly all are in level A (Ibarrola et al. 1997). The available information does not allow us to conclude that the lack of participation in the "teaching career" is connected to the fact that half of the teachers in the system are already receiving double jobs.

Teacher training is the most important element of school success. Mexico recently initiated a reform to improve the training of its future teachers. The process of educational modernization in the different states will undoubtedly influence the future success of schools across the country.

Notes

1. María de Ibarrola, Gilberto Silva Ruiz and Adrián Castelán Cedillo, *¿Quiénes son nuestros profesores? Análisis del magisterio de educación primaria en la Ciudad de México, 1995,* México: Fundación SNTE para la Cultura del Maestro Mexicano, A.C., 1997. The survey was done among 3,724 teachers in 333 schools in Mexico City between October 1994 and June 1995.
2. Secretaría de Educación Pública, *Plan de estudios para la formación inicial de profesores de educación primaria,* México, June, 1997.
3. Information obtained from an interview with an official in the Ministry of Education, Mexico City, August 1993. Access to the results of this exam has not been made available to the research community.
4. Foro Nacional, "Aprendizajes y dilemas de la federalización educativa en México," August 22, 1997, El Colegio de México, México. The forum included case studies of education reform in Guanajuato, Nuevo León, Oaxaca, Aguascalientes and Chihuahua. A book publication by El Colegio de México is expected soon.

Bibliography

Blanco Lerín, Antonio, Adrián Castelán Cedillo, and Gilberto Silva Ruiz. 1996. "La disputa por el salario y carrera magisterial." *Básica* 10 (March–April): 21–28.
Cortina, Regina. 1989. "Women as Leaders in Mexican Education." *Comparative Education Review* 33, no. 3 (August): 357–376.
Gobierno del Estado de Aguascalientes. 1997. *Artículo 6—de la Constitución Política y Ley de Educación del Estado de Aguascalientes.* Instituto de Educación de Aguascalientes, 1997.
Ibarrola, María de. 1996. "Education and Economic Growth: Creating a Culture of Education." Paper presented at the working group on "Reforming Education in Latin America: The Second Wave of Reform." Council of Foreign Relations, New York, NY. March 20, 1996. Table 3: Mexican Teachers' Salaries, 1978–1990.
Ibarrola, María de, Gilberto Silva Ruiz, and Adrián Castelán Cedillo. 1997. *¿Quiénes son nuestros profesores? Análisis del magisterio de educación primaria en la Ciudad de México, 1995.* México: Fundación SNTE para la Cultura del Maestro Mexicano, A.C.

International Labor Organization. 1995. *The Impact of Structural Adjustment Policies on the Employment and Training of Teachers*. Geneva: ILO.

Lockheed, Marlaine. 1996. World Bank presentation for panel on "Designing and Implementing Decentralized Change." Comparative and International Education Society, Annual Meeting, Williamsburg, Virginia, March.

Weiss, Eduardo, and Justa Ezpeleta. 1995. "Las escuelas rurales en zonas de pobreza y sus maestros en las políticas educativas recientes." Paper presented at the Latin American Studies Association International Congress, September 28–30.

Part VII

Conclusion

28

JOAN B. ANDERSON AND LAURA RANDALL

Conclusion: Improving Basic Education in Latin America

There is a clear need for improving basic public education in Latin America. Improved public education increases both national and family income, which affects the next generation's potential for economic and political well-being. Families with high incomes have well-nourished children who can stay in school, increasing their chances of earning higher wages and educating their children in turn. In a virtuous circle, education increases productivity in the work place, leading to higher incomes. Other impacts of education are that as governments in Latin America become more democratic, widespread education among the people is essential for expanding and maintaining those institutions. In addition, it plays an important role in maintaining the cultural and social structure, as well as being a potential force for change in the society, especially with regard to income and wealth distribution. Increasing the quality of basic education, especially for the poor, is the most important investment that can be made toward expanding economic development and allowing countries to compete in a global environment. Improvements in education require both an increase in resources allotted to education and a more efficient use of those resources. This last chapter summarizes some of the policies, detailed in the above chapters, that are currently being applied to improve educational quality with apparent success.

Policies for Improving Educational Structure

With the exception of some poor states and provinces, all four countries have achieved a high level of basic educational coverage. They are implementing policies to improve the quality of education. Policies to increase the amount of time spent in school through some combination of increasing the number of school days in a year, increasing the number of hours per day and/or decreasing the number of shifts in a school are important. A corollary to this is increasing the amount of time dedicated to learning within the school day.

Systems of automatic promotion, flexible promotion and/or school cycles are being implemented in the first years of basic education to allow for flexibility in the rate at which children learn. This has lowered grade repetition rates and has thus reduced age/grade distortions. Chile has had great success with this policy. Expansion of national systems of evaluation can also help focus on quality. There is increasing recognition of the importance of preschool to success in basic and higher education. Preschool is now included as part of compulsory education in Argentina.

Though politically difficult, there is a great need to shift more resources to schools in poor areas. In general, schools in poor areas receive fewer resources and the poorest paid, least trained teachers. Yet children coming from poor and usually uneducated families need more resources in order to learn. Policies such as special federal subsidies for poor districts, student scholarships and school food programs can be of help. In addition, programs of adult literacy for the parents can aid the academic success of the children. Along with this is the need in sparsely populated areas for schools with multi-grade classrooms in order to provide access to a complete school.

Programs for Improving Educational Quality and Lowering Repetition and Dropout Rates

Argentina, Brazil, Chile and Mexico have implemented special programs aimed directly at combating school failure in order to reduce grade repetition and school dropout rates. Given the high association between socioeconomic status and school achievement, the majority (but not all) of these programs are aimed at schools in the lower socioeconomic groups. For example, in Argentina two of the more significant programs are "Better Education for Everyone" and "Improving School Buildings." In Brazil are the "Accelerated Learning" and "Every Child in School" programs. Chile has instituted the "Learning Is Sweet" and "900 Schools" programs, while Mexico has experimented with a "Respectable Schools Program" and a "Program for Remedying Educational Deficits."

There are several major elements offered in these programs. First, there are improvements of the physical environment, such as school repair, supplying materials and sometimes technology (e.g., mimeograph machines, radios, TVs, computers), school libraries, health and nutrition and school lunch programs. Second, some programs like Brazil's Accelerated Learning program, provide special instruction for children who are failing. This can be a special summer school or extra hours before or after school in the subjects where the student is having difficulties. Attempts are made to keep these groups small to allow for individual attention. Third, some programs provide for increased interaction between teachers and parents of children who are at-risk. Fourth, many of the programs provide for improved and increased systems of evaluation. A fifth type of program, small examples of which are found in Brazil and Mexico, provides financial incentives to poor families to keep their school-age children in school. Stipends are paid to families whose children remain in school. Sixth—less common, but a program that has great potential—is the training of school principals and administrators in management techniques. Given the scarce resources allocated to schools, effective management of those resources is of prime importance.

Most of the programs emphasize educational equity and are therefore aimed at schools in poor areas. In all cases these special programs require a strong, sustained financial commitment on the part of government. At the same time, the potential payoff in long-term improved educational and economic performance is high.

Decentralization Issues

To varying degrees, all four countries have partially decentralized their educational systems. They hoped decentralization would reduce public spending by reducing bureaucracy, and would increase the responsiveness of education to local conditions. In Argentina, the impact differed among the provinces according to their educational, financial, and administrative capabilities. In Brazil, decentralization occurred within the context of democratization. The Chilean approach included decentralization of administration, a federal subsidy on a per pupil basis and more flexible curriculum. In Mexico, while administration has been decentralized, finances and much of the curriculum continue to be nationally determined. Decentralization can lead to increased parent participation, as in the Brazilian School Council concept, where each school is governed by a body made up of parents, teachers and administrators.

Given the newness of these policies, their effect on quality and equity are subject to debate. Authors' opinions vary from guarded optimism to negative assessments. Difficulties with decentralization center on an increase in inequality that arises from regional inequities, in particular from a scarcity of people at the local level, especially in poor districts, who are sufficiently trained in management. On the positive side, the flexibility in curriculum that arises is leading to pedagogic innovation. Some of the suggested policies aimed at improving the functioning of decentralization are: (1) keeping debates about the educational system separate from partisan political disputes; (2) engaging local actors in governance of education; (3) increasing financial resources of the educational system and doing so in a way that counterbalances regional inequities; and (4) developing technical management skills through management training for local officials, including school principals.

Improving Curriculum and Teaching

Curriculum incorporates the essential objectives and principles of the educational approaches to guide classroom activities. It determines the nature of the student–teacher interaction as well as the use of time in the classroom. Recent changes in curriculum in Latin America reflect new approaches to education. Each country has a common base of material, but curriculum is becoming more flexible and more interactive. Shifts in orientation from emphasis on memorization to approaches that emphasize interactive teaching methods and the development of thought—"learning how to learn"—are improving the quality of education. Textbooks have been revised and distributed, stressing language and math development in the basic cycle. Teacher guides and in-service training are designed to ensure the effective use of the new materials and to change the teachers' attitudes and behavior in the classroom. Investment in teaching materials and self-study guides yields a high return in educational quality.

Policies for Improving Teacher Training and Careers

Improved quality of education depends on better teaching, which can be obtained by improving teachers' working conditions, enhancing teachers' professional status both by increasing requirements for professional teaching degree and, even more importantly, by increasing teachers' wages. Teachers' salaries have fallen dramatically both in real and relative terms, lowering the quality of personnel that is attracted into teaching. In order to attract and hold highly talented teachers, salaries must be high enough to reflect teaching's professional status and to allow teachers to live on their income from only one job. With low salaries for primary school teachers in public schools, teaching is too often done by those who lack teaching degrees or other adequate teacher training and who often are without sufficient education themselves. Further, salary increases need to be given for improvement, relevant additional education and experience so that a teacher can advance in the career without leaving the classroom for administration.

For innovations in curriculum to be effectively translated into use in the classroom, teachers have to be trained in the new methods and equipment. Continuing education for teachers and teacher in-service trainings are essential for improving educational quality. If teachers are to shift from a transmission model of teaching based on repetition and memorization to an interactive method incorporating learning processes, they must accept and be trained in that methodology. As schools respond to changing educational needs by acquiring computers and other new technologies, teachers must be trained in their effective uses.

The essays in this book help us understand the historical and institutional structure of primary school in Latin America. The most important questions that remain are (1) How much does each factor—school organization and facilities, characteristics of students, teachers' conditions, curriculum, and programs to prevent repetition and increase learning—contribute to increased student achievement? What is the difference in their contribution compared to the achievement of students who do not have the stated characteristics or participate in programs to prevent repetition and increase achievement? and (2) What is the cost/efficiency ratio of each program to prevent repetition and increase achievement of each program? Our continuing research and that of our colleagues and other researchers will attempt to answer these questions.

Increasing the quality of education, especially for the poor, can decrease the amount of economic and social inequality, increase efficiency and productivity of the labor force, and develop the human resources necessary to participate in the technological age. The challenge for Latin American schools is simultaneously to improve the quality of education and to lower grade repetition and dropout rates.

About the Editors and Contributors

Francisco Álvarez Martín holds a licenciado in pedagogy from the Institut Catholique de Paris (1964) and a Licenciado in education from the Universidad Católica de Chile. He is an expert in the design of adult education programs. He teaches at the Escuela de Educación of the Universidad Católica de Santiago. He is a researcher at CIDE in the area of Family-School Management. His publications refer to teacher training and to didactics for globalized teaching.

Ana Lúcia Amaral, teaches at the Universidade Federal de Minas Gerais. She is author (with S.F.R. Castilho) of *Metodologia da Matemática; a aprendizagem significativa nas séries iniciais* (Belo Horizonte: Vigília, 1993. 3v); "Cultural Capital and School Success: a Study of Brazilian Normal Schools," Doctoral Dissertation submitted to the School of Education, Stanford, California, July 1991; "O Plano de Desenvolvimento da Escola," *Revista AMAE Educando,* XXIX, no. 261 (August 1996); "Autonomia da Escola," *Presença Pedagógica* 3, no. 16 (July 1997).

Joan B. Anderson is a professor of economics at the University of San Diego and is co-editor of the *Journal of Borderlands Studies.* She has authored a large number of journal articles on economic development in Latin America, most recently: "Married Women's Labor Force Participation in Developing Countries: The Case of Mexico" (with Denise Dimon), *Estudios Economicos,* no. 25 (January-June 1998); and "Direct Foreign Investment and Mexican Wage Policy" in *Economic Transformation in Emerging Countries: The Role of Investment, Trade and Finance,* ed. Farok J. Contractor (Elsevier, 1998); and a book, *Economic Policy Alterntives for the Latin American Crisis,* 1990. She is a Fulbright Scholar and is past president of both the Association for Borderlands Studies and the Business Association for Latin American Studies. In 1995 she was awarded the Clarence L. Steber Professorship in Business for career accomplishment.

Lúcia Avelar has a Ph.D. in Political Science, with post doctoral studies at Yale University. She is Professora Titular of the Department of Political Science of the University of Brasilia and ex-Professor ad Unicamp, São Paulo. Her books include *O Segundo Eleitorado-Tendências do Voto Feminino no Brasil* (Unicamp, 1989); "Clientelismo de Estado e Política Educacional Brasileira," in *Revista Educaçao e Sociedade*, no. 54. (Cedes/Papirus, 1996); *Mulheres na Elite Política Brasileira*. (Konrad-Adenauer-Stiftung, 1997).

Maria Ligia de Oliveira Barbosa, Universidade Federal de Minas Gerais, is Ph.D. in Social Science from IFCH-UNICAMP. She is co-author (with Marcia Gardênia M. Oliveira and Tania B. Quinatneiro) of *Um toque de Clássicos* (1995); several articles, and technical reports including "A Escola Plural: Alternativa Social?" (CNPq, 1996); "Política Educacional, Gestão Municipal, Desempenho governametnal e desigualdades sociaias" (with Laura da Veiga and Olavo Brasil de Lima Jr.) (World Bank, 1996); and "Crianças e Adolescentes trabalhadores nas ruas centrais de Belo Horizonte" (with Adriano Tostes Macedo) (Associação Municipal de Assistência Social da Prefeitura de Belo Horizonte, 1994); "Os impactos e os limites das políticas educacionais" (with Laura da Veiga) in *Teoria e Sociedade* no. 2 (December 1997) UFMG, Belo Horizonte; "Para onde vai a classe média: um novo profissionalismo no Brasil?"in *Tempo Social*, Revista de Sociologia da USP, 10, no. 1 (May 1998), São Paulo.

Donna Barnes is a professor at the School of Education, University of San Diego. "Bridging the Gap: From Research to Practics; Multi-Aged Grouping," *The Whole Language Teacher* 8, no. 2 (1993); and "What is Whole Language?" in *Handbook: How Every Child Can Learn to Read*, ed. E.M. Swengle.

Teresa Bracho González is a full time researcher at the Center for Teaching and Research in Economics (CIDE). Her publications include 39 articles published in academic journals and 9 chapters in specialized books on education, and one book on education for democracy. Her most recent articles are: 1997 "El gasto familiar en educación. México 1992" (with Andrés Zamudio). *Revista Mexicana de Investigación Educativa*, Vol. II, no. 4, segundo semestre; and 1996 "La formación tecnológica" in *Economia y Políticas en educación*, eds. A. Loyo and J. Padua. (México: Consejo Mexicano de Investigación Educativa). Her research includes educational organizations, education and work, economics of education: Rates of return and its social evaluation, and private costs of education. Recent interests include the consecuences of policies and family decisions on educational inequality and social exclusion.

Cecilia Cardemil Oliva is Professor of Spanish middle school; she holds a Licenciada en Psicologia from the Universidad René Descartes, Paris, France; and Diplomada in Psicología del Aprendizaje de Adultos, Universidad Católica de Louvain, Belgium. As a researcher of the Centro de Investigación y Desarrollo de la Educación (CIDE) she has developed research centered on observations of classroom teaching practices in primary and middle school, on models and processes of learning and transfer of training of teachers. She has several publications, the most recent (in press) is *Bases para el proceso de articulación entre el pre-escolar y los primeros años de enseñanza básica.*

Gabriel Castillo Inzulza is Profesor in Spanish and Latin at the Universidad de Chile. He is an educational and vocational adviser at the Pontificia Universidad Católica de Chile. He holds an M.A. in education from this university, and is a research professor at the Centro de Perfeccionamiento, Experimentación e Investigaciones Pedagógicas (CPEIP). He was an adviser for the Educational Reform of 1965, and to Ministers before the current government. He has been Profesor at the Universidad Católica for more than thirty years. He is the creator of the educational proposal "Educación de Anticipación." He has numeros publications, and has received several awards, and was distinguished by the National Education Award in 1997. He is the director of the Programa Escuela de Anticipación through the Guías de Aprendizaje, CPEIP.

María Celia Agudo de Corsico is Professor of Educational Psychology and Director of the Institute of Educational Research, National University of La Plata. She ia a Member of the Nationals Academy of Education. Her research centers on Cognitive Processes in School Learning and Educational Evaluation. Her books include *Verbs in Educational Evaluation* (1983); *Orthographic Difficulties* (1989); *Linguistic Interaction in the Classroom* (1993); and *Studying in Higher Education* (in press).

Regina Cortina is a faculty member in the Department of Teaching and Learning at New York University. She received her Ph.D. in Education from Stanford University in 1985. She is currently co-editing a book on Gender and Education in Latin America to be published by Garland Publishers. Professor Cortina continues her work on Mexican education and is working on a book, *The New Politics of Mexican Education,* which focuses on the recently enacted law to decentralize public education in Mexico and its effects on local control and democratization.

Ana María Eichelbaum de Babini is a professor of sociology of education at the University of Buenos Aires and other univesities. She was Associate Researcher at the Center for Studies in Education and Development in 1966-67 at Harvard University and is a Plenary member of National Education Academy and the National Council for Higher Education (Consejo Nacional de Educacion Superior). Her recent books include *Sociologia de la educación* (1991); *Los pobres y la escuela* (with Ruth Sautu, 1996); and *La medición de la educación de la unidades sociales* (Academia Nacional de Educacion, 1995).

Alec Ian Gershberg is assistant professor at the Milano School of Management and Urban Policy, a division of the New School for Social Research in New

York City. He teaches education policy and public finance. He is also a Faculty Research Fellow at the National Bureau of Economic Research. He holds a B.A. in Literature and Society from Brown University and a Ph.D in Regional Science from the University of Pennsylvania.

Margarita Gómez-Palacio is Director General of PRONALEES. She holds a Ph.D. in Educational Psychology from the University of Geneva, served as rector of the University of the Americas, and is co-author of Emilia Ferreiro-Margarita Gómez-Palacio, *Nuevas perspectivas sobre los procesos de Lectura y Escritura,* and her recent books include *Español libros de texto para 1o y 2o grado. Español libros para el Maestro 1o y 2o grado. SEP. 1997.*

Mariane Campelo Koslinski is in the Post Graduate Program of the Faculty of Education in UNICAMP (Department of Applied Social Science and Education).

Ruben Klein earned a Ph.D. in mathematics at MIT. He is a researcher at Laboratório Nacional de Computação Científica / CNPq, carrying out research on educational statistics. His publications include: "O Censo educacional e o modelo de Fluxo: o problema da repetência," *Revista Brasileira de Estatística* 52, no. 197/198 (December/January 1991): 5-45, (with Sergio Costa Ribeiro); "Produção e utilização de indicadores educacionais," 2ª versão, presented at the Workshop on Repetition UNICEF/IBE (UNESCO), Genebra, February 1995 (mimeo). "Inidicadores educacionais e disparidades regionais e socio-economicas no Brasil," in *Avaliação e determinação de padrões na educação Latinoamericana,* ed. Helena Bomeny. (PREAL [Programa de Promoção da Reforma Educativa na América Latina], Editora Fundação Getúlio Vargas, 1997), pp 47-86; and "Indicadores educacionais para subpopulações caracterizadas pela cor," *Ensaio* 5 (1998): 495-514, Fundação Cesgranrio, Rio de Janeiro.

Marcela Latorre Gaete, sociologist, is researcher at the Centro de Investigación y Desarrollo de la Educación (CIDE) in Santiago-Chile. She has developed research and evaluation of educational programs and policies which have been implemented by the Ministries of Education in Chile, Ecuador and Paraguay, and has carried out regional evaluation studies, including "Sistemas de Medición de Calidad de la Educación," Unesco/Orealc. Her most recent publication is *Comunidades Educativas donde Termina el Asfalto. Escuelas Fe y Alegría en América Latina* (CIDE-AED, 1998).

Dr. Edith Litwin is Profesora of Education Technology in the Department of Education Science of the School of Philosophy and Letters at the University of Buenos Aires, Argentina. She is director of the Masters in didactics and director of the research program: A new agenda for didactics in the University of Buenos Aires. She is author of *Las Configuraciones Didacticas: una nueva agenda para la* *ensenanza superior,"* (Editorial Paidos); and *Tecnologia Educativa,* (Editorial Paidos), among others.

Ivany Rodrigues Pino is a professor in the Department of Applied Social Sciences and Education (DECISAE) of the Faculty of Education of UNICAMP, Campinas, Brazil. She is president of the Centro de Estudos Educação e Sociedade-CEDES. Her research is on public policy and science, education and technology.

Laura Randall, professor of economics at Hunter College of the City University of New York, is the editor of *The Political Economy of Latin America in the Post War Period; Reforming Mexico's Agrarian Reform; Changing Structure of Mexico; and Economic Development: Evolution or Revolution.* She is the author of *The Political Economy of Brazilian Oil; The Political Economy of Mexican Oil; The Political Economy of Venezuelan Oil; An Economic History of Argentina in the Twentieth Century; A Comparative Economic History of Latin America;* and several articles on Latin American economic development and economic history. She has been awarded four Fulbright grants and several other awards, and served as Co-Chair of the Brazil Seminar of Columbia University.

Maria Umbelina Caiafa Salgado, who holds a master's degree in education, is retired from the Universidade Federal de Minas Gerais. Her most recent publications include "O novo paradigma de organização do trabalho e a formação profissional na área da saúde" in *Saúde, Trabalho e Formação Profissional,* eds. A. Amancio Francisco and C.G.B Moreira (Rio de Janeiro: Editora Fiocruz, 1997); "Educação do Trabalhador: discussões teóricas e prática social," *Tecnologia Educacional* 21, no. 107 (July/August 1992): 11-17; "Políticas de Formação Profissional na década de 70," *Sociedade e Estado* 4, no. 2 (July/December, 1989): 81-102. Currently, she is consultant for elaboration and avaluation of teachers' training programs in projects financed by the World Bank.

Ana Maria Brigido de Sanchez is professor of the sociology of education at the Universidad Nacional de Cordoba.

Ruth Sautu earned a PHD in economic sociology, University of London at London School of Economics and Political Science. She is Professor of Research Methods in Social Science, University of Buenos Aires. Her fields of research are social classes, inequality , and the role of family and school in childrens school performance. Her recent books include *Los Pobres y la escuela* (with A.M.E. de Babini, 1996); *La trastienda de la investigación* (with C. Wainerman, 1997); and *Mujer, trabajo y pobreza* (with M. Di Virgilio and G. Ojeda, 1998).

Ernesto Schiefelbein is Senior Researcher, Universidad Santo Tomás, Chile. His recent publications include *The State of Education in Latin America and the*

Caribbean (Unesco: Santiago, 1996); and "Trends in the Provision and Design of Self-Learning Models of Education" in the *Handbook of Education and Development* (Pergamon, 1997).

Paulina Schiefelbein licenciada en educacion, is a researcher at the Centro de Investigacin y Desarrollo de la Educación (CIDE), Santiago. Her recent publications include *Education in the Americas. Quality and Equity in the Globalization Process* (OAS: Santiago, 1997).

Sylvia Schmelkes is a Mexican sociologist. She has been an educational researcher for 27 years, and presently is a professor at the Departamento de Investigaciones Educativas del Centro de Investigación y Estudios Avanzados del Instituto Politécnico Nacional in Mexico City. Her fields of interest are quality of basic education and adult education. Recent books are *La Escuela y la Formación Valoral Autónoma* (Castellanos, 1997); *The Quality of Primary Education: The Case of Puebla, Mexico* (IIEP, 1996; Fondo de Cultura Económica, 1997); *Hacia una Mejor Calidad de Nuestras Escuelas* (OAS, 1994; Secretaría de Educación Pública 1995).

Min. Paulo Renato Souza is Minister for Education and Sport of Brazil; he is a Ph.D. in Economics, University of Campinas (UNICAMP), S.P., 1980; and is author of several books on economics and economic development.

John Swope, S.J. is Director of the Centro de Investigación y Desarrollo de la Educación (CIDE). He has a Ph.D. in Sociology of Education and is a member of the Counsel of the Southern Educational Research Initiative (SERI). His interests include curriculum, the relation of the school with society, social demand for education, and education about values in public schools. His current research is the evaluation of primary education.

Emilio Tenti Fanfani is Professor of Sociology of Education at the Universidad de Buenos Aires and consultant for UNICEF and researcher for CONICET. He holds a Diploma Superior de Estudios e Investigaciones Politicas in the Tercer Ciclo de la Fundación Nacional de Ciencias Politicas de Paris. He has worked in universities Colombia, Mexico, France and Argentina. He is a researcher at CONICET (Argentina) and professor of sociology at the Universidad de Buenos Aires. His books include *El arte del buen maestro* (Pax-Mexico, Mexico DF, 1986); *Estado y pobreza. Estrategias tipicas de intervención,* (Buenos Aires: Centro Editor de America Latina); *Estado democratico y politica social,* (Buenos Aires: Eudeba, 1989); *La escuela vacia,* (Buenos Aires: Losada, 1995) and *La Argentina de los jóvenes,* (Buenos Aires: Losada, 1998). He is the author of several articles.

Jaime Enrique Vargas Sanchez holds an ingiuser's degree in administration, Univesidad de Chile. He holds an M.A. in Economics from ILADES/Georgetwon University, and a Master of Public Policy from Harvard University. He is Profesor de Economía de las Políticas Sociales in Educación, ILADES/Georgetown University. His recent activities include: 1998: General Manager of Tecnología Productiva Red Cettec S.A., Fundación Chile. 1997: General Coordinator of the Red Latinoamericana de Información y Documentación en Educación (REDUC). 1993–94: Director of the Corporación para el Fomento y Desarrollo de la Pequeña y Mediana Empresa. 1990–94: Researcher of the Programa Trabajo de Asesoría al Congreso Nacional, Tasc Ilades/Georgetown University.

Index

Hidalgo, Mexico, 212, 217, 224
  dropout/absorption rates, 223
  enrollment/terminal efficiency rates,
    218*t*, 222
  "Lectura y Escritura," 221, 222
  preschool education, 221–223
Higher education, redirecting funds from,
    55
Honduras, 19
  grade repetition, 54*t*
Household. *See* Family
Human Development Index (HDI),
    Brazil's use of, 44, 237

I

Illiteracy, adult, 64, 67
"Implementation of the Proposal for
    Learning Reading and Writing"
    (IPALE) (Mexico), 258–260
Implicit costs, 18, 40
"Improving School Buildings"
    (Argentina), 136, 138, 312
"Improving the Quality of Education at
    Schools" (Argentina), 136, 138
In-service education. *See* Teachers, training
Incentive programs
  economic, 37, 40, 149
  teacher (Mexico), 169, 305
Incomplete schools (Chile), 97
Indicators. *See* Education indicators
Indigenous communities, sociocultural
    judgments of, 27
Indigenous language textbooks (Mexico),
    164
Inter-American Development Bank,
    financial aid/loans, 5, 174
Inter-American Dialogue, 27
Interest groups, 45–46
International Federation of Fe y Alegría, 33
International organizations
  educational reform, 53–59
  financial aid/loans, 5–6, 53, 272
  See also Individual organization
IPALE. *See* "Implementation of the
    Proposal for Learning Reading and
    Writing"

K

Knowledge expansion, 251–252

L

Language
  Spanish as a second, 27, 91, 98,
    100
  training strategies for learning (Chile),
    154
Latin America (country comparison)
  curriculum & textbook development,
    10–11
  decentralization, 9–10
  drop out rates, 8–9, 312–313
  educational systems, 6–7, 311–315
  grade repetition, 53, 54*t*, 91, 312–313
  underreporting of, 121–122
  teacher training & salaries, 11–12
Latin American Episcopal Conference
    (CELAM), 35
Learning
  environmental constraints affecting,
    19
  failure in, 18–19
  transmission model of. *See* Transmission
    model
Learning is Sweet program (Chile), 154,
    158–161, 312
Learning sectors, curriculum development
    and, 246–247
Learning Workshops (Chile), 155
"Lectura y Escritura" (Hidalgo, Mexico),
    221, 222
Levin, Henry, 242
Libraries
  Argentina, 235
  classroom, 100
  Mexico, 169, 262
Literacy classes (Brazil), 146
Lo Barnechea, Chile, 295–296
Lo Gallardo School (San Antonio, Chile),
    297–298
Loans. *See* Educational loans
Low-income families
  grade repetition associated with, 131
  inequities in education, 3–4, 23, 24, 64,
    128
  preventive programs (Mexico),
    166–173
  school quality for, 25
  student performance, 26, 69
  See also Socioeconomics
Lunch programs. *See* Meal programs

Pernambuco, Brazil
  curriculum design, 242–243
  grade repetition prevention programs,
    146
  State Four Year Education Plan, 242, 243
Pesquisa Nacional de Amostra por
  Domicílio (PNAD), 127
Piped water supplies, 24
Plan of School Development (PDE)
  (Minas Gerais, Brazil), 242
Plan Social. *See* Social Educational Plan
  (Argentina)
Political elites, 46
Politics, effect on education, 43–50
Poverty. *See* Low-income families
Preschool education programs, 20, 22, 37,
    56
  importance of, 100, 132
  See also Individual country or state
Preventive programs, 36, 39
  See also Individual country or state
Primary education
  Argentina, 63–73, 135
  Brazil, 75–87, 129
  centralization/decentralization for,
    191–199
  Mexico, 107–110, 163
  social returns to, 3
Principals, School Principals' Association
  (Minas Gerais, Brazil), 197
Private management, of public education,
  35
Private schools, 4
Privatization, 56, 57
Pro-Qualidade (Minas Gerais, Brazil),
  195, 198
Program de Educación, Salud y
  Alimentación (PROGRESA)
  (Mexico), 166, 168
Program for Remedying Educational
  Deficits (PARE) (Mexico), 168–172,
  173–174, 312
Programa Escuela Digna (Mexico), 166
"Promoting Alternative Proposals"
  (Argentina), 136
Promotion
  grade. *See* Grade promotion
  teacher. *See* Teachers, promotion of
PRONALEES. *See* National Program for
  Strengthening Reading and Writing
  in Basic Education

"Proposal for Learning Reading and
  Writing" (PALEM) (Mexico),
  258–260
Proyecto Nueva Escuela (Argentina), 233
Psycho-social withdrawal, 27, 28
Psychological counseling. *See* Counselors
  & counseling
Public education, FYA private
  management of, 35

Q

Quality, of school experiences, 18
Quality of education, 24–25, 131–132
  Argentina, 136, 138, 275
  Brazil, 85–86, 195, 238–240
  Chile, 90–91, 95–98, 152–161
  emphasis on, 4
  improving, 8–9, 312–315
  Mexico, 164–165
  student achievement and, 5
Quality of educational materials. *See*
  Educational materials, quality of
Quality of teaching. *See* Teaching, quality
  of
Quinquennial National Plan (Argentina),
  134

R

Re-enrollment (Chile), 95
Regions. *See* Geographic regions
Remedial programs, 37, 39
Renato, Paulo Souza, 239
Repetition. *See* Grade repetition
Residence, affect on performance, 24, 91
"Respectable Schools Program" (Mexico),
  312
Retention. *See* Grade repetition
Rio de Janeiro, Brazil, automatic
  promotion, 129
Rural education systems
  Escuela Nueva (Columbia), 27, 58–59,
    100, 242
  multi-grade classrooms
    Brazil, 149
    Chile, 96–97, 100, 101
  Social Plan (Argentina), 233
Rural MECE program (Chile), 153
Rural residencies
  affect on performance, 24, 91

For Product Safety Concerns and Information please contact our EU
representative GPSR@taylorandfrancis.com
Taylor & Francis Verlag GmbH, Kaufingerstraße 24, 80331 München, Germany

www.ingramcontent.com/pod-product-compliance
Lightning Source LLC
Chambersburg PA
CBHW071833270326
41929CB00013B/1985

9 7 8 0 7 6 5 6 0 2 3 9 8